Anxiety Management

In 10 Groupwork Sessions

Robin Dynes

Speechmark Publishing Ltd
Telford Road, Bicester, Oxon OX26 4LQ, UK

Published by
Speechmark Publishing Ltd, Telford Road, Bicester, Oxon, OX26 4LQ, UK
www.speechmark.net

© Robin Dynes, 2001

First published 2001
Reprinted 2002

002-4178/Printed in the United Kingdom/1010

British Library Cataloguing in Publication Data
Dynes, Robin
 Anxiety management: a practical approach
 1. Anxiety – Treatment   2. Anxiety – Treatment – Popular works
 I. Title
 616.8'5223'06

ISBN 0 86388 222 6

Contents

Contents

Handouts

List of handouts

Acknowledgements

I would like to thank:

◆ All the clients and staff I have worked with over the years – without them this book would not exist.

◆ Stephanie Martin, my editor at Speechmark, for her suggestions and editorial revisions.

◆ My wife Jean for her help, patience and encouragement throughout the writing of the book.

Introduction

This book strives to set out in a straightforward and easy-to-follow manner a guide for anyone wishing to teach anxiety management skills to groups or individuals. Well established cognitive/behavioural methods are used and encouragement is given to learn through the experience of putting the techniques into practice. The book can be used by social workers, probation officers, occupational therapists, care workers, counsellors or anyone who is called upon to respond to people who have anxiety problems.

Why Anxiety Management Training?

Anxiety management training works well because:

1   It is a self-help method. Once learned, it provides each individual with the tools to gain control over and manage anxiety for the rest of their life.
2   Each person remains in control and is responsible for themselves at all times.
3   Results are quick. Progress is made within weeks.
4   It is adaptable to working with groups or individuals. When taught in groups people can support and encourage each other.

Using the Book

The book is divided into two parts:

Part I: Preparing for anxiety management training. This section looks at some issues to consider before beginning an anxiety management group. This includes selecting clients, interviewing, using a co-worker, considering the setting, group cohesion, dealing with common problems, and so on.

Part II: Understanding anxiety management techniques. The aim here is to provide the group leaders with enough information to enable them to facilitate a group and discuss its application. The content for each session is given in detail. Outline session plans are provided for a ten-week programme. Handouts, suggested exercises and assignments are also included. The sessions are adaptable to different client groups and the time available and are planned to encourage the full participation of each person.

Appendixes are included which provide additional material and forms for use in preparing to run the group, for use with the group and for evaluation purposes.

When required, to meet identified additional needs, material from other sources can be added to that provided for the sessions. This may entail increasing the number of sessions to ensure comprehensive cover.

Making the Programme Work

It will be helpful for anyone embarking on running an anxiety management group to read through the whole of this book to familiarise themselves with the material. It is recommended that the order of the material in sessions 1 to 4 is followed as these sessions present the basic information and techniques required by anyone before facing their fears. The material in sessions 5 to 10 is more adaptable to change of order but the order as presented has been found the most useful.

Once the format of the group has been established, it is best to stick to it for the life of the group. Starting each session with participants giving feedback on individual progress sets up an expectancy that set assignments be carried out. It also encourages the building of trust with group members learning from experience and supporting each other. The main body of learning in each session is given as a mixture of presentations and exercises. Do encourage discussion and participation rather than lecturing the group! Each session closes with the setting of assignments. It is important that constant reminders are given that success depends on participants carrying out the assignments and putting the techniques learned into practice. Thus they will learn from experience and will be enabled to manage effectively their anxiety for life.

Preparing for Anxiety Management Training

Preparing to Run a Group

To ensure a successful anxiety management group a number of issues will need to be considered before the group begins.

Selecting Group Members

It is important to match individuals to any treatment. One person may benefit from a particular approach while another may not. An urgent task, therefore, is to assess the suitability of each person being considered for the group. Anxiety management is an educational approach, using cognitive and behavioural methods. When considering individuals it is necessary to assess:

◆ If the person will be able to work constructively in a group. Inhibitors may include: difficulty fitting in because of demanding or disruptive behaviour; fear or embarrassment about sharing thoughts and feelings in a group; lack of ability to concentrate; an unwillingness to make a commitment to attend regularly; substantial cognitive impairment (dementia) or poor verbal skills.

◆ Whether the main problem is one of anxiety or is physically related. Physical problems may include: hormonal changes; the menopause; thyroid problems; infections; anaemia; allergies; pre-menstrual tension and glandular disorders. Unless physically-related conditions are treated, no psychological approach alone will be effective.

- If there are any diagnosed physical conditions which may endanger life, such as severe asthma, pregnancy, colitis or a heart condition. Putting the techniques in this book into practice involves people facing their fears – if anyone has a diagnosed condition their doctor will need to be consulted to ensure it is safe to do this in a gradual way.
- If anxiety is secondary to some other major psychiatric disorder, such as severe depression, and the person has active psychotic symptoms such as delusions, hallucinations, confusion of thought processes, loss of contact with reality or suicidal thoughts. These conditions will need to be treated before the person can begin an anxiety management programme.
- If the individual is taking high doses of sedatives or other medications which will affect their motivation and their ability to concentrate and absorb the content of the course. The person's doctor will need to be consulted for advice about when and how, or even if it is desirable, to reduce medication.
- If the individual is regularly under the influence of alcohol. The person will need to consult their doctor to arrange a detoxification programme before starting an anxiety management group.
- If the problems originate with, for example, marital difficulties, from unresolved issues in the person's life, or are behavioural. Anxiety management on its own will not address these problems.
- If the individual has problems which may be better approached by working with the person on a one-to-one basis, by cognitive therapy, psychotherapy or a combination of two approaches. These might include:
  - specific phobias where a desensitisation programme may be more appropriate.
  - fears related to thoughts such as being a total failure or being rejected. In this case cognitive therapy might be more successful.
  - anxiety based around lack of confidence, assertiveness or social skills. A social skills or assertiveness group might address the issues more directly.
- If the individual is willing to take responsibility for helping themselves and accept the possibility that thought patterns could have some relevance to their anxiety.
- Whether or not the person is able to engage in self-help strategies. The more severe the anxiety the more difficult it is to carry out

assignments and challenge faulty thinking. Initially, one-to-one sessions may be more effective in enabling the person to achieve some success and build confidence.

◆ If the client wishes to explore childhood events or traumas experienced in depth. If they do, then this more action-based approach is unlikely to appeal or produce results.

◆ If the individual feels too threatened by the approach or being in a group. Starting a person on a one-to-one basis and then, when some confidence has been gained, having them in a group where benefits can be gained from sharing and working with other group members can help overcome these problems.

◆ If the individual is able to read and write sufficiently well to be able to understand the material in the way it is to be presented and to complete the assignments. Additional one-to-one help/sessions may be needed or they may have a partner or friend who can assist them. Discreet support may be needed in the group. The programme can be adapted to focus more on behavioural aspects, concepts can be simplified and visual aids provided for presentations to help them understand the material. More time can be allowed for discussion, practice and exercises as required.

◆ If the individual has learning difficulties. It will be necessary to adapt the programme to focus on behavioural aspects, simplify concepts and present the material in a more concrete and visual manner to aid understanding. More time can be allowed for discussion, practice and exercises.

The answers to many of the above issues may be known, depending on the referral system or the setting in which group leaders work. For example, if they work in a day centre they will probably know the group members well and have most of the above information in each person's records.

The Initial Interview

It is usually necessary to have some sort of interview to establish the problem and in order to gather and give information. Also, it provides an opportunity to enable individuals to explore any fears they may have about the process. It will help group leaders to decide whether the person being considered is suitable and give the person an opportunity to decide whether they want to commit themselves. What form the interview takes and how detailed it is will depend largely on the setting and how much information is known about the person. However, even if a substantial amount of information is available it is always safest to confirm it with the person before proceeding.

When identifying problems it is helpful to understand them in the different aspects suggested by P J Lang (1968). These are:

◆ What physical symptoms are being experienced?
◆ What does the person think might happen?
◆ What do the above two reactions cause the person to do? For example: avoid the situation by not going to social occasions.

It is also useful to take into account each person's individual lifestyle. What stress does this cause and what effect does it have on general health and well-being? During the interview explanations will need to be included about what is involved in the programme, what participants will be expected to do and what the benefits will be. Discussion should include:

1 Group members needing to take responsibility for their own learning.
2 The investment of time and energy to complete assignments.
3 What the skills to be learned are. The fact that, once learned, they will need to be practised in anxiety-provoking situations, that this will be uncomfortable at times but, once accomplished, the skills are theirs for life.
4 Commitment to attending each session.
5 Acknowledgement that their thought patterns could have some relevance to the problem.
6 What the person will gain from the programme.

Appendix 1 provides an informal format for obtaining the necessary basic information. This may need to be adapted and changed to suit particular settings. The format should give sufficient information to decide if the programme is suitable. Permission may be needed from the person to gain information about anything group leaders are unsure of, such as a physical condition.

Using a Co-worker

Advantages of using co-workers are:

◆ Two people working together can be more aware of what is happening in the group and pick up on the issues.

◆ They can give each other feedback about their perception of what was happening in the group and use this as a check and to help plan for the next session.

◆ They can give each other feedback about their performance.

◆ They can share the load.

◆ A broader view of what is happening in the group can be obtained.

◆ Two people working together can ensure preparation is more thorough and each participant's needs are taken into consideration.

◆ Two workers make it easier to divide the participants into sub-groups to complete exercises.

◆ Sharing ideas and solving problems together can be more creative than working alone.

Disadvantages of co-working can be:

◆ Power struggles can develop between workers.

◆ Co-workers may collude with each other and not want to give each other honest feedback.

◆ Co-workers may think in ways that are incompatible, or harbour unresolved conflicts.

If two people are going to co-work it is necessary to ensure that they are compatible, feel equal and can work in a complementary way to support each other. Both will need to be involved in planning discussions to provide a basis for predicting compatibility. Views will need to be shared about preferred styles of participation, who will be responsible for leading which parts of the session and what each expects from the other.

Where compatibility exists, with a mutually supportive attitude, experience suggests that it is advantageous and more effective to work with a co-worker – particularly so when working with a large group.

Considering the Setting

Careful thought should be given to the venue where the group is to be held. Consider the following:

- Is the room large enough to seat the group number in comfort?
- Is there enough space for everyone to move around freely and to use a flipchart or chalkboard?
- Is there enough space to do exercises such as relaxation? (Chairs will, preferably, have arm and head rests. Mats or blankets and cushions may be provided so that relaxation can be practised lying down.)
- Is the room suitable for people with any disabilities or special needs? Is there a loop system for people with hearing impairment?
- Will anyone with disabilities be able to access toilets without embarrassment and without disturbing other members of the group?
- Is the room reasonably quiet?
- Does the room enable privacy to be respected?
- Is it possible to ensure that there will be no interruptions from other people using the building?
- Is there adequate heating and ventilation?
- Are there power points for the use of audio-visual aids if you are using them?
- Can equipment be used safely in the room without putting anyone in danger?
- Can drinks be made in the room, if required, during the break?

Attention to the above practical details will help ensure the group members settle down quickly and feel comfortable. It will also eliminate most unwanted interruptions.

Thinking about the Group Size

Having fewer than six people in the group does not allow enough diversity of interaction and reduces the environment needed to achieve change. A small group of this size will also be vulnerable when members are absent or drop out.

A group that is too large makes it difficult to keep track of what is going on and gives each person less time to contribute. Between eight and ten people is about the right number in each session. However, to make allowance for absenteeism and those who stop attending, it is expedient to recruit up to 15 members.

Deciding the Number and Length of Sessions

Option 1 The course has been designed as a cohesive whole, scheduled to take place over a period of ten weeks, using two-hour sessions with a ten-minute break. This may not suit all client groups or situations.

Option 2 If participants are likely to take longer to master the concepts involved, the number of sessions can be doubled. Thus a shorter session each week, of say, one-and-a-half hours could be run, using half of the material but allowing more time for discussion, practice and consolidation. The course would then run for 20 weeks.

Option 3 One session could be used to teach and the following session to consolidate and reinforce material taught at the previous session. This would allow more time for discussion, feedback and practice of the techniques. It also gives more time for the participants to adapt techniques and concepts to their daily lives, practice assignments and effect change. This course would also run for 20 weeks.

Option 4 Have sessions twice a week for the first two weeks, then weekly for four weeks, then fortnightly for the last two sessions. This is more difficult to operate but has the advantage of focusing on the important initial learning and then encouraging more independence as the meetings progress.

Option 5 A more advanced group may obtain more momentum from proceeding at a faster pace. In this case, two sessions each week is suggested, completing the course in five weeks. However, this does mean less time for practising techniques and assignments and to consolidate learning. It may have the advantage of a reduced drop-out rate.

Option 6 It would be exceptional to have a whole group of very severely anxious people. If this is the case, however, then a group of six to eight people is more practical, run over a longer period of time. It will also be necessary to allow extra time at the end of sessions – say about 30 to 45 minutes – for group members who are severely agoraphobic to practise going out from the group, assisted, where necessary, by group facilitators. This enables group members to gain confidence and then build on this success, making it more likely that they will complete assignments. Usually, only one or two members of any group will need this type of support. Also, when a group member has difficulty applying the techniques, a few outings in this manner with a group facilitator supporting and observing can enable solutions to their difficulties to be applied quickly.

Option 7 As the first four sessions present the basic information and techniques required by anyone before facing their fears, it is paramount that these techniques are thoroughly mastered. It can be beneficial to run these four sessions over eight weeks, particularly when the group includes a few more severely anxious people, spending longer on discussion, practice and consolidation and then to proceed at a faster pace for the remaining sessions.

Also, if necessary for those who are more severely anxious, if the first four sessions are run over eight weeks a few additional weeks can be added, solely to enable group members to give feedback on progress, consolidate learning, and to support group members working towards achieving set goals. The remaining sessions can then follow on, or be run as a separate course as required, after success has been achieved with this initial stage.

Option 8 Session 4 (Facing the Fear) is likely to be found the most anxiety raising or difficult by most individuals. It can, depending on the abilities of group members and the degree of difficulty, be useful to spread this one session over two weeks. The other sessions can be run as outlined.

These suggested options will give an indication of how the material may be adapted to suit the needs of participants. It is also necessary to ensure that the time of day the course is run is convenient for everyone. Those who are working may need a course in the evening, while someone looking after children may find late in the morning or early afternoon more suitable.

Looking at Presentation Methods

Anxiety management is basically an educational process that involves a great deal of information-giving. It is helpful, therefore, to use a variety of teaching aids to achieve maximum impact. A flipchart or blackboard is good for brainstorming and showing diagrams or flowcharts. These may be displayed on a wall so as to be kept visible during the whole session. Showing some of the handouts on an overhead projector can also be productive and aid delivery of the material. Simple cartoons to illustrate key issues can enhance and make information more memorable. It is also necessary to have handouts ready so that they can be taken home and gone through at leisure, reinforcing learning and as an aid to memory. Invariably, some sessions may be missed and the handouts will help to fill in these gaps in individual learning. Recommending books to read can also supplement and reinforce the information.

Although visual aids take a lot of time to prepare they are very worthwhile in helping to put across concepts that are difficult to understand. One diagram can clearly put across something that might still remain confusing, even after many attempts at a verbal explanation. Once prepared, diagrams can also be used again and again in any subsequent courses. Visual aids are particularly important when any group members have learning difficulties, literacy problems or when working with adolescents. Concepts and terminology should also be simplified in these cases.

As a lot of material has to be conveyed in a limited time, particularly if the programme timetable is maintained, an energetic but empathetic style of delivery works well. If a more leisurely pace is required, then the programme will have to be adapted. This can be achieved by extending it by two or four weeks as required or using one of the options previously discussed.

Often, once the group has developed some cohesion, the more vocal or dominant members of the group may attempt to extend the feedback and discussion time. This needs to be avoided tactfully, otherwise there will not be sufficient time to cover all the teaching material.

Ensuring Group Cohesion and Interaction

A successful group needs to establish enough cohesion to make it attractive to attend, and to give enough feeling of belonging, comfort, safety and trust to enable personal disclosures to be made and risks taken. Good cohesion can also produce added incentive and encouragement to individuals to keep attending for the whole course. Nevertheless, it is important to guard against the group becoming so cosy it prevents people taking risks. They may fear that raising questions or issues which may evoke difficult discussion within the group will cause dissent and upset the 'pleasant' atmosphere. Group members can sometimes collude in this and avoid addressing issues or being honest with each other.

The need for cohesion makes it essential to encourage the process and make it easy for people to overcome any initial embarrassment and fear and feel reasonably comfortable as quickly as possible. To help to achieve this the initial session includes some introduction exercises to help 'break the ice' and allow people to get to know each other in a fun and unintrusive way. These can, of course, be replaced by other introduction exercises that are known to work well. Agreeing group ground rules is also very important in establishing a safe and comfortable environment in which everyone is aware of what is and what is not acceptable to others.

The relaxation exercise is included in the first session to give people something practical to do to help themselves. They quickly realise they have started on the path to bringing their problem back under control. It will also to help relax them after the anxiety of beginning something new to them, along with the tension of getting to know unfamiliar people.

Other ways of ensuring group cohesion and interaction include:

◆ Ensuring that all members are as involved as possible by encouraging anyone who is not contributing. Asking directly for their opinion, or how they feel while doing something, can prompt them to contribute. How they interact during the break and their progress with assignments should give clues to their attitude. They may be confused, not want to be there or be inclined to listen and watch as a method of trying to sort things out for themselves.

Whatever the reason for non-participation it is important to be aware of it and to address any difficulties.

◆ Making the information-giving sections of the course as participative as possible by asking open questions, and checking personal experience against the information given. Continuous lecturing makes it difficult for people to feel involved: concentration and interest wanes. Participants quickly begin to feel that the group leader is setting themselves up as an authority on their problem. They become dependent and believe that the leader will make it all happen for them, passing over responsibility – and ultimately blame – when they feel the course has been unsuccessful.

◆ A method of increasing the credibility of the course is to invite someone who has completed a previous course successfully to talk briefly about their experience. This can be a really good incentive and motivator for course members.

◆ Sharing tea, biscuits and cakes during the break can help people relate and can be really beneficial in helping to increase group cohesion.

◆ Encouraging group members to comment and congratulate each other when significant progress has been made on difficult tasks by individual members.

◆ Guiding the group. Initially, the group leader will be fairly directive. But as sessions progress and group members interact more and support each other, the role becomes that of a guide.

◆ Following up on members who do not attend. This can make it easier for them to come back to the group. Other group members can become concerned about them or start feeling, if too many drop out, that the group is not much good. In the author's experience it is important to agree ground rules; for example: anyone who is going to be absent should inform the group leader, and if anyone is absent more than once, the group should send them a card. This proves successful in providing added encouragement and incentive to keep people attending.

Do keep in mind when considering the cohesion of the group that, while initially techniques need to be practised in the safe environment of the group, as progress is made there should be a greater emphasis placed on people putting the techniques into practice as they go about their normal lives away from the group.

Dealing with Common Problems

Assignments

Any initial problems with getting group members to complete assignments need to be addressed immediately. Problems can be avoided by:

1 Making it clear from the beginning that techniques practised only within the safety of the group will not achieve anything for anyone.

2 Reminding people that there is no 'race' – each person will succeed in their own time at their own pace.

3 Making the purpose of each assignment explicit, remembering the less able members of the group.

4 Pointing out emphatically that everyone will be expected to report on their progress, share difficulties and encourage each other.

5 Reminding people – this will need to be repeated often – that completing assignments is their responsibility and is the most important part of ensuring success.

Ensuring that group members are aware of the above at the initial interview stage and then repeating it again in the first session should go a long way towards motivating and encouraging individuals to complete their assignments. If avoidance tactics are being used, a general discussion on the effects of avoiding may help. This should include:

◆ What avoidance is.

◆ The effects avoidance has on the quality of life and relationships.

◆ The fact that avoidance of facing fears maintains and increases anxiety.

◆ Asking group members to share their fears about completing assignments and how they deal with them.

There may also be pressure outside the focus of the group or problems of anxiety which influence the person. This may need to be discussed away from the group and appropriate support suggested.

Discussion and feedback

It is essential that there is opportunity given for open discussion and feedback during the sessions. Do explain what is meant by feedback – individual members sharing with the group how they have managed with their assignments and getting supportive comments and suggestions to help with any difficulties encountered. Open questions should be asked to encourage reluctant people to get involved in discussion. These are questions that cannot easily be answered by 'yes' or 'no'. Examples are: 'How did you feel?' and 'What happened next?'. These discussions are important so that individual difficulties can be explored and used as learning points and to clarify any misunderstandings. They also help to keep people motivated.

Encouraging group members to support each other can help ensure that members do not become dependent on the leader. However, it is not appropriate for comments to be given in a critical or judgemental way. To do so can be destructive.

It is imperative that the group remains focused. Some dominant group members may start off-loading emotional material, dwelling on their personal symptoms in great detail or exploring recent crises. Tactfully, but firmly, avoid this, otherwise there is a danger that the session will become aimless, lose its sense of direction or become dominated by individuals. Point out the need to move on to ensure that group objectives are achieved.

Do expect some resistance to people taking responsibility for solving their own difficulties. Some individuals may unconsciously attempt to divert the focus of the group as a means of avoidance. Many may expect to be given a 'cure' which can be a cause of their dropping out.

Relaxation

Relaxation practice should be kept short – no longer than 20 minutes. Concentration is unlikely to last longer for most people. It may also be tempting to fall asleep. Keep in mind that the aim is to train each person to relax within progressively shorter periods of time. In normal daily situations, at work or when out of their home, it is very unlikely that they will be able to lie down and spend a long time doing relaxation or going to sleep. This means learning to relax within a short period – a minute or two – in any sort of situation. Therefore, practice is required while sitting, standing and walking about.

A tendency to fall asleep can be counteracted by making everyone aware why this would be inappropriate before starting relaxation and making sure the light is good. If anyone has a real problem with this, tell the group that if anyone falls asleep they will be woken with a light touch on the arm or leg.

Ensure that group members do not become dependent on the group leader by decreasing the leadership role in relaxation as quickly as possible. Once the basics have been learned this process should begin – the aim is to teach participants to relax independently and in any situation. This can be achieved by:

1 Gradually increasing interference. This means increasing the light and noise levels as progress is made.
2 Ensuring practice is carried out whilst sitting, standing, lying down and so on.
3 Varying the relaxation techniques so that people are not restricted by one method only.
4 Asking participants to take turns in leading relaxation exercises. This can help to ensure that the members do not become dependent on the group leader's voice.
5 Relaxation tapes can be used. Ensure that people do not become too dependent on the tape. This can be avoided by encouraging group members to make recordings using their own voices.

Dealing with poor attendance and avoidance

If someone does not attend they will need to be contacted. If the group is not appropriate for the person, care should be taken to ensure that they do not feel they have failed and that the leader or the other group members do not hold this against them. It may be that the course is not in their best interest at this time and they need guidance to obtain more appropriate help. They may require support to enable them to come back into the group.

There will be occasions when stopping attendance is the positive thing to do. Going ahead with a process that is of no benefit to someone is a waste of time for everyone and will only result in the client feeling that the whole thing is a total failure.

To avoid poor attendance, it is helpful to have discussed in the initial interview what exactly the anxiety-related problem is. Vague terms like 'feeling anxious in some situations' is not sufficient. What this means in cognitive, physical and behavioural terms should be explored and clear, realistic objectives for each person should be established. Tools such as self-rating scales (see Part II, Session 1, Handout 5 – Stress diary/Anxiety rating form) to provide evidence to encourage and reinforce progress can be used. This record will also provide proof, rather than feelings or opinions, that no progress is being made and as an indicator that the approach is not working. The evidence, particularly if combined with irregular attendance, should be followed up to establish whether continued attendance is desirable.

Sometimes group members' mental health may not always remain stable – symptoms may return. This will need to be addressed before the person can continue.

Acknowledge all efforts and successes. Encourage all group members to reinforce this. Participants will have made huge efforts to confront their fears – not an easy task – positive reinforcement is essential to ensure everyone feels supported. Any critical comments will drastically reduce feelings of being supported by the group and make it more difficult for the person to sustain any progress and continue attending.

Avoiding failure

Attention to detail during the initial interview and early sessions can ensure that any sense of failure is cut to a minimum and motivation is maintained. This ensures:

◆ The course and methods used are appropriate for those attending.
◆ Motivation is helped by clarifying each person's objectives and what will be expected from them on the course.
◆ Group members' expectations are realistic.
◆ Group members are clear that results are dependent on their own efforts.
◆ The course is set at an appropriate level and rate of learning for those attending.

Other problems that can impede success and need attention are:

◆ Learning problems.
◆ Individuals becoming dependent on the group leader.
◆ A fear of making changes and a lack of confidence in ability to deal with the consequences of these changes.
◆ A lack of ability to put learning into practice away from the sessions.

If attention is paid to the above most of the difficulties which may lead to anyone feeling that they have failed will have been eliminated.

Ending the Group and Maintaining Change

Often group members will find ending the group difficult. The ground needs to be well-prepared. Group discussion should include:

◆ Plans for how each person will continue to progress in the future. The course has taught them the basic skills, they now need to put them into practice.
◆ Dealing with setbacks which may be encountered.
◆ Maintaining their progress without the support of the group. On the course they might have the support of a partner, friend or a colleague with whom they can maintain contact. Attention will need to be given to ensuring that each person has built their own support network.
◆ A general revision of the main principles.

Endings are easier if one or two follow-up meetings have been planned. These are useful to help evaluate the course and determine how effective it has been after the course has ended.

These follow-up meetings can be tailored to meet the needs of the group. Meeting just the once, three months after the end of the course, may be all that is required. Alternatively, other groups needing a little more weaning may find a meeting a month after the course ends and then a final meeting after another two months helpful. These sessions can be unstructured. They can be used to provide support and to reinforce the general principles taught on the course by revising them again. These meetings have been found to be very effective in helping clients' motivation to maintain progress and change.

Assessing and Evaluating

A combination of different methods can be used at different times. These may include:

◆ An initial interview (a format is given in the appendixes).

◆ Questionnaires completed by the group members at the end of the course and three months after the course has ended (supplied in appendixes).

◆ Verbal feedback in the session each week when individuals report back on their progress with assignments (included in session format).

◆ Using anxiety-rating forms which the group members fill in before starting the course and then again before the course ends. The two forms can then be compared to measure progress (supplied in appendixes).

Assessments, used thoughtfully, provide:

◆ A very effective aid to gathering information.

◆ Help to define the problems and work out solutions.

◆ Information to assist the group leader to provide appropriate material at the correct level and pace.

◆ Motivation for group members.

◆ Sound evidence of progress and change.

◆ Feedback about the effectiveness of the course material.

◆ Information to aid planning for future courses.

◆ Practice-based evidence that can be used for research.

Making an assessment very structured and formal usually results in more reliable information, but can be very off-putting and rigid from the group members' point of view, especially for the less able. Depending solely on subjective observation and intuition risks personal bias, making the information inaccurate and of little use. What seems to work most successfully is a balance combining the group leader's observation and intuition, backed up by the use of some structured methods. In any case, it is unlikely that use of any one method on its own will be sufficient to give accurate measures.

Questionnaires and rating forms are supplied in the appendixes which can be used for assessment and evaluation purposes. However, while these will meet most needs, it may be necessary to consider adapting them or adding additional forms to meet the specific or special needs of a particular group.

Part II

Understanding Anxiety Management Techniques

Sessions

Understanding Anxiety

What is Anxiety?

Everybody experiences feelings of anxiety. It is a normal and natural reaction to something seen as threatening. It is the emotion felt when in a tight corner, under stress or when facing physical, emotional or intellectual danger of some sort.

Difficulties arise when the feelings of anxiety become excessive and:

◆ stop individuals performing at their best
◆ are exaggerated out of proportion to the threat
◆ restrict individuals from being able to do normal everyday activities

Extreme anxiety or fear can be experienced in many different situations and ways. Examples are:

◆ starting a new job
◆ when it is dark
◆ meeting new people
◆ before speaking
◆ when making decisions

◆ when alone
◆ going into a crowded room
◆ walking down a particular street
◆ in confined spaces
◆ going for an interview

Defining anxiety

Dictionaries define anxiety as:

◆ being troubled in mind about some uncertain event
◆ a state of unjustified and excessive uneasiness
◆ fraught with trouble

Other words used to describe anxiety include:

worried	nervous	perturbed	uneasy	fearful
on edge	concerned	alarmed	tormented	upset
distressed	apprehensive	anguished	fraught	on tenterhooks

Exploring Anxiety-Related Behaviour

General feelings of anxiety

Individuals may constantly experience feelings of tension and anxiety. These include feelings of:

- apprehension
- nausea
- an inability to concentrate
- sweating

- continually anticipating disaster
- shakiness
- muscular twitches
- restlessness

Being obsessive

Obsessions are fears fuelled by persistent, unwanted thoughts that keep recurring, despite resistance or knowledge that they are ungrounded. Everyone has them at times. For example, a person may fear that unless they wear a particular colour when they take their driving test they will fail. Sometimes an individual's thoughts can focus around being afraid that they will harm themselves or someone else. When these notions begin to preoccupy the mind so that they disrupt the person's life, they have become a problem.

Performing compulsive rituals

When obsessive thoughts become severe, compulsive behaviour can emerge. These are rituals that the person must carry out, such as counting and recounting something, touching objects or continually washing their hands to avoid germs.

Developing a phobia

A phobia is an intense fear of a particular situation or object which is out of proportion to the reality. It can take many forms such as fear of being attacked, open spaces, hospitals, birds, eating in public or sex. It is beyond voluntary control and leads to avoidance of the situation or object.

Being hyperactive

In a hyperactive state the person is unable to settle down and rest, either physically or mentally. There is a need to keep busy all the time, rapid thoughts keep going through the mind and there is an urge to talk. It can be difficult to live with the energy produced by extreme tension.

Repetitive thoughts

Sometimes ideas and thoughts, which the person is unable to control, keep repeating themselves over and over again in the mind. These may be thoughts such as 'I'm inadequate' or 'I'm a failure.'

Projection of thoughts

This happens when the person fears that actions which another person performs refer to them when, in fact, they do not. An example might be that when the person enters a crowded room, they feel everyone is talking about them. In reality they might not even have been noticed.

Understanding the 'fight or flight' response

This is the term used for the body's reaction to perceived danger or stressful situations. In primitive times people dealt with actual, physical danger either by attacking the aggressor first (fight) or by fleeing the danger (flight). When the danger had passed, the anxiety disappeared and the body switched back to relaxation mode, slowing down and returning to normal functioning. Today, the perceived danger of stressful situations and anxiety can trigger the same response, which is a remnant of the instinct of primitive man.

Reaction in today's world

In modern times anxieties may not warrant the 'fight or flight' response. For example, it would hardly be appropriate for a person to run away from, or attack, an interviewer. It is more likely that their emotional or intellectual well-being would feel threatened.

A physical response still occurs, however, and if the extra energy is not used in a productive manner, the person becomes more tense, remains alert and their adrenalin levels stay high. Uncomfortable feelings such as a dry mouth, nausea, trembling or light-headedness may be experienced. For example, at an interview the person may not be able to think clearly, or their mind goes blank.

Because of the physical effects, worrying thoughts fuel the fire. Even if the person repeatedly tells themselves to calm down, they may very quickly reach the stage when this has no effect. The brain, flooded with adrenalin, is unable to listen to reason. It will not switch to relaxation mode, even though the person knows there is no real danger.

Examining the vicious anxiety chain

The vicious anxiety chain occurs when feelings of anxiety build up to such a pitch that they begin to get out of all proportion to the situation. They become uncontrollable. The process usually begins with the person anticipating the feeling of anxiety. A negative thought goes through the mind. Typical thoughts might be:

'I'm no good at this'
'I'll get upset'

Immediately the body begins to feel tense. A chemical change (release of adrenalin) then starts to take place in the person's body that increases their energy levels in response to the anticipated danger or stress. They have further negative thoughts:

'I'll make a fool of myself'
'I can't do this'

Their heart speeds up, beating faster, to send oxygen-rich blood to their brain and muscles. Their pulse rate increases. They breathe more rapidly to take in extra oxygen and expel carbon dioxide. Their chest starts feeling tight. Their digestive system slows, their mouth feels dry and their stomach is queasy. Negative thoughts increase:

'I feel terrible'
'This is going to get worse'

Arms, legs and back tense, in preparation for action. The oxygen-rich blood, speeding to their brain to help them think and react quickly, starts to make them feel light-headed, giddy and faint.

They may also experience problems with balance or vision. There may be a feeling of unreality, as in a dream – walls and hedges may appear to fall away. They may also sweat profusely. Thoughts are now out of control:

'I'm going to be sick,
'I'm going to die'

Full panic now sets in. They give up, run away or decide it is not worth finishing. The next time they have to face the situation they will find reasons not to do so, thus avoiding facing the fear. Each time they fail to face the fear relief is only temporary and the problem becomes more difficult to face in the future. The longer this continues the more difficult it is to overcome.

Examining anxiety triggers

Other ways in which anxiety responses can be triggered, become exaggerated and do not allow an individual to switch to relaxation mode are:

◆ Experiencing a number of repeated stresses or pressures. These can be conscious or unconscious and originate from work, home, friends, social activities or combinations of these.

◆ Not allowing time for the body to relax and recover from one trauma before they start dealing with a second problem. They rush around trying to cope with one situation after another.

◆ Imagining or anticipating disaster before anything happens. This can have much the same effect as coping with the event itself.

◆ Lack of knowledge about how to relax sufficiently to ensure the body recovers, which means that the body remains tense.

Any one or any combination of the above means that the body remains in a state of alertness all the time. Anxiety and adrenalin levels are constantly higher than normal. The ultimate result is exhaustion, which produces even more anxiety.

Enabling the body to relax

People therefore need to train their bodies to do what they are not doing automatically – kick-starting the slow-down process. This can be done by slowing down their breathing and reducing the amount of oxygen to the brain. This will gradually reduce the adrenalin release and bring their bodily feelings under control. They can then begin controlling their thoughts. Once they can do this it is possible for them to change their behaviour so that they do not continue to avoid the situation and can learn to cope with their anxiety.

Looking at the Effects of Excessive Anxiety

Excessive anxiety can affect people in three ways:

1 Physically (for example, sweating)
2 How they think (for example, 'I'm going to have a heart attack')
3 How they behave (for example, avoiding)

Anxiety affects people from all types of background and often brings about a drastic change in lifestyle or stops people doing what they want to do.

Recognising symptoms

Symptoms people may recognise in themselves include:

Physical	*Thoughts and feelings*	*Behaviour*
chest pain	feeling depressed	lack of interest
tension	thoughts of suicide	seeking attention
ringing in the ears	panic	phobias
facial tics	rapid thoughts	compulsions
indigestion	fear of choking	irritability
missed heart beats	moodiness	being passive
dizziness	lacking in confidence	tearfulness
headaches	paranoia	obsessions
shaking	fear of dying	drinking too much
blurred vision	thinking badly about self	smoking too much
aching jaws	thinking they can't cope	unable to concentrate
constant exhaustion	feeling jumpy	insomnia
sweating	thinking they are crazy	social withdrawal
lack of appetite	feeling nauseous	restlessness
muscular spasms	feeling inadequate	rushing things
high blood pressure	feeling they have no control	accident prone

Changing behaviour

Because of the discomforts, behaviour may have changed. The person no longer:

◆ goes out alone
◆ travels by bus or train
◆ goes to crowded places

- goes into shops
- applies for promotion
- takes risks
- stands up for themselves
- wants to meet new people
- takes part in social events
- trusts others
- says what they feel
- believes in their own worth

Related long-term effects

It is now known that many medical, psychological and social problems can be influenced by long-term stress and excessive anxiety. These include:

- coronary disease
- ulcers
- asthma
- reduced resistance to infection
- psoriasis
- impotence
- cancer
- drug and alcohol abuse
- anxiety and depressive disorders
- psychosis
- frequent minor illnesses
- suicide
- poor performance
- avoidance of social activities
- lethargy

Social anxiety as a natural response

Although the above indicates how exposure to long-term stress and anxiety can influence general health and well-being, anxiety is not, in itself, an illness or harmful. Remember, it is a normal, natural and appropriate reaction to something seen as threatening. In some instances, the perceived threat and response may be inappropriately excessive to any real threat and the person may be unable to switch automatically to a calming response. Even a panic attack – despite what the person may be thinking and feeling at the time – will not harm them unless they also suffer from some serious physical illness or weakness which may be affected by the panic attack.

Using anxiety as a positive force

Being able to get out of the way of danger is a positive use of anxiety. It is also the same burst of adrenalin that enables the sprinter to leave the starting blocks with a burst of speed. Constructive worry can motivate people to prepare for exams, interviews or giving a talk. It urges them to plan ahead and cover as many eventualities as possible. It can guide them not to take risks unnecessarily or regardless of the consequences, such as:

◆ offending people;
◆ driving up a motorway the wrong way;
◆ acting carelessly when operating dangerous machinery.

Performing well

Little or no anxiety (the 'I couldn't care less' attitude) or too much, spoils the ability to perform well. However, a moderate amount of anxiety actually enables individuals to perform at their best.

This, of course, can vary with each person. However, it indicates that people should not be unrealistically striving to get rid of all anxiety but looking to harness energy in the best way possible. The aim, therefore, is to channel anxiety, which makes life difficult, into something that is useful and helps them achieve what they want.

Identifying the Causes of Anxiety

Anxiety is a response to a perceived threat or stress of some sort. This may arise from:

◆ life events
◆ social changes in society
◆ childhood and life experiences

Life events

These are the major events that happen on the journey through life, bringing change with them and, consequently, stress and anxiety. The events can be good or bad. If several changes happen around the same time it may become difficult to cope. These events include:

death of a partner	divorce
prison term	marriage
death of a family member	illness
becoming unemployed	retirement
marital reconciliation	death of a friend
mortgage or loan foreclosure	marital separation
a personal injury	pregnancy
sexual problems	taking on a large mortgage
addition of a new family member	business problems
change in financial state	change of employment
change in living arrangements	change in responsibilities at work
son or daughter leaving home	outstanding personal achievement
trouble with in-laws	partner starting or stopping work
starting or leaving school	trouble with the boss
change in working conditions or hours	change in residence
change of school	change in recreation
change in social activities	taking on a bank loan
change in sleeping habits	change in eating habits
change in number of family reunions	holidays
Christmas	minor violations of the law

Note: The events listed above have been adapted from the Holmes and Rahe 'Social Readjustment Scale', 1967.

Social changes in society

Emotional reaction to moral and social changes in society and the pressures of modern living create uncertainty, fear of inadequacy, role conflicts, time pressures and relationship problems. These include:

♦ Moral beliefs that, in the past, have been used to guide decisions and actions changing.
♦ Family structures being eroded by increasing breakdown of marital relationships.
♦ Elderly people being forced to live alone with minimum or no support.
♦ Constantly rising crime statistics.
♦ People with different cultural beliefs, often with incompatible needs and behaviour, living together in the same communities.
♦ Minority groups asserting their rights.

◆ Both men and women constantly trying to find new roles or defend old ones.

◆ The competitiveness of finding employment. Unemployment is a constant fear.

◆ The accelerated rate at which modern life moves.

◆ The rapid changes in technological development.

Childhood and life experiences

Experiences start from the womb. Psychoanalysts (Klein, 1948; Fairbairn, 1952; Winnicott, 1960) claim that certain early childhood experiences can create adults who are likely to feel more anxious than other people. Erikson (1950) and Fromm *et al* (1944), suggest that anxiety begins as an infant starts to see itself as separate from its mother. Bowlby (1973) postulates further that the first time a child is separated from its mother intense fear is aroused. If the child senses the prospect of further separation a pattern may be set. Sullivan (1938) also thought that anxiety occurs when individuals are disapproved of or expect disapproval from those important to them.

As adults people may have bad experiences which lead them to feel anxious in specific situations, to avoid particular places, and so on.

Assessing Normal and Abnormal Anxiety

A person would be abnormal if they did not worry sometimes. Anxiety triggers vary from person to person. The factory worker worries about the security of their job, the company director over a decision to be made, the receptionist over dissatisfied customers, the single mother or father about how to cope with a tight budget, and so on. It is impossible to live without some kind of anxiety.

Because anxiety is a part of life, each person must learn to live and cope with it. Remember, not everyone tries to avoid it. People such as racing drivers, mountaineers and those involved in other dangerous sports and jobs actively seek it out. It can also aid individuals to perform at their best.

Anxiety is only abnormal when it stops a person going about normal everyday life and stops them doing the things they want to do. This could be expressing an opinion, getting on a bus, going into a café or pub to meet friends for lunch, or putting a viewpoint across in a business meeting.

Hereditary influences

Anxiety cannot be passed on to another person in the same manner as a virus. However, a vulnerability to fears and phobias can run in the family. The chances are increased if, for example, both parents are anxious individuals, although it certainly does not mean that everyone in that family will have a tendency to be anxious.

Another way in which anxiety can be passed on is through example. If a parent has a fear of thunder then their son or daughter may acquire the same fear by observing their behaviour.

Overcoming fear

Most fears can be overcome by using the techniques explained. Even long-standing anxiety can be eased fairly quickly. But do bear in mind that the longer it has been a problem the more persistence and effort is likely to be needed to overcome it.

Evaluating Treatment

Many different techniques have been used to treat anxiety. These include:

drugs	acupuncture	psychoanalysis
group therapy	hypnosis	auto-suggestion
behaviour therapy	electro-shock treatment	homeopathy

Basically there are three types of approach to help:

◆ Physical
◆ Medical
◆ Psychological

Physical treatments, such as electro-shock treatment or psychosurgery, are normally used only in the most extreme cases and usually there are additional problems. Medical treatments – drugs like tranquillisers and sleeping pills – have been shown to be ineffective in treating anxiety and often are addictive, produce side-effects and can be dangerous. However, appropriate medication may be essential when there are complications such as depression, psychosis and so on, which need to be treated. The treatments that are acknowledged to provide lasting improvements use psychological approaches. The methods explained in this book fall into that category and provide a range of techniques which can be used to manage anxiety.

Managing Anxiety

In order to control anxiety people need to learn how to:

1 Relax and bring their bodily feelings under control
2 Control distressing thoughts and faulty thinking
3 Face their fears

Other essential life-skills for people to learn that will enable them to deal effectively with situations that give rise to anxiety, build confidence and self-esteem include:

◆ being assertive
◆ problem-solving
◆ decision-making
◆ communicating effectively
◆ time-management
◆ how to maintain a positive attitude

Looking at the Benefits of Anxiety Management

◆ There are no addictive side-effects, such as those associated with drugs, use of alcohol or smoking. However, if anyone is on medication they must not reduce the dosage or stop taking it without consulting their doctor. To do so could be dangerous.
◆ The skills learned will enable participants to cope with difficult situations when they occur. They can practise the techniques on their own, though it may be helpful for each person to have a friend or family member who will encourage and support them.
◆ The majority of people can experience a reduction in anxiety within a few weeks.
◆ Anxiety management is a self-help approach. People succeed in overcoming their problems due entirely to their own efforts. Knowing they have succeeded by themselves increases both confidence and self-esteem.
◆ Because each person will have learned a range of skills to help them cope with anxiety, it is effective in the long term. Once learned, the skills remain with everyone for life.

Deciding to Make Changes

It is helpful to point out to the group that no one learns how to cope with their anxiety by trying to ignore it or pretending it does not exist. It will not go away on its own! If nothing is done it is likely to become worse. A firm decision needs to be made, otherwise the person becomes a victim. The first step is accepting that they are responsible for themselves.

Here are some signs that can indicate that people are not taking responsibility for how they are, what they do and how they feel. They might:

blame others	get angry	feel impatient
try to control others	want revenge	feel helpless
feel envious	feel shame	comfort eat
avoid confronting issues	feel joyless	feel intimidated
judge others	get upset	drink/smoke to blank out

Being responsible

This means:

1 Not blaming themselves
2 Not blaming others
3 Not expecting someone else, or drugs, to take away the fear
4 Accepting that they can make changes
5 Taking action

Taking time and effort

Point out to the group that in order to succeed time and effort needs to be put into learning the skills required and putting them into practice. Anxiety is a miserable feeling, so few people will find the course easy. The aim is to enable everyone to take control of their own life. The more effort is put in, the quicker and more successful the result will be.

Understanding anxiety

Aims	1 To enable the group to get to know each other and promote group cohesion	
	2 To introduce general concepts relating to anxiety	
	3 To outline the group programme and the format for each session	

Materials Flipchart, magic markers and copies of handouts

CONTENT	Time
Introduce yourself (and co-worker). Give general information regarding toilets, fire procedures and other environmental issues. Include information on the number of sessions in the course, the length of each session, the length of the break in the middle and so on	*10 minutes*
State the aims for the session and introduce a game to enable group members to get to know each other *(Exercise)*	*10 minutes*
Agree group rules *(Exercise)*	*10 minutes*
What is anxiety? *(Presentation – handout 1)*	*15 minutes*
How anxiety affects people *(Exercise)*	*15 minutes*
Break	*10 minutes*
Causes of anxiety *(Exercise)*	*15 minutes*
Outline of course and weekly format. Benefits of anxiety management *(Presentation – handouts 2 & 3)*	*15 minutes*
Progressive relaxation. *(Exercise – handout 4)*	*15 minutes*
Assignments	*5 minutes*

Exercises and Assignments

Introduction games

Choose one of the following games to enable people to get to know each other:

1   Ask each group member, in turn, to share their name and one thing about themselves with everyone. This could be a hobby, a place they have lived or worked, a favourite sport, something liked or disliked and so on.

2   Obtain a soft ball or bean bag. Have each person call out their name as they throw the ball to another group member of their own choice. When everyone has had an opportunity to call out their name players must then start calling out the name of the person they are going to throw the ball to.

3   Have each person, in turn, state their name and what sort of animal they would be if they were an animal. For example: 'My name is George. If I were an animal I'd be a polar bear.'

Group rules

Have a short discussion with the group concerning the rules they would like the group to follow. Use a flip-chart to write down any agreed rules. Ensure discussion includes confidentiality. Other issues people might like to consider are: arriving late and leaving early, smoking, non-attendance, supporting each other and so on.

How anxiety affects people

Using a flip-chart to record comments, ask group members to share how excessive anxiety affects them:

◆   Physically (sweating, palpitations)
◆   How they think (I'm going to have a heart attack)
◆   How they behave (avoiding)

End the exercise with a brief discussion and record comments on the flip-chart on the use of anxiety as a positive force. Examples can include: getting out of the way of danger; motivating us to prepare for examinations or interviews; guiding us not to take unnecessary risks; stopping us acting carelessly and endangering others; athletes starting a race and so on.

Causes of anxiety

Anxiety is a response to a perceived threat or stress of some sort. This may arise from:

- life events (marriage, retirement)
- social changes in society (changes in technology, changes in morality)
- childhood and life experiences (bad experiences)

Discuss each of the above with the group, encouraging them to recognise and acknowledge their own particular sources of anxiety.

Progressive relaxation

Explain that the purpose of this exercise is to make each person aware of the difference between tense and relaxed muscles so that they can learn to recognise when they are tense and then relax in response to this. (Handout 4 gives a detailed format for this exercise.) After the exercise, give the handout to group members so that they can practise the exercise at home.

Assignments

Instruct group members to:

1   Practise progressive relaxation daily (Handout 4)
2   Start a stress diary (Handout 5)

What is anxiety?

Anxiety is a normal and natural reaction to something seen as threatening.

Fight or flight response
This is the name given to the body's reaction to perceived danger. It is geared to preparing the body to deal with danger and to cope with vigorous physical exercise like fighting or running.

Reaction in today's world
In modern times the 'fight or flight' response is no longer the right response in most anxiety-giving situations. It is hardly appropriate to run away from, or attack, an interviewer. It is more likely that your emotional or intellectual well-being would feel threatened. This results in the anxious, pent-up feelings staying with you. You need to react in another, more appropriate way.

The vicious anxiety chain
The vicious anxiety chain occurs when feelings of anxiety build up to such a pitch that they get out of all proportion to the situation. They become uncontrollable.

Typical Anxiety Chain

PANIC
Run away   Blame others   Decide to avoid
Become angry   Decide it isn't worth doing   Rationalise fear

Thoughts intensify   'I'm going to die'
Bodily feelings and thoughts uncontrollable   Start hyperventilating
Palpitations   Blurred vision

More worrying thoughts   'I feel terrible'   Increased body arousal
Faster breathing   Oxygen speeds to brain to help
Faster heartbeat   Think and react   Nausea

Worrying thoughts   Mind alert   'I'm no good at this'
Body arousal   Ready to react   Dry mouth
Release of adrenalin   Tension in muscles

Some anxiety triggers
◆ Repeated stresses
◆ Not allowing your body to relax or recover from one trauma before starting to deal with another
◆ Imagining or anticipating disaster before anything happens
◆ Lack of knowledge about how to relax sufficiently to ensure the body recovers

Outline and weekly format of the course

What you will learn

In order to manage anxiety you will learn to:

1   Relax and bring your bodily feelings under control
2   Control distressing thoughts and faulty thinking
3   Face your fears

Other skills you will learn include:

◆   assertiveness
◆   problem-solving
◆   decision-making
◆   communicating effectively
◆   time management
◆   how to maintain a positive attitude

Format for each session

Review of the past week
You will have an opportunity to discuss how you have managed during the week and what progress you have made with your assignments.

Session core
This will be a mixture of:

Presentations
The presentations will give information about particular aspects of anxiety and techniques for controlling it.

Exercises and discussions
These highlight and explore how the information given relates to you and how you personally experience anxiety.

Skills rehearsal
This is the practice of the techniques presented. Practice will be done as a large group, in smaller groups or in pairs.

Self-help assignments
Each session will end with assignments being agreed, to enable you to practise the rehearsed techniques away from the group in your own time.

◆ There are no addictive side-effects, such as those associated with drugs, use of alcohol or smoking. However, if you are on medication you must not reduce the dosage or stop taking it without consulting your doctor. To do so would be dangerous.

◆ The skills learned will enable you to cope with difficult situations when they occur. You can practise the techniques on your own, though it may be helpful to have a friend or family member who will support and encourage you.

◆ The majority of people can experience a reduction of anxiety within a few weeks.

◆ Anxiety management is a self-help approach. People succeed in overcoming their problems due entirely to their own efforts. You will be able to look back with the confidence of knowing that you have succeeded by yourself.

◆ Because you will have learned a range of skills to help you cope with anxiety, it is effective in the long term. Once learned the skills remain with you for life.

The purpose of this exercise is to raise awareness of the difference between tense and relaxed muscles so that you can learn to recognise when you are becoming tense and relax in response to this.

Sit in a comfortable chair with good back support. Adapt a passive (let it happen) attitude. The idea is to tense a group of muscles, concentrate on the feeling of strain for a few seconds and then relax them. The exercise involves doing this for all parts of the body. Breathe slowly and regularly between stages and during each stage. When ready go through the following stages:

1 **Feet:** pull your toes upwards and tense your feet muscles. Hold, relax and repeat.

2 **Legs:** lift your legs off the floor, straighten them out and bring your toes back towards your face. Hold, relax and repeat. Now point your toes forward and down. Hold, relax and repeat.

3 **Abdomen:** pull your stomach muscles in and tense. Hold, relax and repeat.

4 **Back:** arch and tense your back. Hold, relax and repeat.

5 **Shoulders and neck:** bring your shoulders up towards your ears and tense. Hold, relax and repeat. Press your head back and tense. Hold, relax and repeat.

6 **Arms:** stretch out your arms and hands as far as you can, attempting to touch the walls on each side of the room, and tense. Hold, relax and repeat.

7 **Face:** tense your face by lowering the eyebrows, biting hard and screwing up your face. Hold, relax and repeat.

8 **The whole body:** clench your fists, hold your arms close to your body, press your knees together and tense your whole body. Hold, relax and repeat.

9 **The mind:** now spend a few minutes relaxing your mind. Close your eyes and think about something restful and pleasant, a scene or image which works best for you. Contemplate this image for a moment, then open your eyes, stretch gently and move about in your seat.

Stress diary/Anxiety rating form

Date and time	Anxiety-giving situation	Feelings and thoughts	Strength of anxiety 0–100	How did you cope?	Strength of anxiety after coping 0–100

Controlling physical feelings of anxiety

Releasing Physical Tension

When people become anxious the body's normal 'fight or flight' reaction comes into play. This can result in a number of unpleasant feelings:

tense muscles	tight chest	headaches
breathing difficulties	trembling	stiff neck
aching muscles	dry mouth	irritability

These sensations, in turn, give rise to more anxiety resulting in:

pounding heart	feeling you are going to die	faster breathing
sweating	panic	nausea
constipation	diarrhoea	blurred vision

These feelings are governed by the automatic nervous system, in combination with stress hormones. This is the system automatically knocked into play as part of the 'fight or flight' response. It is possible for a person to intervene and regain control over this response to stress by starting the 'slow-down process'. This is achieved by relaxing the body, slowing the breathing and reducing the amount of oxygen to the brain. The mind and body do not act independently – once a person has learned to relax their body, the mind will also start to become calm. Releasing physical tension from the body will encourage the mind to relax.

Learning to Relax

This ability to relax does not come easily – it is a skill that has to be learned and practised. Group members will need to build these basic skills, first by practising them in a safe environment until they can do them automatically without having to think. Then they can begin to apply them in stressful situations.

They also need to become aware of when they are starting to become tense. That is the time to act – not when feelings are out of control.

Progressive relaxation

Course members should have practised and become familiar with progressive relaxation during the past week.

Release-only relaxation

The time taken to do progressive relaxation can be reduced to about five or six minutes by practising release-only techniques. This is achieved by leaving out the tense stage of the process. Instead of instructing participants to tense and relax, go through the muscle groups one by one and ask them to imagine them relaxing. The ask them to practise the exercise going through the process in their own mind. This should be practised during the week in a variety of positions: standing, sitting, lying down. The more varied the positions and the environments in which it is practised the better.

Mental devices

During the course of a day it may not be possible to stop for long enough to carry out 'progressive' or 'release only' relaxation. It is necessary to learn to relax quickly – within one or two minutes.

As individuals become more experienced in achieving a relaxed state they can begin using even briefer methods. Using mental devices are really useful and should enable a relaxed state to be achieved within one or two minutes. They can be used safely in most circumstances: waiting for a bus, in a dentist's waiting room, waiting to be interviewed, or whatever.

To achieve a relaxed state individuals need to imagine something that they find pleasant and relaxing. This could be:

◆ A special place – by a stream, a view, a garden scene or a room.
◆ An object or ornament that gives pleasure – something given by a family member that reminds them that they are loved and cared for, a favourite painting or object of beauty admired.
◆ A sound – a tune played on the piano, running water, the sound of the sea or an imagined pleasant voice repeatedly saying 'calm'.
◆ A smell – the scent of flowers, freshly baked bread, newly-cut grass, the sea and so on.
◆ Touching something – the feel of wood or some sort of material, water cascading refreshingly over them or the feel of water as they dangle their feet in a stream.

They need to have decided what the imagined mental device will be and practise using it so that it can be easily brought to mind when they feel themselves becoming tense. Instruct them to:

1 Sit down, if possible, and close their eyes.
2 Focus on their breathing and ensure it is even and normal.
3 Think about – and feel – all their muscles relaxing.
4 Bring to mind their imagined mental device and concentrate on it – while breathing naturally.
5 Remain passive and allow calmness to take over. Tell them, if distracting thoughts come to mind, not to dwell on them. Let them drift out of their mind again as they focus on their mental device. Continue in this manner until they feel calm.
6 Open their eyes, when calm. Remain seated for another moment or so before getting up and moving around again.

Rapid relaxation
After a great deal of practice this is a very quick method of relaxation and should take only about 30 seconds. Tell group members to:

1 Take a deep breath and slowly exhale.
2 As they breathe out, imagine the tension and stress draining away with the breath.
3 Repeat this twice.

Advise people not to take more than three deep breaths or they may experience dizziness.

Relieving Tension Through Activity

Severe tension can best be avoided by not allowing it to become extreme. The use of regular exercise, playing a sport or taking part in some sort of leisure activity can assist in this. Physical exercise helps drain away tensions that are building.

The Health Education Authority (*Active For Life Action Pack: General facts on physical activity*, 1996) recommends regular exercise, that is enjoyable, to lessen depression, improve feelings of self-confidence and reduce anxiety. Suppleness, strength and stamina are also improved.

A good way to drain away tensions is to take up an active pursuit such as swimming, cycling or walking. Leisure activities such as gardening, listening to music or fishing are also helpful to release tension built up during the day.

Taking up a sport, some sort of exercise or leisure activity will:

◆ promote a sense of well-being
◆ help build confidence
◆ help relieve tension and anxiety
◆ help people have fun and enjoy themselves

Group members can visit their local library, community or sports and leisure centre to see what activities are available.

Do warn people that when considering an exercise programme, or taking up any sort of vigorous exercise, they need to take it easy at first and gradually build up their strength, keeping within comfortable limits. If anyone is over 35 and unused to exercising they should check with their doctor to confirm it is safe to take up vigorous exercise. Anyone in any doubt as to whether a particular type of exercise is safe should do likewise.

It can be very helpful to do a few gentle loosening up exercises to drain away tensions before doing a relaxation exercise. Fit the exercises to the condition of the participants. Individuals who tend to be restless may find this will make relaxation easier.

Controlling Breathing

Healthy, relaxed people breathe unconsciously. The abdomen swells slightly and the lower ribs expand. The outward breath is usually slightly longer than breathing in, ending with a slight pause. During the process, as much oxygen is absorbed as the body needs – only a fraction of what is breathed in. When they breathe out some of the carbon dioxide in the lungs is exhaled.

This normal, natural process does not have a perfect speed. Each person has their own personal rhythm – usually between 8–12 breaths per minute.

When a person gets into a 'fight or flight' state, in order to cope with an anxiety provoking situation, they start to take quicker and shallower breaths. If an individual moves about to deal with the crisis, the circulation speeds up and the blood is able to absorb the greater amount of oxygen intake. If they do not, then they are breathing in too much oxygen and lowering the carbon dioxide in the bloodstream. This, in turn, causes many unpleasant sensations such as:

dizziness
chest and stomach pain
tingling in hands and face
weakness and trembling limbs

In extreme cases this can lead to hyperventilation.

Feeling anxious, stressed or tense makes people breathe faster. If they are anxious for long periods of time breathing in this manner can become a habit, increasing their feelings of anxiety and discomfort. Also, living in this overly alert state, anxiety has to be increased only slightly and the body begins reacting, producing, for example, uncomfortable feelings of dizziness.

It is, therefore, necessary for people to make themselves aware of their breathing rhythm and learn how to bring it under control when it speeds up. At first, doing this will feel uncomfortable – some people will have been breathing wrongly for so long it has become 'normal' to them to breathe faster.

There is a slight risk that some individuals may feel anxious when beginning to control their breathing and run the risk of hyperventilating. The risk is small but it is worth reminding people when practising that if they feel very uncomfortable they should 'release control' and allow their body to return to its normal breathing pattern.

Exercise 1 provides a breathing exercise to help everyone breathe properly and learn to slow their breathing rate down when they begin to feel anxious. This in turn will restore the right oxygen/carbon dioxide balance. It is well worth timing breathing with a watch – 8–12 breaths a minute – to familiarise people with breathing rhythms.

Emergency measures

If panic is imminent and the person feels unable to take control of their breathing pattern, a paper bag can be used to offset the effect of too much oxygen. The bag needs to be held closely over the nose and mouth and breathed into as naturally as possible. As the person breathes into the bag and inhales carbon-dioxide, the amount of oxygen will be decreased, restoring the proper carbon-dioxide/oxygen balance to the bloodstream.

This is a very useful emergency measure. Practice using it in the group can help build up individual confidence in the procedure. Individuals will then be more willing to take risks in exposing themselves to their fears.

Practising

The necessity of practising breathing control cannot be emphasised enough. It needs to be practised several times each day until it becomes natural. This is vital, so that the person is aware when their breathing is not normal and is therefore able to bring it back under control.

Making the Most of Sleep

Some people will have problems with their sleeping patterns. They may find their mind racing and unable to rest, or they may be physically unable to rest and settle down.

In primitive times life tended to be uncomplicated. People worked hard, then at night eased up and went to sleep for as long as necessary. If woken up, or aroused, they satisfied themselves that there was no danger, and went back to sleep again without worrying. Modern life does not allow people to do this in the same manner! Today life is often lived under pressure – continuously having to keep up with the competition. When a person comes home from work, instead of relaxing, they may continue to rush around in pursuit of pleasure, playing squash, going to an evening class, and so on. They then find it difficult to switch off – to take their foot off the accelerator and rest.

Worrying about sleeping and willing themselves to fall asleep usually makes going to sleep even more difficult. The less bothered they are about going to sleep the more likely they are to do so! Some people worry about the amount of sleep they have. The reality is that everyone varies in the amount of sleep they need. This can range from five or six hours to nine hours in every twenty-four hours. Sleeping patterns also vary. Some people are larks – they like to go to bed early and rise early in the morning. Others are owls – they go to bed late and get up late. None of this matters. As long as they get the amount of sleep they need and are able to fit it into a pattern that suits their time schedule for work, or what they want to do each day, there is no problem. In any case, most people tend to underestimate the amount of time they sleep and overestimate the amount they need.

Our systems can easily cope with a few nights having less sleep than usual. It is only when this becomes continuous that a problem develops.

Preparing for sleep

There are a number of things that can be done to help people slow down or unwind to prepare for sleep. Not all the suggestions will work for everyone. It is often a case of experimenting and finding out what works best for any individual. They could:

◆ Have a milky drink.
◆ Go for a short walk around the block.
◆ Have a regular, unhurried bedtime routine.
◆ Read a book.
◆ Play relaxing music.
◆ Do a relaxation exercise before going to bed.
◆ Ensure that they have taken some physical exercise during the day so that they will feel tired.

◆ Try to avoid napping in the early evening before going to bed.

◆ Be aware of what they eat and drink. Cheese or other food may affect them. Drinking too much liquid may wake them up because of a full bladder. The caffeine in tea or coffee can also have a stimulating effect.

◆ Watch a pleasant video.

Difficulty falling asleep

Suggest people try some of the following. They will need to choose one method and stick with it. Jumping from one to the other in the same evening can have the opposite affect.

◆ Remind themselves that they do not need a good night's sleep every night. It does not matter if they do not fall asleep right away.

◆ Recall a favourite place that they found pleasant and relaxing. This may be sitting by a stream, looking out on a garden or viewing a mountain scene. They should recall and relive the favourite place in detail, soaking up the pleasant atmosphere.

◆ Concentrate on their breathing. Imagine themselves totally relaxed, with any tension draining from them into the mattress.

◆ Practise a gentle breathing exercise.

◆ Imagine listening to their favourite music.

If they wake during the night and cannot get back to sleep, suggest people:

◆ Use any one of the above methods.

◆ Go to the toilet and return to bed.

◆ Get up and have a milky drink.

◆ Use the time to do something – read or listen to soft music.

◆ If concerns keep going through their mind, write them down and resolve to think about them in the morning.

◆ Enjoy being awake! It does not matter if they fall asleep. Lying there relaxed will enable them to rest.

The most important thing for people to remember is not to worry about being awake. Once they stop worrying about it, it is likely that they will quickly fall asleep.

Aims
1 To teach methods of controlling physical tension
2 To explore methods of relieving physical tension
3 To explore ways of dealing with sleeping problems

Materials Flipchart, magic markers and copies of handouts

CONTENT	Time
Discussion on individual progress and homework assignments	*15 minutes*
State the aims of the session and practice 'release-only' relaxation *(Exercise – handout 1)*	*15 minutes*
Practise 'short' relaxation technique *(Exercise – handout 1)*	*10 minutes*
Practise 'rapid' relaxation technique *(Exercise – handout 1)*	*5 minutes*
Relieving physical tension through activity *(Discussion and exercise – handout 2)*	*15 minutes*
Break	*10 minutes*
Controlling breathing *(Exercise – handout 3)*	*15 minutes*
Emergency measures *(Exercise – handout 3)*	*15 minutes*
Making the most of sleep *(Presentation and discussion – handout 4)*	*15 minutes*
Homework assignments	*5 minutes*

2 Session

Exercises and Assignments

Explain the reasoning behind learning to release physical tension and the need to be able to achieve a state of relaxation quickly.

Release-only relaxation exercise

Talk the group through the procedure, as in handout 1, once and then have them do it, going through the procedure in their own minds.

Short relaxation using an imaginary device

Explain the aim of the exercise and talk them through the procedure, as in handout 1.

Rapid relaxation

Explain the aim of the exercise and talk them through the procedure, as in the handout.

Releasing tension through activity

Read through the handout and briefly discuss. Spend five minutes brainstorming on a flipchart which activities group members can think of to help them relieve tension.

Controlling breathing

Explain the breathing process; how bad habits are formed, the outcome of bad habits and how these can lead to hyperventilation. Practise the exercise in handout 3.

Emergency measures

Give each person a paper bag. Ensure everyone is standing by a chair or has someone close by to give a steadying hand. Ask them to take several deep breaths until they are feeling slightly giddy and have begun the process of hyperventilating. When this happens, have them breathe into the bags and see how quickly this returns them to normality. Although some people may be anxious about doing this exercise, it will inspire confidence that it does work.

Making the most of sleep

Have the group state what, if any, sleeping problems they have. Read through handout 4 and discuss.

Homework assignments

Instruct group members to:

1 Complete their stress diary
2 Practise breathing control and the various methods of relaxation.
3 Make notes of any early warning signs that their anxiety levels are starting to rise. (Shorter breathing, tenseness, anxious thoughts and so on. This will enable individuals to identify the point when they should use the relaxation methods taught and avoid anxiety building to a level that is difficult to control.)

Quick relaxation techniques

Release-only relaxation

Relaxation should be achieved within five to six minutes using this method. Instead of using the full tense and relax method, go through each group of muscles, this time imagining each group of muscles, in turn, relaxing and the tension flowing from them. The tense part of the exercise is left out.

This should be practised regularly in a variety of positions: standing, sitting, lying down and so on.

Short relaxation using imagination

The aim of this method is to be able to achieve a state of relaxation within one to two minutes. You will need to have decided on what your imaginary device – a special place by a stream, the scent of flowers or something else – will be in advance. It works like this:

1   Sit down, if possible, and close your eyes.
2   Focus on your breathing and ensure it is even and normal.
3   Think about – and feel – all your muscles relax.
4   Bring to mind your imaginary device and concentrate on it – all the while breathing naturally.
5   Remain passive and allow calmness to take over. If distracting thoughts come to mind, do not dwell on them. Let them drift in and out of the mind again as you focus on your imaginary device. Continue until you feel calm.
6   When calm, open your eyes. Remain seated for another moment or so before getting up and moving around again.

Rapid relaxation

This is a very quick method to help you achieve a state of relaxation. Practice should enable you to relax in about 30 seconds.

1   Take a deep breath and slowly exhale.
2   As you breathe out, imagine the tension and stress draining away with your exhaled breath.
3   Repeat this twice more.

Do not take more than three deep breaths or you may experience dizziness.

Note: The aims of these methods can only be achieved through regular practice.

Relieving tension through activity

Taking up an activity such as swimming, cycling or walking will help to eliminate tensions. Leisure pursuits such as gardening, listening to music or fishing can be just as effective.

Taking up a sport, some sort of exercise or leisure activity will:

◆ Promote a sense of well-being
◆ Help build confidence
◆ Help relieve tension and anxiety
◆ Promote better health
◆ Help you have fun and enjoy yourself

Visit your local library, community or sports and leisure centre to see what activities are available.

Warning: When starting any new activity that includes exercise, such as tennis or cycling, take it easy at first and gradually build up your strength, keeping within comfortable limits. If you are over 35 and unused to exercising you should check with your doctor to confirm it is safe to take up vigorous exercise. If you are in doubt about the safety of any type of exercise, do likewise.

Controlling your breathing

Controlling breathing exercise

1 Place one hand on your stomach.

2 Breathe in through your nose to the silent count of four, allowing your stomach
to swell.

3 Breathe out gently through the mouth to the count of six, allowing the stomach to return to normal.

4 Count to two and inhale again.

5 Try to get a rhythm going, counting to four on the in-breath and to six as you exhale. You are aiming to take about 8–12 breaths per minute.

At first, the above procedure may feel uncomfortable and as though you are not getting enough air. However, with practice, this slower rate of breathing will feel comfortable. Practice will also make you aware of what is your normal breathing rate. When you become anxious and start breathing faster you will then be able to use the exercise to bring your breathing back under control.

Emergency measures

If panic seems imminent, and you feel unable to bring your breathing pattern under control, then a paper bag can be used. Hold the bag closely over your nose and mouth and breathe into it as naturally as possible. As you breathe in from the bag you will inhale carbon dioxide and the amount of oxygen will be decreased, restoring the proper carbon dioxide/oxygen balance to the bloodstream.

Making the most of sleep

Preparing for sleep

Experiment with the following suggestions and find out what works best for you.

1 Have a milky drink.
2 Go for a short walk around the block.
3 Have a regular, unhurried bedtime routine.
4 Read a book.
5 Play relaxing music.
6 Do a relaxation exercise before going to bed.
7 Ensure that you have taken some physical exercise during the day so that you feel tired.
8 Avoid napping in the early evening before going to bed.
9 Be aware of what you eat and drink. Cheese, other dairy products and food may affect you. Drinking too much liquid may wake you because of a full bladder. The caffeine in tea or coffee can also have a stimulating effect.
10 Watch a pleasant video.

If you cannot fall asleep

Try one of the following. Choose one method and stick with it. Jumping from one to another in the same evening could have the opposite effect.

1 Remind yourself that you do not need a good night's sleep every night. It does not matter that you do not fall asleep right away.
2 Recall a favourite place that you found pleasant and relaxing. Remember and relive it in detail, soaking up the pleasant atmosphere.
3 Concentrate on your breathing. Imagine yourself totally relaxed with any tension draining from you into the mattress.
4 Practise a gentle breathing exercise.
5 Imagine yourself listening to your favourite music.

If you wake during the night

1 Use any of the above methods.
2 Go to the toilet and return to bed.
3 Get up and have a drink.
4 Use the time to do something – read or listen to music.
5 If concerns keep going through your mind, write them down and resolve to think about them in the morning.
6 Enjoy being awake! It does not matter if you do not fall asleep. Lying there relaxed will enable you to rest.

The important thing to remember is not to worry about being awake. Once you stop worrying about it, it is likely that you will quickly fall asleep.

Keeping Worrying Thoughts Under Control

Exploring Negative Thinking and Irrational Beliefs

As previously stated, anxiety is extremely useful to protect people from harmful situations. Unfortunately, it also triggers worrying thoughts and makes them think in a negative manner. This has the effect of causing them to want to avoid situations. The more they avoid them, the more negative thoughts they have about them, causing more anxiety and so on.

For example, a friend had an accident on a busy roundabout near where she worked. She drove into the side of another car. It was not a serious accident but she became so nervous about using the roundabout and fearful that she would cause another accident, she started avoiding the roundabout. The more she avoided it the more anxious she became about using it. This is a typical example of how negative thoughts can cause more anxiety.

The thought 'If I use the roundabout I will cause an accident' increased to 'I'll kill someone in an accident'. Finally she was telling herself 'I can't face using the roundabout'.

The physical sensations brought on by anxiety fuel the thoughts. A person may think they are going to faint, become ill or die. The fact is that these very uncomfortable feelings are seldom dangerous and can be overcome with courage and practice.

Facts about negative thoughts

No matter how overwhelming negative thoughts are, they are irrational and rarely match the real facts of the situation. Generally, irrational thoughts fall into one of the following areas:

Catastrophising

This is anticipating total disaster if something minor goes wrong. Examples are: 'My boss wants to see me. I'm going to get the sack!'; 'I've had a headache all morning. I must have a brain tumour!'; 'My husband is late. He's had an accident!'; 'That woman is looking at me. I must look awful!'

Exaggeration

This is magnifying things beyond the limits of truth. For example, the person makes a small mistake and then worries all day in case someone finds out and thinks they are an idiot, or they mispronounce someone's name and worry that the person now dislikes them intensely because of it.

Dismissing the positive

A person dismisses the positive when they turn positive events into a negative. 'He's only saying that to make me feel better.' 'She's only being polite and doesn't want to upset me.' The positive is dismissed when people overlook all their personal strengths and successful experiences, continually ignore achievements and dwell on failures.

Overgeneralisations

Having one bad experience leads a person to believe that every experience will be bad. They perform badly at one interview so they believe that all interviews will be bad. One person refuses a request so they assume everyone will also refuse.

Impossible standards

This is expecting always to be able to do everything perfectly and never make a mistake. The negative thoughts are usually prefixed with words like:

> 'I should cope with …'
> 'I ought to …'
> 'I must …'

These statements are usually followed by thoughts such as 'I'll never be able to do this'; 'I can't do it. I'm a failure.'

Making assumptions
This is making assumptions and jumping to conclusions without regard to the facts. Thoughts include: 'Everyone thinks I'm a fool'; 'Strong men are always in control'; 'Nobody likes me'; 'A caring mother would always be at home with her children.'

What can be done about these negative thoughts? They are unnecessary and unhelpful and stop people from doing what they want to do. They can challenge them and learn to replace them with accurate, realistic and positive thoughts.

Negative thoughts focus on anxiety, creating more and more anxiety until the situation is out of control. Realistic and positive thoughts will reduce anxiety, divert attention and give back control.

Challenging Faulty Thinking

In order to challenge faulty thinking, it is necessary to identify the unreasonable belief that is creating the anxiety and re-evaluate it. For example, someone might think 'I will die with embarrassment if I make a mistake. I will never be able to face anyone again. They'll think I'm a fool. It will be a disaster! I can't do it.'

In order to challenge this, the person can ask themselves: 'Would it be so awful? Everyone makes mistakes now and again. It isn't the end of the world! I can acknowledge the mistake and continue.'

When helping someone challenge their thoughts it can sometimes be useful to ask them what they would think of a person who made a mistake, corrected it and continued. Often individuals can reason something through better if it is made more objective in this manner. The answers they give can then be turned round by saying something like: 'Is it likely, then, that others would think something like that about you?'

Once the thoughts have been worked through in this manner they need to be re-stated in light of the re-evaluation. In this case, more realistic and helpful thoughts to be thinking might be:

'I'm going to feel nervous, but I can cope with that by doing my breathing exercises. I may make a mistake but everyone makes mistakes now and again, so it isn't the end of the world. I'll probably feel a bit embarrassed, but I can acknowledge the mistake, correct it and continue.'

Ways to challenge faulty thinking

Ask the person to examine their thoughts and consider how accurate and realistic they are. Encourage them to:

1 *Look at the evidence.* Is what they are thinking really true? If they intend crossing the road, if they look both ways and make sure no traffic is approaching how likely is it that they will get run over? What evidence do they have that they will always have a panic attack when crossing the road? Get them to remember all the times they have safely crossed the road or experienced only a little anxiety when doing so.

2 *Check their feelings and thinking with other people who cope with similar situations.* These may be colleagues, friends or relatives. Whether they exaggerate, make assumptions, catastrophise, or whatever, they can check the accuracy of their thinking against that of other people.

3 *Challenge what they believe will be the consequence.* Would it really be the end of the world if they made a mistake? If they lost their job would it really be the end of their life? They might have to make some cutbacks, look for another job or whatever. And what about their family, friends, etc.; would they not care?

4 *Look at different ways of interpreting situations.* If they automatically jump to a negative conclusion, have them explore other ways of interpreting the situation. Are their feelings caused by excitement? Did they feel hot because they were hurrying and it was a hot day? The person who did not speak to them may have had some worry of their own on their mind and not heard them. Encourage the practice of looking at alternative ways of interpreting events, rather than automatically assuming the negative one is correct.

5 *Ask themselves if their expectations are realistic.* Are they saying that they must be good at everything? Or that they must be liked and approved of by everyone? Are they expecting never to be anxious or never to make mistakes? These expectations need to be changed to something more realistic. For example, they could be encouraged to think that while it is nice to be liked, everyone does not have to like them, they are still okay.

6 *State what it is realistic to be thinking.* Having examined the thoughts and established that they are exaggerated, or whatever, state what it

is realistic to be thinking in those circumstances. These more accurate thoughts can then be written down on a card and carried with the individual as a reminder. When the negative thoughts come into mind the card can be taken out and the faulty thoughts substituted by repeating the accurate thoughts.

Identifying areas to work on

In order to re-evaluate faulty thinking, individuals need to identify what thoughts are going through their heads both before and when they are feeling anxious. Group members can do this by using the anxious thoughts form (Handout 3). They will already know their feelings and thoughts from keeping their stress diary (Session 1: Handout 5) and have identified the thoughts going through their minds. Sometimes people say their mind is blank but they can usually be helped to identify what they were thinking before the situation arose. Usually they will have been anticipating the event and anxiety will have been building. Alternatively, get them to make themselves aware of their thoughts the next time they are in an anxiety-giving situation.

Next, teach them to challenge these thoughts and unreasonable beliefs. This can be very difficult for some people and will require a lot of practice and work on their part. Some may say: 'I can reason this through now and see that the thoughts are unreasonable, but when I'm in the situation I will not be able to think all this through.' That is why it is important that they reason it through when they are not feeling anxious. Once they have established what it is reasonable to think in the situation, they can write these thoughts down on a card and look at them regularly. When they are in the situation they can take the card out of a handbag or pocket and read it to remind themselves.

After having coped with a situation, it is also useful reinforcement for the person to congratulate themselves. They can do this by saying something like: 'Congratulations! I felt nervous. It was difficult. I made one small error but nobody seemed to mind when I corrected myself. I coped – and next time I will be able to relax a bit more.'

Reassure group members that while initially doing the above can seem false it is effective with practice. Combined with breathing and relaxation techniques, it provides a really powerful technique for coping with the most anxiety-giving situations.

Making Use of Mental Tension Control

The relaxation and breathing techniques, along with the above techniques previously discussed, provide good methods of bringing tension under control. Some additional suggestions are:

◆ Constantly remind group members that the techniques will help them take control of their anxiety and their lives.

◆ Some people may find that worrying thoughts keep running on and on in their mind. When this happens they need to say firmly to themselves: 'Stop!' and replace the thoughts with more realistic and rational ones.

◆ Others may get caught up in procrastinating over why they became anxious. Ask them: 'Does this matter?' They may never know – so why worry! It does not matter as long as they take control of their anxiety now.

◆ Remind people not to expect miracles. Learning to challenge thoughts takes time and practice. There will be setbacks. They will probably have lived with their anxiety for a long time; it will take time and practice to regain control.

◆ Suggest distraction. This means they find something else to occupy the mind and is based on the fact that people can only concentrate on one thing at a time. Therefore, if they focus on something else that is more pleasant or engaging, they cannot think negative thoughts at the same time. Distractions can include:

1 Engaging in some sort of mental activity. Reciting or making up poetry, working out a plan for a job they have to do, doing mental arithmetic, reading a book or keeping a relaxing image in mind.

2 Focusing on what is happening around them. Counting the number of objects they pass on a journey beginning with a letter of the alphabet, listening to other people's conversation, trying to work out from people's appearances as much about them as possible and so on.

3 Keeping physically occupied. Handing round the food at a party, going for a walk, cutting the grass or doing some gardening, doing something for an elderly neighbour. Getting involved in a sporting activity – anything from golf to table-tennis or swimming. Physical activities not only provide good distraction from negative thoughts but help to use up adrenalin that makes group members feel tense.

Distraction works well for a lot of people but is not always the best method for everyone. People will need to experiment to find out if it works for them.

◆ Before going into the anxiety-giving situation, they might try imagining it in as much detail as possible. This entails sitting down quietly, closing their eyes, relaxing and then imagining getting ready for the situation – going on a bus, going into a shop or whatever. They need to imagine it in as much detail as possible, the place itself, other people, going through their chosen coping strategies, dealing really well with the situation, seeing themselves coping as they would like to. They dwell on this image for a while and then congratulate themselves on their success. Rehearsing in this manner can be really helpful and give a big boost to confidence.

◆ Maybe they have particular tense spots such as knots in the stomach, bands around the head, backache and so on. They can imagine the tense spot in their mind as vividly as possible. Imagine the bands around their head loosening, the knots in their stomach being untied, the muscle tissue becoming looser. At the same time, they can imagine the pain or tenseness easing, falling or draining away, letting a feeling of calm gradually wash over them and with it the pain or tenseness disappearing. As they relax it will happen.

◆ Encourage people to congratulate themselves, give themselves treats as a way of saying 'well done' and to acknowledge that they are making progress. This can be reinforced in 'feed-back' sessions by having people report their successes to each other. They must not just wait for other people to acknowledge and congratulate them, but become practised in congratulating themselves. This is important. Initial small steps lead to greater things.

◆ Stopping using delaying and avoiding tactics. Tackling problems right away and putting maximum effort into it avoids going over and over problems in their minds. Instead, they tell themselves they can cope with the situation and do it. This will give them a feeling of being in control. The alternative will be to allow their anxieties to control them and stop them doing what they want to do.

Not all of the above techniques will suit everyone. Individuals will need to experiment and discover what works best for them.

Aims	1 To explore concepts of negative/faulty thinking	
	2 To teach methods of controlling faulty thinking	
	3 To explore methods of controlling mental tension	

Materials Flipchart, magic markers and copies of handouts

CONTENT	Time
Discussion on individual progress and homework assignments	*15 minutes*
State the aims of the session and explain why negative/faulty thinking is unhelpful; go through handout 1 and discuss what negative thoughts group members have. *(Presentation and discussion – handout 1)*	*15 minutes*
Identifying faulty thinking *(Exercise – handout 2)*	*15 minutes*
Explain the process of challenging faulty thinking *(Presentation and discussion – handout 3)*	*15 minutes*
Break	*10 minutes*
Challenging faulty thinking *(Exercise)*	*30 minutes*
Mental tension control methods *(Presentation and discussion – handout 4)*	*15 minutes*
Looking at the gains *(Exercise and discussion)*	*15 minutes*
Homework assignments	*5 minutes*

Exercises and Assignments

Identifying faulty thinking

Give each group member an 'Anxious thoughts form' (handout 2) and ask them to write down what their thoughts are before and during an anxious situation. It will be useful to use stress diary entries and notes from the previous session (assignment 3) to help with this. Some people may also find it helpful to do the exercise with a partner or member of the group.

Challenging faulty thinking

Divide the group into twos and have them assist each other to challenge their negative thoughts using handout 3 as a guide. Once they have gone through the process of challenging the thoughts, have them write on the 'Anxious thoughts form' (handout 2) what would be more realistic and helpful to think in the circumstances. Have each person do this for at least two anxiety-giving situations. Finally, the group comes back together again and each person reads out one situation, what their original thoughts were and what their re-evaluated thoughts are.

Homework assignments

Instruct group members to:

1 Complete their stress diary.
2 Practise mental tension control methods.
3 Continue physical relaxation practice.
4 Use the 'Anxious thoughts form' to make notes of faulty thinking when anxiety begins to take hold. Also, using the challenging procedure, they can re-evaluate the thoughts with more realistic and rational thinking.

Faulty thinking

Common faulty-thinking categories

Irrational and faulty thinking often falls into one of the following areas:

Catastrophising

This is anticipating total disaster if something minor goes wrong. An example is: 'That woman is looking at me. I must look awful!'

Exaggeration

This is magnifying things beyond the limits of truth. You make a small mistake and then worry all day in case someone finds out and thinks you are an idiot.

Dismissing the positive

You dismiss the positive when you turn positive events into a negative. 'He's only saying that to make me feel better.' You dismiss the positive when you overlook all your personal strengths and successful experiences and continually ignore achievements and dwell on failures.

Overgeneralisations

Having one bad experience leads you to believe that every experience will be bad. One person refuses a request so you assume everyone will also refuse.

Impossible standards

This is expecting always to be able to do everything perfectly and never make a mistake. The negative thoughts are usually prefixed with words like:

'I should cope with …'
'I ought …'
'I must …'

These statements are usually followed by thoughts such as: 'I'll never be able to do this.' 'I can't do it. I'm a failure.'

Making assumptions

This is making assumptions and jumping to conclusions without regard to the facts. Thoughts include: 'Everyone thinks I'm a fool.' 'Nobody likes me.'

Anxious thoughts form

Anxious situation	Automatic thoughts before and during anxious situation	How much do you believe the thoughts? 0–100	Realistic alternatives to think	How much do you believe the thoughts now? 0–100

Challenging faulty thinking

Examine your thoughts and consider how accurate and realistic they are. Do this by:

1 *Looking at the evidence.*

2 *Checking your feelings and thinking with other people who cope with similar situations.*

3 *Challenging what you believe will be the consequence.*

4 *Looking at different ways of interpreting situations.*

5 *Asking yourself if your expectations are realistic.*

6 *Stating what it is realistic to be thinking.*

Making use of mental tension control

The relaxation and breathing techniques previously learned provide good methods for bringing tension under control. Some additional suggestions are:

◆ Constantly remind yourself that practising the techniques on this course will enable you to take control of your life.

◆ If worrying thoughts keep running on and on in your mind pull yourself up short and say firmly 'STOP!' Immediately replace the thoughts with more realistic and rational ones.

◆ Do not procrastinate continuously over why you have become anxious. Ask yourself 'Does this matter?' You may never know why – so why worry? It does not matter as long as you take control of your anxiety now.

◆ Do not expect miracles. Learning to challenge thoughts takes time and practice. There will be setbacks.

◆ Distract yourself. This means finding something else to occupy your mind and is based on the fact that you can only concentrate on one thing at a time. Try:
  1 Engaging in some sort of mental activity.
  2 Focusing on what is happening around you.
  3 Keeping physically occupied.
  Distraction works well for a lot of people but it is not always the best method for everyone. You will need to experiment to find out if it works for you.

◆ Rehearse the situation. Imagine it in as much detail as possible, the place itself, other people, going through your chosen coping strategies and dealing really well with the situation. Dwell on this image for a while and congratulate yourself on your success.

◆ If you have particular tense spots such as 'bands' around the head, imagine the band falling away. Let a feeling of calm gradually wash over you and with it the pain or tenseness disappearing.

◆ Congratulate yourself, give yourself treats as a way of saying 'well done' and acknowledging you are making progress. Reinforce this by acknowledging your success to other people in 'feedback' sessions.

◆ Stop using delaying and avoiding tactics. Tackle problems right away and put maximum effort into it.

Not all of the above techniques will suit everyone. You will need to experiment and discover what works best for you.

Facing the Fear

Defining the Fear

The first step in learning to control anxiety is to define the anxiety-giving situation. Statements like 'I get anxious when I go out' or 'I am anxious at work' are too general. Statements need to be specific: 'Going into crowded shops' or 'Eating and drinking with other people'. Group members should have identified a number of these situations in their stress diary.

Using the 'Anxiety-giving situation form' (handout 1), have group members list all the situations in which they feel excessive anxiety. These can include obsessive compulsive activities, phobias and so on. They also need to write down how anxious they are in the situation, on a scale of 0–100. An example would be:

Anxiety-Giving Situation Form

	Anxiety-giving situation	Anxiety rating 0–100
1	Using the phone	50
2	Going into the supermarket each week	85
3	Using public transport	95
4	Staying in the house by myself	70
5	Having a bath or shower	90
6	Locking and closing doors and windows	85
7	Talking to people in authority	80
8	Joining an evening class	88

The list must be specific to each person. They will see from it what situations give rise to their anxiety, and the degree of that anxiety. Do remind people that what may rate high for one person may be low on someone else's list. This is normal. Completing the list will enable individuals to measure their anxiety levels in the same situation in the future and see positive gains. It will also enable them to focus their newly-learned skills on specific goals.

When each person has a complete list, the situations then need to be rewritten on another sheet in order of difficulty – the least anxiety-giving situation at the top and the most anxiety-giving at the bottom. Starting work on the least anxiety-giving situation will provide an opportunity for them to learn that it is not really dangerous or frightening. Practising on a situation which makes them feel uncomfortable or frightened reduces the anxiety provided they go about it in a planned way. This will help to build their confidence, knowing that they can face their fears before progressing to more difficult situations.

Setting Goals

Having selected a goal to work on, this may then need to be broken down into smaller specific steps that can be achieved realistically. Here is an example using the format as shown in the 'Goals Form' supplied in handout 2:

SESSION 4 HANDOUT 2	**Goals form**

Goal   *Go to the shopping centre, go into the shops and make my purchases on my own.*

Steps

1   Walk alone to the end of the road and back.

2   Walk alone to the bus stop, stay there for a few minutes and walk back.

3   Walk alone to the bus stop, get on a bus to the shopping centre and catch the next bus back.

4   Walk alone to the bus stop, get on a bus to the shopping centre and walk around the shopping centre for 30 minutes before coming back.

5   Walk alone to the bus stop, get a bus to the shopping centre, walk around the centre, window shopping, then go into a shop to make a purchase.

And so on.

If the person has really high anxiety levels the above might need to be broken down into even smaller steps. For example:

Steps

1   Walk alone half way to the end of the road and back

2   Walk alone to the end of the road and back

3   Walk alone half way to the bus stop and back

4   Walk alone to the bus stop and back

5   Walk alone to the bus stop and stay there for a few minutes.

6   Walk alone to the bus stop, wait for a bus and travel one bus stop.

And so on.

The number of steps will depend on the individual and the degree of anxiety. Each step should be realistic and achievable. Each step may also need to be completed several times before moving on to the next one. Also, ensure that participants write down when and how often the step they are going to do is to be practised. They should do the same for the second step, before moving on to do it.

It may, for some, be desirable – in the example given – for a companion to accompany the person on the walk at first. Then the next stage might be for the companion to walk on the other side of the road, so they can be seen by the person. This could be followed by the companion walking twenty paces behind, so the person can get used to walking the distance without seeing them. When the person goes on the bus alone it may be desirable for the companion to be at the bus stop when they alight, and so on. For some people who have long-established high anxiety levels, it is necessary to progress in small but achievable steps – this is especially so in the early stages, so that confidence can be built in their ability to deal with their anxiety.

With modifications this process can be applied to all situations. Remember, learning to cope with anxiety is a gradual process that requires practice. Successful small initial steps lead to later larger steps. Once individuals have built confidence in applying their new skills they can then start applying them in more stressful situations.

To be useful, practice needs to be:

◆ *Frequent* enough for the benefits not to be lost. Walking to the bus stop once a week is not going to achieve as much as doing it once a day.

◆ *Repeated* until the person feels comfortable.

◆ *Acknowledged.* This means the person recognising their achievement and rewarding themselves with self-praise and/or a treat.

If a step proves to be too difficult, help the person look for ways of breaking it down into even smaller steps.

Writing down the goals and steps to achieve them in the above manner helps people know what they are aiming for, how they are going to achieve it and indicates how long it is going to take.

Planning to Face the Fear

Once everyone has decided on the goal and the steps they are going to undertake to achieve it, a plan is needed to deal with any anticipated difficulties or things that might go wrong. This may be something that has happened in the past or an unexpected event. Whatever, it is much easier to work out a plan of action beforehand when not under stress so that if anything does happen the person is prepared to deal with it. A 'Solutions form' (handout 3) is supplied to help with this. An example of how it may be filled in is shown on p77.

Encourage people to write down as many alternative solutions as possible to the problem; they can then choose the best one for them.

Each group member should by now have acquired enough skills and done enough planning to begin confronting their fear. They should be working on only one step and goal at a time and have decided:

◆ *When they will confront their fear.* This includes the specific time of day.

◆ *How often they will confront the fear.* Remember, the more often they do so the better. For example, the person walking to the bus stop would benefit more from doing this once or twice a day than from twice a week.

◆ *What they are going to do.* This should be clearly planned.

◆ *Where it will happen.* This needs to be specific.

◆ *Who else will be involved.* This may be a companion to escort the person to the bus stop once, and so on.

**SESSION 4
HANDOUT 3** | **Solutions form**

Goal/step _Walk alone to the end of the road and catch a bus to the shopping centre._

Difficulty	Solutions
Getting short of breath	Rest if caused by physical effort. Bring breathing back under control if caused by anxiety. Stay with the fear until it passes.
Starting to think negatively	Look at a card with realistic thoughts written down.
What if the bus is early and I miss it?	Wait for the next one – there will be another soon.
What if my husband has trouble parking the car and will not be at the bus stop on time to meet me?	Wait. He will be along in a few minutes as soon as he has parked. If the worst happens and he does not turn up I can get the next bus back home.

Facing the Fear

Each person should now be prepared to face their fear. There is nothing left but to put the plan into action. There is bound to be some anxiety but there is a plan to cope. Having plans worked out and knowing what to do when difficulties arise should give the confidence to deal with the situation. Remind people:

1   To congratulate themselves after they have carried out their plan. It does not matter if it went well or there were difficulties – they have faced their fear. That by itself is a success.

2   If there were some difficulties or anxious moments learn from them. Work out what, if anything, went wrong. Because they felt anxious does not mean something went wrong.

◆   They may need to repeat the exercise several times, building more confidence on each occasion until the anxiety begins to subside

◆ They may need to look again at their options for dealing with difficulties – perhaps there is another solution that will work better for them.

◆ They may have misjudged slightly and set too difficult a step. Break it down into two or more smaller steps.

◆ They may not have been feeling very well on the day. We all have bad days on which we perform badly.

Having reviewed the exercise after completion they will need to decide to:

1 Stick with the original plan, or
2 Make some slight adjustment in the light of their experience.

Do emphasise that no matter how badly the event has gone they have not failed. They have begun to face their fear and begun to learn how to cope with it.

Maintaining Progress

Some points to bear in mind to help people maintain progress are:

1 Each person needs to progress at the right pace for them. This will be different for each person. The level of anxiety should never be more than the person feels is manageable. It is better to progress slowly than have a series of overwhelming experiences which are discouraging.
2 Individuals should work on just one goal at a time.
3 They should always work on the least anxiety-giving situation/step first. When they feel comfortable doing this, they then move on to the next situation/step as appropriate.
4 A wide selection of tactics has been taught. Not every one will be useful in every situation. Group members need to plan which tactic they are going to use for each situation.
5 The involvement of a friend or family member is usually most useful in the early stages when an escort may be necessary. Later they can continue to give encouragement and support. However, group members should make sure that the friend understands the purpose of what they are doing. They should not be tempted to hold on to the security provided by someone helping – they are working towards being independent. Also, they should be aware

that the person helping can sometimes become impatient if they do not understand and progress is slow.

6   There will be bad days and setbacks. Maintaining progress means being committed and giving the programme high priority by:

   ◆ practising the exercises regularly
   ◆ learning from setbacks

They must not stop doing the exercises for periods just because one or two events have not gone well. Progress needs to be measured over long periods – not a few days. Accurate progress will be shown with use of the monitoring forms. There may be days or even weeks when symptoms seem worse or a plateau appears to have been reached. There will also be times when there is rapid improvement. It is natural that these 'up and down' fluctuations occur. If the techniques are practised continually the anxiety levels will diminish and progress made over a long period.

Preventing Relapse

Relapse is a serious return of former anxiety levels that individuals have managed to overcome – over and above the normal 'up and down' that occurs in normal recovery.

This can occur for a number of reasons:

1   Irregular practice of the techniques learned. The person will need to set a regular programme as outlined previously and keep to it. They may need some help working out solutions to difficulties.

2   Exposure to new external stresses. These will need to be identified and addressed, following the same process already explained. The new stresses may be caused by life events or other changes outside the individual's control. (Further discussion is provided in Session 9.)

3   Unrealistic expectation that all stress will disappear. This may be linked to the person having difficulty accepting normal levels of stress and mistaking it as a sign of relapse.

4   Vulnerability to stress because of lack of a healthy lifestyle. The person will need to re-examine their lifestyle, ensuring that they are taking exercise, eating a healthy diet and avoiding excessive stimulants. After reviewing their lifestyle the person will need to continue or resume the techniques taught. (Further discussion is provided in Session 8.)

5 Vulnerability to stress because of a physical illness. If there is any doubt about what is wrong, the person should see their doctor for an assessment to ensure the stress is not physically- or medically-related.

6 Vulnerability to stress because of low self-esteem, lack of confidence and ability to be assertive. (This is addressed in Sessions 6 and 8.)

7 Stopping practising anxiety-reducing techniques too soon. The techniques should become each person's coping tactics for the rest of their lives, using them any time they encounter an anxiety-giving situation. They are learned skills which can be brought into play any time they are needed.

8 Stopping taking anti-anxiety medication too soon. Even if the person is experiencing considerable improvement, reducing and stopping taking anti-anxiety drugs should be done only under the supervision of a doctor. If the doctor has reduced the dosage and increased anxiety is experienced, the person must consult their doctor for advice on whether the symptoms will pass quickly or whether they need to increase the dosage again and reduce at a slower rate.

9 Attempting to overcome the problem situation too quickly. Preparation may not be adaquate or the person may be pushing themselves too hard. Have the person rethink the steps – these may need breaking down into smaller more manageable units.

10 Returning to a negative/faulty thinking pattern. They will need to ensure they go through the challenging process again thoroughly and work on building their self-esteem and confidence. They should also be sure they acknowledge and reward themselves for their successes.

11 Depression. Frequently, anxiety and depression are linked. If the symptoms are fairly minor the person will probably be able to sustain motivation to continue with their programme. The bout, if short, may be overcome by concentrating the mind on and doing pleasant things or it might be triggered by negative thoughts. If so skill in challenging these thoughts will help the person overcome it. It will also be helpful to think through any stresses the person faces and work out a strategy to deal with them. If the depression persists or is overwhelming, with the person feeling hopeless or desperate, they must seek other professional help. Medication,

counselling, or a combination of these, or hospital admission, may
be necessary if the depression is very severe.

12 Return of psychotic or acute behavioural disturbances. The person
must consult their doctor to ensure these symptoms are treated.

13 A fear of the change that is occurring and a desire to ensure that
their dependency needs are met. Change can be very frightening;
being able to do things for themselves might mean taking on more
family and other responsibilities. It will bring with it the loss of
their need for their current support system. This will need to be
carefully worked through by the individual.

14 Side effects of sedative medications that cause lack of
concentration and drop in motivation. The person should consult
their doctor who may be able to assist by a planned reduction in
medication, or perhaps give them something to reduce the effects.

It is important that the group leader understands why a client is
relapsing. It may indicate that:

◆ The person was unsuitable for anxiety management training at this
time.
◆ Anxiety management methods need to be adapted to suit the
changing needs of the individual.
◆ Advice should be given or a referral made for appropriate
treatment.

Looking at the Gains

The stage before group members start facing their fears is a good time to
invite them to look at what they will gain from the process. This can then
be used as a motivating instrument and a constant reminder of what
they have to gain – especially when set-backs occur.

A simple chart works well for most people. A blank 'Gains Form'
(Handout 7) is supplied for use in the session. There is an example on p82.

When the 'Gains Forms' have been filled in by everyone, provide
additional positive reinforcement by doing a visualisation exercise. This
is an exercise that individuals can do regularly to help maintain their
motivation and build confidence in achieving their goals. Explain that
visualisation means to rehearse mentally, or see in the mind. It is a way

Gains form

Not learning to cope with my anxiety means:	Learning to cope with my anxiety will enable me to:
Being dependent on other people	Go shopping when I want to
Not having anyone to talk to	Enjoy walks when the weather is nice
Being lonely	Go out and meet other people
Getting depressed	Join an evening class
Feeling helpless	Meet my friend for coffee when I go shopping
Missing out on life	Be independent
Not being able to do the things I want to do	Be responsible
	Have control of my life

of bringing about change in how they see themselves. A clear picture is created in the mind of something they want to happen, change or achieve. The important part of visualisation is imagining the desired changes happening and feeling how it will be when changes, steps or goals have been achieved. The detailed process is given in the exercises and assignment section of the session plans. When the visualisation process is complete ask for feedback about the experience. Did everyone actually see themselves making the changes and achieving their goals?

This is a powerful exercise. However, for it to work people have to believe that they can make changes. It also takes practice and to be most effective needs to be carried out regularly – a few times each day.

It can be very helpful to conclude this activity with a short discussion of what the outcome of negative visualisation might be. What happens when people visualise they cannot do something? Do group members do this often? In what way is it like negative/faulty thinking? How can positive visualisation affect outcome?

Aims
1 To identify anxiety-giving situations
2 To set goals
3 To plan to face the fear

Materials Flipchart, magic markers, copies of handouts and pens

CONTENT	Time
Discussion on individual progress and homework assignments	*15 minutes*
State the aims of the session and do identifying anxiety-giving situations exercise *(Exercise and discussion – handout 1)*	*15 minutes*
Setting goals and working out step-by-step plans to achieve them *(Exercise and discussion – handout 2)*	*15 minutes*
Planning to face your fear *(Exercise and discussion – handout 3)*	*15 minutes*
Break	*10 minutes*
Facing your fear *(Presentation and discussion – handout 4)*	*15 minutes*
Maintaining progress and preventing relapse *(Presentation and discussion – handouts 5 and 6)*	*15 minutes*
Looking at the gains *(Exercise and discussion)*	*15 minutes*
Homework assignments	*5 minutes*

4 Session

Exercises and Assignments

Identifying anxiety-giving situations

Give each group member two copies of the 'Anxiety-giving situation form' (handout 1), explain the reason for using it and how to fill it in. Ask each person to complete one form without worrying about the order of situations and then rewrite them, beginning with the least anxiety-giving situation first and the most difficult last. Group leaders will need to circulate to help anyone having difficulty. Some people may find it helpful to work in pairs. When the task has been completed have the group discuss any difficulties.

Setting goals and working out step-by-step plans

Explain the reason behind working out a step-by-step plan, give out the forms (handout 2) and clarify how to fill them in. Participants then select their first goal and work out a step-by-step plan to achieve it. Some may find it helpful to work in pairs. End by bringing the group back together and discussing any difficulties.

Planning to face your fears

Explain the reason behind working out a plan to deal with any difficulties or things which might go wrong. Give out the 'Solutions form' (handout 3) and explain how to use it. Participants then write down any anticipated difficulties and how they will cope with them. Again, some may find it helpful to work in pairs. When completed, discuss any queries.

Facing your fear

Go through handout 4 and discuss.

Maintaining progress and preventing relapse

Go through handouts 5 and 6 and discuss.

Looking at the gains

Explain why it is helpful to look at gains at this point. Give out the 'Gains form' (handout 7), clarify how to fill it in and then invite the group members to do so. When completed, have a brief feedback discussion.

Now explain the purpose of visualisation, how it works and that the group is going to be talked through the process. It takes about five minutes with a further five minutes afterwards for discussion. When everyone is ready, read out the following instructions, pausing between each step.

Visualisation

Step 1   Focus on the first step on which you have decided to work.

Step 2   Close your eyes, relax and breathe deeply three or four times. Let any tensions flow away as you breathe out.

Step 3   Imagine yourself somewhere that you find peaceful and relaxing. Examples: by a stream, in a favourite room, in a garden, in the mountains or by the sea. Choose a place and think about it for a moment and feel yourself relax.

Step 4   Now imagine yourself achieving your step. If you begin to feel anxious, see yourself using your coping strategies and overcoming the fear. Think about how it feels to be able to do it and achieve what you want.

Wait a moment or two, ask everyone to open their eyes and re-orientate themselves to the group again. Ask participants for feedback from their experience then explain that for the exercise to work they must:

◆ believe that they can make changes
◆ practice the process regularly – several times each day.

Conclude the exercise with a brief discussion on what the outcome of negative visualisation might be. Have the group consider:

1   What happens when people visualise that they cannot do something?
2   How often does each person do this?
3   In what way is it like negative/faulty thinking?
4   How can positive visualisation affect outcome?

Homework assignments

Instruct group members to:

1   Complete their stress diary
2   Practise imaginary visualisation and coping strategies
3   Begin work on selected goals

Anxiety-giving situation form

	Anxiety-Giving Situation	Anxiety Rating 0 – 100
1		
2		
3		
4		
5		
6		
7		
8		
9		
10		
11		
12		
13		
14		
15		
16		
17		
18		

Goals form

Goal _____

_____

_____

_____

Steps

1   _____

_____

_____

2   _____

_____

_____

3   _____

_____

_____

4   _____

_____

_____

5   _____

_____

_____

6   _____

_____

_____

7   _____

_____

_____

8   _____

_____

_____

Note: Include in the first step when you are going to carry it out, how often and when you anticipate completion. When this has been achieved do the same for step two.

Solutions form

Goal/step _____

_____

Difficulty	Solutions

You should now be prepared to face your fear. There is nothing left but to put your plan into action. Remember:

1 To congratulate yourself each time, after you have carried out your plan. It does not matter if it went well or there were difficulties – you have faced your fear. That by itself is a success.

2 If there were some difficulties or anxious moments, learn from them. Work out what, if anything, went wrong. Because you felt anxious does not necessarily mean something went wrong. Review your experience of the exercise.

◆ You may need to repeat the exercise several times, building more confidence on each occasion until the anxiety begins to subside.

◆ You may need to look again at your options for dealing with difficulties – perhaps there is another solution that will work better for you.

◆ You may have misjudged slightly and set too difficult a step. Break it down into smaller steps.

◆ You may not have been feeling very well on the day. Everyone has bad days on which they perform badly.

Having reviewed the exercise you will need to decide to:

1 Stick with the original plan.
2 Make some slight adjustment in the light of your experience.

Remember, no matter how badly the event has gone you have not failed. You have begun to face your fear and to learn how to cope with it.

Maintaining progress

Points to bear in mind to help you maintain progress are:

1 You need to progress at the right pace for you. This is different for each person. The level of anxiety should never be more than you feel is manageable.

2 Work on only one goal at a time.

3 Always work on the least anxiety-giving situation/step until you feel reasonably comfortable with it. Then move on to the next situation/step as appropriate.

4 You have been taught a wide selection of tactics. Not every one will be useful in every situation. You need to plan which tactics you are going to use for each situation.

5 The involvement of a friend or family member is usually most useful in the early stages, when an escort may be necessary. Later, they can continue to give encouragement and support. But do not forget you are working towards being independent.

6 There will be bad days and setbacks. Maintaining progress means being committed and giving your programme high priority:

◆ practising the exercises regularly
◆ learning from setbacks

Relapse is a serious return of former anxiety levels that you have managed to overcome – over and above the normal 'up and down' that occurs in normal recovery. This can occur for a number of reasons:

1 Irregular practice of the techniques you have learned.
2 Exposure to new external stresses.
3 Unrealistic expectation that all stress will disappear.
4 Vulnerability to stress because of a lack of a healthy lifestyle.
5 Vulnerability to stress because of a physical illness. If you have any doubts about what is wrong you should see your doctor for an assessment to ensure it is not physically or medically related.
6 Vulnerability to stress because of low self-esteem, lack of confidence and ability to be assertive.
7 Stopping practising anxiety-reducing techniques too soon. The techniques should become your coping tactics for the rest of your life.
8 Stopping taking anti-anxiety medication too soon. Even if you are feeling a big improvement, reducing and stopping anti-anxiety drugs should only be done under the supervision of a doctor.
9 Attempting to overcome the problem situation too quickly.
10 Returning to negative/faulty thinking patterns.
11 Depression. Frequently, anxiety and depression are linked. If the depression persists or is overwhelming, if you feel hopeless or desperate, you must seek professional help. Medication, counselling,
a combination of these or hospital admission may be necessary if the depression is very severe.
12 Return of psychotic or acute behavioural disturbances. You must consult your doctor to ensure these symptoms are treated.
13 A fear of the change that is occurring and a need to ensure that your dependency needs are met.
14 Side-effects of sedative medications that cause lack of concentration and a drop in motivation. You should consult your doctor.

It is important that you understand why you are relapsing. It may
indicate that:

◆ An anxiety management programme is unsuitable for you at this time.
◆ The anxiety management methods need to be adapted to suit your changing needs.
◆ You should obtain alternate appropriate treatment.

Gains form

Not learning to cope with my anxiety means:	Learning to cope with my anxiety will enable me to:

Solving Problems and Making Decisions

Taking Positive Action

Everyone has problems – no matter who they are. Looking at the newspapers or watching the news raises awareness of some of the problems faced by the rich and successful. No matter who it is, the only way to solve problems is to take positive action.

In previous sessions the group members will have already used a number of problem-solving techniques. This session will look at problem-solving in more detail.

Becoming aware that there is a problem

How do people know that they have a problem? It is usually when they feel discomfort or dissatisfaction of some sort and realise that what they are doing is not working very well. This can show itself in a variety of ways including:

anger	frustration	anxiety
stress	depression	agitation
lack of self-esteem	feeling of life being wasted	lack of control of life

Frequently they may experience the discomfort but remain unaware of what the problem is or what they want or need. They may feel anxious or stressed but be unaware of what is causing the anxiety.

Alternatively, they may be well aware of what is causing the anxiety. This can include everyday issues such as:

arguing with work colleagues   disagreements with partner
shortage of money   lack of company
being always late for appointments   how to get somewhere
what to cook for dinner   how to impress someone

The number of problems that people encounter each day are limitless. Yet how many individuals have been taught how to deal effectively with them? Or how to make themselves aware when they are not sure what is causing the problem?

This session looks at some positive actions that can help people solve the problems encountered. In brief, they are:

Step 1   Recognise there is a problem and state what it is
Step 2   Restate the problem in a way which leads to positive action
Step 3   Accept responsibility for the problem
Step 4   Think of actions which will solve the problem
Step 5   Choose a solution or a combination of solutions
Step 6   Work out a step-by-step action plan
Step 7   Put the plan into action
Step 8   Evaluate and adjust the plan as necessary as the action plan progresses

Blocks to Problem-Solving

Before working through the steps it is helpful to look at some blocks to problem-solving. Many of these blocks prevent individuals from seeing what the problem is or how it can be solved. The group members will recognise some of the blocks and be able to relate them to their own difficulties. Problem-solving is a learned skill. Past experience may have led individuals into poor behaviour patterns which prevent them from being able to solve their problems. This, in turn, may lead to their manipulating other people into trying to solve their problems for them or becoming passive, with the result that the problem increases, as does their discomfort. Blocks include:

1   *Inability to recognise or acknowledge the problem.* Many things can lead to this:
    ◆   Not believing the situation can be changed.
    ◆   Fear of not being able to deal with the problem.

- Pride.
- Ignoring the significance of what they are feeling.
- Not recognising that old behaviour has outlasted its usefulness and the situation has changed.
- Not expecting their feelings to change because they think they ought to feel bad because of their situation and demand to be understood.
- Distorting reality because it clashes with a belief they hold – changing the belief may cause greater discomfort than the problem, so they stick with it. Also include in this catastrophising, exaggeration, dismissing the positive, over-generalisation, setting impossible standards and making assumptions – all of which have been encountered in Session 3.
- Refusing to ask for help.
- Deciding they should always be in control.
- Depending on other people to solve their problems.
- Defending their current actions or situation (many people spend all their energy and time justifying their current situation and feelings).
- Previous experience of failure may not have included information appropriate to solving the problem.
- Rebelling and keeping others from helping them achieve their goal.

2 *Lack of training and knowledge in being able to define problems.* This leads to not being able to define the problem in a solvable way. It is the result of not being taught how to solve problems.

3 *Not taking responsibility for the problem.* Signs that this is happening include:
- Blaming other people for how they feel, think and behave.
- Blaming other people for their inability to resolve the problem.
- Trying to get other people to solve what is their own problem.

4 *Having set rules of thinking.* This limits the alternative choices for action and occurs when a person decides not to think for themselves but let other people do it for them. Alternatively, they may become blinkered by their perspective of the problem and refuse to view it from other angles.

5 *Difficulty in deciding from alternative choices which is the right action to take.* Often caused by lack of training in decision-making methods.

6 *Inability to work out an achievable step-by-step action plan.* Causes include:
- Lack of realism about achievable steps.
- Lack of knowledge about how to structure and work out a plan.

7 *Inability to take action even when a plan has been worked out.* Reasons may include:
- Lack of skills needed to carry out the action plan (a good plan will include the acquiring of any skills needed).
- Lack of personal skills such as time-management, assertiveness, communication, decision-making, self-management and so on.

8 *Inability to learn from experience and take corrective action.* This is the person who repeats the same mistakes over and over again, repeating the same ineffective behaviour. The result is that they begin to feel that nothing they do will succeed. They neglect to evaluate and adjust the action plan as they progress.

Steps to Problem-Solving

Now, having looked at some of the blocks to problem-solving it is time to examine each step in the process of solving a problem.

Step 1: *Recognising that there is a problem and stating what it is.* It is helpful to define what a problem is. For the purposes of these sessions it is an event or situation which produces discomfort for which a person has not developed an automatic response behaviour to enable them to deal with it in a satisfactory way. It follows then that they must develop a strategy to meet that need. If a person feels discomfort and does not know what the problem is they will need to acknowledge the stimuli – both internal and external. Handout 2 can be used to explore whether they are using blocks to avoid the problem. They should start questioning themselves:

- Do I believe the situation can be changed?
- Am I catastrophising?
- Am I putting all my energy into defending my position?

And so on.

Stating the problem is sometimes not as easy as it seems. They may feel anxious or depressed. They may need to question themselves about this:

◆ How long have I felt depressed? (Three months.)
◆ What happened then? (My wife had a promotion and started earning more than I do.)
◆ What did I think about that? (She's a clever woman. She's talking about having to travel and stay away overnight. She's started making new friends. I'm afraid that she'll meet someone else cleverer than me. I want her to get on but I'm afraid of losing her.)

By this process of questioning themselves they can discover what the problem is. If they do not acknowledge it, state what it is and believe they are capable of solving it, they will not be able to find appropriate solutions.

Step 2: *Restate the problem in a solvable way that leads to action.* The way in which a problem is stated can provide a block in itself or make the problem unsolvable. Stating it in a way that leads to taking some action helps avoid this. Stating 'My son had an accident nine months ago. Now I am so worried it will happen again I don't let him go out. He is unhappy if he stays in and I can't cope with the worry if he goes out. It makes me so depressed.' Thinking in this way does not lead to a solution for the problem. If, instead, the person identifies the problem and restates it 'I need to learn to keep my unrealistic and catastrophising thoughts under control when my son goes out.' the problem becomes much more solvable. And a plan can be worked out to do just that. They have identified the problem, which is not depression or the fact that another accident could happen (although unlikely), but their thoughts about it.

It may be that the problem does not seem solvable because it involves elements over which a person has no control: for example, bad weather when they are on holiday. There is nothing anybody can do about bad weather, so it is pointless using energy to try to change it. However, supposing they rethink the problem and restate it in a different way. One way might be: 'What can I do on holiday when the weather is bad?' Now they have a solvable problem and one that they can believe that they can do something about.

Problems can be stated in many ways and it is worthwhile for group members to practise stating them from different viewpoints. The statement that is the right one is the one that leads to action, provides a solution and reduces the discomfort caused by the problem.

Step 3: *Accept responsibility (Whose problem is it?)* If a person is dumping their problem on other people it may be detected in how they speak. 'He makes me feel bad/good …'; 'I make him feel ashamed …'. The idea that someone can make someone else feel good or bad assumes that they have control over them. In reality this is not true. People exposed to the same stimuli will respond differently. If someone drives down the road well below the speed limit it may get different responses from different people. An eager and impatient young driver late for an appointment may respond 'Silly old fool, shouldn't be allowed on the road. People like him cause accidents.' Another person, perhaps a mother collecting a young child from a nearby school might say: 'Ah, if only other people drove as carefully as him the roads would be much safer.' This indicates that individuals can control how they respond if they take responsibility for their feelings.

If a person feels discomfort then the problem must be their responsibility. If two or more people are in the same situation then this might be shared – but each person must accept responsibility for their part of it.

If a person owns the problem then they need to take responsibility for their behaviour (response to it) – that is their thoughts, feelings and actions. If they do not, then they will not be able to solve it or bring about change.

If an individual brings a problem to a friend, the friend may want to help them solve it, but it is not the friend's problem and they do not have any responsibility to solve it. If they try to push it on to their friend, the friend is justified in giving it back to that person. The individual needs to solve the problem, albeit with their friend's help.

Step 4: *Actions that will solve the problem.* Encourage group members to get a sheet of paper and write down anything that comes into their heads that will solve their problems. It does not matter how silly, wild or humorous the idea. Sometimes, the very thing that at first seems silly can lead to real answers. They can put down illogical thoughts – these will help them break out of blinkered thinking. Go for quantity. It is helpful to break out of normal thinking patterns. When they think they have exhausted their ideas have them consider:

◆ combining two or more of the solutions to give other ideas;
◆ looking through the solutions to see if any of them suggest other ideas;
◆ reversing any of the ideas.

Now have them examine all the ideas and choose the ones most likely to solve their problem and write them on the 'Steps to Problem Solving form' (handout 3).

Step 5: *Choose a solution.* This may be one or a combination of solutions. Group members should consider the solution in terms of feasibility and likelihood of success. They should feel it is realistic and be comfortable with it.

Step 6: *Work out a step-by-step action plan.* Group members will already have had practice in doing this in Session 4. They need to ensure that each step is realistic and achievable. Some people may find themselves lacking in particular skills – this may mean inserting a step that enables them to gain the skills and may be achieved by joining an evening class or similar. They will need to think about any barriers there may be and how they will deal with them. Remember shortness of breath and how this was dealt with by slowing down the breathing speed. Other skills that may be needed are assertiveness and time management – both of which are dealt with in later sessions.

Step 7: *Take action.* It needs to be stated on action plans where, when and how long each step is going to take and how long it will take to carry out the whole plan. Action plans are only effective if they are put into action.

Step 8: *Evaluate.* Action plans need to be reviewed and re-evaluated at regular intervals. This enables the plan to be adjusted to allow for changing circumstances – progress may be faster or slower than expected. If something has not worked particularly well then a step may need to be thought through again and some adjustments to the plan made. This is very important and will stop people repeating the same mistake or ineffective behaviour over and over again. If the chosen solution is not working out at all then it may mean looking at the solution list again and choosing another solution in the light of new experience.

If the above procedure does not work, individuals may need to ask themselves:

1   Have I stated the problem in a way that makes it solvable and leads to action?
2   Have I chosen a solution that is really practical/relevant?
3   Am I using blocking tactics at any stage of the process?

A completed sample 'Steps to Problem-Solving Form' (handout 3) appears on pp101–102 to show the whole process.

Making Decisions

Everyone makes lots of decisions every day. These include:

What to eat	How to spend the day	To go for a walk
To get a bus	What clothes to wear	To go on a diet
To ring a friend	To buy a car	To change jobs
To have sex	What to watch on TV	To go to the cinema
To take up a hobby	To employ someone	To get a qualification
To leave home	To get married	To move house

These are only a few of the decisions people make. Some are made without individuals appearing to think about it, some take some thought and others need time and research.

Many things can affect how decisions are made and whether or not they are carried out. These may include:

◆   Past experience
◆   Anxiety about the outcome
◆   Attitude
◆   What other people may think
◆   Motivation

Steps to problem-solving

Step 1 *Recognise that there is a problem and state what it is.*
My boss is always on my back. He makes me feel really anxious when he comes into the office. He's always going on about getting in on time and completing my work on time. I'm totally stressed out. I feel tired, depressed and don't want to come into work most mornings.

Step 2 *Restate the problem in a solvable way that leads to action.*
I need to get to work and complete my work on time.

Step 3 *Whose responsibility is it? (Accept responsibility.)*
Mine.

Step 4 *Action that will solve the problem. (As many alternative solutions as possible.)*
1 Get an alarm clock and go to bed earlier.
2 Discuss my workload with my boss – he may not appreciate just how much I do.
3 Look for another job.
4 Reorganise my social life so that I am not out so late so often.
5 Work overtime.
6 Keep a diary of what I do so that I can reorganise my workload in a more efficient way.
7 Look at our office systems and make some suggestions to make it more efficient and enable me to do more in the time.

Step 5 *Choose a solution (or combination of solutions).*
Consider each solution in terms of consequences, feasibility and likelihood of success. You want a solution that is realistic and with which you feel comfortable.

Solutions 1, 2, 4, 6 and 7.

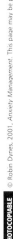

Step 6 *Work out a step-by-step action plan.*
1 Reorganise my social life so that I am not out late so often.
2 Get an alarm clock and go to bed earlier.
3 Keep a diary of what I do so that I can organise my workload in a more efficient way.
4 Having established a pattern of getting in on time, talk to my bosses about my workload so they are aware of what I do. They may then appreciate why some things are late being completed and ensure a fairer distribution of the workload.
5 Work on some ideas of how to reorganise the system to make it more efficient, save time and save (the company) money.

Step 7 *Take action (where, when and how long each step will take).*
1 and 2 This weekend.
3 Start on Monday and keep a diary for the whole week. Reorganise my workload in a more efficient way for the next week.
4 Do this during the third week when I have established better time-keeping and the bosses will be more likely to listen when they see I have made an effort.
5 During the fourth week come up with one or two ideas to change the system to make it more efficient. Make the suggestion and, as other people will be involved, ask for permission to discuss the feasibility of it with them. In the fifth week present the plan and ask for permission to put it into practice.

Step 8 *Evaluate and adjust the plan as necessary.*
Review the above plan each weekend to ensure it is going as intended and adjust it as necessary.

- Pride
- Fear of making the wrong decision
- Ambition
- Fear of change
- Aimlessness
- Self-esteem
- Confidence

Lack of ability to make decisions can result in anxiety, a feeling of helplessness and lack of control and depression.

Handout 4 provides a simple format for making decisions. Group members will need to write at the top of the sheet brief details of what has to be decided. They will need to think about their long – and shorter term – aims and write these down. Aims are important as they give coherence, focus and motivation to decision-making. Aimlessness is very often at the bottom of indecisiveness – even when making every-day decisions. (The process of identifying and setting aims in life will be dealt with in detail in Session 7.)

The next stage of the process is to write down the advantages to be gained and the disadvantages. Each statement will need to be given a rating value out of ten. In order to be aware of advantages and disadvantages the person may need to do some research to ensure they have sufficient information at hand to recognise them. They will also need to list other points to be taken into consideration and give these a rating from –10 to +10. When completed, add up the rating points from the advantages and the disadvantage columns. If this does not give a clear decision use the other points column, adding to the advantage or disadvantage column as appropriate.

This is a very logical way to make decisions that help to clarify the issue, focus the mind and motivate the individual to carry through the decision made. An example showing a completed 'Decisions Form' is shown on p104.

It is clear from the form that this person will make a decision to accept the temporary move.

Decisions form

Statement of decision to be made
Should I accept a temporary move to a different department in a different

store?

What is my long-term aim?
To become manager of my own store.

What is my short-term aim?
To gain wider experience.

Advantages	Rating 1–10	Disadvantages	Rating 1–10	Other points to be taken into consideration	Rating −10 to +10
It is temporary, I can come back to this store if I do not like it.	8	I may find it difficult to fit in.	5	My girlfriend will not like it – she may finish with me.	−7
I will experience working in a bigger, more busy department.	8	I will only be able to come home at weekends	6	I will not be able to play golf during the week with Dad.	−5
It will look good if opportunity for promotion comes up.	9	My department head does not want me to go – he could be difficult when I come back.	5	I will make new friends.	+4
I will make new contacts.	6			It will help me gain more confidence.	+7
I will get paid more.	5				
Total	36	**Total**	16	**Total**	−1

Risk-taking

There will always be the risk of consequences once a decision has been made and put into practice. Remind the group members of what they did when facing their fears. They anticipated what might happen and put contingency plans in place to deal with the situation if anything went wrong. Doing this minimises the risk and ensures measures are in place to deal with anything that goes wrong. The practice of anticipating emergencies and rehearsing what to do is well used for fire emergencies, with first-aid and risk-management in public buildings, the workplace and many other situations. It is well proven and works well when making any sort of decision.

Impulse decisions provide a high risk as the issues have not been thought through, or time given to work out what to do if anything goes wrong.

Deciding not to decide

There are times when it is advisable to delay making significant decisions. These can include:

◆ When angry or upset.
◆ Immediately after a bereavement.
◆ In order to obtain expert advice.
◆ When delay could bring advantages.
◆ When various options have equal weight.
◆ Immediately after an operation.
◆ Immediately after an accident or shock.
◆ During immediate post- and pre-menstrual cycle states, if associated with excitement or mood swings.
◆ During pregnancy or post-pregnancy.
◆ When more information is required to make an informed decision.
◆ When in situations which are strange. These can include: when in hospital; on holiday or in a different setting from the one that is familiar.

This does not mean that a decision is not made but simply that it is delayed until a more favourable time.

It is useful, once the decision has been made, to do a visualisation exercise. That is, they close their eyes and go through the process of visualising themselves carrying the decision through successfully. They will need to include how they will feel both carrying it out and when it has been achieved and take into account what changes it may bring about. This exercise is the same as that practised in the previous session to enable individuals to face their fears. Once the decision is made they can practise it a few times each day until the decision has been carried out. Doing this will aid motivation and confidence.

Aims	1 To explore problem-solving strategies
	2 To look at blocks to problem-solving
	3 To explore decision-making methods

Materials Flipchart, markers and copies of handouts

CONTENT	Time
Discussion on individual progress and homework assignments	*15 minutes*
State the aims of the session and present blocks to problem-solving *(Presentation and discussion – handouts 1 and 2)*	*20 minutes*
Steps to problem-solving *(Discussion and exercise – handout 3)*	*30 minutes*
Break	*10 minutes*
Blocks to making decisions *(Presentation, discussion and exercise)*	*15 minutes*
Making decisions *(Presentation, discussion and exercise – handout 4)*	*20 minutes*
Discuss the use of visualisation to help carry through any decision/action plan	*5 minutes*
Homework assignments	*5 minutes*

Exercises and Assignments

Becoming aware there is a problem

Briefly introduce the topic, go through handout 1 and discuss. It is helpful to write the steps to problem-solving up on the flipchart so everyone can see them during the rest of the session.

Blocks to problem-solving

Go through handout 2 and discuss. Link the blocks to each step of the problem-solving process.

Steps to problem-solving

Give out handout 3 and discuss each step of the process.

Choose one of the following exercises:

1   Provide, or ask the group to suggest, a problem and use the form (handout 3) to go through the process as a group to solve the problem.
2   Ask each group member to use the form (handout 3) to go through the process and solve a problem of their own or one given to them. You will need to circulate and help individuals. When completed, bring everyone back together to discuss any problems.

Blocks to making decisions

Introduce the topic. Use the flipchart to brainstorm:

1   the types of decisions everyone makes every day.
2   the things which block and influence the decision-making process.

Making decisions

Give everyone a copy of the 'Decisions form' (handout 4)) and explain the process. Ensure that risk-taking and the options to decide to delay or not make a decision is included in the discussion.

Choose one of the following exercises:

1   Provide, or ask the group to provide, a decision to be made and go through the process as a group to reach a decision.

2 Give each group member a form and ask them to think of a decision they have to make or give them a decision to make and request they use the form to go through the process. You will need to circulate to help individuals. When completed bring everyone back together again to discuss any problems.

Homework assignments

Instruct group members to:

1 Continue their stress diary.

2 Continue working on anxiety-giving situations.

3 Use the problem-solving method to solve a pending problem.

4 Make a decision using the decision-making process. (This could be a pending decision, one that crops up during the week or one about their future.)

Becoming aware there is a problem

Problems can show themselves in a variety of ways including:

anger	frustration	anxiety
stress	depression	agitation
lack of self-esteem	feeling of life being wasted	lack of control of life

Frequently you may experience the discomfort but remain unaware of what is the problem or what you want or need. You may feel anxious or stressed, but be unaware of what is causing the anxiety.

Alternatively, you may well be aware of what is causing the anxiety. It could be:

arguing with work colleagues	disagreements with a partner
shortage of money	lack of company
being late for appointments	how to get somewhere
what to cook for dinner	how to impress someone

You can take positive steps to help you solve the problems you encounter. In brief these are:

Step 1 Recognise that there is a problem and state what it is

Step 2 Restate the problem in a way which leads to positive action

Step 3 Accept responsibility for the problem

Step 4 Think of actions which will solve the problem

Step 5 Choose a solution or a combination of solutions

Step 6 Work out a step-by-step action plan

Step 7 Put the plan into action

Step 8 Evaluate and adjust the plan as necessary as the action plan progresses

Blocks to problem-solving

Before working through the steps, it is helpful to look at some blocks to problem-solving. Many of the blocks prevent you from seeing what is the problem or how you can solve it.

1 *Inability to recognise or acknowledge the problem.*

2 *Lack of training and knowledge in being able to define problems.*

3 *Not taking responsibility for the problem.*

4 *Having set rules of thinking.*

5 *Difficulty deciding from alternative choices which is the right action to take.*

6 *Inability to work out an achievable step-by-step plan.*

7 *Inability to take action even when a plan has been worked out.*

8 *Inability to learn from experience and take corrective action.*

Steps to problem-solving

Step 1 *Recognise that there is a problem and state what it is.*

Step 2 *Restate the problem in a solvable way that leads to action.*

Step 3 *Whose responsibility is it? (Accept responsibility.)*

Step 4 *Action that will solve the problem. (As many alternative solutions as possible.)*

Step 5 *Choose a solution (or combination of solutions).*

Step 6 *Work out a step-by-step action plan.*

Step 7 *Take action (where, when and how long each step will take).*

Step 8 *Evaluate and adjust the plan as necessary.*

Decisions form

Statement of decision to be made

_____

_____

What is my long-term aim?

_____

What is my short-term aim?

_____

Advantages	Rating 1–10	Disadvantages	Rating 1–10	Other points to be taken into consideration	Rating –10 to +10
Total		Total		Total	

Session 6

Communicating effectively and being assertive

The Need for Good Communication Skills

Whatever people want in life, the ability to communicate effectively with the people around them is essential to achieving it. Communication is fundamental to relationships, expressing feelings, handling conflicts, expressing love and affection, influencing other people's opinions, getting things done and getting needs met. When a person communicates well they feel good; if they do not, their self-confidence and self-esteem are undermined, they can become socially isolated, feel rejected, misunderstood, become anxious and depressed. It could be said that people talk their way through life. However, there is more to it than the verbal aspect. People also communicate using many non-verbal means, such as tone of voice and how they say something. This can include touch, facial expression, posture and gestures to convey liking or disliking.

It is easy to think that some people never have any problems communicating – they seem full of confidence, have a good vocabulary and seem to respond appropriately to any situation in which they find themselves. But people are not born with these skills – getting across to other people what they feel and want and responding to their needs is hard work. To communicate effectively requires that individuals learn and master some basic communication techniques. Even when they have these skills other elements can get in the way. These may include:

◆ Shyness
◆ Embarrassment
◆ Social anxiety
◆ Self-consciousness
◆ Negative self-talk

Group members will have already learned some techniques in previous sessions to help them deal with these problems.

Good communication involves both giving and receiving information; therefore the ideal communicator needs good verbal skills and also to be a good listener. Few people are able to achieve a perfect balance. They may have a natural tendency to talk or prefer to listen. Someone who talks a lot may concentrate only on their own feelings and opinions. They may not respond to the emotions of others, or take trouble to understand what is being said to them. They may be unaware of the effect they are having and misread the situation. Those who mostly listen may not be focusing on the speaker but on their own anxiety or self-consciousness and be missing signals. They may also fall into the trap of thinking they can communicate by subtle hints or innuendoes without stating directly how they feel.

Good communicators:

1 Express themselves clearly, using both verbal and non-verbal skills, ensuring that both methods 'match'.
2 Listen carefully to understand what is being communicated to them and understand how well they have been understood. This includes watching to see that what is being conveyed to them non-verbally matches what is being said.

Using Verbal and Non-Verbal Skills

What people say and how they say it depends on the situation they are in, what is being discussed and what meaning they want to convey.

Situations will vary from being very informal and casual – friends or partners talking in the privacy of their own homes – to the more formal work setting or formal occasion. The language used and how people present what they want to say will also vary depending on the situation and their personal style of communication – how much they say and their personal use of language.

What is being discussed may be very personal and include topics such as sex, expression of dissatisfaction, pleasure, giving instructions, describing an object or a film, political events, organisation of the workplace, promotion, a task to be completed, beliefs or gossip.

Making conversation

Conversation is used to:

◆ Give information – express opinions, attitudes, give instructions and other modes of providing information verbally.

◆ Receive information – listen, ask questions to find out how to do something, know how someone else is feeling, and so on.

◆ Comment on something – agree or disagree, express satisfaction or dissatisfaction.

What do people talk about?

Most conversation is about everyday matters, such as what individuals are doing or situations in which they are involved. They convey experience, feelings and opinions about what is happening to them and in the world at large.

Individuals are usually very aware of what is happening to them but it is helpful, in conversation, for them to be aware also of what is going on around them, what is happening to other people, the local area they live in and the world in general. This should include areas of personal interest such as art, culture, sport, politics, literature, cinema, television, scandal, coming events and celebrations. These provide good conversational topics to help to get to know people. Individuals should try to come to their own conclusions about events and interests, rather than just accepting those of commentators. Doing this gives them opinions to enlarge on in conversation. It also makes them active participants in the process, creating interest, enthusiasm and meaning in what they have to say, rather than passively conveying other people's opinions.

Using non-verbal skills

Facial expression

Facial expression communicates the degree of liking, disliking, interest, involvement, and understanding of a person or situation. People's faces display emotions ranging from joy, pleasure and surprise to guilt, shock, anger and sadness. Even when a person wants to hide their feelings they are often there to be seen.

Facial expressions are a most effective way to provide people with feedback when listening. Listeners can communicate by raising an eyebrow, grimacing, frowning, looking approving or disapproving, nodding, shaking their head or rolling their eyes. It is most important to smile when being introduced to someone. Who wants to have a conversation with someone who looks glum or displeased?

To give a clear message, it is necessary that facial expression and body language matches what is being said. If an individual says one thing and their facial expression and body language indicates something else, the person they are talking to will be confused as to whether they should believe what is being said or the message indicated by body language. Therefore, when body language does not match what is being said, there is a high risk of misunderstanding.

Personal space

Personal space is the amount of space within which a person feels comfortable when talking to someone. If an individual moves into someone else's personal space the other person will usually step back to restate it. If an individual moves too far away from a person that person will be inclined to follow to re-establish a comfortable distance. Space may be thought of as defining the potential threat or warmth which people feel towards each other. In crowded situations such as on a train people mostly cope with unwanted intimacy by avoiding eye contact, not speaking and ignoring each other. A rough guide to personal space tolerances is:

Partners and children	– about 18 inches
Friends, acquaintances and colleagues	– 18 inches to 4 feet
More formal interactions	– 4 to 12 feet

It is helpful for group members to take note of the responses from people around them. If they stand too close other people may feel that they are aggressive. Standing too far away may indicate unfriendliness or coldness. Allowances need to be made for individual differences, as some people seem to need a greater distance around them than others. This may be influenced by how they are feeling at any one time. It may also be affected by height – a tall person talking to a short person may need to stand further away to make eye contact with comfort – whether they are sitting, standing or in any other social context. What is acceptable at a party might not be acceptable the next day in a formal meeting or work situation.

Body position and eye-to-eye contact

Standing or sitting exactly facing each other is the most direct way for people to place themselves when talking. Standing close together, face to face, would indicate an intimate discussion between close friends. People who are not so close or familiar usually find it more comfortable to stand with their bodies at a slight angle to each other. This encourages friendly chat. Standing square on to someone unfamiliar may give a message of being confrontational or aggressive – the other person may feel unable to escape. It can also 'freeze' out a third party who may wish to join the conversation.

A fixed stare can be very disconcerting or be felt to be aggressive. The person who is speaking usually makes frequent eye contact to ensure that the listener is still paying attention and will signal when it is their turn to speak. The listener looks at the speaker to signify attention but glances away briefly, usually over their shoulder, so as not to stare. Glancing away too much, or constantly looking round, might indicate boredom, lack of attention or a wish to escape.

Posture and gesture

The way a person stands, sits, walks and gestures reflects how they feel about other people, and either hinders or helps their communication. Leaning slightly towards the other person indicates taking an interest while leaning back may indicate boredom, disinterest and a wish to disengage. Taking up a closed position with arms folded, feet together or legs tightly crossed, trying to occupy as little body space as possible, may be interpreted as defensive or submissive. Arms folded, with the legs crossed when matched with a defiant expression may mean the person intends to take a firm stand and is not open to suggestion.

Confident people usually adopt open, comfortable postures, using hand gestures to express themselves. They may sit with one hand resting on the arm of their chair whilst making a gesture with the other to emphasise what is being said.

Posture may also indicate emotional state. A tense, rigid stance, combined with a stern look and sharp movements, may indicate anger. Hands in trouser pockets and a slouched posture might indicate indifference. Also, allowances do need to be made for individual styles of posture which reflect personality.

Often, when talking to someone, individuals may mirror the movements of the other person. This usually occurs automatically and shows empathy with that person. If one person leans forward so does the other, and so on. Care needs to be taken with this as overdoing it may have the opposite effect to that intended. The other person may feel that they are being made fun of or, if an individual is talking to their boss, for example, mirroring a dominant gesture could be seen as being competitive.

Appearance

The way people dress and present themselves makes an impression on those around them and will define how seriously their opinions and communications should be taken. There are many prejudices about appearances, fostered by books, magazines and television. People make value judgements based on stereotyped images, often triggered by appearances. If a person wants to be taken seriously, they need to wear something appropriate to the occasion, whether a formal occasion or a party. How they look and what they wear says as much about them as any words. They should avoid making value judgements about people based on stereotype images and appearances. To do so means they will miss out on many rich and meaningful relationships.

To touch or not to touch

This can often present difficulties. Touch is a very important means of communication throughout life. People touch to express love, warmth, sympathy, affection; to give reassurance; to direct and guide people; to greet or say farewell to people. Aggression is expressed through pushing, shoving and hitting. Sometimes emotion is involved and sometimes it is not. Different cultures, groups of people and families have different 'dos' and 'don'ts' regarding touch.

Touching can be appropriate or an intrusion. Generally, when meeting or saying goodbye, a handshake is normal. If both people making the greeting are good friends and feel comfortable with it, a kiss and/or a hug may be appropriate

Touching is a very rewarding form of communication but individuals need to ensure that they act in an appropriate way and that the other person feels comfortable with the degree of intimacy involved.

Right and wrong body language
Body language is not easy to read and everyone makes errors of judgement from time to time – particularly when tone of voice, what is being said, facial expression and other body language do not match. Also, someone may have formed a habit of folding their arms because it is comfortable, not because it is a defensive signal. There may be similar reasons that skew other body language.

Do remind people that there is no 'right' or 'wrong' body language. When communicating with someone, the postures and gestures they use should be suitable to their purpose and the particular situation.

Using verbal skills
Starting a conversation
People do not have to start conversations by trying to impress or showing how witty they are. They might plunge into intimate conversation with someone they know well but most conversations start simply with impersonal topics. This gives time for the other person to begin to adjust and settle down, start to trust and build confidence in them. It is usually most effective to direct the conversation by finding out something safe about the other person. For example:

1   A simple question or request.
     'Hello, have you come far?'

'Did you have a good journey?'
'Do you mind if I join you at this table?'

2 A general comment or greeting .
'That's a lovely dress. Where did you get it?'
'Isn't this view breathtaking! Are you familiar with the area?'
'They've refurbished the lounge since I was here last. Have they made many other changes?'
'I'm impressed. Is this a sign of what is to follow?'

3 A personal comment or greeting.
'You've had your hair done. It really suits you.'
'I'm glad to see you. I've missed your company.'
'It's lovely to see you! You are looking good.'
'Hi, I haven't seen you for ages! What have you been doing?'

4 An exchange of information or an invitation.
'Hello, my name is Bill. What's your name?'
'I'm John, from Sales. Which section are you from?'
'Are you looking for somewhere to sit? Why don't you join us?'
'I've found these leaflets really helpful. Have you found anything useful?

These are everyday comments with which people are familiar and feel comfortable. Once initiated the conversation can continue and may expand into different topics. For example:

Speaker 1: 'That's a lovely dress. Where did you get it?'
Speaker 2: 'In Denton's. It was in the sale.'
Speaker 1: 'Were there many other things worth looking at?'
Speaker 2: 'Yes, there were some of the most beautiful oil paintings for sale in the art gallery.'
Speaker 1: 'Do you paint?'
Speaker 2: 'No, but I enjoy looking at art. I belong to an art appreciation group.'
Speaker 1: 'I don't understand modern art. What do you think of it?'

And so on.

It is important to keep drawing the other person into the discussion with disclosures and questions which give opportunity for the other person to comment. It is important to use as many open questions as possible – that is, questions that ask the person to explain or expand on a topic. Most open questions begin with the words 'How', 'Why', 'What' or 'In what way'. Closed questions allow the person to answer with 'Yes' or 'No' or give a very short answer without expanding on the subject. Most closed questions begin with the words 'When', 'Where', 'Which', 'Who', 'Are' or 'Do'. Although some people will elaborate on closed questions others will not. Putting the question in an open-ended way invites the person to make comment and express their opinions. They feel more relaxed about it knowing that an interest has been shown in what they have to say.

'What do you think of modern art?' is an open question. 'Are you an artist?' is a closed question.

Open questions should be kept specific and relevant to the conversation. Remind people not to keep asking questions repeatedly to the same person as though it were an inquisition. Usually, the person they are talking to will also start asking them questions, giving opportunity for them to make disclosures and express their opinions as well. This gives the conversation balance. They need to ask a question, wait for an answer, give an opportunity for the other person to ask them something and then move the conversation on. Also, they should avoid starting a conversation by holding forth about themselves. Apart from initial introductions, doing this can be very off–putting. It is best to focus and show interest in the other person, giving them opportunity to ask anything they want to know. In this way they can begin to build an enjoyable conversation.

Keeping the conversation going
Good communication is as much about listening as speaking. An individual should not interrupt when another person is speaking except to be supportive. They can do this by saying such things as:

'What did you do then?'
'Did you believe her?'
'Sounds like you enjoyed the experience.'

'Was it painful?'
'What did you say?'
'How did you feel about that?'

People are normally flattered when another person wants to know about them. As an individual finishes speaking, the other person can ask another question or pick up on something that has been said. The person being spoken to should not be tempted to change the subject suddenly or to go off at a tangent on their favourite 'hobby horse'. If they do that, it may make the individual speaking feel that what they have said is being dismissed as unimportant. Jumping in to relate a similar experience of their own may also have a similar effect. It can appear that they are trying to top the other individual's experience and make it seem less important. It can also be very irritating.

If the individual speaking gets into difficulty, or falls silent, they can be helped by the other person asking questions and providing prompts.

Sometimes a number of topics may be explored briefly before one of mutual interest is found and which can be explored in more depth. People should avoid cutting another person off and should respond appropriately to the subject by giving information, disclosing their feelings or asking a relevant question. They can use link statements to move from one topic to another. For example:

'Talking about going to the club on Saturday reminds me: I promised the secretary I'd look into getting a new sound system. I haven't a clue! Do you know anything about them?'

This can be followed by a discussion on sound systems. The other person feels positive about it as their advice is being sought.

There may be occasions when the topic has been exhausted and a suitable pause has occurred. They can then say something like: 'Changing the subject, what do you think about …'

It is best to avoid subjects about which the other person has little or no knowledge. It is better to seek out areas of shared interest and experience.

Disclosures

Everyone has met the person who, within a few minutes, tells all about the intimate details of their lives, ranging from graphic details about their recent operation to their latest sexual exploits and why they are leaving their partner. The opposite is also true; some people disclose very little and it is possible to know them for months and not know they have won national prizes for their favourite sport.

What is disclosed will depend on the situation, how close the relationship is and how each person involved wants the friendship to develop. Generally, in social contexts, it is best to avoid disclosures that:

◆ May be difficult to handle within a social occasion. This includes things like the death of a relative or something which may be embarrassing or in bad taste.
◆ May shock people. This could relate to behaviour or beliefs.
◆ Individuals may later wish they had kept to themselves. Disclosures made public on social occasions are very likely to be repeated.

Ideally disclosures should be appropriate to the conversation and contribute to the sharing of experience and general discussion.

Ending a conversation

Sometimes it can be difficult to withdraw from a conversation. There are subtle signals that can be sent to the other person to bring the conversation to a close without causing offence. These can include:

◆ If good eye contact has been made, glancing away for longer periods to give a discreet signal that they wish to end the conversation.
◆ Briefly summarising what the other person has said, stating key points and then adding an appreciation for the point of view or advice.
◆ Making a statement that brings the conversation to a close and prepares for parting. Examples are: 'It's been nice talking to you.' Or 'I've enjoyed meeting you. I hope we meet again soon.'
◆ Reaching for car keys or something else in preparation for leaving or moving away slightly withdrawing eye contact and using a phrase such as: 'I must rush. Perhaps we can meet again soon. Give me a call.'

When leaving it is best to try to part creating a positive impression. The person departing can smile, pass a compliment, shake hands and be sincere. If there is no intention of meeting the other person again they can avoid saying so; instead they could say something like 'Nice meeting you' or an alternative comment. Remind them that the last impression they make is just as important as the first.

Learning to Listen

Conversation is as much about listening as it is about speaking. One person speaks, the other listens and responds appropriately. Active listening is necessary:

- To understand what is being said.
- To show interest in and express feelings about what the other person has said.
- To provide feedback to the speaker so the person knows how the information is being received and whether or not the message is understood and accepted.
- To provide reinforcement and give support so the conversation can continue.

Ensuring the above happens involves the use of both verbal and non-verbal skills such as asking questions, using phrases like 'Tell me more', agreeing, commenting, making eye contact, using facial expressions such as raising an eyebrow, or nodding. Here are some suggestions to help group members with active listening. They can:

- Briefly restate what the other person has said, to check understanding of what has been said. 'You said that you were late in every day this week.'
- Help the speaker understand their feelings. 'How did you feel when he did that?'
- Avoid interrupting verbally, except to support and encourage.
- Use non-verbal communication to encourage – nods, eye contact, facial expressions.
- Ask if any conclusions reached are correct.
- Ask the person to expand on anything not understood.
- Maintain good eye contact but avoid staring. Glance over the person's shoulder now and then.

- Lean forward slightly towards the person.
- Keep arms and legs uncrossed, indicating openness.
- Face the person so direct eye contact can be made – though not necessarily square on; slightly to one side may be more comfortable.
- Position themselves appropriately, depending on the relationship and the situation. To sit too close together or too far away can cause anxiety. Even if a close friend is in crisis it may be appropriate to give them a cuddle but then move away again to a distance comfortable for both people.
- Refrain from annoying habits such as jangling keys, playing with a pencil, fidgeting, tapping, constantly looking away, watching television while listening, continuing with an activity or any other distracting habits.
- Ask open questions to support and help the other person continue the story.
- Avoid butting in and finishing sentences for the other person, jumping to conclusions or being judgemental. Listen first and ensure that they understand what is being said before responding.

Active listening helps individuals to keep focused and avoid their mind wandering back to what happened earlier or what they intend cooking for the evening meal. Once this happens the other person will quickly become aware and feel that no interest is being shown. Once the mind wanders the eye and facial expressions will reflect what is happening. Eye contact needs to be re-established again and the effort made to engage in active listening.

Being an active listener is essential to good communication. It makes the other person feel special and that interest is being shown, and enables them to respond in a positive manner.

Understanding Assertiveness

What is assertiveness?
Assertiveness is based on an acceptance of personal responsibility, combined with an awareness of the rights of other people. It is the ability to communicate with others in a way that allows an individual to say directly what they really think, feel or want, while taking into account the feelings of others. It enables them to communicate friendship, love, affection, annoyance, anger, pleasure, grief, sadness and to accept praise and criticism.

Assertiveness is being able to:

◆ be honest with everyone
◆ say directly what is wanted
◆ ask for help when it is needed
◆ express opinions and ideas in an open and honest manner
◆ say 'no' when it is justified
◆ give and receive compliments without embarrassment
◆ express both positive and negative feelings
◆ take responsibility for personal actions without blaming other people
◆ negotiate and reach workable compromises where conflict exists
◆ start and finish conversations on personal initiative
◆ respect oneself as equal to other people with equal rights and needs
◆ feel in control of life
◆ have self-respect and respect for other people

Assertiveness is not about:

◆ a person getting their own way at a cost to other people
◆ winning
◆ manipulating others
◆ bullying other people into doing something they do not agree with or do not want to do
◆ being aggressive either verbally or physically
◆ making sarcastic remarks or innuendoes as hidden messages about something a person does not want to say directly
◆ emotionally blackmailing the other person into doing something
◆ giving way to other people to please or placate
◆ controlling other people
◆ humiliating or making other people look small

Lack of assertiveness can lead to:

◆ being unfairly treated by others
◆ bottling things up; this can lead to anger, resentfulness, tension and stress
◆ avoidance; this means not confronting others, not saying what a person feels, not being honest and can result in a barrier building up between people

◆ individuals feeling they are not in control of their life
◆ feeling isolated and lonely, even when in company
◆ anxiety and depression

Styles of Communication and Behaviour

Communication and behaviour can be divided into three styles:

◆ submissive
◆ assertive
◆ aggressive

1 Submissive style

People who behave in a submissive style show lack of respect for themselves by denying their own needs and failing to express their honest feelings and opinions. They may not say 'no' to unreasonable requests, may be unable to ask another person to do something for them and, fearing conflict, may not defend themselves against accusations. Others may express their needs but in an apologetic way that says 'it is not important.' They make poor eye contact, speak in a very soft voice and generally give the impression that they do not matter, or are less important than the person to whom they are speaking.

Submissive-style people usually seek:

◆ to avoid conflict
◆ the approval of others
◆ to avoid responsibility

This is often justified by being thought of as:

◆ nice
◆ easy to get along with
◆ selfless and self-sacrificing

The price paid for this is:

◆ lack of control of life
◆ being led by others, rather than living their own life – life can become empty and meaningless

- being pitied by other people. Others may also become irritated and find it wearing over a period of time
- repressed feelings, such as anger, interferes with a relationship. Resentment and dislike may build for the person for whom sacrifice has been made

2 Assertive style

Assertive behaviour as outlined earlier enables individuals to:

- communicate clearly
- like themselves
- foster good relationships
- encourage intimacy
- reduce fear and anxiety
- live their own life
- stand up for their rights
- build feelings of self-worth
- control their life
- mostly get what they want

3 Aggressive style

An aggressive style is used by people who think of their needs, opinions and feelings as more important than those of people around them. They feel that their needs and opinions must have priority and ignore other people's needs and feelings. They are frequently loud, interrupt others or are sarcastic and rude. They dominate groups and family members, and feel that only their opinion or view is important.

Aggressive people benefit by:

- getting their needs met
- controlling their own lives
- controlling the lives of others

The price paid for this includes:

- provoking aggression from other people
- feeling guilty
- becoming alienated from other people

◆ making many enemies
◆ lack of true friends
◆ feeling vulnerable, threatened and fearful
◆ undermining friendships and relationships
◆ fear of losing control

Becoming Assertive

Being assertive is not easy to put into practice. Difficulties include:

◆ Overcoming cultural and gender behaviours (people are often brought up to be submissive or aggressive; men, in particular, may be encouraged to be more aggressive and women not to argue and be gentle).
◆ Being willing to face some conflict. Being honest is not always easy and may lead to facing issues that are painful.
◆ Allowing themselves to be vulnerable and taking risks.
◆ Re-appraising basic values of 'peace at any price' or 'getting one's own way at any cost to others'.
◆ Developing new ways of communicating and relating.
◆ Not always being 100 per cent certain of getting all that is wanted.

As previously stated, becoming assertive is not easy. Here is a five-step plan to help with the process (see handout 6 for a form).

1 Describe the behaviour to be changed in a non-judgemental way

This is not always as easy to do as it sounds. The individual may be feeling angry, frustrated or upset. Very often the other person involved may not be aware or clear about what has caused the annoyance. Too often angry people say things like 'You know what you're doing' or they are not specific about the behaviour, 'You're always ignoring me', or 'You're always rude'. The statement needs to be specific: 'At the meeting this morning you interrupted me three times before I had finished speaking.' Individuals should avoid making judgements on what the other person's motives were or make accusations about their attitude or character. It can be tempting to say things like 'Were you trying to make me look stupid?' or 'You stupid, ignorant man!'.

They should also avoid sarcasm, accusations of wrong-doing or profanities. It needs to be short and to the point.

2 State how you feel/felt

People should not be tempted to exaggerate this – the emotion must be genuine. A false statement will be detected and will not produce the results that they want. Also, they should not understate it or the other person may be in danger of thinking it is not important. It is not always easy for a person to be aware of how they are feeling and the degree of the feeling. How often do people say that they are irritated by something when really they are on the point of exploding with rage? The emotion they express needs to be genuine and to carry a genuine message. Most statements will begin something like:

> 'I felt humiliated when you ...'
> 'I felt angry when you ...'
> 'I felt it was unfair when ...'

3 Explain what effect the behaviour has/had on you

Most people are willing to change their behaviour if they are aware of what effect it has on the other person. It is usually works best to state an easily recognisable and concrete effect.

> 'It made it appear that I had not prepared the presentation.'
> 'It was unfair because no one else had to make the detour.'
> 'The noise woke the baby up and it took me an hour to get him back to sleep. That's why I feel tired out and irritable today.'
> 'Because it gave the impression you do not support me.'

4 State the behaviour you want

In most cases this step is not necessary – the three steps outlined above will be sufficient to initiate a change in behaviour. However, if that is not enough it can be effective to include this step:

> 'Please come in quietly after eleven o'clock.'
> 'I would like you to raise any criticisms before I do the presentation so it will go smoothly, look professional to the clients and encourage them to order.'
> 'I would like us to discuss and work out our problems in private.'

5 Negotiate and compromise when necessary

Remind people that being assertive is not about 'winning' or making the other person feel 'small'. Appreciating someone else's point of view and resolving a problem with a mutually agreed solution means that both parties feel positive about the solution. Individuals should have in mind what they are prepared to make compromises on and what is not negotiable. This will help them negotiate a satisfactory solution for everyone involved.

Body language

An awareness of body language is important to being assertive. Here are some points for group members to bear in mind. They should:

◆ Make good eye contact.
◆ Ensure that facial expression matches what is being said.
◆ Respect body space.
◆ Not smile when angry.
◆ Watch tone of voice – too loud is aggressive.

  – too soft is passive.
  – keep it calm and assertive.
  – avoid a sarcastic tone.

◆ Talk to people on an equal physical level – avoiding standing over people if they are sitting, ensuring as far as possible that both head levels are the same.
◆ Avoid pointing or other aggressive or unnecessary gestures – use confident gestures to reinforce the verbal message.

Becoming more confident

It will help individuals to feel confident and control the outcome if they are well prepared to put their point of view across. They can do this by:

1 Being clear about what they want to say
2 Working out how they are going to say it
3 Being clear about what outcome they want

If they are not clear about points 1, 2 and 3 they will not give a clear message. Also, if possible, they should choose an appropriate time and place to meet and discuss the issue. Nothing is achieved by embarrassing the other person in front of other people or not being able to say what they want effectively, because the other person is dealing with something urgent or is too busy. Often this can be achieved by saying to the person 'I need to talk to you' and agreeing a time and place.

Repeating the assertion

It is sometimes necessary to stay with the assertion and acknowledge the other person's feelings or situation. Individuals must not allow themselves to be side-tracked or treated as if what they are saying is not important. This may mean repeating the statement in a positive and firm manner. 'I appreciate you are under pressure and it is difficult, but I feel angry ...'

In some cases they may need to repeat the assertion two or three times. When doing so the other person must not be allowed to change the focus – if they make personal comments or deny relevance, it works best to ignore the comments and repeat the statement.

Repeating the statement shows that they will not be side-tracked. Acknowledging the other person's situation shows a respect for them and an understanding of their point of view.

The resolution

Once the message has been communicated it may be accepted, rejected or an alternative arrived at which meets the needs of both parties. When coming to a solution, the original intent must be kept in mind. Active listening skills can be used to reinforce the agreement – this entails repeating what has been agreed to check both parties' understanding of it is the same. It can also be useful for both parties to agree to meet at a specific interval again, to find out if the agreement is working. While this may not always be necessary, it is helpful to thank the other person for their consideration. This fosters good relationships by enabling the other person to feel good. Remind people that assertiveness is not about 'winning'. Both parties should feel good and that their needs are being met.

Aims   1 To explore effective communication skills
            2 To understand assertiveness and practise assertiveness skills

Materials Flipchart, magic markers, copies of handouts and pens.

CONTENT	Time
Discussion on individual progress and homework assignments	*15 minutes*
State the aims of the session and present communicating effectively *(Exercise, presentation and discussion – handouts 1 and 2)*	*30 minutes*
Communication – self-assessment *(Exercise – handout 3)*	*10 minutes*
Break	*10 minutes*
Introduction to assertiveness *(Presentation, discussion and exercise – handouts 4 and 5)*	*25 minutes*
Becoming assertive. *(Exercise and presentation – handouts 6 and 7)*	*25 minutes*
Homework assignments	*5 minutes*

6 Session

Exercises and Assignments

Communicating effectively

Write the words 'Why communicate' in the centre of the flipchart and quickly brainstorm. When complete, using another sheet, write the words 'What happens when we do not communicate' and quickly brainstorm.

Give out handout 1 and discuss.

Give out handout 2 and discuss.

Communication self-assessment

Give out copies of the communication 'Self-assessment form' (handout 3) and allow time to complete.

Introduction to assertiveness

Give out handout 4 and discuss.

Write the heading 'Not being assertive leads to' on the flipchart and have the group call out answers.

Give out handout 5 and discuss.

Becoming assertive

Give out handout 6, 'Being assertive form'. Explain the process. Demonstrate with an example given by the group.

Give out handout 7 and discuss.

Homework assignments

Instruct group members to:

1 Continue with their stress diary
2 Continue working on anxiety-giving situations
3 Select and work on an identified communication difficulty
4 Select and work on an identified assertiveness difficulty

Communicating effectively

Good communicators

1 Express themselves clearly using both verbal and non-verbal skills and ensuring that what is conveyed by both methods match.

2 Listen carefully to understand what is being communicated to them and to know how well they have been understood. This includes watching to see that what is being conveyed to them non-verbally matches what is being said.

Communicating skills

Consider each of the following:

◆ What people talk about

Non-verbal skills

◆ Facial expression
◆ Personal space
◆ Body position and eye-to-eye contact
◆ Posture and gesture
◆ Appearance
◆ To touch or not to touch
◆ Right and wrong body language

Verbal skills

◆ Starting a conversation
◆ Keeping a conversation going
◆ Disclosures
◆ Ending a conversation

Active listening

Conversation is as much about listening as it is about speaking. One person speaks, the other listens and responds appropriately. Active listening is necessary:

◆ To understand what is being said.
◆ To show interest in and express feelings about what the other person has said.
◆ To provide feedback to the speaker, so the person knows how the information is being received and whether or not the message is understood and accepted.
◆ To provide reinforcement and give support so the conversation can continue.

Here are some suggestions to help with active listening:

◆ Briefly restate what the other person has said to check that you understand what they said. 'You said that you were late in every day this week.'
◆ Help the speaker understand their feelings. 'How did you feel when he did that?'
◆ Do not interrupt verbally except to support and encourage.
◆ Use non-verbal communication to encourage – nods, eye contact, facial expressions.
◆ Ask if any conclusions you are reaching are correct.
◆ Ask the person to expand on anything you do not understand.
◆ Maintain good eye contact but do not stare; glance over the person's shoulder now and then.
◆ Lean forward slightly towards the person.
◆ Keep arms and legs uncrossed, indicating openness.
◆ Face the person so you can make direct eye contact – though not necessarily square on; slightly to one side may be more comfortable.
◆ Position yourself appropriately, depending on your relationship and the situation.
◆ Refrain from annoying habits such as jangling keys or playing with a pencil.
◆ Ask open questions to support and help the person continue the story.
◆ Do not jump in and finish sentences for the other person, jump to conclusions or be judgemental; listen first and ensure that you understand what is being said before responding.

Communication – self-assessment form

Indicate if you agree or not with the statements below by ringing 'yes' or 'no'. Do not spend too much time thinking about the statements but do be honest with yourself. This will give you some indication of communication areas you need to work on. Do add other statements of your own as these are not intended to be comprehensive.

General

My feelings are too deep to talk about	Yes	No
I disclose everything about myself to other people	Yes	No
I dislike disclosing information about myself	Yes	No
I am afraid of being wrong	Yes	No
I find it difficult to make compromises	Yes	No
I find it difficult to negotiate with other people	Yes	No
No one understands what I feel	Yes	No
I am afraid to state my opinions	Yes	No
I feel that people should keep their worries to themselves	Yes	No
I feel that my contribution is not valued	Yes	No
I feel resentful when asked how I feel	Yes	No
I feel shy/anxious/embarrassed in social situations	Yes	No
I get annoyed with tactful people	Yes	No
I like to be blunt about what I say	Yes	No
I avoid discussing emotional problems with others	Yes	No
I find it difficult to admit I have made a mistake	Yes	No
I rarely check that I have understood what is being said to me	Yes	No

All the yes answers in the section above indicate areas to work on.

Verbal

I speak louder than necessary	Yes	No
I speak too softly for people to pay attention	Yes	No
I dominate conversations	Yes	No
I constantly jump from one topic to another	Yes	No
I often interrupt other people when they are talking	Yes	No
I ask closed questions	Yes	No
I have difficulty starting conversations	Yes	No
I have difficulty keeping conversations going	Yes	No
I have difficulty ending conversations	Yes	No
I neglect to summarise to make sure I understand what has been said	Yes	No
I do not ask questions to clarify what I do not understand	Yes	No

All the yes answers in this section indicate the areas to work on.

Communication – self-assessment form *(cont)*

Non-verbal

I listen when others are speaking	Yes	No
I maintain good eye contact	Yes	No
My facial expression always matches what I am saying	Yes	No
My posture and gestures match what I am feeling and saying	Yes	No
I stand an appropriate distance from other people	Yes	No
I find it easy to shake hands with others or embrace them	Yes	No
My personal appearance matches what I want other people to know	Yes	No
My tone of voice, pitch and volume appropriately match what I want to communicate	Yes	No
I nod, raise my eyebrows and so on to encourage others to continue talking	Yes	No

All the no answers in this section indicate areas to work on.

What is assertiveness?

Assertiveness is based on an acceptance of personal responsibility combined with an awareness of the rights of other people.

Assertiveness is being able to:

◆ Be honest with yourself and others
◆ Say directly what you want
◆ Ask for help when it is needed
◆ Express your opinions and ideas in an open and honest manner
◆ Say 'no' when you feel justified
◆ Give and receive compliments without embarrassment
◆ Express both positive and negative feelings
◆ Take responsibility for your own actions without blaming other people
◆ Negotiate and reach workable compromises where conflict exists
◆ Start and finish conversations on your own initiative
◆ Respect yourself as equal to other people with equal rights and needs
◆ Feel in control of your life
◆ Have self-respect and respect for other people

Assertiveness is not about:

◆ Getting your own way at a cost to other people
◆ Winning
◆ Manipulating others to get your own way
◆ Bullying other people into doing something they do not agree with or do not want to do
◆ Being aggressive either verbally or physically
◆ Making sarcastic remarks or innuendoes indicating hidden messages about something you do not want to state directly
◆ Emotionally blackmailing the other person into doing something
◆ Giving way to other people to please or placate
◆ Controlling other people
◆ Humiliating or making other people look small

Assertiveness – styles of communication and behaviour

Styles of communication and behaviour

Communication and behaviour can be divided into three styles:

1 *Submissive style*

People who behave in a submissive style show lack of respect for themselves by denying their own needs and failing to express their honest feelings and opinions.

If you are submissive you will usually seek:

◆ To avoid conflict
◆ The approval of others
◆ To avoid responsibility

This is often justified by being thought of as:

◆ Nice
◆ Easy to get along with
◆ Being selfless and self-sacrificing

The price paid for this is:

◆ Lack of control of life
◆ Being led by others rather than living your own life – life can become empty and meaningless
◆ Being pitied by other people. They may also become irritated and find it wearing over a period of time
◆ Repressed feelings such as anger interfere with the relationship. Resentment and dislike may build for the person for whom sacrifice has been made

2 *Assertive style*

Assertive behaviour as outlined earlier (handout 4) enables you to:

◆ Communicate clearly
◆ Like yourself
◆ Foster good relationships
◆ Encourage intimacy
◆ Reduce fear and anxiety
◆ Live your own life
◆ Stand up for your rights
◆ Build feelings of self-worth
◆ Control your life
◆ Mostly get what you want

3 *Aggressive style*

An aggressive style is used by people who think of their needs, opinions and feelings as more important than those of people around them.

If you are inclined to an aggressive style you tend to:

◆ Feel that your needs and opinions must have priority
◆ Ignore other people's needs and feelings
◆ Frequently be loud, interrupt others, sarcastic and rude
◆ Dominate groups and family members
◆ Feel that only your opinion or view is important

You will usually benefit by:

◆ Getting your needs met
◆ Controlling your own life
◆ Controlling the lives of others

The price for this includes:

◆ Provoking aggression from other people
◆ Feeling guilty
◆ Becoming alienated from other people
◆ Making many enemies
◆ Lack of true friends
◆ Feeling vulnerable, threatened and fearful
◆ Undermining friendships and relationships
◆ Fear of losing control

Being assertive form

1 *Describe the behaviour to be changed in a non-judgemental way*

_____
_____
_____
_____
_____
_____

2 *State how you feel/felt about the behaviour*

_____
_____
_____
_____
_____
_____
_____

3 *Explain what effect the behaviour has/had on you*

_____
_____
_____
_____
_____
_____
_____

4 *State the behaviour you want*

_____
_____
_____
_____
_____
_____

5 *What are you willing to negotiate and compromise on?*

_____
_____
_____
_____
_____

Being assertive is not easy to put into practice. Difficulties you may encounter include:

◆ Overcoming cultural and gender behaviours.
◆ Having to face some conflict.
◆ Allowing yourself to be vulnerable and taking risks.
◆ Re-appraising your basic values of 'peace at any price' or 'getting your own way at any price to others'.
◆ Developing new ways of communicating and relating.
◆ Not always being 100 per cent certain of getting all that you want.

Body language

An awareness of body language is important to being assertive. Points to bear in mind:

◆ Make good eye contact.
◆ Ensure that facial expression matches what is being said.
◆ Respect body space.
◆ Do not smile if you feel angry.
◆ Watch your tone of voice – too loud is aggressive.
                      – too soft is passive.
                      – keep it calm and assertive.
                      – avoid a sarcastic tone.
◆ Talk to people on an equal physical level – do not stand over people if they are sitting; ensure as far as possible that both head levels are the same.
◆ Avoid pointing or other aggressive or unnecessary gestures – use confident gestures to reinforce the verbal message.

Becoming more confident

Boost your confidence and ability to control the outcome by preparing to put your point across. Do this by:

1 Being clear about what you want to say
2 Working out how you are going to say it
3 Being clear about what outcome you want

If you are not clear about these you will not give a clear message.

Repeating your assertion

Stay with it and acknowledge the other person's feelings or situation. Do not allow yourself to be side-tracked or treated as if what you are saying is not important. This may mean repeating the statement in a positive and firm manner. 'I appreciate you are under pressure and it is difficult, but I feel angry …'

The resolution

Once you have communicated your message it may be accepted, rejected or an alternative arrived at which better meets the needs of both parties. When coming to a solution:

◆ Keep your original intent in mind.

◆ Use active listening skills to reinforce the agreement – repeat what has been agreed to check that both parties' understanding of it is the same.

◆ Agree to meet at a specific interval again to find out if the agreement is working.

◆ Thank the other person for their consideration. This fosters a good relationship by enabling the other person to feel good.

◆ Remember at all times that being assertive is not about 'winning'. Both parties should feel good and that their needs are being met.

Identifying aims and managing time

Why Have Aims in Life?

The reason most people do not get what they want from life is usually because they have not worked out what they really do want. They may have a feeling of being dissatisfied, know something is not right, feel that life is being wasted or is empty. This can cause stress, anxiety, depression, restlessness, irritability, loss of confidence and self-esteem. However, it is not enough for people to know what they want (have an aim) from life; they also need to be able to convert these desires into an action plan and act on it.

In addition, an individual's aims in life influence and make sense of their life. Aims enable them to:

◆ Make decisions (ensuring the decisions are in tune with their aims and values).

◆ Avoid wasting time with purposeless pursuits.

◆ Identify how to make best use of their time.

◆ Be motivated.

◆ Control their lives.

◆ Identify the skills they need to achieve their aims.

◆ Have a sense of purpose and achievement.

◆ Increase their feelings of self-worth.

◆ Plan to get what they want.

◆ Feel satisfied with life.

◆ Solve problems in a way that is in tune with their aims and values.

◆ Make the best use of their energy and resources.

Blocks to Achieving Aims

Many of the blocks will be similar to those encountered in problem-solving and may include:

◆ Fear of making changes and not being able to deal with any problems.
◆ A belief that nothing works out.
◆ A belief that no one will help.
◆ Lack of resources/experience/qualification/skills/money.
◆ Ignoring feelings.
◆ Not believing that aims can be achieved.

Any blocks will need to be examined and action taken to resolve them. If this does not happen, any action plan will be sabotaged by them. Doing this is difficult, as many people will be challenging what past experience has led them to think and feel. It is only by taking some risks, experiencing small successes at first and then building on this positive experience, that this can be overcome.

Working Out Aims

Handout 5 provides a format to help people work out their aims and plan to achieve them. The process enables individuals to look at past events in their lives and learn about the causes of past anxieties. They then look at their values and establish aims that are in harmony with these. Where conflict exists between a value and an aim individuals will have to make a decision to compromise on either their value or aim to avoid a source for future anxiety. They may, of course, decide that it is an anxiety with which they can live. They will, at least, be aware of what is causing the anxiety and may decide at a later date to make changes if the anxiety becomes too uncomfortable.

The format asks each person to think through the following steps:

1 *The main events in my life have been:*

This is the process of taking stock of life so far – doing a 'This is my life' review. It needs to take into account all the major events that have happened in each person's life. An exercise is included in the session to help people do this. It is important that both high and low points are included and for them to be aware of how they felt about each event. Questions they ask themselves should include:

◆ Was the event stressful? Why?
◆ Did they choose to do it?
◆ Was it forced on them?
◆ Did they take a risk?
◆ Did it result in their having a belief such as 'nothing ever works out'?
◆ How realistic is that belief?
◆ Have they been led along?
◆ Did they drift from one event to another?
◆ Have they done the things they wanted to?
◆ Was what they were doing in 'conflict' or 'harmony' with what they wanted?
◆ Was what they were doing in 'conflict' or 'harmony' with personal values?
◆ What does all this tell them about their life?

2 *My values and beliefs are:*

Values tend to drive people's lives and determine their behaviour. Therefore, it is important for them to know what their values are, yet few people consciously sit down and consider them. These values often change as people travel through life and experience different events. Values that take priority early in life may matter less later and other values may come to the forefront.

It is important that people are aware of their values, so that they can ensure that their aims and how they intend to achieve them conform. People will not be well motivated to achieve something that is in conflict with their values or beliefs. It is more likely to cause them great anxiety.

It is also possible that they hold different values that are in conflict – usually a 'negative' conflicts with a 'positive'. An example might be: a person believes that life should be 'fun', but because of a recent experience they have become 'cynical' or developed a 'pessimistic' outlook or feel 'guilty' about enjoying themselves. There is conflict here that will demotivate, create anxiety and stop the person achieving their aims. They will need to rethink their values and resolve these issues where conflict exists. Examples of values that may be important are:

being honest	loyalty	having fun
having choice	being noticed	having friendships
being fair	having ambition	helping others
looking after oneself	having lots of money	being hard-working

An exercise is included in the session to help group members become aware of their values.

3 *What I want in the future is:*

This needs to encompass all areas of life, including:

- social/leisure
- spiritual
- physical
- mental
- work
- finance
- personal

As people write down what they want, encourage them to treat it like a 'fantasy' list – let ambition run free, inhibitions fall away and truthfulness come to the fore. Ideally, there should be no constraints. These are the things people really would like for the future. Reassure them that they will not have to share their thoughts with the group unless they want to.

An exercise is included in the session to help people brainstorm their needs. It is important that they spend time on this. Some things they might have a burning desire to do, other things less so, some may be long-term, others short-term. These are the options they will have to choose from and plan to achieve.

4 *What will help me achieve my aims?*

These are the resources the person has to assist them achieve their aims and may include: savings, support of a partner, values and beliefs, determination and so on. Skills acquired through leisure, interests and work are also often transferable. Everything that could be helpful should be listed. It is important to make the list as full as possible as it will assist the person to be realistic, to judge how realistic their aims are and to work out an action plan. There is no point in setting aims that there is no hope of achieving; neither should anyone underestimate themselves and what they can achieve. They may also need to consider what they are prepared to sacrifice in order to get what they want.

5 *What will hinder me achieving my aims?*

These are the blocks that will need to be overcome and may include:

◆ a belief that nothing works out
◆ lack of resources (money, support of partner and so on)
◆ anxiety about meeting people
◆ negative self-talk
◆ shyness
◆ lack of particular skills

and so on.

People will need to take all the above into account when working out their action plan and use problem-solving techniques to overcome any difficulties.

6 *My chosen aims are:*

From the options already outlined, the person now chooses what their main aims in life will be. They will need to ensure that the aims are:

◆ compatible with their values
◆ realistic and achievable
◆ what they really want to pursue
◆ if short-term, that they contribute to long-term aims

The longer-term the aim, the greater the commitment will need to be to keep working towards it. However, backed by a strong sense of values and motivation, the ultimate aim can be reached. It is also especially important with long-term aims to have a number of steps clearly mapped out and a number of evaluations built in to show progress, make adjustments and to include rewards for achievement.

7 *My step-by-step action plan is:*

This will include all the things the person will need to do to achieve their aims. Some research may need to be done to find out what is required. Where skills are lacking, training may be needed, and so on. All the difficulties identified will need to be taken into account and a plan created to deal with them. Where the aim is long-term, take into account life events as much as possible. These are the life changes to be gone through while achieving the aims (see 'life changes' section below for more details about this. Also, dealing with changes is dealt with fully in Session 9). Consider who else will be affected – partners, family, friends and so on. Do not forget that the person will have their own feelings to deal with as well. It is always best to keep the steps small, realistic and to set time limits on achieving them.

8 *Put the plan into action.*

Each person will have to ensure that what they do corresponds with their action plan and leads them towards their main aim. It is very easy to be side-tracked, especially when difficulties are encountered.

9 *Evaluate and adjust the plan as necessary.*

Pre-set times are required to take stock of how things are going. Helpful questions to answer might include:

- What has been successful? Why?
- What has not been successful? Why?
- Do some steps need to be broken down into smaller steps?
- Have any aims or values changed? (Sometimes, especially over a long period, a lack of motivation can be caused by a change in aims or values due to new experiences – this may have a positive or negative effect.)
- How can the plan be adjusted to take into account what has been learned?

Life Changes

It is helpful for individuals to look again at their aims and values as they pass from one stage of adult development to another. These are the times when aims and values are most likely to undergo changes and consequently plans to achieve them will need to be adjusted. During this period, as their aims and values are questioned, individuals may feel distress. Feelings of anxiety at these times are usually 'normal' and are not caused by wrong decisions. What they need to do is stay with it until they have adjusted. Do bear in mind that not everyone develops at the same pace or makes changes at the same age. Also, it may be different for men and women. The comments below on the stages of adulthood changes are only intended as a rough guide.

Stages of adulthood changes

20–30

This is the stage when people have usually become independent, are committed to work, marriage and buying a house. They may start raising a family and take on other responsibilities. Their aims and values are very much influenced by upbringing, education, reading, films and mentors from their youth. At around 30 years of age they may begin to question commitments, aims and values. Life has become more complex. They may want to change career or lifestyle, and marital life may not be what was expected.

Some people will make just a few adjustments in some areas and renew their commitment. Other people may decide to make more changes in many areas of life. When aims and values have changed and no adjustments are made people may find themselves anxious, stressed or unhappy with their lot.

30–40

Once through the crisis in the early 30s there is a tendency to get on with life. As people move towards 40 they start becoming aware that they are not immortal and that time may be running out. If life has not worked out as expected they may start asking themselves if there is still time to change or whether this is it.

40–45

Mid-life crisis has hit. Where individuals are going to succeed and what is not going to be achievable becomes clearer. Children are likely to have grown up and are becoming independent. Individuals may want to be accepted for what they are and not what everyone expects them to be. They may be asking themselves 'Is there still time to make my dreams come true?' They may want to start a new career, or take a new direction in different areas of life. This can be a very painful and anxiety-ridden time.

45–55

This is a more settled time. Things may not seem so urgent any more, values may have changed, money, objects or promotion may be less important.

55–65+

People start coming to terms with what they have and have not achieved. They start thinking about retirement, what to do, how to cope with a smaller income and a change in lifestyle. They may lose friends with retirement, parents may need looking after or die. They become aware of the ageing process and may start suffering from ill-health.

People who do not follow the expected pattern of changes at the same time as their friends and colleagues may feel out-of-step. An individual who is not married by 30–35 may feel less of a person than their friends who are married and have children. This can be a cause of feeling different and give rise to anxiety.

Why Manage Time?

Now that each person has established what they want from life and has started establishing a plan to achieve it they will need to know how to manage their time effectively. Is it being used in a way that will enable them to achieve their aims? Or is a lot of time being spent doing things that are not in tune with either aims or values? Is this bringing about periods of stress and anxiety?

Managing time is a skill that is often associated with high-powered business people who have many demands made on their time. However, everyone – housewives, parents, carers or whoever – need time-management skills. Otherwise, they are likely to look back when they are elderly with many regrets about things they have not done, decisions not taken, or a life that has taken an accidental course with all the major decisions being taken by someone else.

Time management is therefore related to all the other skills taught in these sessions and will enable group members to:

◆ Avoid any unnecessary stress and anxiety
◆ Relate the use of time to what they want from life
◆ Make better decisions
◆ Have a sense of purpose in daily life
◆ Value time and self
◆ Be motivated
◆ Be more in control of themselves
◆ Have a sense of personal progress
◆ Have a sense of achievement
◆ Raise their self-esteem
◆ Make sure that life is balanced to meet their needs

Investigating how Time has been Spent

Group members will have learned about completing their life-line in an exercise earlier in the session (handout 3). This will give some idea about how they have been spending time. It is helpful if they consider their past life in terms of what can be learned about how they have used time. Questions they might ask themselves include:

◆ What were the times I enjoyed most? Why?
◆ What were the worst times? Why?
◆ What decisions did I make?
◆ What decisions were made for me?
◆ Did I drift from one thing to another?
◆ What did I plan?
◆ What made the good times good?
◆ What made the bad times bad?
◆ Am I happy with how I have spent time?
◆ What changes do I want to make?

These questions may be difficult for some people and cause them some distress. Some may not want to share their answers. Individual encouragement will need to be given. It is important that people give full and honest answers to reinforce the importance of how time is spent and its relation to:

- Aims in life
- Decision-making
- Having control of their lives
- How they experience events
- Stress and anxiety
- Identifying changes they want to make

and all the other benefits achieved through time management.

Examining Use of Current Time

This is a useful exercise to carry out at least once a year and may be helpful every six months. Use the sheet provided (handout 8) to enable each person to record their current use of time each day for one week. This will entail each person having seven sheets. The record should include time spent:

washing	work	sleeping
sport	dressing	exercising
housework	doing hobbies	relaxation
leisure activities	courses	chatting with friends
studying	watching television	reading

People do not need to stop what they are doing each half-hour to do the recording. It is better to have set times during the day to do it – lunchtime, late afternoon and before going to bed are good times. Individuals will need to note their anxiety level during each activity and give it a priority rating on a scale of 1-10 in terms of importance in light of their aims and values, and an urgency rating of A, B or C (with A being the most urgent and C the least) in terms of not being able to postpone it.

They will have to examine their charts and identify:

- Activities that are in conflict with their aims and values (is this giving rise to anxiety?).

◆ Activities that cause high anxiety.

◆ Activities that are in line with aims and values, which should be given priority.

◆ Things which have to be done (work, cleaning, washing and so on).

◆ What they want to do.

◆ If there is a balance in the time given to work, social, leisure, home life and other essential tasks (time for self often gets left out).

◆ What time they have control over and could change to ease pressure, give a better balance or to do what they want to do.

◆ Time wasted that could be used for things which give more satisfaction (remember, doing too little may result in boredom and anxiety).

◆ Activities which have little value and could be substituted for activities that have more value.

◆ Activities that could be done at different times or in a different way to free up time or balance the day or week better.

It is important that all the above is completed, keeping in mind long-term aims and values, otherwise there will be little motivation to work on changing how time is spent.

Surprisingly often, people do not have a lot of ideas about how to use their leisure time. It is helpful to have lots of ideas handy – a list of leisure activity suggestions is supplied (handout 9).

SESSION 7 | Identifying aims and managing time

Aims
1 To examine the importance of having and setting aims in life
2 To explore personal use of time
3 To plan use of time to achieve personal aims and avoid anxiety

Materials Flipchart, magic markers, copies of handouts and pens

CONTENT	Time
Discussion on individual progress and homework assignments	*15 minutes*
State the aims of the session and give an introduction to setting aims *(Presentation, discussion and two exercises – handout 1)*	*15 minutes*
Identifying life aims *(Lifeline, values, 'What I want' and identifying life aims exercises – handouts 2, 3, 4 and 5)*	*30 minutes*
Break	*10 minutes*
Introduction to managing time *(Exercise)*	*15 minutes*
Examining how time has been spent *(Exercise – handout 6)*	*15 minutes*
Examining how current time is spent *(Exercise – handouts 7, 8 and 9)*	*15 minutes*
Homework assignments	*5 minutes*

Exercises and Assignments

Introduction to setting aims

Exercise 1   Give a brief introduction using handout 1. Then, using the flipchart, have the group brainstorm the benefits of having aims in life.

Exercise 2   Using another flipchart sheet, brainstorm what blocks there might be to stop them achieving their aims. Briefly explore ways they have learned to overcome these.

Lifeline exercise

Give out handout 2 and a copy of the lifeline in handout 3. Now have each person write on the chart all the major events of their life so far – both good and bad. Good events should be written on one side of the line and bad on the other side. Once this has been completed, ask them to examine their lifeline using the suggested questions in handout 2 and make notes of anything they have learned. Make it clear that no one is going to be asked to share their conclusions and that it is important they are honest with themselves.

Values exercise

Quickly have the group brainstorm values that they might hold in life. These might include:

loyalty	having lots of money	having fun
being happy	being honest	having a family
being noticed	being useful	being hard working
having friendships	helping others	looking after oneself

Once some ideas have been explored have each group member write down personal values they hold in life. They may not be able to complete this in the time given as it will take some thought over a period of time. It can be completed as a homework assignment.

'What I want ...' exercise

Give out handout 4 and have each person write down what they want in the future in all the categories listed. Alternatively, have each person complete their lifeline writing in what they want in the future. Ensure that they include aims in the categories of social/leisure, spiritual, physical, mental work, financial and personal ambitions.

Identifying life aims exercise

Give out handout 5. The form can be completed using the information gained from the previous exercises. Emphasise the importance of the action plan.

Note: It is unlikely that people will be able to finish these life-aim exercises fully in the allotted time as they need considerable thought given over a few days. As long as each person understands the process, they can be completed as part of the homework assignments.

Introduction to managing time

Give a brief introduction to this section. Using the flipchart, have the group brainstorm why it is important to manage time effectively.

Examining how time has been spent

Using handout 6 and the lifeline (handout 3) worked on earlier in the session, have the group members examine how they have spent time in the past.

Examining how current time is spent

Give out copies of handout 7 and the daily time record sheets (handout 8). Each person will need seven copies of the daily time record sheets – one for each day of the week. Also consider giving out handout 9 (suggested leisure activities). Explain how the daily record sheets are to be completed and have each person fill in, as far as possible, a sheet for the current day. The remaining sheets will need to be filled in as a homework assignment. Request that each person brings back their conclusions about their use of time and what changes they propose making as feedback to the next session.

Homework assignments

Instruct group members to:

1 Continue with their stress diary.

2 Continue to work on anxiety-giving situations.

3 Complete aims exercises (lifeline, values, 'What I want' and identifying life aims).

4 Complete daily record of time for seven days and analyse use of time.

The reason most individuals do not get from life what they want is because they have not worked out what they do want. Even when you have worked out what your aims and values are, it is helpful to look at them again as you pass from one stage of adulthood to another. These are the times when your aims and values are most likely to undergo changes and, consequently, your plans to achieve them will need to be adjusted.

Stages of adulthood changes

20–30
This is the stage when you will usually have become independent, are committed to work, marriage and buying a house. At around 30 years of age you may begin to question your commitments, aims and values. Life has become more complex. You may want to change career or lifestyle and marital life may not be what you expected.

You may make just a few adjustments in some areas and renew your commitments. Or you may decide to make more changes in many areas of life. When your aims and values have changed and no adjustments are made you may find yourself anxious, stressed or unhappy with your lot.

30–40
Once through the crisis in your early 30s you will tend to get on with life. As you move towards 40 you start becoming aware that you are not immortal and that time may be running out. If life has not worked out as you expected you may start asking yourself if there is still time to change or whether this is it.

40–45
Mid-life crisis has hit. Where you are going to succeed and what is not going to be achievable becomes clearer. Your children will probably now have grown up and are becoming independent. You may want to start a new career, or take a new direction in different areas of life. This can be a very painful and anxiety-ridden time.

45–55
You become more settled. Things may not seem so urgent any more, values may have changed, money, objects or promotion may be less important.

55–65+
You start coming to terms with what you have or have not achieved. You begin thinking about retirement, what to do, how to cope with a smaller income and a change in lifestyle.

If you have not followed the expected pattern of changes as your friends and colleagues have, you may feel out-of-step. If you were not married by 30–35, you may feel less of a person than your friends who are married and have children. This can be a cause of feeling different and give rise to anxiety.

Life review questionnaire

When taking stock of each major event of your life, questions you might ask yourself are:

- Was the event stressful? Why?
- Did I choose to do it?
- Was it forced on me?
- Did I take a risk?
- Did it result in my having a belief such as 'nothing ever works out'?
- How realistic is that belief?
- Was I led into the event?
- Have I done the things I wanted to? If not, why not?
- Was what I did in 'conflict' or 'harmony' with what I wanted?
- Was what I did in 'conflict' or 'harmony' with my personal values?
- What does this tell me about my life?

Lifeline chart

0 — 10 — 20 — 30 — 40 — 50 — 60 — 70 — 80

What I want in the future is

SOCIAL/LEISURE

SPIRITUAL

PHYSICAL

MENTAL

WORK

FINANCIAL

PERSONAL

Identifying life aims

1 The main events in my life have been:

2 My values and beliefs are:

3 What I want in the future is:

4 What will help me achieve my aims?

5 What will hinder me achieving my aims?

6 My chosen aims are:

7 My step-by-step action plan is:

Step 1 _____

Completion date _____

Step 2 _____

Completion date _____

Step 3 _____

Completion date _____

Step 4 _____

Completion date _____

Step 5 _____

Completion date _____

8 Put the plan into action

9 I will evaluate and adjust the plan as necessary on:

Examining how time has been spent

You will have completed your lifeline earlier in the session – this will give you some idea about how you have been spending time in the past. It is helpful if you consider your past life in terms of what can be learned about how you have used time. Questions you might ask yourself include:

◆ What were the times I enjoyed most? Why?
◆ What were the worst times? Why?
◆ What decisions did I make?
◆ What decisions were made for me?
◆ Did I drift from one thing to another?
◆ What did I plan?
◆ What made the good times good?
◆ What made the bad times bad?
◆ Am I happy with how I have spent time?
◆ What changes do I want to make?

These questions may be difficult and cause some distress. You may not want to share answers, but it is important that you give full and honest answers to reinforce the importance of how you spend your time and its relation to:

◆ Aims in life
◆ Decision-making
◆ Having control of your life
◆ How you experience events
◆ Stress and anxiety
◆ Identifying changes you want to make

and all the other benefits you get from time management.

Examining how current time is spent

This is a good exercise to carry out at least once a year and may be helpful every six months. Use the 'Daily time record forms' (handout 8) to record your daily use of time.

Have set times during the day to do the recording. Note your anxiety levels during each activity, give it a priority rating on a scale of 1-10 in terms of importance in light of your aims and values, and an urgency rating of A, B or C (A being the most urgent and C the least) in terms of not being able to postpone it. When your charts are completed you will need to examine them and identify:

◆ Activities that are in conflict with your aims and values (is this giving rise to anxiety?).
◆ Activities that cause high anxiety levels.
◆ Activities that are in line with your aims and values, which should be given priority.
◆ Things which have to be done (work, cleaning, washing and so on).
◆ What you want to do.
◆ If there is a balance in the time given to work, social, home life and other essential tasks (time for self often gets left out).
◆ What time you have control over and could change to ease pressure, give a better balance or to do what you want to do.
◆ Time wasted that could be used for things which give more satisfaction (remember, doing too little can also result in boredom and anxiety).
◆ Activities which have little value and could be substituted for activities that have more value.
◆ Activities that could be done at different times or in a different way to free up time or balance the day or week better.

It is important that all the above is completed, keeping in mind your long-term aims and values, otherwise there will be little motivation to work on changing how time is spent.

Some suggestions for leisure activities are given in handout 9.

Daily time record

Date _____ Day _____

Time	Activity	Anxiety levels 0–10	Priority of aims 0–10	Urgency A, B, C
0600–0630				
0630–0700				
0700–0730				
0730–0800				
0800–0830				
0830–0900				
0900–0930				
0930–1000				
1000–1030				
1030–1100				
1100–1130				
1130–1200				
1200–1230				
1230–1300				
1300–1330				
1330–1400				
1400–1430				
1430–1500				

Date _____   Day _____

Time	Activity	Anxiety levels 0–10	Priority of aims 0–10	Urgency A, B, C
1500–1530				
1530–1600				
1600–1630				
1630–1700				
1700–1730				
1730–1800				
1800–1830				
1830–1900				
1900–1930				
1930–2000				
2000–2030				
2030–2100				
2100–2130				
2130–2200				
2200–2230				
2230–2300				
2300–2330				
2330–2400				

Time record activity review

PRIORITY		URGENCY			Anxiety levels
		A	B	C	
	1				
	2				
	3				
	4				
	5				
	6				
	7				
	8				
	9				
	10				
	11				
	12				
	13				
	14				
	15				

Leisure activities

swimming	decorating	archery
restoring antiques	animal training	sculpturing
woodcarving	giving lectures/talks	candle-making
joining a committee	wine-making	hang-gliding
collecting stamps/coins	dancing	calligraphy
running for local council	gardening	organising outings
walking/hiking	planning and giving parties	camping
football/cricket/hockey	horse riding	caravanning
cycling	mountain climbing	photography
ice-skating	jogging	genealogy
chess/draughts/bridge	dressmaking	archaeology
philosophy	voluntary work	rambling
taking part in Guides/Scouts	learning a musical instrument	writing short stories/poetry
squash	tennis/badminton	rugby
raising funds for charity	sailing	snooker
socialising with friends	visiting places of interest	darts
motor-cycle racing	motor racing	doing competitions
bicycle racing	brass rubbing	visiting exhibitions
joining a drama group	going to see plays/concerts	yoga
joining clubs	joining activity groups	drawing/painting
pottery	joining an evening class	photography
woodcarving	making jewellery	bowling

Developing a support network and a healthy lifestyle

What is a Support Network?

A support network is comprised of the people or groups of people who help, support and share their lives with each other. Support networks can include:

teachers	counsellors	parents
friends	clubs	doctor
day centre	support group	work colleagues
sons/daughters	grandparents	relatives
students	education classes	employers
social workers	landlords	neighbours

Knowledge of how to develop support networks and have individual needs met through them is a skill.

Why Have a Support Network?

There are many situations in life in which it is helpful to have support. These include:

dealing with stress	learning new skills
overcoming drink problems	when upset
going through a bereavement	decorating the house

solving problems	obtaining expert opinions
getting emotional support	getting spiritual support
providing encouragement	sharing ups and downs

Frequently, individuals come together as a group to support each other – they may face a common problem, have a similar interest or have a common need.

Handout 1 provides an illustration of how a psychologist, Maslow (1970), thought needs should be classified. He suggested that people need to look after the basic needs of shelter, food and safety first, before meeting other needs. According to Maslow's hierarchy of needs, everyone needs to think very carefully about how they build up and develop personal support networks as they work towards self-actualisation. As they develop support, it is also important that they not only take support and help from others but that they reciprocate in kind, helping and supporting each other. This accepting and giving support enables individuals to feel part of a community and is very significant in the development of self-esteem.

When the group considers why it is important to have a support network ensure they bear in mind the advantages of:

◆ feeling other people care
◆ having someone to share disappointments and achievements
◆ having someone to encourage and support them
◆ getting help to solve a problem
◆ having someone with whom to talk things through
◆ having someone to teach them a new skill
◆ having guidance
◆ having someone with whom to enjoy a good time

Isolation makes any situation more stressful. If a person feels that they have the help, understanding and support of people around them they feel more able to deal with any problems that may arise.

Examining Personal Support Networks

In order to assess their personal support networks group members need to look at what support they have. In order to do this, it is helpful to draw their own personal network. Handout 2 can be used for this purpose. Here is an example:

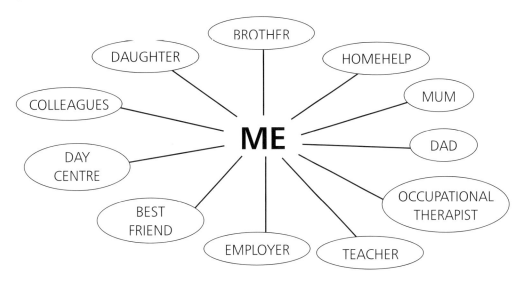

Now using handout 3 ('My support network') have group members write down each type of current support they have, how each person supports them and what they offer in return. What they give back is very important in the process of maintaining and developing a support network. Remind everyone that it is also plays an essential role in building self-esteem and giving them a sense of belonging to others. Where they feel that they do not offer anything in return ask them to leave the space blank. Here is an example:

SESSION 8 HANDOUT 3	My support network	
My current support	**How they support me**	**What I can offer in return**
Mum	Helps me keep things realistic and in perspective	Encouragement and support to get back to work
Dad	Listens and encourages	I am teaching him computer skills
Brother	Cheers me up	Talk his problems with girlfriends through with him
Work colleague	Helps with my workload when I get behind	

The next step is to have group members draw on their personal support chart in a different colour pen any additional support that will be needed, or that they would like, to help them achieve their aims in life. They must always keep their life aims in mind so that they can prioritise any support needed and ensure the support is appropriate for what they want from life and to achieve. They then transfer any identified support needed to handout 4 ('How can I strengthen my support network?'). This may also mean strengthening some of their existing support. For example, if they are getting support from someone but giving nothing in return they may want to strengthen this by considering what they can offer the other person. This can include difficult relationships – they might want to look at ways of overcoming the difficulties. When they think about what can be offered to others have them take into account:

◆ Personal qualities, such as friendship, listening and encouraging, loyalty, sharing good and bad times together, having fun, leisure time, helping to solve problems and so on.
◆ Skills they can share such as gardening, decorating and art. These can include hobbies, interests and so on.
◆ Personal qualities and skills they want to develop and want to share as part of relationships with other people.

Group members will need to complete handout 4, filling in ideas to strengthen current relationships and to develop new support. They will then need to work out an action plan to enable them to achieve their goals (Session 4, handout 2). It is advisable that:

◆ Only one or two goals are worked on at any one time.
◆ The action plan has a stated goal, with realistic steps which are achievable and a date for completion is included.
◆ A date is set to evaluate progress and take corrective action if required, to ensure the plan succeeds.

Why is a Healthy Lifestyle Important?
There are many ways that a healthy lifestyle incorporating sensible exercise, diet and leisure can benefit everyone. These include:

◆ Reduction of anxiety and stress
◆ Looking better and feeling good

- Avoiding muscular tension building up
- Helping with sleep problems
- Maintaining good health
- Keeping fit
- Helping to control blood pressure
- Reducing the risk of coronary disease and strokes
- Helping with weight control
- Maintaining and improving mobility and strength
- Maintaining joint flexibility
- Helping build and maintain self-esteem
- Giving value to self
- Maintaining resistance to infection and illnesses
- Preventing unnecessary stress on the heart
- Maintaining effective metabolism
- Avoiding stress on the respiratory system
- Building stamina and energy
- Giving pleasure and enjoyment
- Giving a sense of well-being and achievement

Taking Exercise

According to the Health Education Authority Physical Activity Evaluation Panel Survey (1995), most people do not take enough exercise to benefit their health. Some people complain that they have highly active lives and do not have enough time for physical activity. It therefore makes sense for individuals to build physical activity into their daily routine. It is recommended (Health Education Authority, *Active For Life Action Pack: General Facts on Physical Activity*, 1996) that everyone participates in at least 30 minutes of moderate intensity activity on at least five days each week. The fact sheets also highlight the benefits of exercise in helping to:

- reduce stress, anxiety and depression
- cope better when under pressure
- control weight
- look better and feel good
- control blood pressure
- reduce the risk of coronary heart disease and strokes
- improve and maintain good health

and many other gains.

If group members have not taken exercise for years they will need to start slowly and build up gradually. If they are over 35, or have had any recent health problems, they will need to check with their doctor before taking up any strenuous sports, exercises or activities. Taking physical exercise does not necessarily mean going to a gym, spending hours doing exercises or pumping iron. For example, to start gradually and enable a person to build more exercise into their daily routine they could:

◆ Park the car some distance from their workplace or a destination and walk the remainder of the way.
◆ Get off the bus a stop early and walk the rest of the way.
◆ Use stairs instead of lifts.
◆ Go swimming.
◆ Plan pleasurable walks each week.
◆ Take up a hobby or leisure activity such as rambling, bowling, cycling, dancing, basketball and so on.
◆ Join an exercise class (there are classes for all ages).
◆ Use exercise videos, tapes, books if they prefer to do a routine at home.
◆ Use an exercise machine.
◆ Walk instead of using the car for short journeys.

Information about activities available in different areas is usually available in local libraries and recreation and leisure facilities. Each person's daily activities will show up the most suitable ways in which exercise can be incorporated into routines. Strenuous exercise should not be undertaken immediately after meals – the body needs about an hour to digest food. Also, before exercising vigorously individuals should always warm up with some gentle running on the spot or stretches.

To ensure that exercise is effective and to help the body adapt to what is being asked of it, advise group members to start any exercise, no matter how gentle, gradually. For example, if a person decides to do some extra walking, they should begin with the normal distance and pace they walk, and time themselves doing this. They could then, during week one, walk the same distance a minute faster. The following week they may choose to walk a slightly longer distance and so on. It is safe for them to feel slightly breathless, but not gasping for air. Obviously, each person's capabilities will differ depending on age, fitness and current health.

Eating a Sensible Diet

When under stress, everyone's digestive system slows down. They may not feel like eating or may eat 'comfort foods' such as chocolate – these provide little or no nourishment. Stress depletes the body's resources, making it essential to eat properly to ensure resources are replaced. Also, anxiety or stress may affect the digestive system, making it more beneficial to eat a number of small meals throughout the day.

The main rules people need to be aware of to ensure healthy eating and to obtain all the nutrients they need are as follows. They should:

- Eat regularly – it is better to eat three moderate meals a day rather than one large meal.
- Eat a variety of foods.
- Enjoy their food.
- Eat the right amounts to maintain a healthy weight.
- Avoid eating too much fat.
- Avoid eating too many sugary foods.
- Eat plenty of food rich in carbohydrate and fibre.

There are five main groups of food from which they can choose. These are:

1 *Starchy foods or carbohydrates.* This group includes bread, breakfast cereals (oats are particularly good), pasta, rice, noodles, potatoes, beans and lentils and dishes made from maize, millet and cornmeal. These foods should be the main part of each meal and are good for keeping up energy levels.

2 *Fruit and vegetables.* This includes all fresh and frozen fruit and vegetables, salad vegetables, fruit juices and dried fruit. They should aim for five or six portions per day.

3 *Dairy foods.* These foods are milk, cheese, yogurt and fromage frais. Advise people to choose lower fat versions when available and to aim for two or three portions per day.

4 *Meat, fish, poultry and alternatives.* This group incorporates beef, pork, bacon, lamb, sausages, beef burgers, meat pies, all poultry, fish (frozen and canned), fish fingers, liver, kidneys, eggs, baked beans, chick peas, lentils, nuts and nut products, textured vegetable protein and other alternatives. They should aim for two or three portions each day.

5 *Foods containing fat and sugar.* These are foods such as butter, margarine, low-fat spreads, cooking oils, mayonnaise, oily salad dressings, biscuits, cakes, puddings, ice cream, chocolate, sweets, crisps, sugar and sweetened drinks. A small amount of fat is essential for good health; it also adds flavour and a pleasant texture to some foods. All these foods should be used sparingly. Sugary foods can be enjoyed as treats but not too often, and should be limited to small amounts.

Advise people to drink plenty of water. A moderate amount of alcohol (one or two units each day) is not harmful and, some say, can be helpful. The same applies to caffeine. There is a need to be cautious about drinking large quantities of low-calorie drinks – some sugar substitutes can affect some people, making them hyperactive. This is not good when combined with stress and anxiety. Lastly, salt should be used sparingly – it tends to raise blood pressure.

Benefiting from Leisure
It is essential that everyone make time for leisure activities, hobbies or whatever they find relaxing and enjoyable. Many of these activities (swimming, cycling, walking, bowls, golf etc) may also help with providing exercise. A large number of alternative suggestions will be found in Session 7, handout 9 ('Leisure activities').

It is well worthwhile for each person to review their daily time record sheet and ensure that there is sufficient time given each week to leisure pursuits. These are times to help them unwind and allow their mind to focus on activities they enjoy and find relaxing. It is especially important that they allow time to have sufficient sleep.

Making Lifestyle Changes
Having a healthy lifestyle does not mean suddenly doing lots of exercises, working out or going on drastic diets; changes should be incorporated gradually and one at a time. It is much less stressful to plan any changes by merging them into daily routines and making them easy to achieve. Approached in this way, a healthy lifestyle will benefit everyone, regardless of age, size, shape or disability. Handout 8 provides a lifestyle changes chart to help individuals look at what they are doing

now and what changes they can make to ensure a healthy lifestyle. Remind group members that it is better that changes are:

◆ Made gradually over a period of time (they should make a step-by-step action plan).

◆ Incorporated into a daily routine.

Aims
1 To explore the importance of having and maintaining a support network
2 To produce a plan to develop personal support networks
3 To explore the importance of a healthy lifestyle
4 To enable each person to examine their lifestyle and plan appropriate changes

Materials Flipchart, magic markers and copies of handouts

CONTENT	Time
Discussion on individual progress and homework assignments	*15 minutes*
State the aims of the session and introduce developing a support network *(Exercise – 'What is a support network?')*	*5 minutes*
Why have a support network? *(Exercise – handout 1)*	*10 minutes*
Examining personal support networks *(Exercise – handouts 2 and 3)*	*15 minutes*
Developing and strengthening support networks *(Exercise – handout 4)*	*15 minutes*
Break	*10 minutes*
Why is a healthy lifestyle important? *(Exercise)*	*5 minutes*
Exercise, diet and leisure *(Presentation – handouts 5, 6, 7 and handout 9 from session 7)*	*25 minutes*
Making lifestyle changes *(Exercise – handout 8)*	*15 minutes*
Homework assignments	*5 minutes*

Exercises and Assignments

Introduction to developing a support network

Introduce developing a support network and brainstorm on the flipchart what a support network is.

Why have a support network?

Brainstorm why having a support network is helpful. Give out handout 1 and briefly discuss the role of a support network in relation to self-esteem and working towards self-actualisation. Ensure that the importance of giving, as well as receiving, support is discussed.

Examining personal support networks

Give out handout 2 and have each person draw in their personal support network. Now have them fill in the 'My support network chart' (handout 3).

Developing and strengthening support networks

Ask each person to keep their life aims in mind and fill in handout 4 ('How can I strengthen my support network?). It may be necessary for each person to give this some thought and complete the exercise at home.

Why is a healthy lifestyle important?

Using the flipchart, brainstorm the benefits to be achieved from a healthy lifestyle.

Exercise, diet and leisure

Do a presentation using handouts 5, 6, 7 and handout 9 from session 7 ('Leisure sheet').

Making lifestyle changes

Give each person a copy of the 'Lifestyle changes chart' (handout 8) and have them write out the changes they want to make concerning exercise, diet and leisure. They then complete the action plan section of the form. Again, group members may need to complete the action plan at home.

Homework assignments

Instruct group members to:

1 Continue with their stress diary.
2 Continue to work on anxiety-giving situations.
3 Plan and put into action one method of strengthening or developing their support network.
4 Plan and put into action one change to their lifestyle to incorporate exercise, diet or leisure.

MY NEEDS

5 ↑

SELF-ACTUALISATION
Being creative. Making decisions. Using your full potential and having control of your personal and working life.

4 ↑

SELF-ESTEEM
Being given recognition, having opportunities, getting approval from others, giving praise to others, sharing with others, feeling worthwhile and respected, being able to admit to making mistakes.

3 ↑

BELONGING
Being accepted, part of a group, important to others, getting and giving love and affection, having caring friends.

2 ↑

SAFETY
Protection from threat and danger, a secure job or source of income and relationships.

1 ↑

PHYSIOLOGICAL
Sufficient food and water, somewhere to live, good health, physical fitness.

ME

My support network

My current support	How they support me	What I can offer in return

How can I strengthen my support network?

Relationships to strengthen	What I can offer in return	Ideas to do this

New support to develop to achieve my aims

New support	What I can offer	Ideas to achieve this

It is recommended (Health Education Authority, *Action For Life Action Pack: General Facts on Physical Activity,* 1996) that everyone has at least 30 minutes of moderate intensity activity on at least five days each week. The fact sheets also highlight the benefits of exercise in helping people to:

◆ reduce stress, anxiety and depression
◆ cope better when under pressure
◆ control weight
◆ look better and feel good
◆ control blood pressure
◆ reduce the risk of coronary heart disease and stroke
◆ improve and maintain good health

and many other gains.

If you have not taken exercise for years you will need to start slowly and build up gradually. If you are over 35, or have had any recent health problems, check with your doctor before taking up any strenuous sports, exercises or activities. To start gradually and enable you to build more exercise into your daily routine you could:

◆ Park your car some distance from your workplace or a destination and walk the remainder of the way.
◆ Get off the bus a stop early and walk the rest of the way.
◆ Use stairs instead of lifts.
◆ Go swimming.
◆ Plan pleasurable walks each week.
◆ Take up a hobby or leisure activity such as rambling, bowling, cycling, dancing, basketball and so on.
◆ Join an exercise class (there are classes for all ages).
◆ Use exercise videos, tapes or books if you prefer to do a routine at home.
◆ Use an exercise machine.
◆ Walk instead of using the car for short journeys.

Diet

When under stress, your digestive system slows down. Stress depletes the body's resources, making it essential to eat properly to ensure that resources are replaced. Also, anxiety or stress may affect the digestive system, making it more beneficial to eat a number of small meals throughout the day.

The main rules you need to be aware of to ensure healthy eating and to obtain all the nutrients you need are to:

◆ Eat regularly – it is better to eat three moderate meals a day than one large meal.
◆ Eat a variety of foods.
◆ Enjoy your food.
◆ Eat the right amounts to maintain a healthy weight .
◆ Avoid eating too much fat.
◆ Avoid eating too many sugary foods.
◆ Eat plenty of food rich in carbohydrate and fibre.

There are five main groups of food from which to choose. These are:

1 *Starchy foods or carbohydrates.* This group includes bread, breakfast cereals (oats are particularly good), pasta, rice, noodles, potatoes, beans and lentils and dishes made from maize, millet and cornmeal. These foods should be the main part of each meal and are good for keeping up energy levels.
2 *Fruit and vegetables.* This includes all fresh and frozen fruit and vegetables, salad vegetables, fruit juices and dried fruit. Aim for five or six portions per day.
3 *Dairy foods.* These foods are milk, cheese, yogurt and fromage frais. Choose lower-fat versions when available. Aim for two or three portions per day.
4 *Meat, fish, poultry and alternatives.* This group incorporates beef, pork, bacon, lamb, sausages, beef burgers, meat pies, all poultry, fish (frozen and canned), fish fingers, liver, kidneys, eggs, baked beans, chick peas, lentils, nuts and nut products, textured vegetable protein and other alternatives. Aim for two or three portions each day.
5 *Foods containing fat and sugar.* These are foods such as butter, margarine, low-fat spreads, cooking oils, mayonnaise, oily salad dressings, biscuits, cakes, puddings, ice cream, chocolate, sweets, crisps, sugar and sweetened drinks. A small amount of fat is essential for good health; it also adds flavour and a pleasant texture to some foods. Try to use all these foods sparingly. Sugary foods can be enjoyed as treats but not too often and should be limited to small amounts.

Drink plenty of water. A moderate amount of alcohol (one or two units each day) is not harmful and, some say, can be helpful. The same applies to caffeine. Be cautious about drinking large quantities of low-calorie drinks – sugar substitutes can affect some people, making them hyperactive. This is not good when combined with stress and anxiety. Lastly, use salt sparingly – it tends to raise blood pressure.

It is essential that you make time for leisure activities, hobbies or whatever you find relaxing and enjoyable. Many of these activities (swimming, cycling, walking, bowls, golf, etc) may also help with providing exercise. A large number of alternative suggestions can be found in session 7, handout 9. ('Leisure activities').

It is well worth reviewing your daily time record sheets to ensure that there is sufficient time given each week to leisure pursuits. These are times to help you unwind, let your mind focus on things you enjoy and find relaxing. It is especially important that you allow time to have sufficient sleep.

Lifestyle changes chart

	What I do now	What I can do
Exercise		
Diet		
Leisure		

Action plan

Step 1_____ Completion date_____

Step 2_____ Completion date_____

Step 3_____ Completion date_____

Step 4_____ Completion date_____

Step 5_____ Completion date_____

Managing common situations and adapting to change

This session is aimed at helping group members apply all that has been learned so far to common everyday experience, and to use the techniques to cope with that experience.

Coping with Social Activities

Taking part in social and leisure activities can present many difficulties for many people. The experience of extreme anxiety may result in the person feeling that it is not worthwhile, as there is little or no pleasure for them in the event. This may seriously handicap individuals in many ways, as social events are not always just for fun. Events may be related to:

◆ Work
◆ Training
◆ Being important to their child's education
◆ A partner's work
◆ Making career progress
◆ Maintaining friendships

Most social and leisure situations fall into one of the following groups:

◆ Small informal gatherings in peoples' homes
◆ Social events in public places
◆ Eating out

- Entertainment
- Sports and physical activities
- Clubs and societies
- Educational events such as evening classes

Preparing to go out

Being well prepared will give confidence, enable the person to feel in control and allow them to enjoy the social occasion. This means knowing such things as:

- Where the event is to be held
- What sort of event it is
- Who will be there
- What time they are expected
- Whether there will be a formal meal or a buffet
- How long the event will last
- What clothes are appropriate

And:

- Having a plan to deal with difficulties (feelings of panic, negative thoughts and so on)
- Being ready slightly early (this gives time to practise breathing/relaxation/visualisation before leaving)

Small informal gatherings in people's homes

An anxious person can feel trapped in small informal gatherings. It is difficult to escape – there is not usually a bar as in a hotel, or places to walk around if the person needs a few minutes to themselves. There may be people in the room whom they dislike or find it difficult to engage in conversation. The room may be crowded, hot and uncomfortable with people crushed in together. But the chances are they will know most or some of the people invited, so it will be easier to greet them and start conversations. The procedure is always similar:

1   The host introduces arrivals to at least a few people, unless they are well known
2   They choose somewhere to sit
3   A drink may be offered

If they do begin to feel panic coming on they will have the plan they worked out to deal with it. Remember, a panic attack will not do them any harm, they will feel relief when it is over and it is highly unlikely anyone will even notice.

Social events in public places

These will include weddings, anniversaries, dinners, work outings, parties and other events. Again, being prepared is essential for feeling comfortable. The event needs to be rehearsed in the mind with the person able to see themselves coping successfully. Events in public places usually present easier avenues of escape to enable the person to be alone briefly, and it is less likely body space will be crowded. The host usually greets arrivals and introduces them to one or two people. The chances are they will know some of the other guests anyway. If not, they will need to introduce themselves to others and make some conversation. Having a plan to manage the difficulties will enable them to manage the situation effectively.

Eating out

Eating out is probably one of the most common social occasions and may vary from a casual snack at lunchtime to dining more formally in restaurants or hotels. The casual lunch meeting, for most, will be easier than the formal occasion. Nevertheless, it is eating in public and can present similar difficulties. The plan will have to take into account some of the following:

◆ What they will do if they arrive a little early or their host or guest is a few minutes late
◆ Being conducted to a table by the waiter
◆ Having to order drinks
◆ Making greetings
◆ Ordering food
◆ There may be a greater feeling of being on show – especially on formal occasions
◆ Conversations will have to be started and sustained
◆ Requests and refusals for more drinks and food
◆ Compliments and thanks given or received
◆ Farewells made

It is well worth reminding group members that, if they feel slightly light-headed, sweaty or their stomachs are rumbling when they go out for a meal, it may be caused by:

1   Low blood sugar (especially if they have not eaten for a few hours)
2   The restaurant being crowded and hot
3   An overactive intestine

Entertainment

Most public entertainment happens in cinemas, theatres, community centres and concert halls. These are all very public arenas, often with wide open spaces, lots of people and noise.

The cinema is probably the easiest to cope with for most people. Even so, there may be a lot of obstacles to be overcome. These may include:

◆   Getting there
◆   Purchasing a ticket
◆   Mixing and/or sitting with a crowd of people
◆   Feeling disorientated
◆   Feelings of panic
◆   Noise (the soundtrack may be very loud)
◆   Getting home afterwards

It may be helpful for the person, initially, to go with a friend for support. They can then build on this by going alone and often, choosing different cinemas and going at different times, including when the cinema is busy.

The theatre is similar but may present some additional problems:

◆   It is more difficult to leave in the middle of an act
◆   It is more formal
◆   There is usually an interval

An advantage is that they can choose and book their seat in advance.

Concerts can vary greatly from very informal affairs to the more serious classical concerts. With pop concerts the biggest problem is likely to be with the crowd and noise. People can obtain a seat near an exit if that is a problem. With more formal concerts the problem may be the slow, quiet moments. Practising breathing and relaxation at these times is helpful, as is allowing themselves to be absorbed by the music.

Sports and physical activities

If someone goes along as a spectator to a sporting event the main problem may be dealing with the crowd. At most sporting events a spectator does not have to speak to anyone if they do not want to. They can applaud and shout if they feel like it and get caught up in the excitement.

People may want to take part in a sporting activity – football, swimming, keep fit, table tennis, bowls and so on. Difficulties may then include:

◆ Going to a strange place
◆ Meeting new people
◆ Having performance judged
◆ Risk of appearing foolish
◆ Being trapped in a situation which is difficult to control
◆ For some sports – changing out of clothes

Breaking into sports groups is not easy but can be made easier if people have someone to go with. If possible, it is helpful for them to go along as a spectator first and see what might be expected of them. However, with anything involving physical activity, there is a big plus – once they start doing the activity it will distract them so that they will not have time to think about their symptoms. Physical activity is also good for confidence-building and improving self-image as well as improving health.

Clubs, societies and education classes

Most clubs, societies and education classes welcome newcomers. They often have hosts or hostesses who make it easy for newcomers by introducing them to other members and making them feel welcome. Tutors will do the same in classes when people join. Most gatherings of this sort have a feeling of a social get-together. At first, individuals may feel like an outsider but they will soon get to know a few people. Having a similar interest to talk about will make the initial contact easier. It would be unrealistic of them to expect to like everybody in the club or society. They may retain a nodding acquaintance with some and get to know others really well. It is also okay for them to try out clubs and societies. They need to decide what they want from joining and then go along. The initial visits will enable them to decide if it will give them what they want. Most clubs and societies allow people to have initial visits before they join. If someone decides a particular club does not provide what they want, there is no obligation. If it does not suit them, they can look out for another club or class that will meet their needs.

Using strategies

The group members will have already discussed strategies (starting a conversation, keeping it going, and so on) to use on social and other occasions. Here are a few more they can practise and use. Have them:

- Stand at the edge of a group for a few seconds, listen to the conversation and then break into it by making an observation, giving an opinion or making a disclosure.
- Ask if anyone wants a drink or food
- Touch someone lightly on the arm or make eye contact, say 'Hello' and introduce themselves.
- Just observe the interaction going on around them and then decide who or which group to break into, if they want to. It is okay, sometimes, not to be in a group or engaged in conversation.

When people first join a club, society, go to an evening class or a party, they can flit from one person or group to another just getting to know others. They may or may not enter into arguments or discussion. Doing this will help to build confidence approaching others and starting conversations.

Dealing with Relationships

During the course of everyone's life they have many relationships with a great many people. Generally these fall into three categories:

1 Friendships
2 Family relationships
3 Work relationships

Some people focus their lives mostly around their partner and family relationships. They may see friendships as less important and not really consider it worth developing and maintaining friendships. Other people see friends as very important in providing extra support, affection, to test their views and opinions against and with whom to have fun. Friends may also help to solve problems, give advice in times of difficulty and invoke a sense of belonging and sharing of life. However, starting and maintaining relationships can give anxieties to many people, not least ensuring that the effect that they have on others is the effect that they intended. Also having to cope with how relationships change can cause anxiety.

Friendships

Anxiety may form around many difficulties. Changes may include friends moving away, getting married, leaving home, getting involved in different interests, changing jobs and so on. Other difficulties may include:

getting to know someone new	fear of trusting other people
fear of being let down	having to support another person
fear of making disclosures	fear of commitment
fear of being thought silly	fear of being criticised
fear of saying what you feel	dealing with rejection
fear of being inadequate	fear of getting into conflict
feeling awkward	not feeling equal to others
having to say 'no'	fear of hurting the other person
fear of being deceived	expressing affection

Family relationships

Family relationships include partners. As the years pass, these relationships go through many changes. For example, everyone is very dependent upon their parents in their early years. As individuals grow up they become more independent, eventually leave home or get married, and then as their parents grow older, the parents become dependent on them.

Many of the difficulties are similar to those for friendships, but may be on a much more intimate, deeper level and include sexual anxieties. Family relationships are usually much less inhibited. Also, the sense of commitment may not be chosen, as with friends, but out of a sense of duty. People do not choose their relations.

Family relationships are not easy, Honesty, understanding and genuine give-and-take is required. Often, in times of trouble, it is on family members that people depend.

Work relationships

Again, there are similar and different elements at play in workplace relationships. A person is unlikely to be able to choose their work mates – unless they are the boss. Changes occur, a colleague may be promoted, they may be promoted and their relationships with their colleagues change. A friend may leave and a new employee start. Tensions may form around:

◆ Fear of making a mistake
◆ Not being clear about what is expected
◆ Being bullied
◆ Having extra work dumped on them
◆ Being blamed for something they did not do
◆ Feeling isolated
◆ Being thought too friendly with the boss
◆ Not having the right attitude
◆ Being ignored
◆ Not being listened to
◆ Not being part of a clique
◆ Fear of being thought difficult
◆ Fear of being thought weak
◆ Having to work with people they do not like

Making it work

In different types of relationships, the use of language will be varied. Family, friends and people at work all have to be approached differently. It will be different again in the workplace. There are different boundaries about what is said and done. When talking to an employer, a person may be more formal and think before they comment. When talking to a friend, they are usually friendly, but polite, and hold some things back. With family members they are likely to be more direct, authoritative and hold less back. In all relationships, if people act too passively they run the risk of offending, being taken advantage of, or ignored. If they are aggressive they are in danger of being destructive, avoided and disliked.

The key elements in overcoming anxiety and making all these relationships work include:

◆ Wanting them to work
◆ Knowing boundaries and limits
◆ Using breathing and relaxation techniques
◆ Challenging negative thoughts and replacing them with realistic thinking
◆ Using decision-making skills
◆ Being assertive
◆ Using problem-solving skills
◆ Communicating well

Successful relationships are a fine balancing act which people do not always get right – but with practised use of the above skills they can overcome misunderstandings, control anxieties and ensure success most of the time.

Overcoming Anxiety at Work

Social occasions associated with work have been dealt with. It is now time to look at the job itself. There are many things that can affect people, some elements they may be able to control or influence, others they may not. These can include:

◆ Fear of losing their job
◆ Conflicts with colleagues
◆ Having to deal with complaints/criticisms
◆ Having to stand up for their rights
◆ Fear that colleagues may dislike them
◆ Fear that they cannot cope with changes
◆ Fear that work will pile up and be overwhelming
◆ Shift work
◆ Bad working conditions
◆ Lack of staff facilities
◆ Boring repetitive tasks
◆ Personal values in conflict with the management
◆ Unrealistic expectations being made of them
◆ Poor training
◆ Unclear job descriptions

- Bad communication systems
- Lack of clear guidelines
- Poor professional relationships within the company

Techniques learned during previous sessions will enable group members to deal with or influence all these difficulties. For example: having to stand up for their rights requires assertiveness skills; having to work to deadlines requires time-management, communication and assertiveness skills to negotiate realistic deadlines and, probably, problem-solving skills.

It may not always be within their power to make changes to company policy – but they may be able to influence it. This will depend on the approach used, the size of the company and systems within the company. There may already be a process within the company to help them do this. Even if there is not, all companies are interested in being able to achieve more and increase their profit margins. It is surprising what can be achieved along with earning the gratitude of colleagues. For example – a suggestion about how a work area can be reorganised to create greater efficiency and safety is likely to be welcomed. A manager does not want to have to deal with accidents. Any suggestions that help to improve efficiency and the work-place safety at the same time may well be adapted.

Although stress in the workplace is ultimately the responsibility of the organisation, it is possible to influence it. This is not about individuals putting themselves in conflict with managers, but showing managers that, by making working practice changes, the company and the individual both win. However, people must not expect this always to be successful. What they can influence and how involved they can be may depend on their position within the company.

Tips to help reduce stress at work
People can:

- Practise breathing and relaxation techniques.
- Avoid becoming overtired or fatigued.
- Ensure that deadlines are realistic.
- Plan and create systems that will help deal with unexpected events.

◆ Always keep some energy in reserve – avoid working for long periods 'flat out'.

◆ Learn to say 'no' when demands become too much.

◆ Recognise limitations and stay within them.

◆ Learn to recognise what is causing anxiety or stress and find ways to change the situation or cope better with it.

◆ Use problem-solving skills and work out a plan of action to deal with situations.

◆ Use communication skills to good advantage.

◆ Balance rest and activity.

Adapting to Change

Change is a part of everyday experience. Session one indicated that anxiety often arises from:

◆ Life events (marriage, retirement)

◆ Social changes (changes in technology, morality and so on)

◆ Childhood and life experiences (good and bad experiences)

Some of these changes are normal as people progress through life. Examples are: leaving school, starting a job, getting married, growing older and retirement. There is the day-to-day management of life-adapting to new technology, new working practices, moving home, new relationships, and even how people shop. Sometimes changes are planned in advance, other changes are unexpected, like accidents or being made redundant, and these throw most people into crisis. Some changes may be thought of as good and others as bad. Changes thought of as good can create problems and anxiety. These might include getting married, having a child or getting promotion. Changes initially thought of as bad can, in the long term, result in good outcomes. These might include losing a job which, in the long term, could result in getting a better job or forcing a person to take a risk to do something different, or something they have always wanted to do.

How well people experience change may be influenced by:

◆ Whether or not it was planned

◆ Wanting the change

◆ Accepting the change

- Resenting the change
- Pace of the change – gradual or quick
- How big a change it is

What stops people making changes?

Many individuals hesitate, even from making good changes. The reasons can include:

- Fear of taking risks/the unknown
- Lack of confidence
- Lack of self-esteem
- Feeling more comfortable with what is known
- Lack of motivation
- Not being sure of what they want from life
- Earlier bad experiences of change
- Lack of belief in self
- Not looking for benefits in change
- Thinking negatively about change
- Catastrophising
- Not being able to take action, even when a plan has been worked out
- Not taking responsibility for action

Choosing to make changes

Many people choose to make changes. Reasons may include:

- Not being satisfied with their present life (being lonely, broke, anxious)
- Boredom
- Wanting to keep a relationship
- Wanting to keep a job
- Wanting promotion
- Wanting to start a family
- Wanting different experiences
- Wanting to improve living standards
- Wanting to do or achieve something

Making changes

As group members have been working through the sessions they will have been making changes to their lives. If they think back over their lives, they be will able to think of changes made – some imposed by events outside their control, personal changes such as growing up, social, technological, political. They will also be able to think of changes that they want to make or have to face in the near or distant future. These might involve 'life event' changes. Sometimes a person can be in a life event change without being aware of how it is affecting them. They know something is wrong but are not sure what it is. As with problem-solving, it may be necessary to question themselves to discover what is causing the distress. Here is a process to enable individuals to plan for and deal with the process of change. It is similar to the problem-solving process, but with a few differences (see handout 4 for a copy of the 'Making changes form').

1 *Acknowledge and state the change being made.* It does not matter if the change is anticipated, desired, undesired or sudden. Individuals state the change briefly in a positive and achievable way. This may be 'I need to adjust to living on my own', 'I want to have a better social life', 'I want to spend more time with my family', 'I want to have a new career, earn more money and start a family'.

2 *Accept responsibility for making the change.* The change may be caused by circumstances not under their control but making the change is their responsibility.

3 *State the long-term aim.* Stating this will add to motivation and help adopt a positive attitude. It is the reason they are making the change. This may be 'to start a family'.

4 *State what is the short-term aim?* Stating this will help the person to see that what they are doing now will fit in with their long-term aim, help them make any decisions and not waste effort. An example of a shorter-term aim might be: 'To earn enough money to pay the bills and go back to college to enable me, later, to start a new career and earn more money to support a family.'

5 *State anything that might hinder the change.* Here they state anything that might hinder their doing what they want to do. This might include: fear of taking the risk, lack of some skills, lack of confidence, negative thinking or more practical things such as lack of transport, lack of support from their family, lack of access to a computer to do assignments and so on. They list any of the resources they do not have at present that will be needed to succeed. They will need to take all into account when they do their action plan and use problem-solving techniques to overcome any difficulties.

6 *State everything that will help make the change.* These are all the
resources they have that will assist and work for them and may
include: support of friends, savings, skills they have such as ability
to manage on a small budget, ability to study and so on. The older
they are the more skills they are likely to have. They should not
discount the skills they have gained through experience,
employment and interests. Many skills are transferable. Also,
remind people not to forget determination, wanting to succeed.
They list everything they can think of that might help them
achieve what they want. It is important to do this because it will
help them to be realistic when they work out their action plan and
judge targets to set. It will also help them to assess how realistic
their aims are. There is no point in a person setting aims that they
have no hope of achieving – to do so is to set themselves up to fail.

7 *Action ideas/options to enable the changes to be made.* Here individuals
brainstorm thoughts, ideas and options. It does not matter how
silly or impossible the ideas seem. They can get a friend or friends
to help them do this. Two or three minds will come up with more
ideas than one person can on their own.

8 *Work out a step-by-step action plan.* Using the ideas, the person now
chooses the most suitable options and works out a step-by-step
plan to enable them to make the changes. They should ensure that
each step and the time set to achieve it is realistic. Also, they need
to take into account the difficulties they are aware they will have
and plan how to deal with them. The plan, as well as being
practical, should allow for feelings and how they will deal with
them. They can use the resources they have listed to assist with
this. It is also helpful to plan rewards for themselves as each step is
achieved.

9 *Put the plan into action.* No plan is any good unless it is carried out.

10 *Evaluate and adjust the plan as necessary.* As with the problem-solving
process, they will need to make adjustments as they go. Dates
need to be set to do this. They may have miscalculated the pace of
change slightly. The person may need to adjust some steps – speed
them up or slow them down. It may be necessary to include extra
steps to deal with something they had not anticipated, or a step
may not be working as well as they thought it might. As each step
is completed, they will learn from the experience.

It is important that each person does this evaluation as planned. It will enable them to learn from experience, re-shape the plan to take that experience into account and avoid getting stuck.

Aims
1 To explore common anxiety-giving situations
2 To apply techniques learned to these situations
3 To explore methods of dealing with change

Materials Flipchart, magic markers, copies of handouts and pens

CONTENT	Time
Discussion on individual progress and homework assignments	*15 minutes*
State the aims of the session and introduce coping with social activities *(Exercise and discussion – handout 1)*	*20 minutes*
Dealing with relationships *(Exercise, discussion and presentation – handout 2)*	*20 minutes*
Overcoming anxiety at work *(Exercise and discussion – handout 3)*	*20 minutes*
Break	*10 minutes*
Handling life events and managing change *(Exercise and presentation – handout 4)*	*30 minutes*
Homework assignments	*5 minutes*

Exercises and Assignments

Coping with social activities

Write the words 'Why cope with social activities?' at the top of the flipchart and quickly brainstorm. Discuss the different types of social situations listed in handout 1 briefly and write up on a clean flipchart sheet a list of the problems encountered in them. Take one example of a social situation and brainstorm on another sheet with the group the sort of things that might be included in an action plan to cope with it. Use the 'preparing to go out' section of handout 1 as a springboard for ideas.

Dealing with relationships

Divide a flipchart sheet into three sections or have three separate sheets. Using the headings (one heading to a sheet) 'friendships', 'family relationships' and 'work relationships', discuss briefly, brainstorm and write down anxiety-giving difficulties under each heading. Take one example that has been highlighted and, using a clean sheet, write down suggestions that might be included in an action plan to overcome the difficulty.

Give out handout 2 and discuss any relevant points.

Overcoming anxiety at work

Brainstorm with the group all the things that they feel cause them anxiety at work – these are things to do with the job itself – and discuss briefly. Some elements they may feel they are able to influence, others they may not because of company policy or lack of authority. Take one item that has been highlighted by the group and ask for suggestions that might be included in an action plan to limit or overcome the anxiety caused by it.

Give out handout 3 and discuss any relevant points.

Adapting to change

Using the flipchart, quickly brainstorm and discuss the following:

1 What is change? (Ensure that life events, social change and life experiences are included.)
2 What makes it a good or bad experience?

3 What stops us making changes?

4 Why would we choose to make changes?

Give out copies of the 'Making changes form' (handout 4). Go through the form and explain the process. Use a sample experience of a change to be made as an example.

Homework assignments

Instruct group members to:

1 Continue with their stress diary.

2 Continue to work on anxiety-giving situations.

3 Plan a change they would like to make and put it into action.

4 Make a note of any aspects from the sessions that they are not sure about to ask in the next session.

Coping with social activities

Types of social and leisure situations

◆ Small informal gatherings in peoples' homes
◆ Social events in public places
◆ Eating out
◆ Entertainment
◆ Sports and physical activities
◆ Clubs and societies
◆ Educational events such as evening classes

Preparing to go out

Being well prepared will give confidence, enable you to feel in control and allow you to enjoy the occasion. This means knowing such things as:

◆ Where the event is to be held
◆ What sort of event it is
◆ Who will be there
◆ What time you are expected
◆ Whether there will be a formal meal or a buffet
◆ How long the event will last
◆ What clothes are appropriate

And:

◆ Having a plan to deal with difficulties (feelings of panic, negative thoughts and so on)
◆ Being ready slightly early (this gives time to practise breathing/relaxation/ visualisation before leaving)

Dealing with relationships

Making it work

In different types of relationships the use of language will be different. When talking to an employer you may be formal but polite and think before commenting. When talking to a friend you will be friendly, but polite, and hold some things back. With family members you are likely to be more direct, authoritative and hold less back. In all relationships, if you act too passively you run the risk of offending, being taken advantage of, or ignored. If you are aggressive you are in danger of being destructive, avoided and disliked.

The key elements in overcoming anxiety and making relationships work include:

◆ Wanting them to work
◆ Knowing boundaries and limits
◆ Using breathing and relaxation techniques
◆ Challenging negative thoughts and replacing them with realistic thinking
◆ Using decision-making skills
◆ Being assertive
◆ Using problem-solving skills
◆ Communicating well

Successful relationships are a fine balancing act that you cannot always expect to get right – but with practised use of the above skills you can overcome misunderstandings, control your anxieties and ensure success most of the time.

Overcoming anxiety at work

Think about the following suggestions and how they might apply to you, and add other ideas:

- ◆ Practise breathing and relaxation techniques.
- ◆ Do not allow yourself to become overtired or fatigued.
- ◆ Ensure that deadlines are realistic.
- ◆ Plan and create systems that will help you deal with unexpected events.
- ◆ Always keep some energy in reserve – do not work for long periods
  'flat out'.
- ◆ Practise assertiveness – learn to say 'no' when demands become too much.
- ◆ Recognise your limitations and stay within them.
- ◆ Learn to recognise what is causing your anxiety or stress and find ways to change
  the situation or cope better with it.
- ◆ Use problem-solving skills and work out a plan of action to deal with situations.
- ◆ Use your communication skills to good advantage.
- ◆ Balance rest and activity.

1   Acknowledge and state the change to be made

2   Accept the responsibility for making the change

3   My long-term aim is:

4   My short-term aim is:

5   What might hinder my making changes:

6   What will help me make the changes:

7   Action ideas/options that will enable me to make the changes are:

8 My step-by-step action plan is:

Step 1 _____

_____

Completion date _____

Step 2 _____

_____

Completion date _____

Step 3 _____

_____

Completion date _____

Step 4 _____

_____

Completion date _____

Step 5 _____

_____

Completion date _____

9 Put the plan into action

10 Evaluation and adjustments to plan (set dates to do this)

Controlling anxiety for life

Becoming Stressproof

The earlier a person becomes aware that anxiety or stress is developing the easier it is to deal with it. Each individual needs to become an expert at recognising early warning signs so that these can be dealt with effectively before they become a problem. Warning signs may be different for different people. General indicators they can recognise are:

Physical

◆ feeling tense – tense neck and shoulders

   clenched jaws

   grinding teeth

   clenching fists

   shaking foot or leg

◆ feeling tired and lethargic
◆ breathlessness
◆ sweating

Thoughts and feelings

◆ feeling irritable and intolerant
◆ mood swings
◆ feeling aggressive
◆ blaming themselves
◆ feeling angry without real cause
◆ feeling disorganised
◆ thinking they cannot cope
◆ feeling they are losing control
◆ thinking everyone is trying to get at them
◆ lacking motivation

◆ thinking and feeling that they are making a bad impression
◆ feeling guilty

Behaviour
◆ rushing around without any real purpose
◆ bursting into tears
◆ smoking excessively
◆ drinking more alcohol than usual
◆ avoiding doing things, going places or meeting people
◆ constantly checking things
◆ eating more than usual (comfort eating)
◆ loss of appetite
◆ wanting to sleep more than usual
◆ being unable to sleep

These are the more common signs to watch for – some may apply, but each person needs to be aware of their own early warning signs. Having recognised the signs they then need to question themselves about what is causing the anxiety. They may ask themselves questions such as:

'When did I first start to feel anxious?'
'What was I doing then?'
'What was going on in my life?'

The causes may be:

◆ a developing situation
◆ a disagreement with someone
◆ having to make a difficult decision
◆ anticipation of a difficult situation
◆ doing something or going somewhere unfamiliar
◆ fear of a change which is about to happen
◆ an unhealthy lifestyle
◆ poor time management
◆ conflict between what they are doing and their life values
◆ committing themselves to something they do not want to do
◆ over-committing themselves
◆ additional external stresses over which they have little or no control
◆ trying to do too much too soon

- avoiding facing fears
- poor physical health

Having identified the source of the anxiety, action must then be taken to resolve it. This involves the person writing down all the options available that might solve or deal with the problem and then working out a step-by-step action plan. Handout 2 provides a planning sheet to help individuals through this process. Having worked out an action plan the steps must then be put into action.

Keeping a Positive Attitude

Maintaining a positive attitude is essential to creating high self-esteem and maintaining the good work begun. It is important that individuals respond to events in a positive way without undermining themselves and how they see the world around them. A negative attitude results in:

lack of energy	feeling anxious
not wanting to bother	feeling defeated
depression	thinking badly about self
poor relationships	neglecting self
not enjoying life	feeling unable to make changes
low self-esteem	thinking badly about others
feeling unworthy	not being able to cope

A positive attitude results in:

feeling energetic	enthusiasm
interest in others	feeling good
feeling able to make changes	wanting to do things
high self-esteem	enjoying life
better relationships	looking after self

What can people do to prevent themselves forming a negative attitude and to promote a positive attitude? They can do this by:

- Challenging negative thinking.
- Having realistic aims in life that are in line with values.
- Anticipating events, planning and rehearsing how to deal with them.

◆ Using visualisation to see themselves being successful.

◆ Taking exercise.

◆ Being aware of strengths, acknowledging and using them.

◆ Repeating positive statements about what is to be achieved (I am good at what I do, I will do this task well. I will get the job. I coped okay yesterday, I can cope today.).

◆ Having a good support system.

◆ Communicating needs effectively.

◆ Having a sense of purpose.

◆ Maintaining a healthy lifestyle.

◆ Managing stress.

◆ Facing fears.

◆ Being assertive.

◆ Having positive aims.

◆ Looking after themselves.

◆ Identifying and saying positive things about themselves (I enjoyed doing that. I have a good sense of humour. I am a good friend.).

◆ Having leisure interests.

◆ Having good relationships.

◆ Congratulating themselves on achievements, no matter how small.

◆ Sharing successes with friends.

Group members will be able to identify many more ways that help develop, reinforce and maintain a positive attitude to keep themselves motivated to continue the work they have begun. It is helpful for individuals to identify particular ways that work best for them and to use them regularly.

Looking Back

The aim of this part of the session is to help group members revise and reflect on the main principles covered during the course, enabling them to raise any points or ask questions about issues on which they are unclear. They will also have the handouts to refer to for revision and for future requirements. Some 'memory joggers' are given in the handout of the main areas covered (Handout 4: Looking back). These can be used to prompt discussion.

The end of this revision section is a good time to congratulate everyone on staying with the course all the way through, and on progress so far.

Point out that individual progress has been due to their personal effort and hard work.

Maintaining the Good Work

The next question is: 'How can the good work be maintained in the future?' This needs to be explored with the group. Some goals will have been achieved, others will be still being worked on and others will need to be worked on in the future. The anxiety management group will have provided group members with the basic knowledge to tackle anxiety problems and demonstrate that it is possible to face their fears and change their lives to enable them to do what they want to do. They now need to continue practising these techniques and continue to build on what has been achieved. The skills should be put into practice for life. Many people will find that as their situation changes over time they will gain new and helpful insights by going through the general principles again, long after the group has been disbanded.

Here are some suggestions that the group might consider to help support them as they keep up the good work and to reinforce learning. The group leaders will need to be clear about what they are prepared to commit themselves to, in the way of follow up or support.

- A list of books can be provided (see handout 6). It is worth checking with the local library and bookshop to see what additional titles are available. Group leaders may also have a number of books that they can loan out.
- Should the group have follow-up meetings – how many and when? Should these be structured or informal? Will they involve the group leader? Should reminder letters be sent out in advance of any arranged meetings? If so, who will do this? It is usually helpful at these meetings at least to review performance, discuss areas with which people are having difficulties or have forgotten and also to have a relaxation practice.
- Some groups may wish to continue meeting regularly, without the group leader, to support each other. Often meetings can be arranged in their own homes or a hired room. If they do this they may wish to call on the group leaders for guidance sometimes – especially in the early stages.

- If the whole group does not want to meet together, two or three people may wish to get together or keep in touch to support each other on a regular basis. Separate small groups may form in this manner.

- It may be desirable for some members to attend other groups or classes in the community for support, or to help them develop their skills further. It is helpful if group leaders are aware of other courses in the area and can put members in touch with them. In some areas there may be 'phobic' groups, or other similar support groups, which meet regularly. Adult education and other classes may be useful for people to further develop skills to meet needs.

Ending the Group

Either of the exercises provided with the session plan will provide a suitable ending to the session and give opportunity for group members to say goodbye in a way appropriate to any arrangements made for the future.

The group members will have looked at what they have achieved and made plans for the future. Some will be well on their way to achieving their goals. Others may have to continue working hard to consolidate what they have begun. Some members may also be faced with feelings of separation and loss now the formal group is ending. Even if everybody has not been able to achieve all they had expected during the life of the course, it will have provided them with the knowledge to enable them to control and manage their anxiety for the rest of their lives.

Aims   1 To become aware of personal early warning signs of anxiety and stress and learn to take immediate action
2 To examine the effects of both negative and positive attitudes and each person to become aware of what helps them maintain a positive attitude
3 To revise the main points and principles covered in the course
4 To plan how group members will support themselves and maintain their progress now that the course is ending

Materials Flipchart, magic markers, copies of handouts and pens

CONTENT	Time
Discussion on individual progress and homework assignments	*15 minutes*
State the aims of the session and introduce becoming stressproof *(Exercise and discussion – handouts 1 and 2)*	*20 minutes*
Keeping a positive attitude *(Exercise – handout 3)*	*20 minutes*
Break	*10 minutes*
Looking back *(Discussion – handout 4)*	*30 minutes*
Maintaining the good work *(Discussion – handouts 5 and 6)*	*15 minutes*
Ending the group *(Exercise)*	*10 minutes*

10 Session

Exercises

Becoming stressproof

Give out handout 1, discuss briefly and then have each person identify their own personal indicators of anxiety or stress. Give out handout 2 ('Early-warning action plan') and explain how to use it.

Keeping a positive attitude

Introduce the subject. Draw a vertical line down the centre of a flipchart sheet. Write the headings 'A negative attitude results in:' on one side of the line and 'A positive attitude results in:' on the other side. Now have the group brainstorm each. Discuss and then on a separate sheet brainstorm ways to promote a positive attitude. Have individuals identify methods that work for them. Give out handout 3.

Looking back

Introduce the idea of revision, give out handout 4 and provide opportunity for questions and discussion as you quickly summarise the listed memory-joggers.

Maintaining the good work

Give out handout 5 and 6 and discuss how the group members are going to ensure continued progress, support and reinforce learning now that the course has come to an end.

Ending the group

Choose one of the following exercises:

1   Have a round of statements beginning with one of the following:
    'Before I go I would like to say …'
    'The thing I will remember most from the group is …'
    'The most important thing I have learned from the group is …'
    'What I have gained from the group is …'
2   Give each participant a sheet of paper and an envelope. Ask them to write down what they would like to achieve during a set period of time. This may be one month, three months, or by when the group have next decided to meet. When completed, ask them to seal the envelopes, write their names and addresses on them and

exchange envelopes with someone else in the group. When they attend the next meeting in one month's time, the envelopes can be opened and progress discussed. If group members do not wish to meet as a group again the letters can be posted to each other and individuals encouraged to make contact and discuss progress.

Becoming stressproof

The earlier you become aware that anxiety or stress is developing the easier it is to deal with it. You need to become expert at recognising early-warning signs that you are becoming anxious or stressed so it can be dealt with effectively before it becomes a problem. Warning signs may be different for different people. Examine the general indicators below and then write down your own personal early warning indicators of anxiety or stress.

GENERAL AND PERSONAL INDICATORS OF STRESS	
General indicators of stress or anxiety	Personal indicators of stress or anxiety
Physical Feeling tense – tense neck and shoulders clenched jaws grinding teeth clenching fists shaking foot or leg Feeling tired and lethargic Breathlessness Sweating	
Thoughts and feelings Feeling irritable and intolerant Mood swings Feeling aggressive Blaming yourself Feeling angry without real cause Feeling disorganised Thinking you cannot cope Feeling you are losing control Thinking everyone is trying to get at you Lacking motivation Thinking and feeling that you are making a bad impression Feeling guilty	
Behaviour Rushing around without any real purpose Bursting into tears Smoking excessively Drinking more alcohol than usual Avoiding doing things, going places or meeting people Constantly checking things	

Becoming stressproof (cont)

GENERAL AND PERSONAL INDICATORS OF STRESS	
General indicators of stress or anxiety	**Personal indicators of stress or anxiety**
Eating more than normal (comfort eating) Loss of appetite Wanting to sleep more than usual Being unable to sleep	

These are the signs of which you need to be aware. Having recognised the signs you then need to question yourself about what is causing the anxiety. Ask yourself questions such as:

◆ 'When did I first start to feel anxious?'
◆ 'What was I doing then?'
◆ 'What was going on in my life?'

This may be:

◆ a developing situation
◆ a disagreement with someone
◆ having to make a difficult decision
◆ doing something or going somewhere unfamiliar
◆ fear of a change that is about to happen
◆ an unhealthy lifestyle
◆ poor time management
◆ conflict between what you are doing and your life values
◆ committing yourself to something that you do not want to do
◆ over-committing yourself
◆ additional external stresses over which you have little or no control
◆ trying to do too much too soon
◆ avoiding facing fears
◆ poor physical health

Having identified the source of the anxiety you must then take action to resolve it. Write down all the options available to solve or deal with the problem and then a step-by-step action plan can be worked out. Handout 2 ('Early-warning action plan') provides you with a planning sheet to help you through this process. Having worked out an action plan put it into practice immediately.

Early-warning action plan

Warning signs	What is causing my anxiety?	What I can do about it
Physical		
Thinking and feeling		
Behavioural		

Action plan

Step 1_____ Completion date_____

Step 2_____ Completion date_____

Step 3_____ Completion date_____

Step 4_____ Completion date_____

Step 5_____ Completion date_____

Maintaining a positive attitude is essential for creating high self-esteem and maintaining the good work you have begun throughout life. It is important to respond to events in a positive way without undermining yourself and how you see the world. A negative attitude results in:

lack of energy	feeling anxious
not wanting to bother	feeling defeated
depression	thinking badly about yourself
poor relationships	neglecting yourself
not enjoying life	feeling unable to make changes
low self-esteem	thinking badly about others
feeling unworthy	not being able to cope

A positive attitude results in:

feeling energetic	enthusiasm
interest in others	feeling good
feeling able to make changes	wanting to do things
high self-esteem	enjoying life
better relationships	looking after yourself

What can you do to prevent forming a negative attitude and to promote a positive attitude? You can:

◆ Challenge negative thinking.
◆ Have realistic aims in life that are in line with your values.
◆ Anticipate events, plan and rehearse how to deal with them.
◆ Use visualization to see yourself being successful.
◆ Take exercise.
◆ Be aware of your strengths, acknowledge and use them.
◆ Repeat positive statements about what is to be achieved (I am good at what I do, I will do this task well. I will get the job. I coped okay yesterday, I can cope today.).

Keeping a positive attitude *(cont)*

◆ Have a good support system.

◆ Communicate your needs effectively.

◆ Have a sense of purpose.

◆ Maintain a healthy lifestyle.

◆ Manage stress.

◆ Face fears.

◆ Be assertive.

◆ Have positive aims.

◆ Look after yourself.

◆ Identify and say positive things about yourself (I enjoyed doing that. I have a good sense of humour. I am a good friend.).

◆ Have leisure interests.

◆ Have good relationships.

◆ Congratulate yourself on achievements, no matter how small.

◆ Share successes with friends.

You will be able to identify many more ways that help develop, reinforce and maintain a positive attitude and keep yourself motivated to maintain the work you have begun. Identify particular methods that work well for you and use them regularly.

The aim of this handout is to help you revise and reflect on the main principles covered during the course and raise any points or ask questions about any part of it on which you are not clear. It is strongly recommended that you retain and read through all the handouts given out from time to time, so that you become and remain really familiar with the information. The following is intended to jog your memory about what has been covered.

- Everybody experiences anxiety. It is a normal reaction to something that is seen as threatening.
- The 'fight or flight' response is geared to preparing the body to deal with danger or stress.
- The 'vicious anxiety chain' begins by anticipating the feelings of anxiety with negative or faulty thinking.
- Be aware of your anxiety triggers.
- Use relaxation and breathing techniques to 'kick start' the slow-down process and bring bodily feelings under control.
- Challenge distressing thoughts and faulty thinking.
- Set goals to work on and break these down into step-by-step action plans.
- Plan to face your fears so that you are prepared to deal with anything that may go wrong.
- Use visualisation techniques to rehearse completing the plan successfully and boost your confidence.
- Review the plan regularly, learn from your experience and adjust it accordingly to ensure you succeed.
- Reward and congratulate yourself on each step achieved.
- Be prepared for 'ups and downs' and 'setbacks' and keep going. Progress will not always go in a straight line.
- Recognise and acknowledge problems, state them in a solvable way and work out a realistic step-by-step plan to deal with them.
- When making difficult decisions consider advantages and disadvantages in relation to both long- and short-term aims.
- Communicate effectively using both verbal and non-verbal skills.
- Assertiveness is the ability to communicate with others in a way that allows you say directly what you really think, feel or want, while taking into account the feelings of others.
- Work out your aims in life ensuring that they are in line with your values and beliefs.
- Regularly review how you manage time, taking into account your aims and values in life. Bear in mind leisure and relaxation, daily routine tasks, and work.
- Develop a healthy lifestyle, take exercise and ensure a healthy diet.
- Apply the knowledge gained to everyday situations and learn to manage change.
- Make yourself aware of your early warning signs of anxiety, deal with the cause immediately and develop a positive attitude.

Maintaining the good work

Here are some suggestions for you to think about to ensure continued progress, support and to reinforce learning.

◆ Keep the handouts and read through them at regular intervals.
◆ Make full use of personal support systems.
◆ Read books on the topics covered on the course (see handout 6). Your local library or bookshop may have additional titles or be able to acquire them for you. The group leaders may have recommended titles available for you to borrow.
◆ Consider having follow-up meetings. This may be with or without the group facilitators. You will need to decide how many, when and where they are to take place and if they are to be formal or informal. It is usually helpful at these meetings at least to review performance, cover issues with which people are having difficulties or have forgotten and have a relaxation practice. Do reminder letters need to be sent out in advance of the meetings and who will do this?
◆ Do you want to go on meeting regularly on your own to support each other without the group facilitators? Meetings can be arranged in private homes or a hired room. Will you want to call on the group facilitators for guidance from time to time?
◆ If the whole group does not want to meet you may want to get together with one or two other group members from time to time or keep in touch to support each other on a regular basis. Separate small groups may form in this manner.
◆ Consider attending other groups or classes in the community for support or to help you develop your skills further. In some areas there may be 'phobic' or other similar support groups which meet regularly. Adult education classes may also be useful for you to further develop skills to meet your needs.

Below is a list of books that you may find helpful. There are many others available which you may be able to obtain through your local library or any good bookshop.

Bolton R, 1979, *People Skills,* Simon & Schuster, New York.

Butler J & Hope T, 1995, *Manage Your Mind: The Mental Health Fitness Guide,* Oxford University Press, Oxford.

Charlesworth E & Nathan R, 1997, *Stress Management – A Comprehensive Guide To Wellness,* Souvenir Press, London.

Cleghorn P, 1996, *Secrets of Self-Esteem,* Element Books, Shaftesbury.

Ffeifer V, 1989, *Positive Thinking,* Element Books, Shaftesbury.

Garner A, 1997, *Conversationally Speaking,* Lowell House, New York.

Glass L, 1991, *Confident Conversation,* Piatkus, London.

Greener M, 1996, *The Which? Guide To Managing Stress,* Which? Books, London.

Hayward S, 1998, *Stress Solutions,* Ward Lock, London.

Hewitt J, 1982, *The Complete Relaxation Book,* Rider, London.

Holdsworth N & Paxton R, 1999, *Managing Anxiety and Depression: A Self-help Guide,* Mental Health Foundation, London.

Jeffers S, 1991, *Feel The Fear and Do It Anyway,* Arrow, London.

Kennedy H, 1997, *Overcoming Anxiety,* Robinson, London.

Lindenfield G, 1995, *Assert Yourself,* Thorsons, London.

Lindenfield G, 1995, *Self-Esteem,* Thorsons, London.

Marks I M, 1978, *Living With Fear,* McGraw Hill, New York.

Nelson-Jones R, 1990, *Human Relationship Skills,* London.

Rachman S & De Silva P, 1996, *Panic Disorders: The Facts,* Oxford University Press, Oxford.

Sharpe R, 1991, *Self-help For Your Anxiety,* Souvenir Press, London.

Silove D & Manicavasagar V, 1997, *Overcoming Panic,* Robinson, London.

Trickett S, 1989, *Coping With Anxiety And Depression,* Sheldon Press, London.

Walmsley C, 1992, *Assertiveness – The Right To Be You,* BBC Books, London.

Weekes C, 1972, *Peace From Nervous Suffering,* Hawthorn Books, London.

Weekes C, 1992, *Understanding Obsessions and Compulsions,* Sheldon Press, London.

Weekes C, 1992, *Body Language In Relationships,* Sheldon Press, London.

Weekes C, 1995, *Enjoy Healthy Eating,* Health Education Authority, London.

Appendixes

Appendixes

Name _____   Telephone no _____

Address _____   Date of birth _____

_____

_____

Married/single/
partner _____   Referred by _____

Children/age/sex _____   Date referred _____

Occupation _____

Medical history

This should include any previous anxiety treatment – if it did not work then you will need to know why, any current medical treatments including sedative drugs being taken, and any physical problems such as heart conditions.

Description of problem

Detail the current problem and situation and how it affects the person. Explore current lifestyle, relationships, stresses and so on.

Problem history

Find out when the first episode occurred, what triggered it and what stresses were influencing the person's life at that time. Has the problem got worse? How has this developed and what has influenced it? How has it affected the person's life? (The longer the problem has been established the more difficult it will be for the person to deal with.)

Personal history

Start with childhood and continue through early school, teenage years, up to the present time. Include education, work experience and leisure activities and their attitude to these. Note throughout the history how the person has related to family members, work colleagues and friends.

Anxiety/Symptom Rating Form

1 Behavioural

Do you find any of the following situations difficult? Please tick the appropriate rating column. Use the blank spaces to add additional personal ratings.

	Never	Sometimes	Frequently	Always
1 Travelling on public transport				
2 Going into shops				
3 Walking down the street				
4 Meeting people at parties				
5 Meeting people at work				
6 Going into shopping centres				
7 Going into restaurants or cafes				
8 Eating/drinking with people				
9 Being on your own				
10 Driving a car				
11 Going into a room full of people				
12 Leaving your home				
13 Going to unfamiliar places				
14 Being with people you do not know well				
15 Being with friends				
16				
17				
18				
19				
20				

2 Physical

Have you recently experienced any of the following symptoms? Please tick the appropriate rating column. Use the blank spaces to add additional personal ratings.

	Never	Sometimes	Frequently	Always
1 Dry mouth				
2 Difficulty swallowing				
3 Pounding/racing heart				
4 Tremors				
5 Wobbly legs				
6 Tense muscles (neck, shoulders, jaws)				
7 Dizziness				
8 Headaches				
9 Sweating				
10 Feeling nauseous				
11 Diarrhoea				
12 Tiredness				
13 Problems sleeping				
14 Shortness of breath				
15 Sexual difficulties				
16				
17				
18				
19				
20				

Anxiety/Symptom Rating Form *(cont)*

3 Thoughts

Have you recently experienced worrying thoughts about any of the following? Please tick the appropriate rating column. Use blank spaces to add additional personal ratings.

	Never	Sometimes	Frequently	Always
1 Fainting				
2 Losing control				
3 The impression you are making				
4 Dying				
5 Having a panic attack				
6 Not being able to cope				
7 Being unable to breathe				
8 Being embarrassed				
9 Going mad				
10 Talking to people				
11 Choking				
12 Vomiting				
13 Having an incurable disease				
14 What other people are thinking about you				
15 Being different				
16				
17				
18				
19				
20				

4 General

Have you recently experienced any of the following? Please tick the appropriate rating column. Use the blank spaces to add any additional personal rating.

	Never	Sometimes	Frequently	Always
1 Feeling guilty				
2 Tearfulness				
3 Blaming yourself				
4 Anger				
5 Moodiness				
6 Impatience				
7 Lack of confidence				
8 Feelings of being disorganised				
9 Avoiding people				
10 Feeling passive				
11 Accident proneness				
12 Boredom				
13 Changes in how you relate to other people				
14 Depression				
15 Feelings of confusion				
16 Aggressiveness				
17 Rushing around				
18 Drinking more than normal				
19 Eating more than normal				
20 Smoking more than normal				

	Never	Sometimes	Frequently	Always
21 Avoiding going out				
22 Hiding away				
23 Resorting to taking extra medication				
24 Sleeping more than normal				
25 Irritability				
26				
27				
28				
29				
30				

Please assist us to evaluate and improve the effectiveness of what we do by giving us feedback from your experience of the group.

What did you want to achieve?

_____

_____

_____

_____

_____

What have you achieved?

_____

_____

_____

_____

_____

What has not been achieved?

_____

_____

_____

_____

_____

Please rate the following aspects

	Poor	Fair	Good	Very good	Excellent
Venue					
Presentation of information					
Style of facilitators					

What aspects of the group have been the most useful?

_____

_____

_____

_____

What has been the least useful?

_____

_____

_____

_____

What could be changed or improved?

_____

_____

_____

_____

What do you plan to do to follow up on what has been achieved?

_____

_____

_____

_____

Please make any additional comments you think may be helpful.

_____

_____

_____

_____

Thank you for contributing to the evaluation. Please return this form to the organisers.

Group Evaluation/Satisfaction Form 2

Please assist us to evaluate and improve the effectiveness of what we do by giving us feedback from your experience since you attended our anxiety management group.

When the regular group meetings ended you planned to: (Group leader to complete from evaluation/satisfaction form 1)

_____

_____

_____

_____

_____

What have you achieved?

_____

_____

_____

_____

_____

What has not been achieved?

_____

_____

_____

_____

_____

What has helped you most since the group ended?

_____

_____

_____

_____

_____

Group Evaluation/Satisfaction Form 2 *(cont)*

What has hindered you most?

_____

_____

_____

_____

_____

What do you plan to do to follow up on what you have achieved so far?

_____

_____

_____

_____

_____

Please make any additional comments you think may be helpful.

_____

_____

_____

_____

_____

Thank you for contributing to the evaluation. Please return this form to the organisers.

Bibliography

Bowlby J, 1973, *Attachment and Loss Vol II: Separation, Anxiety and Anger,* Hogarth Press, London.

Erikson E, 1950, *Childhood and Society,* Norton, New York.

Fairbairn WRD, 1952, *Psychoanalytic Studies of the Personality,* Tavistock Publications, London.

Fromm E, 1944, Individual and Social Origins of Neurosis, *American Socialogical Review* IX (4)

Health Education Authority, 1995, *Physical Activity Evaluation Panel Survey.*

Health Education Authority, 1996, *Active For Life Action Pack: General Facts on Physical Activity.*

Holmes TH & Rahe RH, 1967, The Social Readjustment Rating Scale, *Journal of Psychosomatic Research* 11, pp213-218.

Klein M, 1948, *Contributions to Psychoanalysis,* Hogarth Press, London.

Lang PJ, 1968, 'Fear Reduction and Fear Behaviour: A Construct', in J M Shlien (ed), *Research in Psychotherapy,* Vol 3, American Psychological Association, Washington DC.

Maslow AH, 1970, *Motivation and Personality,* (3rd Edition), Harper Collins, New York.

Sullivan HS, 1938, Introduction to the Study of Interpersonal Relations, *Psychiatry* 1, pp121-134.

Winnicott DW, 1960, *The Theory of the Parent-Infant Relationship,* Hogarth Press, London.

Read Write Inc.

Handbook 2

Series developed by
Ruth Miskin

OXFORD

OXFORD
UNIVERSITY PRESS

Great Clarendon Street, Oxford, OX2 6DP, United Kingdom

Oxford University Press is a department of the University of Oxford.
It furthers the University's objective of excellence in research, scholarship,
and education by publishing worldwide. Oxford is a registered trade mark of
Oxford University Press in the UK and in certain other countries.

British Library Cataloguing in Publication Data

Data available

978-0-19-837430-5

7 9 10 8

Printed and bound in Great Britain by Bell and Bain Ltd, Glasgow

Acknowledgements

The Author would like to thank Jenny Roberts for all her excellent support
in compiling the Handbook and, in particular, for developing
the grammar and vocabulary activities.

Illustrations: Tim Archbold

Photographs: by kind permission of Ruth Miskin Training.

FSC
www.fsc.org

MIX
Paper from
responsible sources
FSC® C007785

Subscribe to *Read Write Inc. Phonics* on Oxford Owl to access the
vital online part of the *Read Write Inc. Phonics* programme, including
essential teaching resources. To purchase your subscription visit
www.oxfordowl.co.uk

Contents

Dear Reading Teacher,

Have you ever failed to teach a child to read? I have. As a Reception teacher I failed a few children every year – and it wasn't a great feeling. My failure gave me the reading bug. It made me obsess over finding a way that would work for every child. I tried different methods and schemes in five different schools, but it was only when I became a headteacher that I had the time to trial and research the most effective methods. Twenty-five years ago – first in Leeds and then in Tower Hamlets – I took my first steps towards creating *Read Write Inc.*

But it wasn't just about finding the right system. As you'll know, children learn to read more easily when they enjoy it. I loved teaching reading so they loved learning – enthusiasm is catching. I was passionate about their progress. And, as a head, I needed all the teachers to feel the same as me. Children feel our passion for them – they know when we're on their side. They know when we will stick with them until they succeed.

Every school needs teachers who are passionate about getting children to read – teachers who will take up the challenge of getting every child to read. You!

Be prepared – the first year of teaching *Read Write Inc.* is the hardest, while you learn the new systems. However, by the second year, you will have the confidence to teach any child to read and write.

I hope you will love teaching *Read Write Inc. Phonics* and share my passion for teaching children to read and write.

Best wishes,

Ruth Miskin

Read Write Inc. Phonics resources

This handbook includes everything you need to teach *Read Write Inc. Phonics* from Yellow to Grey Level. This chart gives an overview of all the resources in the programme.

Learning the letters and sounds

Speed Sounds Cards Sets 1, 2 and 3	Picture-Sound Cards	Sound-Picture Frieze
Set 1 Cards have pictures that are in the same shape as the letters. Sets 2 and 3 Cards show a picture and phrase.	Pictures that start with the first letter of the Speed Sounds, e.g. m for moon.	Colour wall chart with the same pictures as the Speed Sounds Set 1 and 2 Cards.

Learning to blend sounds into words

Magnetic Sound Cards	Fred Frog Beanie
Small magnetic tiles to help children identify letter shapes and develop skills of blending and segmenting.	Beanie toy of Fred the Frog used to teach Fred Talk.

Applying phonic knowledge to reading and writing

Red Ditty Books and Ditty Photocopy Masters	Storybooks	Get Writing! Books
Short decodable passages to give children practice in sound blending: an important bridge between reading single words and reading stories.	75 core decodable Storybooks matched to children's phonic knowledge.	*Get Writing!* Books for children to embed their phonic knowledge, spelling, punctuation, and for composition activities based on oral rehearsal and role-play.

Teacher support for *Read Write Inc. Phonics*

Phonics Handbook 1	Phonics Handbook 2
Guidance for teaching Red to Orange Levels, including the Speed Sounds Lessons, Ditty blueprints, step-by-step Storybook and *Get Writing!* lessons for each book and a section on teaching handwriting.	Guidance for teaching Yellow to Grey Levels, including the Speed Sounds Lessons, step-by-step Storybook and *Get Writing!* lessons for each book and a section on teaching handwriting.

Speed Sounds Posters

Simple and Complex Sounds Posters for quick reviews of letter-sound correspondences.

Desktop Speed Sounds Chart

A small desktop sound chart which includes all of the Speed Sounds.

My Speed Sounds Books

Pocket-sized books for children to take home so they can practise reading and writing the sounds they have learnt with a parent or carer.

Phonics Green Word Cards

Word Cards for use in the Speed Sounds Lessons, for children to practise word blending for reading.

Red Word Cards

Word Cards featuring common words with an uncommon spelling, e.g. *ai* in *said*.

Sound Blending Books

10 Sound Blending Books for practising blending words made up of Speed Sounds Set 1.

Non-fiction Books

35 Non-fiction books for further phonic practice, at home and at school.

More Storybooks

15 Set A Storybooks for further practice.

Book Bag Books

75 decodable Book Bag Books matched to the phonic content in the Storybooks for additional reading practice at home.

Reading Leader Handbook

Guidance for the Reading Leader on all aspects of their role.

Read Write Inc. Phonics Online

Includes files for handwriting, assessment, Story Green Words, Speedy Green Words, writing prompts and Storytime and Poetry Time.

To subscribe, go to: www.oxfordowl.co.uk

Introduction to *Read Write Inc. Phonics*

In *Read Write Inc. Phonics* lessons, children learn to read accurately and fluently with good comprehension. They learn to form each letter, spell correctly, and compose their ideas step-by-step.

Throughout the programme, children learn the English alphabetic code: the 150+ graphemes that represent 44 speech sounds. They rapidly learn sounds and the letter, or groups of letters, they need to represent them in three sets of Speed Sounds Lessons. Simple and enjoyable mnemonics help all children to grasp the letter-sound correspondences quickly, especially those who are at risk of making slower progress or those who are new to learning English. This learning is taught and consolidated every day. High frequency words that are not phonically regular are taught as 'tricky' words (we call them Red Words) and are practised frequently.

Lively phonic books are closely matched to children's increasing knowledge of phonics and 'tricky' words so that, early on, they experience plenty of success. Repeated readings of the texts support their increasingly fluent decoding.

A thought-provoking introduction and prompts for thinking out loud and discussion help children comprehend what they are reading.

Teachers read aloud and discuss picture books with similar themes to those in the Storybooks, so children build up background knowledge ready for the next Storybook.

Reading

Children read the story three times. On the first read, children focus on accurate word reading; the second, on developing fluency; and the third, on comprehension. Fluency and comprehension increase with each repeated reading.

Accuracy

Children learn to:

- read new sounds and review previously taught sounds;
- sound out the names of characters and unfamiliar words;
- understand the meanings of new words;
- read the story (first read).

Fluency

Children learn to:

- read the words in the story speedily;
- track the story, 'jumping in' when the teacher hesitates;
- read the story with increased speed (second read).

Comprehension

Children learn to:

- predict the outcome, after listening to a story introduction;
- discuss and compare key moments in the story;
- read the story with a storyteller's voice (third read);
- answer questions about the story;
- read the same story at home;
- build background knowledge, ready to read the next *Read Write Inc.* Storybook.

Writing

As with reading, the alphabetic code is embedded first, so that children can write simple words early on and build on their success. The children write every day, rehearsing out loud what they want to write, and composing sentence by sentence, until they are confident enough to write independently. They write at the level of their spelling knowledge: that is, they use their knowledge of the alphabetic code and the 'tricky' words they have learnt. They practise handwriting every day: sitting at a table comfortably, learning correct letter formation and joining letters speedily and legibly.

In every lesson, children rapidly build up their spelling knowledge so that soon they are able to spell complex words confidently. The children can use adventurous vocabulary in their writing because they have encountered such language in their reading and they have talked about what the words mean.

Transcription

Children learn to:

- develop a confident handwriting style;
- spell common words with common graphemes and suffixes;
- spell common words with unusual graphemes;
- write prepared sentences with correct spelling and punctuation.

Composition

Children learn to:

- build and rehearse their own sentences based on ideas from the story;
- apply new grammar concepts linked to the story;
- use new vocabulary in their writing;
- edit their writing to correct their grammar and punctuation;
- write a composition based on the Storybook they have just read;
- edit their own and their partner's writing.

Teacher modelling and participation

The teacher explains and uses direct instruction for every activity – 'My turn Your turn' **(MTYT)** – ensuring that all the children in the group are watching and mirroring what the teacher is doing. The children then turn to their partners (**TTYP** – 'Turn to your partner') to either practise what they have been taught or discuss a new idea. The teacher observes and listens carefully, picking up on any errors or uncertainties. The teacher repeats the activity until all the children are confident at every step. Revision and consolidation at the start of the next day's lesson are vital in embedding the learning, step-by-step.

Grouping

Children are assessed and grouped according to their phonic knowledge. Each child reads books that match their phonic knowledge. Ongoing assessment means that groups are constantly adjusted to ensure the best progress for each child.

Training for *Read Write Inc. Phonics*

A key element of the *Read Write Inc.* approach is that practice across the school is completely consistent. This is achieved because the headteacher and all the teachers and teaching assistants, from Reception to Year 6 (P1–P7), are trained to teach reading and writing.

This means that everyone has a shared understanding of the 'Simple View of Reading', how letters and sounds in English are related (the alphabetic code), and how to teach all children to read and write.

After the training, the trainer shows the Reading Leader how to coach the staff in your school to ensure that everyone is teaching as effectively and as consistently as possible. The headteacher and the Reading Leader learn how to monitor progress until every child can read. They help you to ensure that no child is left behind to struggle.

The most successful *Read Write Inc.* schools attribute the rapid progress of their children to the partnership they build with the trainers. Your Reading Leader will choose the most appropriate training route for your school, and there is further guidance on this in the *Reading Leader Handbook*.

What to expect on the training day

The trainers:

- model lessons and practise with you so you are prepared to teach;

- demonstrate the reading, writing and spelling process step-by-step;

- examine footage of real lessons;

- demonstrate consistent management strategies that speed up progress;

- ensure you know how to get *all* children reading and writing – whatever their background or need.

Overview – route through *Read Write Inc. Phonics*

The chart below shows a summary of the progression of sound teaching in *Read Write Inc. Phonics*.

New Speed Sounds to learn	Speed Sounds to review	Progression of Storybooks and Get Writing! Books	Extra practice if needed: Non-fiction	Extra practice if needed: Fiction
Set 1 + blending				
	Set 1 + blending	Sound Blending Books (1 -10) Red Ditty Books (1–10) Get Writing! Red Ditty Books (1–10)		Ditty Photocopy Masters
Set 2	Set 1 + blending	Storybooks Green Set 1 (1–10) Get Writing! Green Book	Green Non-fiction	Green Set A
Set 2	Set 1 + blending	Storybooks Purple Set 2 (1–10) Get Writing! Purple Book	Purple Non-fiction	Purple Set A
Teach letter names*	Sets 1 and 2	Storybooks Pink Set 3 (1–10) Get Writing! Pink Book	Pink Non-fiction	Pink Set A
Teach Set 3	Sets 1 and 2	Storybooks Orange Set 4 (1–12) Get Writing! Orange Book	Orange Non-fiction	
Teach Set 3	Sets 1 and 2	Storybooks Yellow Set 5 (1–10) Get Writing! Yellow Book	Yellow Non-fiction	
Teach Set 3	Sets 1 and 2	Storybooks Blue Set 6 (1–10) Get Writing! Blue Book	Blue Non-fiction	
Teach Set 3	Sets 1 and 2	Storybooks Grey Set 7 (1–13) Get Writing! Grey Book	Grey Non-fiction	

Once children are fluent readers and have completed the Grey Storybooks they can move on to *Read Write Inc. Literacy and Language* and *Read Write Inc. Spelling*.

For example, once children have learnt the Set 1 Speed Sounds and can blend words made up of these sounds, they can start on the Sound Blending Books, then the Red Ditty Books and the *Get Writing!* Red Ditty Books. When they move onto the Green Storybooks and *Get Writing!* Green Book they are taught the Set 2 Speed Sounds and continue to review Set 1 Speed Sounds and blending.

*Note: Teach letter names by singing the alphabet song with the whole class. (Not in *Read Write Inc.* lessons.) Do not hold up the Speed Sounds Cards while you do this.

The five principles

Read Write Inc. Phonics shows you both *how* to teach a child to read and write, and also *how to keep their attention.*

We have five core principles to teaching and learning. These are to:

1. know the **PURPOSE** of every activity and share it with the children, so children know the **one** thing they should be thinking about;

2. be **PASSIONATE** about teaching so you can engage children emotionally;

3. teach at an effective **PACE** and devote every moment to teaching and learning;

4. ensure that every child **PARTICIPATES** throughout the lesson. Partner work is fundamental to learning;

5. **PRAISE** effort and progress – not ability.

Read Write Inc. is particularly effective when the school adopts the routines and signals outlined below consistently across the whole school.

1. Purpose

We can only pay attention to *one new* thing at a time. If we are asked to learn too much at once, we give up. Each activity in the programme has one very clear purpose. It is important to set the purpose at the beginning of each activity so the children understand what they are learning and why.

2. Passion

Emotional engagement is necessary for children to learn something new. The greater their engagement the more they learn. Children mirror your mood. When you are enthusiastic, children are too. Show your passion for teaching.

- Smile. If you aren't enjoying the lesson, the children won't either.
- Love the children who need winning over – they need you more than all the others. When you enjoy having them in your lesson, they misbehave less.
- Prepare thoroughly so you can concentrate on children's progress.

3. Pace

Signals to keep the pace

We need children's minds to be free to learn to read and write. This means practising routines until they become second nature.

Silent signals

Praise children for routines they do quickly and quietly. However, once children know the routines, acknowledge their co-operation with a nod, a smile or a thank you.

Team stop signal

The team stop signal helps us stop children in a calm manner, ready for what's next. Use this signal to gain attention. Practise until children respond in under five seconds and in silence. It replaces all other stopping techniques: clapping, clicking, singing rhymes, shaking maraca, shouting, shushing, singing, dance routines, counting back.

Use the stop signal at playtime, in assembly, in lessons, during transitions, at lunchtime, on trips and in staff meetings. See Glossary, p.22.

Turn to your partner (TTYP) signal

Partner work should be used consistently in all lessons. This signal indicates children should turn to their partners to answer the question. See 'Participation' below and Glossary, p.22.

My turn Your turn (MTYT) signal

Use this silent signal when you want the children to repeat something after you. See Glossary, p.20.

1, 2, 3 signal

Use this silent signal to move the children silently from tables to carpet in under 15 seconds. See Glossary, p.18.

Silent handwriting signal

Use this silent signal to indicate that children should sit in the correct handwriting position. See Glossary, p.21.

4. Participation

Teamwork

We want children to be motivated to work together, teach each other, practise together, talk together, give feedback to each other. Teamwork is key.

Partnerships

1. Articulating a thought forces children to engage. It makes them organise what they know and what they don't know. This is why we want all children to practise what they have been taught with a partner throughout every lesson. They practise every activity and answer every question together.

   Organise new partnerships every four to six weeks. Pair up assertive children – so they can battle it out. Pair up shy children – someone has to talk. Mix boys and girls, first and second language learners.

2. Children need to pay attention to their partners. They only do this if they feel comfortable working with them. Use a Partner Quiz to help new partners build a relationship: ask partners to find out their partner's favourite food/TV programme/film/computer game/story and what makes them cross, happy...and so on.

3. Praise effective partner work throughout the day, until it becomes 'what you do'.
   (See **Praise**, below.)

4. Some partnerships are more successful than others, but stick with it – if you take partnerships seriously, the children will too.

No hands-up, thumbs-up, chests-up!

We strongly discourage hands-up or thumbs-up (or chests-up!) as a technique for answering questions. In 'hands-up' classrooms, few children respond to questions. Children who don't raise their hands are unlikely to pay attention.

We also discourage the 'pull out the stick' technique. Again, any one question is only answered by a few children.

We gain and keep children's attention throughout the lesson by using three techniques: choral work, partner practice and partner talk.

Choral work: My turn Your turn (MTYT)

We use choral work when we want children to copy what we've just said.

Partner Practice

This is used in the Partner Practice word activities, First Read, Second Read, Jump-in and Third Read.

Children are asked to recall what we have just taught them by teaching their partners. You are then able to check if your teaching has been successful – or not.

Model and then practise the routines. Ensure partners know who is Partner 1 and 2. (Give out numbered cards to remind partners, if necessary.)

Routines for Partner Practice

The teaching partner:

- places one Storybook between them;

- points accurately to each sound/word with a lolly stick;

- prompts their partner to correct an error and sound out new words, using Fred Talk.

While children read, move around the group. Don't sit with one partnership. You have given the 'teacher' a job to do, and you want them to take responsibility for teaching their partner. Always talk to the partner who is teaching. Don't intervene and teach the partner who is reading.

Partner talk

Children pay attention because they know they will be expected to answer every question with their partner and could be called upon to share their response with the rest of the group.

Partner talk is used in: the Story Introduction, Think About the Story, Questions to Read and Answer, Build a Sentence and Write About.

Routines for partner talk

1. Ask the question.

2. Use the **TTYP** silent signal (see Glossary, p.22).

3. Listen as children prepare an answer with their partner.

4. Use the stop signal (see Glossary, p.22).

5. Select feedback methods.

Explain that you expect both partners to prepare an answer and that *you* will choose how feedback is collected, i.e. you will no longer choose children to answer questions who raise their hands or thumbs. Observe partners as they talk – don't get stuck with one partner.

Feedback methods

Use **Choose Two** (see Glossary, p.18) for responses requiring explanations and reasons. Select two partners who have answers you can build upon. (Choose children who have not raised their hands/ thumbs to answer.)

Use **Choral Response** (see Glossary, p.18) when there is only one correct answer. Ask children to respond together by gesturing towards them with both hands (Your turn signal).

Paraphrase some of the children's responses that you heard during **TTYP** to keep the discussion moving or when you want to feed back on behalf of a child who isn't yet confident to talk to the whole group.

Use **Popcorn** (see Glossary, p.20) for one-word answers with multiple responses. Ask children to call out their answers – calling out when no one else is. It should sound like popcorn cooking.

Use **Word Wave** (see Glossary, p.22) for one-word answers with multiple responses. Ask children to call out their answers as you move your hand across the group.

5. Positive teaching

It is really worth winning over children who might potentially be unco-operative. Check these children are near you in your direct line of vision. Give them responsibility. For example, ask the child to help you model correct partner behaviour or to start the stop signal – and praise them for working well as a team.

Praise effort

There is no field of learning where a huge amount of practice is not essential: sport, music, dancing, science, mathematics – and learning to read and write is no exception.

Children must understand that effort is always required to learn something new and that sometimes things *are* hard to learn and therefore they need to practise *even* harder. Children feel good when they are working hard and succeeding.

So praise effort and be specific, for example:

- *"Well done, I can see that you've worked very hard on learning those sounds."*
- *"You're putting in a lot of effort into remembering your sentence."*
- *"You've really improved the sentence by changing that word."*

Praise the child quietly. For every child you praise loudly, there are another three children who are disappointed you didn't praise them.

Be genuine – only praise when there is a good reason. Children know when they deserve your praise.

Praise partner work

The more children help each other, the quicker the team learns. One of the best ways to check if you know something is if you can explain it to someone else.

Given that there is only one of you, you need the children's help to teach each other. You want to praise the partners for working well together to elevate their status. When partners can effectively teach each other, you have 30 teachers in one class.

Praise children for the way partners work together. For example:

"Great team work:

- *You can **both** read the sounds/words quickly now."*
- *You **both** listened carefully to each other."*
- *You **both** have an answer."*
- *You **both** worked so hard."*

Team cheers

Use cheers to celebrate great teamwork. Use them at the end of an activity or at the end of a lesson to show how much you value their co-operation and teamwork.

Ask partners to do joint cheers: for example, double high fives, shake hands – saying *"Great job, partner"*, short clapping rhythm with words: *"Two heads are better than one"/"Together we win"/"Teamwork means dream work!"*

Praise that doesn't work

Don't praise children's ability!

If you praise children for being clever at something, you draw attention to 'ability' as something that is in short supply, i.e. only some children have it.

The *not-praised-for-being-clever-children* think: 'I'm not clever. I can't do this. It's not worth trying.'

The *praised-for-being-clever-children* think: 'I am clever. I find it easy.' However, when things get hard they think: 'Uh-oh. This is difficult. If I were really clever I wouldn't have to try hard. Maybe I am not clever.'

Behaviour that stops children learning

If you do this then you will get rewards: stickers, tokens and points

Stickers, tokens and points do not help children learn in the long term. By rewarding an activity that should be intrinsically rewarding, we send the message to children that the activity, i.e. reading, is not pleasant and that nobody would do it without a bribe.

Given that our core purpose is to ensure that children read for pleasure, we must avoid, at all cost, building a culture of payment for learning.

Children who receive stickers think: 'I get stickers for reading. No one else gets them. I can't be clever.' Or 'I like stickers. I will work hard for the next sticker but if I don't get a sticker I won't work hard.'

Anger

Anger and anxiety disable children's ability to learn and work hard. It puts them into the debilitating mode of freeze, flight or fright. Teachers who use punishments, sanctions, criticism, shouting, sarcasm, belittlement, rudeness and frowning may achieve *compliance* from children but destroy any willingness to learn.

Use positive teaching methods combined with the other principles to ensure that you do not have to resort to anger in lessons. If you have particularly potentially challenging children in your group, work with your Reading Leader to win these children over and continue to embed positive teaching in your lessons.

Glossary

We use the following key terms and signals in *Read Write Inc.*

1, 2, 3 transitions

Move the children silently from carpet to table in under 15 seconds.

- Hold up one finger: children stand.
- Hold up two fingers: children walk and stand behind their chairs.
- Hold up three fingers: children sit down and prepare to read or write.

And in reverse, move the children from table to carpet in under 15 seconds.

- Hold up one finger: children stand behind their chairs.
- Hold up two fingers: children walk to the carpet.
- Hold up three fingers: children sit down beside their partners.

Challenge Words

A few 'challenge' words appear in Yellow, Blue and Grey Storybooks. Challenge Words are low frequency words that include a low frequency grapheme or one that has not been taught. These are topical words that the author needed to include in the story.

There are very few of these and they have an asterisk next to them.

Choose Two

Use this to gather responses that require explanations and reasons as a feedback mechanism after **TTYP**. Select two partners who have answers you can build upon. (Choose children who have not raised their hands/thumbs to answer.)

Choral Response

Use this when there is only one correct answer, as a feedback mechanism after **TTYP**. Ask children to respond together by gesturing towards them with both hands (Your turn signal).

Feedback methods after TTYP

See entries for **Choose Two, Choral Response, Paraphrase, Popcorn, Word Wave.**

Fred Fingers

Fred Fingers are used to spell Green Words in both the Speed Sounds Lessons and in Yellow, Blue and Grey *Get Writing!* Books. (These words are found in the Spelling panel.)

Children say the sounds as they press the sounds onto their fingers.

In Speed Sounds Set 1 Lessons, the teacher tells the children how many fingers they will need to show.

In Speed Sounds Sets 2 and 3 and in Yellow, Blue and Grey Storybooks, children count the number of sounds in the word and then show the corresponding number of fingers.

Fred in your head

Once children can sound out a word, we teach them to say the sounds in their heads.

Hold up the word to give the children time to mime the sounds, and then push the word forward as a signal to say the word together, until they can say the word straight away.

We show them how to do this by:

1. whispering the sounds and then saying the whole word;

2. mouthing the sounds silently and then saying the whole word;

3. saying the whole word straight away.

Fred Talk

Fred the Frog helps children read and spell. He can say the sounds in words, but he can't say the whole word, so children have to help him.

To help children read, Fred (the teacher) says the sounds and then children say the word. For example, Fred says *c-a-t*, children say *cat*, Fred says *l-igh-t*, children say *light*.

Teachers are encouraged to do Fred Talk through the day, so children learn to blend sounds. For example:

Play Simon Says: *Put your hands on your h-ea-d/f-oo-t/kn-ee.*

Put on your c-oa-t/h-a-t/s-c-ar-f.

Set the table with a b-ow-l/f-or-k/s-p-oo-n.

Freeze Frame

This drama device helps children focus on a key moment in the story. Children are asked to freeze frame, in silence, a character's expression and body language in response to an event.

Linked Storybooks

Each *Read Write Inc.* Storybook is matched to three of our favourite 'real' storybooks. The stories provide background knowledge for the next story.

My turn Your turn (MTYT) signal

This silent signal is used when you want the children to repeat something after you.

My turn: gesture towards yourself with one or two hands.

Your turn: gesture towards the children with one or two open palms.

Explain to the children that this signal is yours and not theirs.

Nonsense words

Nonsense words (also called pseudo words, non-words and alien words) are used to assess children's knowledge of sounds. We use made-up words to ensure that children have not read or heard the words before.

As children's reading develops, they will need to work out longer real words that include some syllables that, on their own, have no meaning, e.g. fan-*tas*-tic, e-*nor*-mous.

Paraphrase

Paraphrase children's responses that you have heard during **TTYP** – to keep the discussion moving or when you want to feed back on behalf of a child who isn't yet confident to talk to the whole group.

Popcorn

Use for one-word answers with multiple responses, as a feedback mechanism after **TTYP**.
Ask children to call out their answers – they need to try to call out when no one else is.
It should sound like popcorn cooking.

Punctuation mimes

Full stops

Exaggerate how your voice drops at the end of a sentence.

Mime action: punch the air.

Capital letters

Make a triangle shape with your arms above your head – fingers together and elbows apart.

Exclamation mark

Mime action: Make a downward stroke as you say *"wiiiith"*, then punch as you say *"feeling"*.
Ask the children: *"Did you hear my excitement/astonishment/conviction/surprise…?"*

Question mark

Exaggerate the raise in pitch of your voice.

Mime action: raise eyebrows as you draw a question mark in the air.

Commas

Mime action: twist a wrist.

Speech marks

Mime action: open speech marks with two fingers of your right hand and close the speech marks with two fingers of the left.

Ellipsis

Mime action: make three short pokes with a forefinger while miming the words 'wait and see'.

Red Rhythms

Red Rhythms are used to spell Red Words ('tricky' words – see below and list of Red Words with circled graphemes on p.242). These Red Words for spelling are found in the Spelling panel in Yellow, Blue and Grey *Get Writing!* Books.

Use **MTYT** to spell out the word using letter names, and place emphasis on the letters making up the tricky grapheme, e.g. in:

said, say the letter names in a rhythm, S-AI-D, with 'A-I' in an exaggerated manner

would, say the letter names in a rhythm, W-OUL-D, with O-U-L in an exaggerated manner.

Red Words

Red Words ('tricky' words) are common words with a low-frequency grapheme, e.g.

- s**ai**d: the sound 'e' is written with the grapheme ai;

- s**o**n: the sound 'u' is written with the grapheme o;

- y**our**: the sound 'or' is written with the grapheme our.

Only the most common graphemes are included on the Speed Sounds poster.

Red Words are printed in red in the Storybooks up to Orange Level.

Silent handwriting signal

Once children are sitting at their tables, hold up a pencil – real or imaginary – in a pencil grip with the non-writing hand flat – holding imaginary paper.

This signal indicates that children sit with their:

- feet flat on the floor

- bottom at the back of the chair

- body one fist from the table

- shoulders down and relaxed

- back leaning forward slightly

- left/right hand holding the page

- left/right hand holding a pencil, ready in a tripod grip.

Special friends

Special friends are a combination of two or three letters representing one sound, e.g. *ck, ph, ay, igh* (digraphs and trigraphs). Ensure children always say the sound and not the letter names, e.g. *ck* not *c* and *k*.

Speedy Green Words

Speedy Green Words are common words with common graphemes that are included frequently in the Storybooks. These words are *always* taught first by sound-blending. The children practise reading the words at speed so they can read the story without sounding out each word. The children's effort can then go into understanding the story.

Please note that this activity is *not* the same as teaching children to work out the word 'on sight'. Children must be able to sound out the word before building up speed.

There are Speedy Green Word Cards available for Red, Green, Purple, Pink and Orange Storybooks, as well as printable versions in the Storybook files in *Read Write Inc. Phonics* Online.

Story Green Words

Story Green Words are low frequency words with sounds the children have been taught. They include names and words that are particular to the Storybook. They allow children to practise decoding unfamiliar words and to learn new vocabulary. Only use the dots and dashes side when really needed.

These words should be printed from the online files. (They can be found in the Storybook files in *Read Write Inc. Phonics* Online.)

Team stop signal

Use this signal to gain attention. Practise until children respond in under five seconds and in silence.

1. Hold one hand in the air with a flat palm. Do not clap or talk.

2. Scan the room to check every child has responded.

Every child:

- raises one hand in response
- checks that their partner and others at their table have also raised their hands – gently tapping an arm if necessary
- looks attentively at you – eyes locked into yours to show they are ready to listen
- sits up tall, beside their partners.

3. Lower your hand and scan to check everyone is looking at you attentively, ready to listen. Do not start talking until you have their attention.

Think out loud (TOL)

'Thinking out loud' shows children the thinking necessary to work something out. They can 'see' what you think and how you work things out – as if you have a thought bubble coming out of your head. Use it to show children, for example, how you connect one part of the story to another, make decisions about what a character is thinking and feeling, recall the spelling of a word or decide the best word to write.

Try not to make it look too easy. Hesitate, ask yourself questions and ponder as you formulate an answer.

Turn to your partner (TTYP) signal

Partner work should be used consistently in all lessons.

Hold both hands pointing forward as if they are two open gates. Close the gates as soon as you have finished asking the question.

Practise this signal until children turn automatically to their partners to answer the question. Avoid saying the words 'turn to your partner' once children are familiar with the signal.

Children should turn their heads towards their partners, not their whole body or chair.

Word Wave

Use this for one-word answers with multiple responses, as a feedback mechanism after **TTYP**. Ask children to call out their answers as you move your hand across the group.

22

Using *Read Write Inc. Phonics* Online

Read Write Inc. Phonics Online is on the Oxford Owl for schools website. To subscribe, go to www.oxfordowl.co.uk. *Read Write Inc. Phonics* Online contains a wealth of teaching support materials that you will need. Key content areas of the online resource are as follows.

Speed Sounds Lesson resources

These resources support the teaching of Speed Sounds Lessons. They include: Speed Sounds slideshows; a video of how to pronounce pure sounds; printable nonsense words, multi-syllabic words and additional Speed Sounds cards for assessment; a Phonics Screening Check assessment; and two printable Parent Booklets to send home with children to explain how to use the Speed Sounds to new parents.

Storybook files

Each Storybook has an accompanying online file. The file consists of a number of tabs, labelled a, b, c, etc. The tabs correspond to activity types and follow in a sequential order so that you can tab through them in the lessons. (They are also referenced in the teaching notes.) The Storybook online files contain the following content to help you teach your lessons:

Speedy Green Words	Animated files that bring up the words as a slideshow to use with children
Story Green Words	Illustrated words to help explain new vocabulary to children
Build a Sentence	Picture prompts for this activity
Think About the Story	Picture prompts for this activity
Write About…	Files to support modelling writing for children
Proofread – spelling	Display files that you can use to show answers and discuss corrections
Printable files	Printable versions of the Storybook introduction, Speedy Green Words and Story Green Words

Handwriting files

There are printable files with detailed guidance on teaching handwriting for you to use alongside the guidance on pp.25–28 of this handbook.

Storytime and Poetry Time files

These are all the files you need for teaching *Read Write Inc. Phonics* Storytime and Poetry Time (see p.30): the printed story and poetry texts, artwork for display and audio readings of all of the poems. There are accompanying teaching activities for developing oral language and comprehension. Search by Reception or Year 1 to find the files you need.

One-to-one files

Closely matched to the One-to-one Tutoring Kit, there is extensive video support and guidance for one-to-one tutoring of the programme in the online files.

Comprehension and Grammar files

There are six printable Comprehension and Grammar tests for practice and assessment.

Assessment and guidance on marking

Assessing children's reading

Your Reading Leader will organise reading assessment and grouping for your school. Please see the *Reading Leader Handbook* and 'Assessment' in *Read Write Inc. Phonics* Online.

Marking children's writing

We mark children's writing to show them that we care about their efforts and the progress they make. Marking helps them understand how and why their writing is successful and how it can be improved. Marking is vital in assessing the effectiveness of our teaching – what children have understood and what we need to teach them next. Marking prompts a dialogue between you and the child and, therefore, further opportunities for assessment.

Marking methods in *Read Write Inc. Phonics*

Children mark their own work with guidance from you

- *Spell test*: children tick each **sound** spelt correctly and correct own errors.
- *Hold a Sentence*: children tick words spelt correctly and correct words with **sounds** spelt incorrectly by writing out the whole word above. They insert a missing word with an upturned V (^).
- *Proofread for spelling and punctuation:* children tick corrected errors and correct any missed edits.

Responding orally to children's writing progress during the lesson

While children are writing, move around the room, quietly responding to children's progress. Keep a check on how you divide your attention – ensure that you spend some time with every child. If not, you should spread your attention over two weeks.

You could comment on children's interesting word choices and ideas, as well as challenging the children to develop their ideas. Do not speak too loudly while children are writing so they can pay attention to their own work without being distracted.

Assess and mark children's writing after the lesson

It is not always possible to give enough attention to every child in every lesson. Make sure you mark the children's writing and keep a track of their progress on the 'Assessment Grid – Writing' (search for this in *Read Write Inc. Phonics* Online by the title).

For the Build a Sentence and Write About activities, you should:

1. Tick interesting vocabulary.
2. Draw a line under any misspelt words that you expect children to spell correctly.
3. Use ^ to indicate that a word needs to be inserted.
4. In Red to Orange *Get Writing!* Books, avoid correcting words containing graphemes not yet taught.
5. In Yellow to Grey *Get Writing!* Books, correct misspelt adventurous words by writing the correct spelling lightly in pencil above them.
6. Write positive comments about the children's ideas, use of vocabulary and sentence structure.

Ask children to write their favourite words in the 'Words to keep' section at the end of the Write About.

Assess children's writing progress

1. Keep an assessment notebook to jot down common errors and steps to inform future teaching.
2. For Yellow, Blue and Grey Storybooks consider writing a prompt for children to respond to in the next lesson, e.g. *Why do you think Barker is a good pet?*
3. Use the 'Assessment Grid – Writing' (see above). Select one recent Write About every half term and complete the writing grid. Use a different-coloured pen each term to show progress.

Handwriting

There are regular timetabled slots for handwriting to ensure that children build up their handwriting skills every day.

We make the *physical* process of writing – handwriting – enjoyable from the start, so children see themselves as 'writers'. We use mnemonics – memory pictures – to help children visualise the letter or join before they write it down. Children need to practise handwriting under the guidance of a teacher so they do not develop habits that will be difficult to undo later.

Please don't ask children to copy letters or words. We need their attention to be focused on their own formation of letters and joins.

Please ensure you allow 5 to 10 minutes for every handwriting session marked on the timetable.

There are three handwriting stages.

Stage 1

Stage 1 lessons are in *Phonics Handbook 1*. These lessons are taught while children read the Red, Green, Purple, Pink and Orange Storybooks. The online checklists for each letter are in the Handwriting files in *Read Write Inc. Phonics* Online.

Stage 1a: Children practise correct letter formation.

Stage 1b: Children learn where to place the letters on the writing line.

Stage 2

Stage 2 lessons are in this handbook. These lessons are taught while children read the Yellow, Blue and Grey Storybooks. The online checklists for each letter are in the Handwriting files in *Read Write Inc. Phonics* Online.

Children learn a mature style of writing that will lead to joined-up writing.

Stage 3

Stage 3 lessons are also in this handbook. These lessons are also taught while children read the Yellow, Blue and Grey Storybooks. The online checklists for each letter are in the Handwriting files in *Read Write Inc. Phonics* Online.

Children learn the two basic joins: the arm join (diagonal) and the washing line join (horizontal) and the two variables for each join.

Handwriting position

Teach children that when you use the handwriting signal (see p.21) they should automatically go into the perfect handwriting position:

- feet flat on the floor
- bottom at the back of the chair
- body one fist from the table
- shoulders down and relaxed
- back leaning forward slightly
- left/right hand holding the page
- left/right hand holding a pencil, ready in a tripod grip.

> See *Phonics Handbook 1* for Handwriting Stage 1.

Handwriting Stage 2

Explain to children that they are going to use new characters to help them develop a grown-up style of writing that will lead to joined-up writing. New pictures will help them to visualise the new shapes.

See 'Handwriting Stage 2' in the Handwriting files in *Read Write Inc. Phonics* Online.

Introduce the formation family: six sisters, two uncles and their two pets.

The six sisters – Annie, Dina, Gabi, Olivia, Carina and Queenie – all look the same. Their mother tells them that they must all have a different haircut so people can tell them apart!

The uncles – Uncle Umberto and Uncle Yaseen – look just like the sisters, except they are bald on the top of their heads.

The family have a dog and a bunny whose faces are very similar too, but they have long ears.

The lesson plan

Practise the letters in the handwriting order. (See 'Handwriting Stage 2' in the Handwriting files in *Read Write Inc. Phonics* Online.)

Use the following routine for every lesson. (This is an example lesson for the letter **d**.)

Demonstrate

1. **TOL** as you use your mental checklist to write the letter **d**.

✓ start at her hair bobble on top of her head

✓ all the way over the top of her head

✓ curve down her face

✓ round chin

✓ join the chin by her ear

✓ up to the bobble

✓ straight tall spiky hair – up and down

✓ curve at the line and draw small flick (not curvy)

Repeat a few times using **MTYT**.

2. Ask the children to **TTYP** to say the mental checklist.

3. Take feedback.

4. Ask two partners to tell you how to write the letter **d**.

Repeat a couple more times until the children can say the mental checklist to each other.

Practice

1. Use the handwriting signal to check that the children are still sitting in the perfect handwriting position.

2. Rub out the picture and any letters from the board – the children must not copy.

3. Ask the children to write one letter, slowly and carefully. (Do not ask them to draw the handwriting picture.)

4. Model again how you repeat writing the letter, getting a bit quicker each time.

5. Go round the room praising what you see so others can hear. Don't sit with one child. For example: *"Nice round chin there! Love the long straight hair. What a great curl."*

Review

1. Write the letter on the board and make one error, drawing on children's common errors.

2. Ask the children to **TTYP** to find your 'two best bits', for example, you remembered to start at the bobble. Then ask children to **TTYP** to find 'one to fix'.

3. Rewrite the letter perfectly, correcting using children's feedback.

4. Ask children to practise again.

5. Ask children to find 'two best bits' and 'one to fix' in each other's work.

On the next day, choose a new focus letter, and review one or two previously taught letters.

Handwriting Stage 3

Explain to children that there are two basic joins:

- the arm join (diagonal)
- the washing line join (horizontal).

The arm join has three variations:

- arm to boat *ai*
- arm to sun *ab*
- arm to sister. *ic*

The washing line join has three variations:

- washing line to boat *wr*
- washing line to sun *wh*
- washing line to sister. *va*

See 'Handwriting Stage 3' in the Handwriting files in *Read Write Inc. Phonics* Online.

The lesson plan

Use the following routine for every lesson. (This is a sample lesson for joining **a** to **i**.)

See 'Handwriting Stage 3' in the Handwriting files in *Read Write Inc. Phonics* Online for the joins to practise.

Demonstrate

1. Demonstrate how to write the letters.

- **TOL** about where to start **a** – level with the top of the boat. Recall the checklist for Annie as you write the letter.
- **TOL** as you write the join – not too spiky, not too round, not too squeezed, not too spaced.
- **TOL** as you write **i**. Recall the checklist for **i**.

2. Ask children to **TTYP**: What size is each letter? (*Boat, sun* or *water.*) What is good about your join?

3. Take feedback.

Practice

1. Use the handwriting signal to check that the children are still sitting in the perfect handwriting position.

2. Rub out the joined letters from the board – the children must not copy.

3. Ask the children to write each letter and the join, slowly and carefully.

4. Model again how you repeat writing the letters and join, getting a bit quicker each time.

5. Go round the room praising what you see so others can hear. Don't sit with one child. For example: *"I love the spacing of your join and the join is not too spiky or too round."*

Review

1. Write the letters and join on the board and make one error, drawing on children's common errors.

2. Ask the children to **TTYP** to find your 'two best bits'. Then ask them to **TTYP** to find 'one to fix'.

3. Rewrite the letters and join perfectly, correcting using children's feedback.

4. Ask the children to practise again.

5. Now ask them to find 'two best bits' and 'one to fix' in each other's work.

Storytime and home reading

Overview of Storytime

Make the best possible use of Storytime so that children encounter high-quality literature outside of their phonics lessons. The more you read to them the sooner their oral comprehension, knowledge of stories and vocabulary will grow.

There is no other way to get children excited about reading stories than reading to them. Listening to stories must feel like a treat – for everyone – especially for you!

Tips for reading aloud to children

When you share a story:

- Show curiosity in what you're going to read. *"This should be funny – it's about a little boy queuing for the loo."*

- Read the whole story the first time without stopping too much. If you think children might not understand something say, for example, *"Oh I think what's happening here is that…"*

- Chat about the story.
  - *"I wonder why he did that…"*
  - *"Oh no, I hope she's not going to…"*
  - *"I wouldn't have done that. Would you?"*
  - *"I bet she's feeling desperate now…"*

- Link stories to your own and children's experiences and then link these experiences to other stories you have read to them. *"This reminds me of…"*

- Read favourite stories over and over again. Encourage children to join in with the bits that they know. Build the suspense each time, hesitating so they can jump in before you say the word.

- Read with enthusiasm. Try out different voices.

- Don't stop reading to children when they can read for themselves. Select some books that are at a higher level than those they can read on their own. What you read to them today they might choose to read tomorrow.

- Read with enjoyment. If you're not enjoying it, you've chosen the wrong book!

The three types of Storytime in *Read Write Inc. Phonics*

1. *Linked text to be read to children in the phonics lessons*

Share a linked text with children after every Storybook. (This will be either every three days or every five days, depending on the Storybook level.) These stories prepare the children to read their next *Read Write Inc. Phonics* Storybook. For example, before reading *Black Hat Bob*, the children listen to a story about pirates.

Read other stories to children when they are back in class too.

2. *Your storytimes*

Read your favourite stories every day with the whole class, at the end of the day. Build a collection of stories that become class favourites.

3. *Read Write Inc. Storytime and Poetry Time*

This is a twice-termly resource that you can find in the Storytime and Poetry Time files in *Read Write Inc. Phonics* Online. It provides ideas to develop fairy stories and poetry. These include:

- six short stories for Reception (P1)
- six short stories for Year 1 (P2)
- six poems for Reception (P1)
- six poems for Year 1 (P2).

There are online files with artwork to accompany the stories and poems, as well as audio versions of the poems. The texts can also be printed from the online files to make a mini book.

There are teaching notes to accompany each story or poem with suggestions for activities. These activities are to develop *oral language and comprehension only*; they are not writing activities.

Home reading

Please ensure that the reading books that children take home match closely with the sounds they know.

Children should take home one of the following at least every two days:

- the last *Read Write Inc.* Storybook that they have read, or
- an earlier *Read Write Inc.* Storybook, or
- a *Read Write Inc.* Book Bag Book that matches the last Storybook that they have read (or an earlier Storybook)

as well as a picture book that they know well.

Last Read Write Inc. Storybook read

Children need to practise what they can already read. Put the black and white version of the Storybook into their book bag once they have read the story three times in class. There are brief notes to parents/carers in these books to help them use the books successfully with their child.

Do explain to parents/carers that children can read this story very well because they have practised. Please ask parents/carers not to say, "This book is too easy for you!"

You can also send home *Read Write Inc.* Storybooks that children have previously read. The children enjoy re-reading stories that they know well. Their fluency improves on every reading.

Read Write Inc. Book Bag Books

Each R*ead Write Inc.* Book Bag Book is a story or non-fiction text that has been carefully matched to each of the *Read Write Inc.* Storybooks and *Get Writing!* activities. The Book Bag Books give children additional reading practice at home.

Put the matching Book Bag Book into their book bags once they have completed the *Get Writing!* activity in class, and taken home the black and white version of the Storybook.

Picture books

Ensure children choose books from the selection that you have already read aloud a few times. This means that, if their parents/carers are too busy, the child can retell the story from the pictures. (Children are not expected to read the story as this is beyond their decoding ability.)

You may also find the traditional tales in the Storytime files of *Read Write Inc. Phonics* Online (see 3. above) useful to send home. These can be printed out for parents/carers to read aloud and talk about with their child. The stories will be familiar to the children once you have read to them as part of your storytime, but, as with picture books, will be beyond the children's decoding ability.

How to use the lesson plans

This handbook contains lesson plans for teaching:

- Speed Sounds Sets 2 and 3

- Yellow Storybooks, Non-fiction books (two titles) and *Get Writing! Yellow Book*

- Blue Storybooks, Non-fiction books (two titles) and *Get Writing! Blue Book*

- Grey Storybooks, Non-fiction books (two titles) and *Get Writing! Grey Book*

Speed Sounds Lesson Plans

There are blueprint lesson plans for each type of sound (e.g. Set 3 special friends, Set 3 split digraphs). A chart summarises all of the information you will need for each individual sound in Sets 2 and 3. See p.32 for more detailed guidance.

Storybook, Non-fiction and *Get Writing!* Book lesson plans from Yellow Level onwards

Detailed lesson plans are given for the first two titles in each level. The cycle of activities that underpins the teaching repeats each time. From the third title in each level, a shorter version of the lesson plan is given, outlining only the things that will change for the teaching of that particular book.

Resources

In the margin of the lesson plans, there are icons to show which resources you will need for that part of the lesson. See p.53 for the key.

Purposes

The list of activities is summarised separately to the main lesson plans. See p.73 for the list of purposes for each activity.

Speed Sounds Lesson Plans – Introduction

The Speed Sounds Lessons give clear guidance on how to teach children the sounds they need to read the Storybooks and to follow the activities in the *Get Writing!* books. Please practise saying the sounds clearly before you start teaching. (See www.ruthmiskin.com or search for Pure Sounds in *Read Write Inc. Phonics Online*).

How many sounds should I teach each day?

Teach 2–3 new sounds per week for Sets 2 and 3. Older children coming to phonics late usually manage to learn a few new sounds every day.

How do I keep track of children's phonic progress?

Full details of assessment and grouping are in the *Reading Leader Handbook*.

Organisation

Children should sit on the carpet or at tables near the board, and always at tables for the writing tasks within the lesson. Sit easily distracted children in your direct line of vision.

Check that children keep up from the very beginning. If you let a child get behind in the first few days, they will still be behind a year, or three, later. Provide one-to-one 5–10-minute sessions in the afternoon until they can keep up with the rest of the group.

If more than two or three children are falling behind, ask the Reading Leader to support you. See the *Reading Leader Handbook* for further information.

Purpose

The activity headings state the purpose of the activity so you can make it clear to children what they are learning and why. Make sure the children also know the overall purpose of the Speed Sounds Lessons – that they are learning to read and write sounds so they can read and spell words containing these sounds.

Fred

We use a character called Fred to help. Fred can only speak words in sounds and the children say the word. For example, Fred says *c-a-t*, children say *cat*, Fred says *l-igh-t*, children say *light*.

Dos and Don'ts

Do

- Praise children for working hard.
- Check that children's palms are facing them when they are spelling with Fred Fingers.
- Carry a set of Speed Sounds Cards for the sounds you have taught in your pocket – you can get them out at any moment during the day for children to practise them quickly.
- Practise Fred Talk throughout the day, using other one-syllable words, e.g. l-u-n-ch, b-r-ea-k, p-l-ay.

Don't

- Use letter names when you are teaching Speed Sounds Sets 1 and 2.
- Use capital letters in the Speed Sounds Lessons.

> See *Phonics Handbook 1* for Set 1 Speed Sounds Lesson Plans.

Set 2 Speed Sounds Lesson Plans

Introduction

Set 2 Speed Sounds should be taught as soon as children can read Set 1 Speed Sounds speedily and blend words with four sounds. Continue to practise reading words containing Set 1 Speed Sounds, in particular the digraphs sh, th, ch, ng, nk.

> ## Resources
>
> Display these resources at the front of the classroom, at children's eye level:
> - Simple Speed Sounds poster
> - Picture frieze of Speed Sounds Set 2
>
> You will also need:
> - A flipchart/board to model writing
> - Speed Sounds Set 2 Cards
> - Phonics Green Word Cards for Set 2 (labelled '2' in the corner of the cards)
>
> Children will need an exercise book and a sharp pencil to complete the writing tasks within the lesson.

Order of teaching

Use the blueprint lesson plan below, including the Word Time lesson, to teach all the Set 2 sounds. Subsitute the information in grey text in the blueprint with the details in the chart. Use the appropriate Phonics Green Word Cards – see chart on pp.52–55.

The Set 2 Speed Sounds should be taught in this order: **ay ee igh ow oo *oo* ar or air ir ou oy**.

Blueprint lesson plan

Speed Sound: ay

 Say the sound

1. Say the sound *ay*, without showing the Speed Sound Card. Ask children to repeat.

2. Show the Speed Sound Card (picture side). Explain the picture, e.g.
   This little girl wants to play. She says ... may I play? Say: *ay – may I play?*
   Ask children to repeat.

3. Say one of the words listed on the Speed Sound Card in Fred Talk. Ask the
   children to repeat in Fred Talk, and then to say the whole word. Repeat for
   three to four words.

 Read the sound

1. Show the Speed Sound Card (picture side). Say: *When we look at this side
   we say the phrase: may I play?*

2. Show the letter side. Say: *When we look at this side we say the sound: ay*.

3. Explain that when there are two or more letters together they make just
   one sound, e.g. *ay*. Tell the children that these letters are 'special friends'
   (digraphs or trigraphs).

4. Point to the sound on the Simple Speed Sounds poster. Say the sound.

5. Flip the card a few times and ask the children to say the sound or the phrase.

 Review the sounds

Hide the new sound in the pack of sounds taught so far. Include some Set 1 sounds which
need further practice. Ask the children to read the sounds and spot the new sound. Gradually
increase the speed as children gain confidence.

Word Time

 Read the words

Use the Phonics Green Word Cards below.

> spray, play, day, way, may, say

1. Hold up the first card (dots and dashes side), e.g. **spray**, and ask children to tell you the sound of
   the 'special friends', e.g. **ay**.

2. Ask them to say the sounds in Fred Talk, e.g. *s-p-r-ay*, and then say the word, e.g. *spray*.

3. Say the word with exaggerated pronunciation. Ask children to repeat it. If necessary, explain
   the meaning of the word.

4. Repeat for all the words.

Review the words

Ask children to read words from previous Set 2 lessons and Word Time Lessons 1.6 and 1.7. Ask them to read words without the dots and dashes and use 'Fred in your head' to gain speed. (If necessary, flip to the dots and dashes side of the card to help children.) Gradually increase the speed.

 Reading assessment

1. Ask children to read a few nonsense words that you have printed from the online file. (Search for Set 2 Nonsense Words in *Read Write Inc. Phonics* Online.) Tell children that the word they are about to read belongs to an alien language.

2. Show the word and ask them to tell you the sound of the 'special friends', if applicable.

3. Ask children to say the sounds and read the word.

Note any sounds that need further practice in the next Speed Sounds Lesson.

 Spell with Fred Fingers

> spray, play, day, way, may, say

1. Say the word, e.g. *spray* and ask children to repeat it.

2. Ask children to:
   - Hide their fingers as they count the sounds on them.
   - Hold up their fingers, palms facing them, when you say *fingers*.
   - Repeat the word, then pinch their fingers as they say the sounds, e.g. *s-p-r-ay*.
   - Write the word as they say the sounds, underlining any 'special friends'.

3. Ask children to say the sounds as you write the word on the board, underlining any 'special friends'.

4. Ask children to tick/correct the spelling of each sound in their own work.

5. Repeat with two or three words from the list provided.

 Spell review

Ask children to write two or three previously taught words using the steps in Spell with Fred Fingers, above.

Summary lesson plans for teaching Set 2 Speed Sounds

Use the blueprint lesson plan on pp.34–35 to teach the Speed Sounds in the chart below.
You will need to substitute the information in grey text in the blueprint lesson with the details below.

Speed Sounds				Word Time			Spell with Fred Fingers	Spell review
Sound	Say the sound	Read the sound	Review the sounds	Read the words	Review the words	Reading assessment		
ay	See blueprint lesson on p.34.							
ee	ee – what can you see? *Choose 3–4 words:* see, three, been, green, seen, keep, need, sleep, feel	ee	Spot the new sound in the pack.	see *Use Phonics Green Word Cards:* see, three, been, green, seen, sleep	spray Words from previous Set 2 lessons and Word Times 1.6 and 1.7.	blig Ask children to read a few nonsense words printed from online. (Search for Set 2 Nonsense Words in *Read Write Inc. Phonics Online.*)	*Words to spell (choose 2–3):* see, three, been, green, seen, sleep	Ask children to write two or three previously taught words.
igh	igh – fly high *Choose 3–4 words:* high, night, light, fright, bright, sight, might	igh	Spot the new sound in the pack.	high *Use Phonics Green Word Cards:* high, night, light, fright, bright, might	see Words from previous Set 2 lessons and Word Times 1.6 and 1.7.	blig Ask children to read a few nonsense words printed from online. (Search for Set 2 Nonsense Words in *Read Write Inc. Phonics Online.*)	*Words to spell (choose 2–3):* high, night, light, fright, bright, might	Ask children to write two or three previously taught words.

Speed Sounds

Sound	Say the sound	Read the sound	Review the sounds	Word Time		Reading assessment	Spell with Fred Fingers	Spell review
				Read the words	Review the words			
ow	ow – blow the snow Choose 3–4 words: blow, snow, slow, show, know, flow, glow	ow	ow Spot the new sound in the pack.	blow Use Phonics Green Word Cards: blow, snow, low, show, know, slow	high Words from previous Set 2 lessons and Word Times 1.6 and 1.7.	blig Ask children to read a few nonsense words printed from online. (Search for Set 2 Nonsense Words in Read Write Inc. Phonics Online.)	Words to spell (choose 2–3): blow, snow, low, show, know, slow	Ask children to write two or three previously taught words.
oo	oo – poo at the zoo Choose 3–4 words: too, zoo, mood, fool, pool, stool, moon, spoon	oo	oo Spot the new sound in the pack.	too Use Phonics Green Word Cards: too, zoo, food, pool, moon, spoon	blow Words from previous Set 2 lessons and Word Times 1.6 and 1.7.	blig Ask children to read a few nonsense words printed from online. (Search for Set 2 Nonsense Words in Read Write Inc. Phonics Online.)	Words to spell (choose 2–3): too, zoo, food, pool, moon, spoon	Ask children to write two or three previously taught words.
oo	oo – look at a book Choose 3–4 words: took, look, book, shook, cook, foot	oo	oo Spot the new sound in the pack.	took Use Phonics Green Word Cards: took, look, book, shook, cook, foot	too Words from previous Set 2 lessons and Word Times 1.6 and 1.7.	blig Ask children to read a few nonsense words printed from online. (Search for Set 2 Nonsense Words in Read Write Inc. Phonics Online.)	Words to spell (choose 2–3): took, look, book, shook, cook, foot	Ask children to write two or three previously taught words.

Summary lesson plans for teaching Set 2 Speed Sounds

Speed Sounds		Word Time						
Sound	Say the sound	Read the sound	Review the sounds	Read the words	Review the words	Reading assessment	Spell with Fred Fingers	Spell review
ar	ar – start the car Choose 3–4 words: car, bar, star, park, smart, start, sharp, spark	ar	ar Spot the new sound in the pack.	car Use Phonics Green Word Cards: car, start, part, star, hard, sharp	took Words from previous Set 2 lessons and Word Times 1.6 and 1.7.	blig online Ask children to read a few nonsense words printed from online. (Search for Set 2 Nonsense Words in Read Write Inc. Phonics Online.)	Words to spell (choose 2–3): car, start, part, star, hard, sharp	Ask children to write two or three previously taught words.
or	or – shut the door Choose 3–4 words: sort, short, worn, horse, sport, snort, fork	or	or Spot the new sound in the pack.	sort Use Phonics Green Word Cards: sort, short, horse, sport, fork, snort	car Words from previous Set 2 lessons and Word Times 1.6 and 1.7.	blig online Ask children to read a few nonsense words printed from online. (Search for Set 2 Nonsense Words in Read Write Inc. Phonics Online.)	Words to spell (choose 2–3): sort, short, horse, sport, fork, snort	Ask children to write two or three previously taught words.
air	air – that's not fair Choose 3–4 words: fair, stair, hair, air, lair, chair	air	air Spot the new sound in the pack.	fair Use Phonics Green Word Cards: fair, stair, hair, air, chair, lair	sort Words from previous Set 2 lessons and Word Times 1.6 and 1.7.	blig online Ask children to read a few nonsense words printed from online. (Search for Set 2 Nonsense Words in Read Write Inc. Phonics Online.)	Words to spell (choose 2–3): fair, stair, hair, air, chair, lair	Ask children to write two or three previously taught words.

Speed Sounds

Sound	Say the sound	Read the sound	Review the sounds	Word Time		Reading assessment	Spell with Fred Fingers	Spell review
				Read the words	Review the words			
ir	ir – whirl and twirl *Choose 3–4 words:* girl, bird, third, whirl, twirl, dirt	ir	Spot the new sound in the pack.	**girl** *Use Phonics Green Word Cards:* girl, bird, third, whirl, twirl, dirt	**fair** Words from previous Set 2 lessons and Word Times 1.6 and 1.7.	blig Ask children to read a few nonsense words printed from online. (Search for Set 2 Nonsense Words in *Read Write Inc. Phonics Online*.)	*Words to spell (choose 2–3):* girl, bird, third, whirl, twirl, dirt	Ask children to write two or three previously taught words.
ou	ou – shout it out *Choose 3–4 words:* out, shout, loud, mouth, round, found	ou	Spot the new sound in the pack.	**out** *Use Phonics Green Word Cards:* out, shout, loud, mouth, round, found	**girl** Words from previous Set 2 lessons and Word Times 1.6 and 1.7.	blig Ask children to read a few nonsense words printed from online. (Search for Set 2 Nonsense Words in *Read Write Inc. Phonics Online*.)	*Words to spell (choose 2–3):* out, shout, loud, mouth, round, found	Ask children to write two or three previously taught words.
oy	oy – toy for a boy *Choose 3–4 words:* toy, boy, enjoy	oy	Spot the new sound in the pack.	**toy** *Use Phonics Green Word Cards:* toy, boy, enjoy	**out** Words from previous Set 2 lessons and Word Times 1.6 and 1.7.	blig Ask children to read a few nonsense words printed from online. (Search for Set 2 Nonsense Words in *Read Write Inc. Phonics Online*.)	*Words to spell (choose 2–3):* toy, boy, enjoy	Ask children to write two or three previously taught words.

Set 3 Speed Sounds Lesson Plans

Introduction

Set 3 Speed Sounds should be taught as soon as children can read Set 2 Speed Sounds speedily.

The children have learned one grapheme for each sound so far. They can read using these sounds. They are now going to learn more ways of writing the same sounds.

Resources

Display this resource at the front of the classroom, at children's eye level:

• Complex Speed Sounds poster

You will also need:

• A flipchart/board to model writing
• Speed Sounds Set 3 Cards
• Phonics Green Word Cards for Set 3 (labelled '3' in the corner of the cards)

Children will need an exercise book and a sharp pencil to complete the writing tasks within the lesson.

Order of teaching

The Set 3 Speed Sounds should be taught in this order: **ea oi a͡-e i͡-e o͡-e u͡-e aw are ur er ow ai oa ew ire ear ure tion tious/cious**.

A blueprint lesson plan, including a Word Time lesson, is given for:

• teaching Set 3 special friends (blueprint – ea)
  – oi aw are ur er ow ai oa ew ire ear
• teaching Set 3 special friends – split digraphs (blueprint – a͡-e)
  – i͡-e o͡-e u͡-e
• teaching multi-syllabic words (blueprint – ure)
  – tion tious/cious.

Substitute the information in grey text in the blueprint with the details in the chart on pp.46–51. Use the appropriate Phonics Green Word Cards – see the chart.

Explain the Complex Speed Sounds poster to the children.

Explain that they will be learning different ways to read and spell the same sound.

Explain that they will be using letter names as well as sounds for the spelling.

Blueprint lesson plan – special friends

Speed Sound: ea

 Say the sound

1. Say the sound *ea*, without showing the Speed Sound Card. Ask children to repeat.

2. Show the Speed Sound Card (picture side). Explain the picture, e.g. ***The child is saying ... cup of tea!*** Say: *ea – cup of tea*. Ask children to repeat.

3. Say one of the words listed on the Speed Sound Card in Fred Talk. Ask the children to repeat in Fred Talk, and then to say the whole word. Repeat for three to four words.

Read the sound

1. Show the Speed Sound Card (picture side). Say: *When we look at this side we say the phrase:* **cup of tea!**

2. Show the letter side. Say: *When we look at this side we say the sound: ea.*

3. Explain that when there are two or more letters together they make just one sound, e.g. *ea*. Tell children that these letters are 'special friends'.

4. Point to the sound on the Complex Speed Sounds poster. Say the sound.

5. Flip the card a few times and ask the children to say the sound or the phrase.

Review the sounds

Hide the new sound in the pack of sounds taught so far, including some Set 2 sounds that need further practice. Ask the children to read the sounds and spot the new sound. Gradually increase the speed as children gain confidence.

Word Time

Read the words

Use the Phonics Green Word Cards below.

> clean, dream, seat, scream, real, please

1. Hold up the first card (dots and dashes side), e.g. **clean**, and ask children to tell you the sound of the 'special friends', e.g. **ea**.

2. Ask them to say the sounds in Fred Talk, e.g. *c-l-ea-n*, and then say the word, e.g. *clean*.

3. Say the word with exaggerated pronunciation. Ask children to repeat it. If necessary, explain the meaning of the word.

4. Repeat for all the words.

Review the words

Ask children to read words from previous Sets 2 and 3 lessons that need further practice. Ask them to read words without dots and dashes, and use 'Fred in your head' to gain speed. (If necessary, flip to the dots and dashes side of the card to help children.) Gradually increase the speed.

Reading assessment

1. Ask children to read a few nonsense words that you have printed from the online file. (Search for Set 3 Nonsense Words in *Read Write Inc. Phonics* Online.) Tell children that the word they are about to read belongs to an alien language.

2. Show the word and ask them to tell you the sound of the 'special friends'.

3. Ask children to say the sounds and read the word.

Note any sounds that need further practice in the next Speed Sounds Lesson.

Spell with Fred Fingers

> clean, dream, seat, scream, real, please

1. Say the word, e.g. *clean* and ask children to repeat it.

2. Ask children to:

   • Hide their fingers as they count the sounds on them.
   • Hold up their fingers, palms facing them, when you say *fingers*.
   • Repeat the word, then pinch their fingers as they say the sounds, e.g. *c-l-ea-n*.
   • Write the word as they say the sounds, underlining any 'special friends'.

3. Ask children to say the letter names as you write the word on the board, underlining the 'special friends'.

4. Ask children to tick/correct the spelling of each sound in their own work.

5. Repeat with two or three words from the list provided.

 Spell review

Ask children to write two or three previously taught words using the steps in Spell with Fred Fingers, above.

Blueprint lesson plan – special friends (split digraph)

Speed Sound: a͡-e

 Say the sound

1. Say the sound *a͡-e (ay)*, without showing the Speed Sound Card. Ask children to repeat.

2. Show the Speed Sound Card (picture side). Explain the picture, e.g. *The child is saying ... ma͡ke a ca͡ke*. Say: *a͡-e – ma͡ke a ca͡ke*. Ask children to repeat.

3. Say one of the words listed on the Speed Sound Card in Fred Talk. Ask the children to repeat in Fred Talk, and then to say the whole word. Repeat for three to four words.

 Read the sound

1. Show the Speed Sound Card (picture side). Say: *When we look at this side we say the phrase: ma͡ke a ca͡ke.*

2. Show the letter side. Say: *When we look at this side we say the sound a͡-e.*

3. Explain that these letters are 'special friends', but they need to be split up because they are too chatty. They are two letters that make one sound, but they are not side-by-side.

4. Point to the sound on the Complex Speed Sounds poster. Say the sound.

5. Flip the card a few times and ask the children to say the sound or the phrase.

 Review the sounds

Hide the new sound in the pack of sounds taught so far, including some Set 2 sounds that need further practice. Ask the children to read the sounds and spot the new sound. Gradually increase the speed as children gain confidence.

Word Time

 ### *Read the words*

Use the Phonics Green Word Cards below.

> make, cake, name, same, late, date

1. Hold up the first card (dots and dashes side), e.g. make, and ask children to tell you which letters are the 'special friends', e.g. a͡-e (ay).

2. Ask them to say the sounds in Fred Talk, e.g. m-a-k͡-e, and then say the word, e.g. make.

3. Say the word with exaggerated pronunciation. Ask children to repeat it. If necessary, explain the meaning of the word.

4. Repeat for all the words.

 ### *Review the words*

Ask children to read words from previous Sets 2 and 3 lessons. Ask them to read words without dots and dashes, and use 'Fred in your head' to gain speed. (If necessary, flip to the dots and dashes side of the card to help children.) Gradually increase the speed.

 ### *Reading assessment*

 1. Ask children to read a few nonsense words that you have printed from the online file. (Search for Set 3 Nonsense Words in *Read Write Inc. Phonics* Online.) Tell children that the word they are about to read belongs to an alien language.

2. Show the word and ask them to tell you the sound of the 'special friends'.

3. Ask children to say the sounds and read the word.

Note any sounds that need further practice in the next Speed Sounds Lesson.

 ### *Spell with Fred Fingers*

> make, cake, name, same, late, date

1. Say the word, e.g. *make* and ask children to repeat it.

2. Ask children to:
   - Hide their fingers as they count the sounds on them.
   - Hold up their fingers, palms facing them, when you say *fingers*.
   - Repeat the word, then pinch their fingers as they say the sounds, e.g. *m-ay-k.*
   - Write the word as they say the sounds, drawing an arc between any 'special friends' who have been split up.

3. Ask children to say the letter names as you write the word on the board, drawing an arc between any 'special friends' who have been split up while saying *Where's my friend? He's on the end.*

4. Ask children to tick/correct the spelling of each sound in their own work.

5. Repeat with two or three words from the list provided.

 ### *Spell review*

Ask children to write two or three previously taught words using the steps in Spell with Fred Fingers, above.

Blueprint lesson plan – multi-syllabic words

Speed Sound: ure

Say the sound

1. Say the sound *ure*, without showing the Speed Sound Card. Ask children to repeat.

2. Show the Speed Sound Card (picture side). Explain the picture, e.g. ***The witch is saying … sure it's pure.*** Say: *ure – sure it's pure.* Ask children to repeat.

Read the sound

1. Show the Speed Sound Card (picture side). Say: *When we look at this side we say the phrase:* **sure it's pure.**

2. Show the letter side. Say: *When we look at this side we say the sound:* **ure.**

3. Flip the card a few times and ask the children to say the sound or the phrase.

Review the sounds

Hide the new sound in the pack of sounds taught so far. Ask the children to read the sounds and spot the new sound. Gradually increase the speed as children gain confidence.

Word Time

Read the words

Use the Phonics Green Word Cards below.

> pic|ture, mix|ture, crea|ture, fu|ture, ad|ven|ture, tem|per|a|ture

1. Fold the card 'picture' and hold it up so only the first syllable is showing. Ask children to read the syllable – only using Fred Talk if necessary.

2. Repeat with the next syllable.

3. Unfold the card and ask children to read the whole word, tweaking the pronunciation if necessary. If children do not know what the word means, explain it to them.

4. Repeat for the other words in the list above.

Review the words

Ask children to read words from previous Sets 2 and 3 lessons. Ask them to read words without the dots and dashes, and use 'Fred in your head' to gain speed. (If necessary, flip to the dots and dashes side of the card to help children.) Gradually increase the speed.

Reading assessment

1. Ask children to read a few nonsense words that you have printed from the online file. (Search for Set 3 Nonsense Words in *Read Write Inc. Phonics* Online.) Tell children that the word they are about to read belongs to an alien language.

2. Show the word and ask them to tell you the sound of the 'special friends'.

3. Ask children to say the sounds and read the word.

Note any sounds that need further practice in the next Speed Sounds Lesson.

Spell with Fred Fingers

> pic|ture, mix|ture, crea|ture, fu|ture, ad|ven|ture, tem|per|a|ture

1. Say the whole word, *mixture*, and ask children to repeat it.

2. Say the word in syllables: *mix-ture* and ask children to repeat it.

3. Say the first syllable and ask children to repeat it, then hide their fingers as they count the sounds in the syllable. When you say *fingers*, they show their fingers. Then ask them to write the syllable and underline any 'special friends'.

4. Repeat with each syllable.

5. Write the word on the board and ask children to tick/correct the spelling of each sound in their own work.

6. Repeat with two or three words from the list above.

 Spell review

Ask children to write two or three previously taught words using the steps in Spell with Fred Fingers, above.

45

Summary lesson plans for teaching Set 3 Speed Sounds

Use the appropriate blueprint lesson plan to teach the Speed Sounds in the chart below.
You will need to substitute the information in grey text in the blueprint lesson with the details below.

Speed Sounds					Word Time				
Sound	Say the sound	Read the sound	Review the sounds		Read the words	Review the words	Reading assessment	Spell with Fred Fingers	Spell review
ea (special friends)	See blueprint lesson on p.40.								
oi (special friends – see p.40)	oi – spoil the boy. *Choose 3–4 words:* join, coin, voice, choice, noise	oi	oi Spot the new sound in the pack.		join *Use Phonics Green Word Cards:* join, voice, coin	clean Words from previous Set 2 and 3 lessons.	blig online. Ask children to read a few nonsense words printed from online. (Search for Set 3 Nonsense Words in *Read Write Inc. Phonics Online.*)	*Words to spell (choose 2–3):* join, voice, coin	Ask children to write two or three previously taught words.
a-e (special friends: split digraph)	See blueprint lesson on p.42.								
i-e (special friends: split digraph – see p.42)	i-e – nice smile. *Choose 3–4 words:* shine, white, fine, hide, smile, nice, wide, like, mine, time	i-e	i-e Spot the new sound in the pack.		smile *Use Phonics Green Word Cards:* smile, white, nice, like, time, hide	make Words from previous Set 2 and 3 lessons.	blig online. Ask children to read a few nonsense words printed from online. (Search for Set 3 Nonsense Words in *Read Write Inc. Phonics Online.*)	*Words to spell (choose 2–3):* smile, white, nice, like, time, hide	Ask children to write two or three previously taught words.

Speed Sounds				Word Time					
Sound	Say the sound	Read the sound	Review the sounds	Read the words	Review the words	Reading assessment	Spell with Fred Fingers	Spell review	

Sound	Say the sound	Read the sound	Review the sounds	Read the words	Review the words	Reading assessment	Spell with Fred Fingers	Spell review
o-e (special friends: split digraph – see p.42)	o-e – phone home *Choose 3–4 words:* home, hope, rose, spoke, note, broke, stole, rope, those	o-e	o-e Spot the new sound in the pack.	home *Use Phonics Green Word Cards:* home, hope, spoke, note, broke, phone	smile Words from previous Set 2 and 3 lessons.	blig Ask children to read a few nonsense words printed from online. (Search for Set 3 Nonsense Words in *Read Write Inc. Phonics Online*.)	*Words to spell (choose 2–3):* home, hope, spoke, note, broke, phone	Ask children to write two or three previously taught words.
u-e (special friends: split digraph – see p.42)	u-e – huge brute *Choose 3–4 words:* tune, rude, huge, mule, brute, use, June, dude, accuse, excuse	u-e	u-e Spot the new sound in the pack.	tune *Use Phonics Green Word Cards:* tune, rude, huge, brute, use, June	home Words from previous Set 2 and 3 lessons.	blig Ask children to read a few nonsense words printed from online. (Search for Set 3 Nonsense Words in *Read Write Inc. Phonics Online*.)	*Words to spell (choose 2–3):* tune, rude, huge, brute, use, June	Ask children to write two or three previously taught words.
aw (special friends – see p.40)	aw – yawn at dawn *Choose 3–4 words:* saw, raw, law, straw, dawn, paw, crawl, jaw, claw, yawn	aw	aw Spot the new sound in the pack.	saw *Use Phonics Green Word Cards:* saw, law, dawn, crawl, paw, yawn	tune Words from previous Set 2 and 3 lessons.	blig Ask children to read a few nonsense words printed from online. (Search for Set 3 Nonsense Words in *Read Write Inc. Phonics Online*.)	*Words to spell (choose 2–3):* saw, law, dawn, crawl, paw, yawn	Ask children to write two or three previously taught words.

47

Summary lesson plans for teaching Set 3 Speed Sounds

Speed Sounds				Word Time					
Sound	Say the sound	Read the sound	Review the sounds	Read the words	Review the words	Reading assessment	Spell with Fred Fingers	Spell review
are (special friends – see p.40)	are – care and share *Choose 3–4 words:* care, share, dare, bare, spare, scare, flare, square, Clare, software	are	Spot the new sound in the pack.	share *Use Phonics Green Word Cards:* share, dare, scare, square, bare, care	saw Words from previous Set 2 and 3 lessons.	blig Ask children to read a few nonsense words printed from online. (Search for Set 3 Nonsense Words in *Read Write Inc. Phonics Online*.)	*Words to spell (choose 2–3):* share, dare, scare, square, bare, care	Ask children to write two or three previously taught words.
ur (special friends – see p.40)	ur – nurse with a purse *Choose 3–4 words:* burn, turn, lurk, hurl, burn, burp, slurp, nurse, purse, hurt	ur	Spot the new sound in the pack.	burn *Use Phonics Green Word Cards:* burn, turn, spurt, nurse, purse, hurt	share Words from previous Set 2 and 3 lessons.	blig Ask children to read a few nonsense words printed from online. (Search for Set 3 Nonsense Words in *Read Write Inc. Phonics Online*.)	*Words to spell (choose 2–3):* burn, turn, spurt, nurse, purse, hurt	Ask children to write two or three previously taught words.

Speed Sounds

Sound	Say the sound	Read the sound	Review the sounds	Word Time — Read the words	Review the words	Reading assessment	Spell with Fred Fingers	Spell review
er (special friends – see p.40)	er – a better letter. *Choose 3–4 words*: over, never, better, weather, after, hamster, litter, proper, corner, supper	er	er — Spot the new sound in the pack.	never — *Use Phonics Green Word Cards*: never, better, weather, after, proper, corner	burn — Words from previous Set 2 and 3 lessons.	blig — Ask children to read a few nonsense words printed from online. (Search for Set 3 Nonsense Words in *Read Write Inc. Phonics Online*.)	*Words to spell (choose 2–3)*: never, better, weather, after, proper, corner	Ask children to write two or three previously taught words.
ow (special friends – see p.40)	ow – brown cow. *Choose 3–4 words*: howl, how, down, brown, cow, town, crowd, drown, now, gown	ow	ow — Spot the new sound in the pack.	how — *Use Phonics Green Word Cards*: how, down, brown, cow, town, now	never — Words from previous Set 2 and 3 lessons.	blig — Ask children to read a few nonsense words printed from online. (Search for Set 3 Nonsense Words in *Read Write Inc. Phonics Online*.)	*Words to spell (choose 2–3)*: how, down, brown, cow, town, now	Ask children to write two or three previously taught words.
ai (special friends – see p.40)	ai – snail in the rain. *Choose 3–4 words*: paid, snail, tail, drain, paint, Spain, chain, train, rain, stain	ai	ai — Spot the new sound in the pack.	snail — *Use Phonics Green Word Cards*: snail, paid, tail, train, paint, rain	how — Words from previous Set 2 and 3 lessons.	blig — Ask children to read a few nonsense words printed from online. (Search for Set 3 Nonsense Words in *Read Write Inc. Phonics Online*.)	*Words to spell (choose 2–3)*: snail, paid, tail, train, paint, rain	Ask children to write two or three previously taught words.

Summary lesson plans for teaching Set 3 Speed Sounds

Speed Sounds		Word Time					
Sound	Say the sound	Read the sound	Review the sounds	Read the words	Review the words	Reading assessment	Spell with Fred Fingers	Spell review
oa (special friends – see p.40)	oa – goat in a boat. *Choose 3–4 words:* toad, oak, road, cloak, throat, roast, toast, loaf, coat, coal, coach	oa	oa. Spot the new sound in the pack.	goat. *Use Phonics Green Word Cards:* goat, boat, road, throat, toast, coat	snail. Words from previous Set 2 and 3 lessons.	blig (online). Ask children to read a few nonsense words printed from online. (Search for Set 3 Nonsense Words in *Read Write Inc. Phonics Online*.)	*Words to spell (choose 2–3):* goat, boat, road, throat, toast, coat	Ask children to write two or three previously taught words.
ew (special friends – see p.40)	ew – chew the stew. *Choose 3–4 words:* new, knew, flew, blew, few, crew, newt, screw, drew, grew, stew	ew	ew. Spot the new sound in the pack.	chew. *Use Phonics Green Word Cards:* chew, new, blew, flew, drew, grew	goat. Words from previous Set 2 and 3 lessons.	blig (online). Ask children to read a few nonsense words printed from online. (Search for Set 3 Nonsense Words in *Read Write Inc. Phonics Online*.)	*Words to spell (choose 2–3):* chew, new, blew, flew, drew, grew	Ask children to write two or three previously taught words.
ire (special friends – see p.40)	ire – fire, fire! *Choose 3–4 words:* fire, hire, wire, spire, bonfire, inspire, conspire	ire	ire. Spot the new sound in the pack.	fire. *Use Phonics Green Word Cards:* fire, hire, wire, bon|fire, in|spire, con|spire	chew. Words from previous Set 2 and 3 lessons.	blig (online). Ask children to read a few nonsense words printed from online. (Search for Set 3 Nonsense Words in *Read Write Inc. Phonics Online*.)	*Words to spell (choose 2–3):* fire, hire, wire, bon|fire, in|spire, con|spire	Ask children to write two or three previously taught words.

50

Speed Sounds

Sound	Say the sound	Read the sound	Review the sounds	Word Time — Read the words	Review the words	Reading assessment	Spell with Fred Fingers	Spell review
ear (special friends – see p.40)	ear – hear with your ear. *Choose 3–4 words*: ear, hear, dear, fear, gear, near, rear, tear, year, spear	ear	ear. Spot the new sound in the pack.	hear. *Use Phonics Green Word Cards*: hear, dear, fear, near, year, ear	fire. Words from previous Set 2 and 3 lessons.	blig. Ask children to read a few nonsense words printed from online. (Search for Set 3 Nonsense Words in *Read Write Inc. Phonics Online*.)	*Words to spell (choose 2–3)*: hear, dear, fear, near, year, ear	Ask children to write two or three previously taught words.
ure (multi-syllabic)	See blueprint lesson on p.44.							
tion (multi-syllabic – see p.44)	tion – pay attention: it's a celebration	tion	tion. Spot the new sound in the pack.	conversation. *Use Phonics Green Word Cards*: con|ver|sa|tion, cel|e|bra|tion, ex|plor|a|tion, tradi|tion, con|grat|u|la|tion, a|tten|tion	picture. Words from previous Set 2 and 3 lessons.	blig. Ask children to read a few nonsense words printed from online. (Search for Set 3 Nonsense Words in *Read Write Inc. Phonics Online*.)	*Words to spell (choose 2–3)*: con|ver|sa|tion, cel|e|bra|tion, ex|plor|a|tion, tradi|tion, con|grat|u|la|tion, a|tten|tion	Ask children to write two or three previously taught words.
tious/cious (multi-syllabic – see p.44)	tious – scrumptious; cious – delicious	tious cious	tious cious. Spot the new sound in the pack.	delicious. *Use Phonics Green Word Cards*: de|li|cious, sus|pi|cious, vi|cious, pre|cious, fe|ro|cious, scrump|tious	conversation. Words from previous Set 2 and 3 lessons.	blig. Ask children to read a few nonsense words printed from online. (Search for Set 3 Nonsense Words in *Read Write Inc. Phonics Online*.)	*Words to spell (choose 2–3)*: de|li|cious, sus|pi|cious, vi|cious, pre|cious, fe|ro|cious, scrump|tious	Ask children to write two or three previously taught words.

Five-day timetable for teaching Yellow, Blue and Grey Level books

Timings within a session

The session for each day should last for about an hour, once children are in Year 1 (P2) and above.

Allocate timing within this as follows:

- Daily Speed Sounds Lesson – 10 minutes

- Handwriting – 5 minutes

- Write About – 20–30 minutes (Day 4); 30–40 minutes (Day 5)

- Linked Text – 10 minutes (Day 5)

The timing for the other activities can be flexible depending on your children's progress.

Day 1	Day 2	Day 3	Day 4	Day 5
Daily Speed Sounds Lesson	Daily Speed Sounds Lesson	Daily Speed Sounds Lesson	Daily Speed Sounds Lesson	Daily Speed Sounds Lesson
Speed Sounds from the Storybook	Speedy Green Words	Partner Practice – Speedy Green Words and Red Words	Spell Check	Spell Test
Story Green Words	Red Word Cards		Grammar	Write About… *(continue writing here)*
Speedy Green Words	Partner Practice – Speedy Green Words and Red Words	Think About the Story	Vocabulary	
Red Word Cards	Jump-in	Third Read – Children	Proofread – Spelling and Grammar	
Partner Practice – Story Speed Sounds, Story Green Words and Red Words	Second Read - Children	Questions to Talk About	Write About… *(start writing here)*	
Story Introduction	Fred Fingers – Spelling Green Words	Questions to Read and Answer		
First Read – Children	Red Rhythms – Spelling Red Words			
Read Aloud – Teacher	Hold a Sentence (2 sentences)	Build a Sentence		Partner Proofread
Red Rhythms – Spelling Red Words				Words to Keep
Handwriting	Handwriting	Handwriting	Handwriting	Linked Text

Resources

 Read Write Inc. Phonics Online resource

 Printable resource

[S|B] Storybook

[G|W] *Get Writing!* Book

Storybook, Non-fiction and *Get Writing!* Book lesson plans from Yellow Level onwards

Detailed lesson plans are given for the first two titles in each level. The cycle of activities that underpins the teaching repeats each time. From the third title in each level, a shorter version of the lesson plan is given, outlining only the things that will change for the teaching of that particular book.

Summary of activity purposes

Activity title	Children's purpose
Reading activities	
Speed Sounds in the Storybook	*To practise reading the sounds in the story*
Story Green Words	*To practise reading the Story Green Words and learn the meanings of new words*
Speedy Green Words	*To read the Speedy Green Words without sounding them out loud*
Red Word Cards	*To read the Red Words speedily*
Partner Practice – Speed Sounds and Story Green Words	*To help our partners read the sounds and Story Green Words*
Story Introduction	*To find out what is going to happen in the story*
First Read – Children	*To help our partners read every word in the story correctly*
Read Aloud – Teacher	*To enjoy listening to the whole story*
Partner Practice – Speedy Green Words and Red Words	*To help our partners read the Speedy Green Words and Red Words without using Fred Talk*
Jump-in	*To join in with our teacher, and get ready to read the story with greater fluency*
Second Read – Children	*To read the story more speedily, without using Fred Talk*
Think About the Story	*To think about what is happening in the story*
Third Read – Children	*To read the story in a storyteller's voice*
Questions to Talk About	*To find answers to questions in the book*
Questions to Read and Answer	*To help our partners answer questions about the story*
Writing activities	
Red Rhythms – Spelling Red Words	*To spell Red Words correctly*
Fred Fingers – Spelling Green Words	*To spell Green Words correctly*
Hold a Sentence – 1 and 2	*To 'hold' a whole sentence in our heads before writing it with correct spelling and punctuation*
Build a Sentence	*To build a sentence out loud before writing it down*
Spell Check	*To check we can spell the Red and Green Words (from the Spelling panel in the Get Writing! Books)*
Grammar	*To learn and practise new grammar skills*
Vocabulary	*To learn new and interesting vocabulary to use in our writing*
Write About... Note – there are six key steps for each 'Write About' (see *Reading Leader Handbook*).	*To write a composition based on the book*
Proofread – spelling; Proofread – grammar	*To correct spelling and punctuation errors*
Spell Test	*To celebrate the words we can spell and (for our teacher) to identify words that need further practice*
Partner Proofread	*To edit our own writing*
Words to Keep	*To select our favourite words from our Write About to use in future writing*

Storybook and Non-fiction Teaching Notes

This section contains the teaching notes for the following Storybooks and Non-fiction books:

Yellow

- Yellow Storybook 1 The duckchick
- Yellow Storybook 2 Off sick
- Yellow Storybook 3 Tom Thumb
- Yellow Storybook 4 The gingerbread man
- Yellow Storybook 5 Robin Hood
- Yellow Storybook 6 Lost
- Yellow Storybook 7 Do we have to keep it?
- Yellow Storybook 8 Danny and the Bump-a-lump
- Yellow Storybook 9 Grow your own radishes
- Yellow Storybook 10 The foolish witch
- Yellow Non-fiction 1 In the park
- Yellow Non-fiction 5 A mouse in the house

Blue

- Blue Storybook 1 Barker
- Blue Storybook 2 The poor goose
- Blue Storybook 3 Hairy fairy
- Blue Storybook 4 King of the birds
- Blue Storybook 5 Our house
- Blue Storybook 6 The jar of oil
- Blue Storybook 7 Jade's party
- Blue Storybook 8 Jellybean
- Blue Storybook 9 A box full of light
- Blue Storybook 10 The hole in the hill
- Blue Non-fiction 3 On your bike
- Blue Non-fiction 5 At the seaside

Grey

- Grey Storybook 1 Rex to the rescue
- Grey Storybook 2 The lion's paw
- Grey Storybook 3 I dare you
- Grey Storybook 4 Looking after a hamster
- Grey Storybook 5 How silly!
- Grey Storybook 6 Wailing Winny's car boot sale
- Grey Storybook 7 Toad
- Grey Storybook 8 Andrew
- Grey Storybook 9 Dear Vampire
- Grey Storybook 10 Vulture culture
- Grey Storybook 11 A celebration on planet Zox
- Grey Storybook 12 A very dangerous dinosaur
- Grey Storybook 13 The invisible clothes
- Grey Non-fiction 1 A job for Jordan
- Grey Non-fiction 5 A place in space: the Moon

The duckchick

Teacher's Preparation

1. Print out the Story Green Words (see online file '5.1 The duckchick', starting with tab a) and stack them into your pocket chart: *Mama, nest, cluck, hatch, crack, chick, quack, pond, quick as a flash, bank, upset, duckchick, pecked, shocked, grubs, flapped, stretched, crusts, hopped, grabbed.*

2. Display these Red Word Cards in your pocket chart: *some, saw, her, to, all, was, they, watch, of.* These are the Red Words in the Storybook text.

3. Practise reading the Storybook Introduction (below and printable online file 5.1a) and the whole story with expression, for reading aloud to children.

4. Prepare sticky notes you may need for activities such as Think About the Story, Build a Sentence and Write About How Mama Hen Got a Shock. Ideas are provided but you may wish to add your own.

DAY 1

Daily Speed Sounds Lesson

1. Review one Set 3 Speed Sound with a particular focus on spelling. See pp.40–51.

2. Review Set 2 and 3 Speed Sounds. See pp.33–51.

Speed Sounds from the Storybook

Find the circled focus graphemes on p.4 of the Storybook. Point to each focus grapheme on the Complex Speed Sounds poster and use **MTYT (My turn Your turn)** to say them: *wr, qu, tch.*

Story Green Words

Follow the steps below to read the Story Green Words (printed from online) with the children. After they have read each Story Green Word, explain the meaning of any new words. Definitions for some of the words can be found in the Vocabulary Check on p.7 of the Storybook.

Names and single-syllable words

1. Hold up the first card, e.g. 'cluck', and ask children to tell you the 'special friends' (digraph – *ck*) or shake their heads if there aren't any. If children have difficulty spotting the 'special friends', show them the side of the card with the dots and dashes to give them a quick reminder.

2. Ask them to say the sounds *c-l-u-ck* and say *cluck*.

3. Say the word *cluck* with exaggerated pronunciation. Ask children to repeat it.

4. Repeat for the other words.

Multi-syllabic words

1. Fold the card 'upset' and hold it up so only the first syllable is showing. Ask children to read the syllable – only using Fred Talk if necessary.

2. Repeat with the next syllable.

3. Unfold the card and ask children to read the whole word, tweaking the pronunciation if necessary.

4. Repeat for the other word.

Root words and suffixes

1. Fold the card 'pecked' so you can only see the root word ('peck') and hold it up. Ask children to read it without Fred Talk.

2. Repeat with the suffix (-ed).

3. Unfold the card and ask children to read the whole word, tweaking the pronunciation if necessary.

4. Repeat for the other words.

 Speedy Green Words

1. Display the first Speedy Green Word (online file 5.1b).

2. Tell children to first read the sounds silently using 'Fred in your head'. Then ask them to say the word aloud when the word animates, or when you push the word towards them if you have printed out the words.

3. Repeat Steps 1 and 2 with the other Speedy Green Words, increasing the pace as children become more confident.

4. Review Speedy Green Words from a previous Storybook that need further practice.

Red Word Cards

1. Hold up the first card, e.g. 'some'.

2. Say the word *some* and ask children to repeat it.

3. Point to the card and say the sounds you can hear, *s-u-m* and say *some*. Ask children to repeat.

4. Help children to spot the tricky letter ('o').

5. Say the word again. Ask children to repeat it.

6. Repeat for the other Red Words.

 Partner Practice

Children practise the Speed Sounds and Story Green Words on pp.4–6. Ensure partners sit at the table with one Storybook between them and one lolly stick for pointing.

1. Ask one partner to teach the sounds out of order using **MTYT**. Ensure that children point accurately underneath the sounds.

2. Ask the other partner to teach the words out of order using **MTYT**.

3. During the activity, note any sounds/words that need further practice and review together at the end of the activity.

On subsequent books, ask a different partner to start teaching the sounds.

Next, children practise the Red Words on p.8. Note that the grid contains Red Words from the Storybook text, plus some revision Red Words.

1. Ask partners to take turns reading the words across the rows or down the columns. Ensure that children point accurately underneath the words. (Partners help each other if stuck.)

2. Repeat until they can read all the Red Words at speed.

 Story Introduction

Read the introduction (below and printable online file 5.1a) to children using expression. Explain the meaning of any words children may be unsure of. Ask children to **TTYP (Turn to your partner)** to discuss the question and then select two pairs to feed back (Choose two – see p.18).

> In spring, Mama hen laid six eggs. One day, when she was busy keeping them warm in her nest, she noticed that egg 6 was bigger than the others.
>
> 'Why is it so big?' she clucked to herself.
>
> The first five eggs soon began to hatch and out popped five soft, fluffy chicks. Then there was another very big *cccc-r-a-ck* and egg 6 hatched too. But this chick wasn't soft and fluffy like the rest. Mama hen was shocked. This chick was a duckchick!
>
> "Cluck!" went Mama hen, and the chicks clucked too.

> "Quack!" went the duckchick.
> Mama hen took all the chicks down to the pond. She showed them how to peck grubs from the mud, but the duckchick wasn't interested. He flapped his long wings, stretched his long neck and jumped into the water.
> "Cluck!" went Mama hen and the chicks.
> "Quack!" went the duckchick.
> When they had eaten as many grubs as they could, Mama hen led the chicks onto a log. They were having so much fun hopping along, they didn't notice a fox spying on them from a nearby bush...
>
> **TTYP:** What do you think will happen to the chicks?

First Read – Children

Ensure partners sit at the table with one Storybook between them and one lolly stick for pointing.

1. Ask Partner 1s to:

   – point to the words while their partner reads the first page of the story.

   – prompt their partner to Fred Talk words they read incorrectly.

2. Swap roles on the second page. Continue to swap roles page by page.

3. Remind children who finish quickly to re-read the story.

4. Note any words that need further practice and review these when children have finished reading.

Read Aloud – Teacher

1. Ask children to close their Storybooks.

2. Read the whole story aloud with expression.

TTYP: How did the duckchick save the chicks?

Red Rhythms – Spelling Red Words

The children should keep their *Get Writing! Yellow* Book closed. However, you will need to use the Red Words in the panel on p.3 of the *Get Writing!* Book: *some, saw, her, all, watch.*

1. Write the first word on the board or flipchart.

2. Say the word and ask children to repeat it.

3. Point to each sound as you say it, then say the whole word. Ask children to repeat.

4. Help children to spot any tricky letters that aren't on the Speed Sounds Chart and circle these.

5. Point as you say the letter names in a rhythm (exaggerating the tricky letters) and then say the word.

6. Repeat with all the Red Words in the panel on p.3 of the *Get Writing!* Book.

7. Hide the words that are on the board or flipchart. Say the first Red Word again. Ask children to say the letter names as they write the word in their exercise book. Write the word on the board and ask children to tick/correct the spelling of each sound. Repeat with the other Red Words.

Handwriting

Follow the handwriting lesson plan on pp.25–28 to review Stage 2/3 handwriting.

Daily Speed Sounds Lesson

1. Review one Set 3 Speed Sound with a particular focus on spelling. See pp.40–51.

2. Review Set 2 and 3 Speed Sounds. See pp.33–51.

Speedy Green Words

Repeat as for Day 1. Increase the speed children read these words by reducing the 'Fred in your head' time. To do this, display them at a faster speed or, if using the cards, push the card forward sooner each time until children can read them almost immediately.

Red Word Cards

Repeat the Red Word Cards activity from Day 1, increasing the speed.

S B **Partner Practice**

Ensure partners sit at the table with one Storybook between them and one lolly stick for pointing. Children practise the Speedy Green Words on p.18 and the Red Words on p.8.

1. Ask partners to take turns reading the words across the rows or down the columns. Ensure that children point accurately underneath the words.

2. Repeat until they can read all the Speedy Green Words correctly without Fred Talk and the Red Words at speed.

S B **Jump-in**

1. Ask one partner to track under the words with a lolly stick as you read the story aloud, but ask both partners to 'Jump-in' and read the words when you hesitate on four/five words per page.

2. Ask partners to swap roles after each page.

S B **Second Read – Children**

Ask partners to read the whole story again, taking turns to read alternate pages. (See Day 1 First Read.) Ask Partner 2s to point on the first page this time.

Fred Fingers – Spelling Green Words

The children should keep their *Get Writing!* Book closed. However, you will need to use the Green Words in the panel on p.3 of the *Get Writing!* Book. Ask children to write the spellings in their exercise books.

Single-syllable words

wrong, quick

1. Say the word *wrong* and ask children to repeat it.

2. Ask children to:

   – Hide their fingers as they count the sounds on them.

   – Show their fingers when you say *fingers*.

   – Repeat the word, then pinch their fingers as they say the sounds.

   – Write the word as they say the sounds, underlining any *special friends*.

3. Write the word on the board and ask children to tick/correct the spelling of each sound in their own work.

4. Repeat for the next word.

Multi-syllabic words

problem, began, very

1. Say the whole word *problem* and ask children to repeat it.

2. Say the word in syllables: *prob-lem* and ask children to repeat it.

3. Say the first syllable and ask children to repeat it, then hide their fingers as they count the sounds in the syllable. When you say *fingers*, they show their fingers. Then ask them to write the syllable and underline any 'special friends'.

59

4. Repeat with each syllable.

5. Write the word on the board and ask children to tick/correct the spelling of each sound in their own work.

6. Repeat for the other words.

Red Rhythms – Spelling Red Words

Repeat the Red Rhythms activity in Day 1, with the same Red Words.

 ### Hold a Sentence – 1 and 2

(**1**) Things began to go wrong in the spring.

1. Say the sentence above and ask children to repeat it.

2. Use **MTYT** until children can remember the whole sentence, and then add punctuation mimes (see p.20).

3. Write the sentence on the board and ask children to help you:

   – Use Fred Fingers to spell Green Words.
   – **TOL (Think out loud)** about how to spell any Red Words.
   – Use punctuation and finger spaces.
   – Re-read the sentence to check it makes sense.

4. Hide the sentence and ask children to write it on p.2 of their *Get Writing!* Book.

5. Display the sentence again and help children to mark each word of their own work.

6. Repeat Steps 1 to 5 with the sentence below.

(**2**) The duckchick flapped his long wings and jumped into the pond.

Handwriting

Follow the handwriting lesson plan on pp.25–28 to review Stage 2/3 handwriting.

DAY 3

Daily Speed Sounds Lesson

1. Review one Set 3 Speed Sound with a particular focus on spelling. See pp.40–51.

2. Review Set 2 and 3 Speed Sounds. See pp.33–51.

 ### Partner Practice

Ensure partners sit at the table with one Storybook between them and one lolly stick for pointing. Repeat as for Day 2, practising the Speedy Green Words on p.18 and the Red Words on p.8.

Think About the Story

Children do not need their Storybooks. Display the Storybook pictures (online file 5.1c) as you read the story aloud from your Storybook. Use your prepared notes for **TOL, MTYT, TTYP** and Freeze Frames to reinforce children's understanding. For example:

p.9   **TOL** about why Mama hen is worried about egg 6.

p.10   **TOL** about what the chicks look like as they hatch.

p.11   Freeze Frame Mama hen's expression.
   TTYP: How does Mama hen feel, and why? *Surprised because the chick looks so different from the others.* (Ensure children understand that the reason the duckchick looks different is because it's a baby duck, not a chicken.)

p.12 **TOL** about why Mama hen and the other chicks are shocked when duckchick jumps into the pond.

MTYT (with feeling): *The duckchick **flapped** his long wings, **stretched** his long neck, and – **"Splash!"** – **jumped** into the pond.*

p.13 **TOL** about why Mama hen and the other chicks don't go into the pond.

p.14 **TOL** about why they are so scared.

p.15 **TOL** about how duckchick saves the other chicks.
Freeze Frame Mama hen's expression.

TTYP: How does Mama feel now, and why? *Grateful to the duckchick for saving the chicks.*

S B Third Read – Children

Ask partners to read the whole story again, taking turns to read each page. (See Day 1 First Read.) Ask Partner 1s to point on the first page this time.

S B Questions to Talk About

Read out the questions on p.16 of the Storybook. For each question, direct children to the correct page to find the answer. Ask them to **TTYP** and to respond using 'Fastest finger' (FF) where they find the answer in the text or 'Have a think' (HaT) where they have to justify their answer/opinion.

S B Questions to Read and Answer

Ask children to turn to p.17 in the Storybook.

1. Show partners how to take turns to read the questions and find the answers in the text. They should swap roles after each question.

2. After children have completed the questions with their partner, take feedback.

GW Build a Sentence

Tell children that tomorrow they will write about how Mama hen felt about her duckchick. Explain that today you are going to help them build up a sentence that Mama hen might have said when the duckchick hatched.

1. Display the picture of the duckchick hatching (online file 5.1d). **MTYT:** *Who is this in my nest?*

2. **TTYP:** What does the duckchick look like? Draw out responses such as *He is big/has a long neck/ a big beak/long wings.* Demonstrate how to include details in the sentence, e.g. *Who is this in my nest with a big beak and a long neck?*

3. **TTYP:** What noise does the duckchick make? Draw out responses such as *quack/squawk/squeak*, and model how to include them in the sentence, e.g. *Who is this in my nest with a big beak, a long neck and a loud squawk?*

4. Ask partners to decide on their own sentence and to practise saying it until they can remember it. Select a few partners to say their sentences to the group.

5. Ask children to write their own sentence on p.2 of their *Get Writing!* Book. Encourage children to spell new words using their phonic knowledge. Accept phonically-plausible spellings.

Handwriting

Follow the handwriting lesson plan on pp.25–28 to review Stage 2/3 handwriting.

 Daily Speed Sounds Lesson

1. Review one Set 3 Speed Sound with a particular focus on spelling. See pp.40–51.

2. Review Set 2 and 3 Speed Sounds. See pp.33–51.

Spell Check

Ask children to turn to the panels of Red and Green Words on p.3 in the *Get Writing!* Book.

1. Ask Partner 1s to:

   – choose and say one of the Red or Green Words, then cover it up

   – help their partner to write the word in their exercise book

   – look back at the listed word and help their partner tick/correct the spelling of each sound.

2. Ask partners to swap after each word, so that each partner writes five words.

 Grammar

1. Tell (or remind) children that a verb shows us what someone or something is doing, e.g. *swims, runs, hops, jumps, shouts.* Explain that verbs can be in the **present** tense (to explain what is happening now) or can be in the **past** tense (to explain what has already happened).

2. **TOL** about how verbs in the past tense often end in -ed, e.g. *pecked, grabbed, flapped, stretched, jumped, hatched.* Recall some common past tense verbs that don't end in -ed, e.g. *went, said, fell, saw, swam.*

3. Ask children to complete the Grammar activity on p.3 of their *Get Writing!* Book.

4. Ask children to **TTYP** to check if they have underlined the same words and if not, to discuss which answers are correct and why.

5. Tell children the correct responses and explain any difficult points. (They should have underlined: *flapped, stretched, jumped, pecked, watched, fell.*)

 Vocabulary

1. Explain that good writers try to develop a wide vocabulary and use a variety of words to make their writing more interesting for the reader.

2. Write *flapped* on the board. Use **MTYT** to say the word. Give the context of the word in the story: The duckchick flapped his long wings. Write three more words next to *flapped*, e.g. *snored, shut, shook.* Ask children which one means almost the same as *flapped (shook).*

3. Ask children to turn to the Vocabulary activity on p.3 of their *Get Writing!* Book. Talk through the activity, explaining any words that they are unsure of. Then ask children to complete the activity.

4. Ask children to **TTYP** to check if they have circled the same words and if not, to discuss which answers are correct and why.

5. Tell children the correct responses and explain any difficult points. (They should have circled: *dropped, fast, clutched, looking at.*)

 Proofread – Spelling

1. Display the sentences on screen (online file 5.1e) and read them to the children.

2. Ask partners to spot the errors.

3. Take feedback and show how to correct the errors.

4. Hide the sentences and ask children to correct the sentences in their *Get Writing!* Book on p.4.

5. Display the sentences written correctly and help children to check their own corrections.

 Proofread – Grammar

Use online file 5.1f. Follow as for the Proofread – Spelling activity.

Write About How Mama Hen Got a Shock

Note that this activity should be started on Day 4 and completed on Day 5.

1. **TOL** about how anxious you feel when you take children on a school trip and have to make sure that everyone is safe.
   TOL about how Mama hen must have felt when she took all her little chicks out on a walk.
   TTYP: How did she feel? *Proud/Anxious to keep them safe/Watchful.*

2. Use online file 5.1 (tab g onwards) for this activity. Tell children that they are Mama hen. Explain that they will be writing, in role as Mama hen, about how she felt about the duckchick when he hatched and when he saved her chicks from the hungry fox. Talk about the word *rescue*. Explain that it means to save or help someone when they are in trouble. Ask children to turn to pp.4–5 in their *Get Writing!* Book. Explain that they are going to use the questions and sentence starters to help them write about how Mama hen's feelings towards the duckchick changed.

3. Ask children questions and encourage them to respond in the role of Mama hen. Develop this as a conversation. **TTYP** and then draw out responses from children, using **MTYT** to create full sentences.

   – What did you say when the duckchick hatched out of the big egg? *I said…"Gosh, what a large chick"/"He's so big"/"He doesn't look like my other chicks!"*

   – What did the duckchick look like? *The duckchick had… a large beak, a long neck, brown fluffy feathers and big webbed feet.*

   – What noise did the duckchick make? *He made such a… loud quack/squeak/squawk.*

   – How did you feel when you saw the duckchick? *I felt… very surprised/shocked/curious when I first saw him.*

   – What happened when you got to the pond? *When we got to the pond… the duckchick jumped into the water/my chicks hopped along a log/I saw a fox who looked very hungry/we were scared and my chicks fell into the water.*

   – How did the duckchick save your chicks? *The duckchick saved my chicks by swimming into the water and pulling them to the bank.*

   – How do you feel about the duckchick now? *The duckchick is so brave/He saved my chicks/I'm so grateful to him/I love him to bits!*

4. Repeat the first question and use the online file (tab g) to model how to write a response on the board, e.g. *I said, "Gosh, what a large chick."* Keep re-reading as you write to make sure it makes sense.

5. Hide your writing. Ask children to decide on their first sentence and to practise saying it aloud with their partner until they can remember it. Select a few partners to say their sentences to the group. Then children can write their own first sentence, using the sentence starter on p.4 of their *Get Writing!* Book. Point out the Useful words and encourage children to use some of these words in their writing. Encourage children to spell new words using their phonic knowledge. Accept phonically-plausible spellings.

6. Repeat Steps 4 and 5 (demonstrate how you write, then ask children to write) with all the questions.

Handwriting

Follow the handwriting lesson plan on pp.25–28 to review Stage 2/3 handwriting.

 Daily Speed Sounds Lesson

1. Review one Set 3 Speed Sound with a particular focus on spelling. See pp.40–51.

2. Review Set 2 and 3 Speed Sounds. See pp.33–51.

Spell Test

1. Choose one of the Red or Green Words listed in the panels on p.3 of the *Get Writing!* Book. Say it aloud and ask children to write it in their exercise book. Remind them to use Fred Fingers if necessary.

2. Write the word on the board.

3. Ask children to tick/correct the spelling of each sound.

4. Repeat with the other nine listed words.

 ### Write About How Mama Hen Got a Shock (continued)

Complete the writing activity started on Day 4.

Partner Proofread

1. Remind children of the proofreading activity they did on Day 4.

   TTYP: What sort of things do we check when we proofread our work?

2. Share responses and note features to check on the board. These may include:

   – spaces between words

   – capital letters (**TOL** – at the start of a sentence, for proper nouns and the pronoun *I*)

   – full stops (**TOL** – at the end of a sentence)

   – question marks or exclamation marks (**TOL** – to show a question or exclamation)

   – spelling.

3. If necessary, model how to correct a sentence that contains common errors made by the class. Do not use any of the children's work, but create your own sentence to correct.

4. Ask Partner 1s to place their exercise book on top of Partner 2's. Tell partners they have three minutes to proofread Partner 1's writing, together. Encourage Partner 1s to mark any corrections in their own exercise book.

5. Repeat for Partner 2's work.

 ### Words to Keep

Ask children to re-read their writing and select the words they are most proud of, or words they might want to use again. Then ask them to write these in the 'Words to keep' section on p.5 of their *Get Writing!* Book.

Linked Text

Read the linked text for the next Storybook.

Off sick

Teacher's Preparation

1. Print out the Story Green Words (see online file '5.2 Off sick', starting with tab a) and stack them into your pocket chart: *Sam, sick, ha ha, ring, ill, felt, glass, nap, crisps, pick, film, humph*, sandwich, o'clock, swimming, popped, hugged, kissed, biggest.*
Note that Challenge Words are marked with an asterisk.

2. Display these Red Word Cards in your pocket chart: *watch(es), was, to, all, said, want, you, are, of, school, her, they.* These are the Red Words in the Storybook text.

3. Practise reading the Storybook Introduction (below and printable online file 5.2a) and the whole story with expression, for reading aloud to the children.

4. Prepare sticky notes you may need for activities such as Think About the Story, Build a Sentence and Write About Being Ill. Ideas are provided but you may wish to add your own.

 DAY 1

Daily Speed Sounds Lesson

1. Review one Set 3 Speed Sound with a particular focus on spelling. See pp.40–51.

2. Review Set 2 and 3 Speed Sounds. See pp.33–51.

Speed Sounds from the Storybook

Find the circled focus graphemes on p.4 of the Storybook. Point to each focus grapheme on the Complex Speed Sounds poster and use **MTYT** to say them: *ph, rr, ve, gg.*

Story Green Words

Follow the steps below to read the Story Green Words (printed from online) with the children. After they have read each Story Green Word, explain the meaning of any new words.

Definitions for some of the words can be found in the Vocabulary Check on p.7 of the Storybook.

Names and single-syllable words

1. Hold up the first card, e.g. 'Sam', and ask children to tell you the 'special friends' or shake their heads if there aren't any. (There aren't any for this word, but if children have difficulty spotting the 'special friends', show them the side of the card with the dots and dashes to give them a quick reminder.)

2. Ask them to say the sounds *S-a-m* and say *Sam*.

3. Say the word *Sam* with exaggerated pronunciation. Ask children to repeat it.

4. Repeat for the other words.

Multi-syllabic words

1. Fold the card 'sandwich' and hold it up so only the first syllable is showing. Ask children to read the syllable – only using Fred Talk if necessary.

2. Repeat with the next syllable.

3. Unfold the card and ask children to read the whole word, tweaking the pronunciation if necessary.

4. Repeat for the other word.

Root words and suffixes

1. Fold the word 'kissed' so you can only see the root word ('kiss') and hold it up. Ask children to read it without Fred Talk.

2. Repeat with the suffix (-ed).

3. Unfold the card and ask children to read the whole word, tweaking the pronunciation if necessary.

4. Repeat for the other words.

Challenge Words

Follow the steps as for the Red Word Cards, below.

Speedy Green Words

1. Display the first Speedy Green Word (online file 5.2b).

2. Tell children to first read the sounds silently using 'Fred in your head'. Then ask them to say the word aloud when the word animates, or when you push the word towards them if you have printed out the words.

3. Repeat Steps 1 and 2 with the other Speedy Green Words, increasing the pace as children become more confident.

4. Review Speedy Green Words from a previous Storybook that need further practice.

Red Word Cards

1. Hold up the first card, e.g. 'watches'.

2. Say the word *watches* and ask children to repeat it.

3. Point to the card and say the sounds you can hear, *w-o-ch-e-z* and say *watches*. Ask children to repeat.

4. Help children to spot the tricky letter ('a').

5. Say the word again. Ask children to repeat it.

6. Repeat for the other Red Words.

SB Partner Practice

Children practise the Speed Sounds and Story Green Words on pp.4–6. Ensure partners sit at the table with one Storybook between them and one lolly stick for pointing.

1. Ask one partner to teach the sounds out of order using **MTYT**. Ensure that children point accurately underneath the sounds.

2. Ask the other partner to teach the words out of order using **MTYT**.

3. During the activity, note any sounds/words that need further practice and review together at the end of the activity.

On subsequent books, ask a different partner to start teaching the sounds.

Next, children practise the Red Words on p.8. Note that the grid contains Red Words from the Storybook text, plus some revision Red Words.

1. Ask partners to take turns reading the words across the rows or down the columns. Ensure that children point accurately underneath the words. (Partners help each other if stuck.)

2. Repeat until they can read all of the Red Words at speed.

Story Introduction

Read the introduction (on the following page and printable online file 5.2a) to children using expression. Explain the meaning of any words children may be unsure of. Ask children to **TTYP** to discuss the question and then select two pairs to feed back (Choose two – see p.18).

Eva was ill. Her head was hot and her tummy hurt, so Mum rang up the school and told Miss Flint she'd be staying in bed.

'Ha ha!' thought Eva as she watched her brother Sam go off to school.

She lay in bed until midday, when her mum brought her an egg and a glass of milk. Even though she was still too ill to get up, she was starting to feel bored.

"Can I watch TV?" she asked Mum.

"No," said Mum, "you must just rest in bed."

Eva ate a bit of the egg, had a sip of the milk and took a long nap.

At 4 o'clock, Sam came home from school. He told her about his day. Then he had a sandwich and a hot drink and watched TV.

"I'm going swimming with Dad," he told Eva. Eva didn't like being in bed anymore. She was fed up with it! She wanted to go swimming with Dad too!

"Mum, let me get up!" she said.

"No, not yet."

"But I am OK!" she complained. "I want to go swimming with Dad and Sam!"

TTYP: Do you think Eva was allowed to go swimming that day? Why or why not?

S B **First Read – Children**

Ensure partners sit at the table with one Storybook between them and one lolly stick for pointing.

1. Ask Partner 1s to:

   – point to the words while their partner reads the first page of the story.

   – prompt their partner to Fred Talk words they read incorrectly.

2. Swap roles on the second page. Continue to swap roles page by page.

3. Remind children who finish quickly to re-read the story.

4. Note any words that need further practice and review these when children have finished reading.

Read Aloud – Teacher

1. Ask children to close their Storybooks.

2. Read the whole story aloud with expression.

TTYP: Why did Eva get fed up with being ill?

Red Rhythms – Spelling Red Words

Children should keep their *Get Writing! Yellow* Book closed. However, you will need to use the Red Words in the panel on p.7 of the *Get Writing!* Book.

1. Write the first word on the board or flipchart.

2. Say the word and ask children to repeat it.

3. Point to each sound as you say it, then say the whole word. Ask children to repeat.

4. Help children to spot any tricky letters that aren't on the Speed Sounds Chart and circle these.

5. Point as you say the letter names in a rhythm (exaggerating the tricky letters) and then say the word.

6. Repeat with all the Red Words in the panel on p.7 of the *Get Writing!* Book.

7. Hide the words that are on the board or flipchart. Say the first Red Word again. Ask children to say the letter names as they write the word in their exercise book. Write the word on the board and ask children to tick/correct the spelling of each sound. Repeat with the other Red Words.

Handwriting

Follow the handwriting lesson plan on pp.25–28 to review Stage 2/3 handwriting.

Daily Speed Sounds Lesson

1. Review one Set 3 Speed Sound with a particular focus on spelling. See pp.40–51.

2. Review Set 2 and 3 Speed Sounds. See pp.33–51.

 Speedy Green Words

Repeat as for Day 1. Increase the speed children read these words by reducing the 'Fred in your head' time. To do this, display them at a faster speed or push the card forward sooner each time until children can read them almost immediately.

Red Word Cards

Repeat the Red Word Cards activity from Day 1, increasing the speed.

`S B` **Partner Practice**

Ensure partners sit at the table with one Storybook between them and one lolly stick for pointing. Children practise the Speedy Green Words on p.18 and the Red Words on p.8.

1. Ask partners to take turns reading the words across the rows or down the columns. Ensure that children point accurately underneath the words.

2. Repeat until they can read all the Speedy Green Words correctly without Fred Talk and the Red Words at speed.

`S B` **Jump-in**

1. Ask one partner to track under the words with a lolly stick as you read the story aloud, but ask both partners to 'Jump-in' and read the words when you hesitate on four/five words per page.

2. Ask partners to swap roles after each page.

`S B` **Second Read – Children**

Ask partners to read the whole story again, taking turns to read alternate pages. (See Day 1 First Read.) Ask Partner 2s to point on the first page this time.

Fred Fingers – Spelling Green Words

Children keep their *Get Writing!* Book closed. However, you will need to use the Green Words in the panel on p.7 of the *Get Writing!* Book. Ask children to write the spellings in their exercise books.

Single-syllable words

milk, have

1. Say the word *milk* and ask children to repeat it.

2. Ask children to:

   – Hide their fingers as they count the sounds on them.

   – Show their fingers when you say *fingers*.

   – Repeat the word, then pinch their fingers as they say the sounds.

   – Write the word as they say the sounds, underlining any 'special friends'.

3. Write the word on the board and ask children to tick/correct the spelling of each sound in their own work.

4. Repeat for the next word.

Multi-syllabic words.

cannot, tomorrow

1. Say the whole word *cannot*, and ask children to repeat it.

2. Say the word in syllables: *can-not* and ask children to repeat it.

3. Say the first syllable and ask children to repeat it, then hide their fingers as they count the sounds in the syllable. When you say *fingers*, they show their fingers. Then ask them to write the syllable and underline any 'special friends'.

4. Repeat with each syllable.

5. Write the word on the board and ask children to tick/correct the spelling of each sound in their own work.

6. Repeat for the other word.

Root words with a suffix

swimming

1. Say the whole word *swimming*, and ask children to say the root.

2. Ask children to:
   - Hide their fingers as they count the sounds in the root word until you say *fingers*.
   - Repeat the root word and pinch their fingers as they say the sounds.

3. Ask children to write the root word, underlining any special friends.

4. Write the root on the board and **TOL** about how you would add the suffix, noting any letters that need doubling.

5. Ask children to write the suffix.

6. Ask children to tick/correct the spelling of each sound in their own work.

Red Rhythms – Spelling Red Words

Repeat the Red Rhythms activity in Day 1, with the same Red Words.

GW **Hold a Sentence – 1 and 2**

(**1** Mum said I cannot go swimming with Dad and Sam today.)

1. Say the sentence above and ask children to repeat it.

2. Use **MTYT** until children can remember the whole sentence, and then add punctuation mimes (see p.20).

3. Write the sentence on the board and ask children to help you:
   - Use Fred Fingers to spell Green Words.
   - **TOL** about how to spell any Red Words.
   - Use punctuation and finger spaces.
   - Re-read the sentence to check it makes sense.

4. Hide the sentence and ask children to write it in on p.6. of their *Get Writing!* Book.

5. Display the sentence again and help children to mark each word of their own work.

6. Repeat Steps 1 to 5 with the sentence below.

(**2** Tomorrow you can have sweets and pick a film from the shop.)

Handwriting

Follow the handwriting lesson plan on pp.25–28 to review Stage 2/3 handwriting.

> **Daily Speed Sounds Lesson**
>
> 1. Review one Set 3 Speed Sound with a particular focus on spelling. See pp.40–51.
>
> 2. Review Set 2 and 3 Speed Sounds. See pp.33–51.

S B Partner Practice

Ensure partners sit at the table with one Storybook between them and one lolly stick for pointing. Repeat as for Day 2, practising the Speedy Green Words on p.18 and the Red Words on p.8.

Think About the Story

Children do not need their Storybooks. Display the Storybook pictures (online file 5.2c) as you read the story aloud from your Storybook. Use your prepared notes for **TOL**, **MTYT**, **TTYP** and Freeze Frames to reinforce children's understanding. For example:

p.9   **TOL** about why the girl isn't going to school and what happens at 9 o'clock.
Freeze Frame the girl's expression.
TTYP: How is she feeling? *Miserable because she is so poorly/Hot/Wants to be sick.*

p.10   **TOL** about how she spends her time from 12 o'clock.

p.11   Freeze Frame her expression when Sam gets back from school.
TTYP: How is she feeling, and why? *Jealous/Miserable because she can't watch TV or go swimming.*

pp.12–13   **TOL** about how she tries to convince her mum that she should get up.
MTYT (with feeling): *But I **am** OK! I **am**! Yes, my tum is **OK**. **No**, I do not want to be sick. **No**, I am not too hot.*

p.14   **TOL** about how Sam makes her feel even worse.

p.15   **TOL** about how her mum and dad make her feel better.
Freeze Frame the girl's expression.
MTYT (with feeling): *It's not **that** bad, being off sick.*

S B Third Read – Children

Ask partners to read the whole story again, taking turns to read each page. (See Day 1 First Read.) Ask Partner 1s to point on the first page this time.

S B Questions to Talk About

Read out the questions on p.16 of the Storybook. For each question, direct children to the correct page to find the answer. Ask them to **TTYP** and to respond using 'Fastest finger' (FF) where they find the answer in the text or 'Have a think' (HaT) where they have to justify their answer/opinion.

S B Questions to Read and Answer

Ask children to turn to p.17 in the Storybook.

1. Show partners how to take turns to read the questions and find the answers in the text. They should swap roles after each question.

2. After children have completed the questions with their partner, take feedback.

Build a Sentence

Tell children that tomorrow they will write about being ill. Explain that today you are going to help children build up a sentence to describe what it's like being ill.

1. Display the picture of Eva ill in bed (online file 5.2d). Ask children to imagine that they are Eva. Say the simple sentence: *I am ill.*

2. Use **MTYT** each time you expand the sentence using the children's ideas. **TTYP**: How do you feel? Draw out responses such as *hot/tired/itchy/hurting*. Demonstrate how to build the children's ideas into the sentence, e.g. *I am hot and tired.*

3. **TTYP**: Where do you lie? Draw out responses such as *in bed/on the sofa/snuggled under the covers/under my duvet.* Model how to include suggestions in the sentence, e.g. *I am hot and tired so I snuggle under a blanket on the sofa.*

4. **TTYP**: What do you do? For example, *sleep/read my favourite book/watch TV/listen to stories/ read a comic/do some colouring.* Demonstrate how to add some of the children's ideas to the sentence, e.g. *I am hot and tired so I snuggle under a blanket on the sofa and listen to stories.*

5. Ask partners to decide on their own sentence and to practise saying it until they can remember it. Select a few partners to say their sentences to the group.

6. Ask children to write their sentence on p.6. of their *Get Writing!* Book. Encourage children to spell new words using their phonic knowledge. Accept phonically-plausible spellings.

Handwriting

Follow the handwriting lesson plan on pp.25–28 to review Stage 2/3 handwriting.

> **Daily Speed Sounds Lesson**
>
> 1. Review one Set 3 Speed Sound with a particular focus on spelling. See pp.40–51.
>
> 2. Review Set 2 and 3 Speed Sounds. See pp.33–51.

[GW] **Spell Check**

Ask children to turn to the panels of Red and Green Words on p.7 of the *Get Writing!* Book.

1. Ask Partner 1s to:
   - choose and say one of the Red or Green Words, then cover it up
   - help their partner to write the word in their exercise book
   - look back at the listed word and help their partner tick/correct the spelling of each sound.

2. Ask partners to swap after each word, so that each partner writes five words.

[GW] **Grammar**

1. Tell (or remind) children what an **apostrophe** looks like (a comma in the air). **TOL** about how an apostrophe can show that some letters are missing in words. When we push two words together, we sometimes drop one or two letters, but an apostrophe shows the place of the missing letters.

2. On the board write *I am* and *I'm.* Use **MTYT** to say each word. Point out that the apostrophe shows where the letter *a* has been dropped. If appropriate to the year group, use the word 'contraction' to explain this shortening of words.

3. Ask children to complete the Grammar activity on p.7 of their *Get Writing!* Book.

4. Ask children to **TTYP** to check if they have written the same words and if not, to discuss which answers are correct and why.

5. Tell children the correct responses and explain any difficult points. (They should have written: *I am, I will, he is* or *he has, it is* or *it has.*)

Vocabulary

1. Explain that good writers try to develop a wide vocabulary and use a variety of words to make their writing more interesting for the reader.

2. Write *hot, warm* and *cold* on the board. Tell children that two of these words have quite similar meanings, but the other one doesn't. Ask them to **TTYP** to decide which is the odd one out *(cold).*

3. Ask children to turn to the Vocabulary activity on p.7 of their *Get Writing!* Book. Talk through the activity, explaining any words that they are unsure of. Then ask children to complete the activity.

4. Ask children to **TTYP** to check if they have underlined the same words and if not, to discuss which answer is correct and why.

5. Tell children the correct responses and explain any difficult points. (They should have underlined: *run, slip, sleep, happy, glad* and *fit*.)

 Proofread – Spelling

1. Display the sentences on screen (online file 5.2e) and read them aloud.

2. Ask partners to spot the errors.

3. Take feedback and show how to correct the errors.

4. Hide the sentences and ask children to correct the sentences in their *Get Writing!* Book on p.8.

5. Display the sentences written correctly and help children check their own corrections.

 Proofread – Grammar

Use online file 5.2f. Follow as for the Proofread – Spelling activity.

 Write About Being Ill

Note that this activity should be started on Day 4 and completed on Day 5.

1. **TOL** about your own experience of waking up feeling really poorly. Describe how you ached all over, felt really hot and tired, and how thirsty you were. **TTYP:** Have you ever woken up and felt terrible? Which bits of you ached? Were you hot or cold? Did you feel thirsty? Did you feel sick? Did you have spots? Were you itchy?

2. Use online file 5.2 (tab g onwards) for this activity. Tell children they are going to write a diary entry about being ill. Ask them to turn to p.8 in their *Get Writing!* Book. Point out the clocks showing different times of the day on pp.8–9. Explain that they are going to talk about how they feel at each time and what happens.

3. Ask children to imagine they have just woken up. It is 7 o'clock. Mum is shouting for them to get up, but they can't. They feel awful. Ask children to Freeze Frame how they look, e.g. *droopy eyes, sad mouth, sleepy, heavy head.* **TTYP:** How do you feel? Use **MTYT** to build children's responses into sentences, e.g. *At 7 o'clock I wake up feeling very sick and hot.*

4. **TOL** about how you complete the first sentence. Repeat it a few times, then use the online file (tab g) to model how to write it. Keep re-reading as you write to ensure it makes sense. Ask children to **TTYP:** What do you say to Mum when she calls for you to get up? Model how to add this to the first sentence, e.g. *At 7 o'clock I wake up feeling very sick and hot. I say to Mum, "I don't want to get out of bed. I feel poorly."*

5. Hide your writing. Ask children to practise their own sentences aloud with their partner until they can remember them. Select a few partners to say their sentences to the group. Then children can write their own sentences on p.8 of their *Get Writing!* Book. Point out the Useful words box in their *Get Writing!* Book. Encourage children to spell new words using their phonic knowledge. Accept phonically-plausible spellings.

6. Repeat Steps 3, 4 and 5 (ask each question, demonstrate how you write, then ask children to write) with the different times on pp.8–9 of the *Get Writing!* Book, as children write their own diary entries.

Handwriting

Follow the handwriting lesson plan on pp.25–28 to review Stage 2/3 handwriting.

> **Daily Speed Sounds Lesson**
>
> 1. Review one Set 3 Speed Sound with a particular focus on spelling. See pp.40–51.
>
> 2. Review Set 2 and 3 Speed Sounds. See pp.33–51.

Spell Test

1. Choose one of the Red or Green Words listed in the panels on p.7 of the *Get Writing!* Book. Say it aloud and ask children to write it in their exercise book. Remind them to use Fred Fingers if necessary.

2. Write the word on the board.

3. Ask children to tick/correct the spelling of each sound.

4. Repeat with the other nine listed words.

 ## Write About Being Ill (continued)

Complete the writing activity started on Day 4.

Partner Proofread

1. Remind children of the proofreading activity they did on Day 4. **TTYP**: What sort of things do we check when we proofread our work?

2. Share responses and note features to check on the board. These may include:

    – spaces between words

    – capital letters (**TOL** – at the start of a sentence, for proper nouns and the pronoun *I*)

    – full stops (**TOL** – at the end of a sentence)

    – question marks or exclamation marks (**TOL** – to show a question or exclamation)

    – spelling.

3. If necessary, model how to correct a sentence that contains common errors made by the class. Do not use any of the children's work, but create your own sentence to correct.

4. Ask Partner 1s to place their exercise book on top of Partner 2's. Tell partners they have three minutes to proofread Partner 1's writing, together. Encourage Partner 1s to mark any corrections in their own exercise book.

5. Repeat for Partner 2's work.

 ## Words to Keep

Ask children to re-read their writing and select the words they are most proud of, or words they might want to use again. Then ask them to write these in the 'Words to keep' section on p.9 of their *Get Writing!* Book.

Linked Text

Read the linked text for the next Storybook.

Tom Thumb

Teacher's Preparation

Prepare as for p.56. Print out and display the Story Green Words (see online file '5.3 Tom Thumb', starting with tab a): *Tom Thumb, in fact, thumb, wrong, gulp, bank, rod, string, chef*, guest*, matchbox, elastic, insects, velvet, banquet, goblet, splendid, among*, finches, visiting, spotted, presented.*

Note that Challenge Words are marked with an asterisk.

Display these Red Word Cards in your pocket chart: *small, was, to, do, said, of, what, their.*

DAY 1

Day 1 timetable	a. Daily Speed Sounds Lesson	g. **Story Introduction**
See guidance below for activities in **bold**. See pp.56–58 for other Day 1 activities.	b. Speed Sounds from the Storybook	h. First Read – Children
	c. Story Green Words	i. Read Aloud – Teacher
	d. Speedy Green Words (online file 5.3b)	j. **Red Rhythms – Spelling Red Words**
	e. Red Word Cards	k. Handwriting
	f. Partner Practice	

Story Introduction

This is the story of Tom Thumb, who was so small that he was barely the size of a man's thumb. He used a matchbox as a bed and an eggcup as a bath. When he got dressed, he wore a button as a cap, an elastic band as a belt and a tiny jacket, which he borrowed from a doll.

Tom Thumb loved to play outside with the insects. He would skip along the bank of the pond, where he chatted to the finches and visited the frogs.

One day, when he was jumping into the pond with his frog friends, a big fish spotted him, and gulped him up, thinking he would make a tasty snack.

"Help!" yelled Tom Thumb from inside the fish's tummy, but no one heard him.

Not long after, a man caught the fish with his rod and sold it to the King's chef. As he cut it open to prepare it for a banquet, out stepped tiny Tom Thumb.

The chef thought for a while about what he could do with the tiny boy, before he had an idea: 'Maybe I could put him into a dish for the King!'

TTYP: What do you think the King will say when he finds Tom Thumb in his dish?

Red Rhythms – Spelling Red Words See *Get Writing! Yellow*, p.11.

DAY 2

Day 2 timetable	a. Daily Speed Sounds Lesson	f. Second Read – Children
See guidance below for activities in **bold**. See pp.58–60 for other Day 2 activities.	b. Speedy Green Words (online file 5.3b)	g. **Fred Fingers – Spelling Green Words**
	c. Red Word Cards	h. Red Rhythms
	d. Partner Practice	i. **Hold a Sentence – 1 and 2**
	e. Jump-in	j. Handwriting

Fred Fingers – Spelling Green Words See *Get Writing!* Book, p.11.

Hold a Sentence – 1 and 2

> **1** He skipped with the insects and chatted with the frogs.

> **2** Get me out of this fish!

See *Get Writing!* Book, p.10.

Day 3 timetable	a. Daily Speed Sounds Lesson	e. Questions to Talk About
See guidance below for activities in **bold**. See pp.60–61 for other Day 3 activities.	b. Partner Practice	f. Questions to Read and Answer
	c. Think About the Story	**g. Build a Sentence**
	d. Third Read – Children	h. Handwriting

 Think About the Story

p.9 TOL about the size of Tom Thumb.

p.10 TOL about what he wore and did for fun.

p.11 TOL about what happened when Tom was visiting the frogs.
Freeze Frame Tom's expression as he is snapped up by the fish.
TTYP: What is he feeling and why? *Shock/ Fear and terror because he might die.*
TOL about how awful it must be to be in the fish's tummy. Speculate on what might happen next.

p.13 TOL about what the King's chef decides to do with Tom.

p.14 TOL about what the King wants Tom to do for him.
MTYT (with feeling – as the King): *"What a **splendid little chap**! He can do **tricks** for my **guests** when I have a **banquet**!"*

p.15 TOL about what Tom might be thinking as he performs for the King.
TTYP: Will Tom Thumb be happy staying with the King?

  Build a Sentence

Tell children that tomorrow they are going to write a poster to help find Tom Thumb. Explain that today you are going to help children build up a sentence to describe him.

1. Display the picture (online file 5.3d). Say the simple sentence: *Tom Thumb is small.*

2. Use **MTYT** each time you expand the sentence using the children's ideas. **TTYP:** How small is Tom Thumb? Draw out responses such as *tiny/teeny weeny/pocket-sized.* Model how to build the children's ideas into the sentence, e.g. *Tom Thumb is tiny.*

3. **TTYP:** What things are the same size as Tom Thumb? For example, *eggcup/matchbox/teaspoon/ tomato/potato/apple.* Demonstrate how to incorporate the children's ideas into the sentence, e.g. *Tom Thumb is as tiny as a teaspoon.*

4. Ask partners to decide on their own sentence and to practise saying it until they can remember it. Select a few partners to say their sentences to the group.

5. Ask children to write their own sentence on p.10 of their *Get Writing!* Book. Encourage children to spell new words using their phonic knowledge. Accept phonically-plausible spellings.

Day 4 timetable	a. Daily Speed Sounds Lesson	e. Proofread – Spelling
See guidance below for activities in **bold**. See pp.61–63 for other Day 4 activities.	b. Spell Check	f. Proofread – Grammar
	c. Grammar	**g. Write a Poster For Tom Thumb**
	d. Vocabulary	h. Handwriting

Grammar

1. Tell (or remind) children when to use capital letters (e.g. at the start of a sentence, for people's names, for the word *I*). Write a few lowercase letters on the board and ask children to write the equivalent capital letters – either on the board or in their exercise books.

2. Ask children to complete the Grammar activity on p.11 of their *Get Writing!* Book.

3. Ask children to **TTYP** to check if they have circled the same words and if not, to discuss which answers are correct and why.

4. Tell children the correct responses and explain any difficult points. (They should have circled: *Tom, Thumb, The, Ben, King, Fred, What, I.*)

 Vocabulary

1. Explain that good writers try to develop a wide vocabulary and use a variety of words to make their writing more interesting for the reader.

2. Write *cut* on the board. Use **MTYT** to say the word. Give the context of the word in the story: *The king's chef cut the fish up.* Write three more words adjacent to *cut*, e.g. *ate, smelt, chopped.* Ask children to **TTYP** to decide which one means the same as *cut (chopped).*

3. Ask children to turn to the Vocabulary activity on p.11 of their *Get Writing!* Book. Talk through the activity, explaining any words that they are unsure of. Then ask children to complete the activity.

4. Ask children to **TTYP** to check if they have circled the same words and if not, to discuss which answer is correct and why.

5. Tell children the correct responses and explain any difficult points. (They should have circled: *talked, put, tugged, shouted, stunned.*)

 Write a Poster for Tom Thumb

Note that this activity should be started on Day 4 and completed on Day 5.

1. **TOL** about how you felt when you lost a pet. **TTYP:** Have you lost anything precious to you? How did you feel when you lost it? For example, *panicky, worried, sad, cross.*

2. Use online file 5.3 (tab g onwards) for this activity. Explain to children that they are going to write a poster. Tell them that Tom Thumb is lost. His mum is very worried about him and she needs help to write a poster to try to find him. Display the online file (tab g) and read the first line: *Please help me find Tom Thumb.* Ask children to turn to p.12 in their *Get Writing!* Book.

3. Ask children to imagine they are Tom's mum answering questions from the police. **TTYP:** Why are you worried about Tom Thumb? Draw out responses such as *I am worried because... he's so small birds might peck him/cats might catch him/feet might step on him.* Encourage children to expand their ideas beyond what happens in the story. Repeat with all the questions on pp.12–13 of the *Get Writing!* Book, using **MTYT** to create full sentences based on children's ideas.

4. Go back to the first question and use the online file (tab g) to model how to write one of the children's responses on the board. **TOL** as you write and keep re-reading it to make sure it makes sense.

5. Hide your writing. Read out the first question again and ask children to respond with their partners. Ask partners to decide on their first sentence and to say it aloud until they can remember it. Select a few partners to say their sentences to the group. Then children can write their own sentence in their *Get Writing!* Book, where they will also find a box of Useful words. Encourage children to spell new words using their phonic knowledge. Accept phonically-plausible spellings.

6. Repeat Steps 4 and 5 (demonstrate how you write, then ask children to write) with all the questions, so that children complete the poster.

DAY 5	**Day 5 timetable**	a. Daily Speed Sounds Lesson	d. Partner Proofread
	See Day 4 for guidance on the activity in **bold**. See pp.63–64 for other Day 5 activities.	b. Spell Test	e. Words to Keep
		c. Write a Poster For Tom Thumb (continued)	f. Linked Text

 Write A Poster for Tom Thumb (continued)

On Day 5, children continue the writing activity that they began on Day 4.

The gingerbread man

Teacher's Preparation

Prepare as for p.56. Print out and display the Story Green Words (see online file '5.4 The gingerbread man', starting with tab a): *test, fresh, crisp, cloth, felt like lead, currants, buttons, crafty, dusty, oven*, gingerbread*, finished, winked, pulled, sniffed, lifted, sticky, gasped, grinned, licked.*

Note that Challenge Words are marked with an asterisk.

Display these Red Word Cards in your pocket chart: *to, was, her, said, you, of, they, their.*

You may like to bring in a gingerbread man to show the children.

DAY 1

Day 1 timetable	a. Daily Speed Sounds Lesson	**g. Story Introduction**
See guidance below for activities in **bold**. See pp.56–58 for other Day 1 activities.	b. Speed Sounds from the Storybook	h. First Read – Children
	c. Story Green Words	i. Read Aloud – Teacher
	d. Speedy Green Words (online file 5.4b)	**j. Red Rhythms – Spelling Red Words**
	e. Red Word Cards	k. Handwriting
	f. Partner Practice	

Story Introduction

One day, Ann and Seth decided to make gingerbread men. They rolled the dough between their fingers to make the hands, the legs and the head, and used currants to make the buttons. Then they laid them out on a tin tray and flattened them with a rolling pin. As Seth pushed the tin into the hot oven, the last gingerbread man winked, but Seth was so busy he didn't notice.

When the gingerbread men were fresh out of the oven, Seth put them on the side to cool and went to read his paper. As he left the room, the last gingerbread man peeled his sticky head off the bottom of the tin. He stood up, jumped out of the tin and onto the floor, and ran as fast as he could out of the kitchen.

Seth and Ann gasped. "Stop!" they yelled, but the gingerbread man ran on. Seth and Ann raced after him, running like the wind.

"Run, run, as fast as you can! You can't catch me. I'm the gingerbread man!" he sang.

Seth and Ann chased him across fields and over hills, slipping under fences and jumping over hedges. They ran so fast that their legs felt like lead. Finally, they stopped to rest.

The gingerbread man kept running until he came face to face with a crafty old fox.

"Stop!" yelled the fox, licking his lips. "Let me help you, gingerbread man!"

TTYP: How do you think the fox might trick the gingerbread man?

Red Rhythms – Spelling Red Words See *Get Writing! Yellow*, p.15.

DAY 2

Day 2 timetable	a. Daily Speed Sounds Lesson	f. Second Read – Children
See guidance below for activities in **bold**. See pp.58–60 for other Day 2 activities.	b. Speedy Green Words (online file 5.4b)	**g. Fred Fingers – Spelling Green Words**
	c. Red Word Cards	h. Red Rhythms
	d. Partner Practice	**i. Hold a Sentence – 1 and 2**
	e. Jump-in	j. Handwriting

Fred Fingers – Spelling Green Words See *Get Writing!* Book, p.15.

Hold a Sentence – 1 and 2

1 He jumped out of the tin and ran from the kitchen.

2 He stopped running and looked at the fox.

See *Get Writing!* Book, p.14.

Day 3 timetable	a. Daily Speed Sounds Lesson	e. Questions to Talk About
See guidance below for activities in **bold**. See pp.60–61 for other Day 3 activities.	b. Partner Practice	f. Questions to Read and Answer
	c. Think About the Story	**g. Build a Sentence**
	d. Third Read – Children	h. Handwriting

 Think About the Story

p.9 TOL about why Seth doesn't notice the last gingerbread man wink.

p.10 TOL about what Seth does after he gets the gingerbread men out of the oven.

p.11 Freeze Frame Seth's expression when he sees the gingerbread man jump up. TTYP: How is Seth feeling and why? *Amazed/Shocked/Cross.*

pp.12–13 TOL about what the gingerbread man does and says.
MTYT (with feeling): *"Run, run, as fast as you can! You can't catch me. I am the gingerbread man!"*

p.13 Who helped Seth and Ann chase the gingerbread man? TTYP: Why did the gingerbread man keep on running?

p.14 TOL about what the fox offers and why the gingerbread man accepts.

p.15 TOL about what the fox is going to do with the gingerbread man.
TTYP: Do you think the gingerbread man is clever or foolish? Explain why.

  Build a Sentence

Tell children that tomorrow they will write about what happened to the gingerbread man. Explain that today you are going to help them build up a sentence in role as the gingerbread man as he runs away.

1. Display the picture of the runaway gingerbread man (online file 5.4d). Say the simple sentence: *You can't catch me.*

2. **TTYP:** Where do you go? For example, *over hills/through woods/across a river/up a tower/into the bushes/under fences/across fields/along a train track.* Use ideas to build up the sentence, e.g. *You can't catch me as I run under fences and race through the woods.* Encourage children to add as many ideas as they can.

3. Ask partners to decide on their own sentence and to practise saying it until they can remember it. Select a few partners to say their sentences to the group.

4. Ask children to write their own sentence on p.14 of their *Get Writing!* Book. Encourage children to spell new words using their phonic knowledge. Accept phonically-plausible spellings.

Day 4 timetable	a Daily Speed Sounds Lesson	e. Proofread – Spelling
See guidance below for activities in **bold**. See pp.61–63 for other Day 4 activities.	b. Spell Check	f. Proofread – Grammar
	c. Grammar	**g. Write About the Gingerbread Man**
	d. Vocabulary	h. Handwriting

Grammar

1. Tell (or remind) children that when we are writing about things that happened in the past, we add the suffix -ed to the end of some verbs.

2. On the board write *I look at my friend.* Use **MTYT** to say the sentence. Use **TTYP** for children to identify the verb *(look)*. Point out how this is in the present tense. Demonstrate how to turn the verb into the past tense by adding -ed *(looked)*.

3. Ask children to complete the Grammar activity on p.15 of their *Get Writing!* Book.

4. Ask children to **TTYP** to check if they have written the same words and if not, to discuss which answers are correct and why.

5. Tell children the correct responses and explain any difficult points. (They should have written the words: *jumped, walked, ran.*)

 Vocabulary

1. Explain that good writers try to develop a wide vocabulary and use a variety of words to make their writing more interesting for the reader.

2. Tell (or remind) children that **adjectives** can describe people, animals or things. Use **MTYT** to say the sentences: *The first tortoise was slow. The second tortoise was slower. The third tortoise was the slowest.* Point out how the endings -er and -est help us to compare things.

3. Ask children to turn to the Vocabulary activity on p.15 of their *Get Writing!* Book. Talk through the activity, explaining any words that they are unsure of. Then ask children to complete the activity.

4. Ask children to **TTYP** to check if they have written the same words and if not, to discuss which are correct and why.

5. Tell children the correct responses and explain any difficult points. (Children should have written: *fastest; colder, coldest.*)

Write About the Gingerbread Man

Note that this activity should be started on Day 4 and completed on Day 5.

1. **TOL** about when you have had to run to catch something or to get somewhere in time, e.g. to catch a bus, a dog, your little brother or sister at the park, getting to school on time. Explain how you felt, e.g. *out of breath, tired, a sense of urgency.* **TTYP:** When have you had to run quickly? What did you feel?

2. Use online file 5.4 (tab g onwards) for this activity. Tell the children that Seth has returned home without finding the gingerbread man. His mother comes to visit him later in the evening and she asks him lots of questions about what happened. Ask children to take on the role of Seth, telling the story of his day while you play the role of Seth's mum. Explain that after the talk, children will write down their own account of what happened to the gingerbread man. Ask children to turn to p.16 in their *Get Writing!* Book.

3. Ask the first question and encourage children to respond orally. Prompt them to expand their answers into full sentences and to add extra detail with their own ideas. Continue to talk through all the questions, using **MTYT** to create full sentences based on children's ideas.

4. Go back to the first question and use the online file (tab g) to model how to write one of the children's responses on the board. **TOL** as you refer to some of the Useful words on p.16 of the *Get Writing!* Book. Keep re-reading the sentence as you write to make sure it makes sense.

5. Hide your writing. Ask children to discuss their first sentence with their partner and say it aloud until they can remember it. Select a few partners to say their sentences to the group. Then children can write their own sentence on p.16 of their *Get Writing!* Book. (Encourage them to not to simply copy your sentence, but to create their own.) Point out the Useful words and encourage children to use some of these words in their writing. Encourage children to spell new words using their phonic knowledge. Accept phonically-plausible spellings.

6. Repeat Steps 4 and 5 (demonstrate how you write, then ask children to write) with all the questions on pp.16–17 of the *Get Writing!* Book, modelling possible responses for as long as children need support.

Day 5 timetable	a. Daily Speed Sounds Lesson	d. Partner Proofread
See Day 4 for guidance on the activity in **bold**. See pp.63–64 for other Day 5 activities.	b. Spell Test	e. Words to Keep
	c. Write About the Gingerbread Man (continued)	f. Linked Text

GW **Write About the Gingerbread Man (continued)**

On Day 5, children continue the writing activity that they began on Day 4.

Robin Hood

Teacher's Preparation

Prepare as for p.56. Print out and display the Story Green Words (see online file '5.5 Robin Hood', starting with tab a): *Robin Hood, band of Merry Men, John* Little, poor, crook, brags, sprang, strength*, bridge*, rooks, brook, contest, arrow, grunted, gasped, whacked, happened.*
Note that Challenge Words are marked with an asterisk.
Display these Red Word Cards in your pocket chart: *your, who, tall, you, of, to, want, they, said, call, all, one, was, are.*

DAY 1	**Day 1 timetable**	a. Daily Speed Sounds Lesson	**g. Story Introduction**
	See guidance below for activities in **bold**. See pp.56–58 for other Day 1 activities.	b. Speed Sounds from the Storybook	h. First Read – Children
		c. Story Green Words	i. Read Aloud – Teacher
		d. Speedy Green Words (online file 5.5b)	**j. Red Rhythms – Spelling Red Words**
		e. Red Word Cards	k. Handwriting
		f. Partner Practice	

Story Introduction

Robin Hood lived in the woods with his band of Merry Men. He spent his days robbing from rich people and giving what he stole from them to poor people. The poor people loved him but the rich people thought he was a crook.

One day a man called John Little was bragging to his friends. "I could win any sort of contest with the famous Robin Hood," he boasted. His friends just laughed. Not long after, John Little came face to face with Robin Hood when he was crossing a wooden bridge above a fast-running brook. When Robin tried to pass, John would not let him.

"Let me get past, will you?" Robin asked politely.

"I will not," grunted John.

"I will shoot an arrow at your chest!" Robin told him, taking an arrow from his belt.

But John shook his head. He told Robin Hood they could have a contest, but with sticks, not arrows, to make it a fair fight. "I will set upon you, and I will win!" John bragged.

TTYP: Who do you think won the contest, and why?

Red Rhythms – Spelling Red Words See *Get Writing! Yellow*, p.19.

DAY 2	**Day 2 timetable**	a. Daily Speed Sounds Lesson	f. Second Read – Children
	See guidance below for activities in **bold**. See pp.58–60 for other Day 2 activities.	b. Speedy Green Words (online file 5.5b)	**g. Fred Fingers – Spelling Green Words**
		c. Red Word Cards	h. Red Rhythms
		d. Partner Practice	**i. Hold a Sentence – 1 and 2**
		e. Jump-in	j. Handwriting

Fred Fingers – Spelling Green Words See *Get Writing!* Book, p.19.

Hold a Sentence – 1 and 2

> **1** Let me get past!

> **2** Will you put that arrow back and get a stick?

See *Get Writing!* Book, p.18.

See *Get Writing!* Book, p.18.

DAY 3

Day 3 timetable	a. Daily Speed Sounds Lesson	e. Questions to Talk About
See guidance below for activities in **bold**. See pp.60–61 for other Day 3 activities.	b. Partner Practice	f. Questions to Read and Answer
	c. Think About the Story	**g. Build a Sentence**
	d. Third Read – Children	h. Handwriting

 Think About the Story

p.9 TOL about what Robin Hood did for the poor and why the rich thought he was a crook.
TOL about why John Little wanted to have a contest with Robin Hood.

p.10 TOL about how John and Robin met. Freeze Frame Robin's expression when he saw the size of John Little.
TTYP: How was he feeling? *Surprised at his size.*

p.11 TOL about why John wanted Robin to put down his arrow.
Freeze Frame John's expression.
TTYP: How was he feeling and why? *Determined but jolly. He wanted to test his strength against Robin Hood, but he wasn't a bad man.*

pp.12–13 TOL about who won the contest and how they became friends.

p.14 TOL about why Robin wanted John to join the Merry Men.
MTYT (with feeling): *"A man who can win a contest with **me** is a good man to have for a pal."*

p.15 Freeze Frame Robin's expression.
TTYP: How was he feeling and why? *Pleased to have a new friend/Pleased to have more in his band of Merry Men.*
Freeze Frame John's expression.
TTYP: How was he feeling and why? *Glad to have a new friend/Pleased to be part of the Merry Men.*

  Build a Sentence

Tell children that tomorrow they will write about an argument with someone. Explain that today you are going to help them build up some sentences that could be used in an argument.

1. Display the picture of a brother and sister arguing (online file 5.5d). Explain that this brother and sister are always arguing and their dad gets fed up with listening to them. He always hears: *It's not me, it's him* or *It's not me, it's her!* Ask children to repeat these sentences.

2. Take on the role of Dad and ask partners to take on the role of the brother and sister: *What are you two arguing about now?* Draw out responses such as *She/He… took more cake than me/won't take turns with the TV controls/broke her promise/took up too much room on the sofa/pulled a face at me/won't walk to school with me/won't let me play/took my dish/said I was mean.*

3. Model how to build some responses into the sentences, e.g. *It's not me, it's her! She took more cake than me.* Encourage children to add more reasons, e.g. *It's not me, it's her! She took more cake than me and then she pulled a face at me.*

4. Ask partners to decide on their own sentences and to practise saying them until they can remember them. Select a few partners to say their sentences to the group.

5. Ask children to write their own sentences on p.18 of their *Get Writing!* Book. Encourage children to spell new words using their phonic knowledge. Accept phonically-plausible spellings.

Day 4 timetable	a. Daily Speed Sounds Lesson	e. Proofread – Spelling
See guidance below for activities in **bold**. See pp.61–63 for other Day 4 activities.	b. Spell Check	f. Proofread – Grammar
	c. Grammar	**g. Write About Falling Out**
	d. Embolden	h. Handwriting

Grammar

1. Tell (or remind) children that a **prefix** is a group of letters that we add to the start of a word to make a new word.

2. Write the word *kind* on the board. Use **MTYT** to say the word, then ask children to **TTYP** to say what it means *(friendly/generous/caring/helpful)*. Now write the word *unkind* on the board. Use **MTYT** to say the word, then ask children to **TTYP** to say what that means. Draw out that it means the opposite of *kind*. Point out that adding the prefix un- to a word changes it to the opposite meaning, and give a few more examples in sentences, such as: *unwrap, undress*.

3. Ask children to complete the Grammar activity on p.19 of their *Get Writing!* Book.

4. Ask children to **TTYP** to check if they have written the same words and if not, to discuss which answers are correct and why.

5. Tell children the correct responses and explain any difficult points. (They should have added these new words: *unwell, unpacked, unhappy, unlock*.)

Vocabulary

1. Explain that good writers try to develop a wide vocabulary and use a variety of words to make their writing interesting for the reader.

2. On the board write the word *said*. Use **MTYT** to say the word. Ask children to **TTYP** to think of other words that could be used instead of *said*. (Draw out examples such as *bragged/called/shouted/whispered/grunted/yelled/sniggered/cried/giggled*.)

3. Write on the board *"I will win," said John.* Ask children to **TTYP** to decide what you could write instead of *said* in this sentence, e.g. *bragged/boasted/shouted/laughed.* Show how other words bring extra meaning to the sentence, e.g. *"I will win," boasted John* – using *boasted* shows that John is confident and proud.

4. Ask children to turn to the Vocabulary activity on p.19 of their *Get Writing!* Book. Talk through the activity, explaining any words that they are unsure of. Then ask children to complete the activity.

5. Ask children to **TTYP** to check if they have written the same words and if not, to discuss which are correct and why.

6. Tell children the correct responses and explain any difficult points. (Children should have written: *grunted, yelled, giggled, asked*.)

Write About Falling Out

Note that this activity should be started on Day 4 and completed on Day 5.

1. **TOL** about your own experiences of arguing with a brother or sister or friend when you were young. Tell children about the silly things you used to argue about, how sometimes you didn't speak to each other for hours or even days afterwards but how you made up in the end. **TTYP:** What sort of things do you argue about with your brother or sister or friend? How do you make up in the end?

2. Use online file 5.5 (tab g onwards) for this activity. Explain to children that they are going to write a story about arguing with a brother or sister. **TTYP:** What is the name of your brother or sister, in the story? Ask children to turn to p.20 in the *Get Writing!* Book.

3. Ask children the first question: How did the argument begin? Draw out responses and use **MTYT** to create sentences such as *It began when he wanted to use my new football but I said no because I knew he would lose it.* Ask children: What did they do to annoy you? Use **MTYT** to encourage them to build on the first sentence to show how the argument escalated, e.g. *On Monday, he took my football anyway to play with his friends.*

4. Use the online file (tab g) to model how to write the first sentences. **TOL** as you write, and keep re-reading to make sure it makes sense.

5. Hide your writing. Ask children to practise their own sentences aloud with their partner until they can remember them. Select a few partners to say their sentences to the group. Then children can write their own sentences on p.20 of their *Get Writing!* Book. Point out the Useful words on p.20 of their *Get Writing!* Book. Encourage children to spell new words using their phonic knowledge. Accept phonically-plausible spellings.

6. Repeat Steps 3, 4 and 5 (ask each question, demonstrate how you write, then ask children to write) until children have completed their story.

DAY 5

Day 5 timetable	a. Daily Speed Sounds Lesson	d. Partner Proofread
See Day 4 for guidance on the activity in **bold**. See pp.63–64 for other Day 5 activities.	b. Spell Test	e. Words to Keep
	c. Write About Falling Out (continued)	f. Linked Text

GW **Write About Falling Out (continued)**

On Day 5, children continue the writing activity that they began on Day 4.

Lost

Teacher's Preparation

Prepare as for p.56. Print out and display the Story Green Words (see online file '5.6 Lost', starting with tab a): *Kay West, Ray Brooks, Jay, plump, check, sheds, stray, hay, shock, fond, glad, kiss, string, grey*, visit, Catkin, Malaya, playful, praying.*
Note that Challenge Words are marked with an asterisk.
Display these Red Word Cards in your pocket chart: *they, call, all, are, your, you, her, what, do, to, brother, of, were.*

DAY 1

Day 1 timetable	a. Daily Speed Sounds Lesson	**g. Story Introduction**
See guidance below for activities in **bold**. See pp.56–58 for other Day 1 activities.	b. Speed Sounds from the Storybook	h. First Read – Children
	c. Story Green Words	i. Read Aloud – Teacher
	d. Speedy Green Words (online file 5.6b)	**j. Red Rhythms – Spelling Red Words**
	e. Red Word Cards	k. Handwriting
	f. Partner Practice	

Story Introduction

Kay West lives at 24 Clayton Villas. One day she found a grey mouse hiding under her fridge. She tried to pick it up and put it outside, but it ran between her feet and disappeared under the sofa.
  "I'll get a cat," she decided, "to keep the mouse away."
  Kay went to the pet shop. There were big cats, small cats, and cats of all different colours. She spotted a playful plump black cat purring in the corner of the room.
  "What's that one called?" she asked the lady in the pet shop.
  "Catkin," she told her.
  Catkin was just right. As soon as Kay brought Catkin home, the mouse went away.
  Kay and Catkin grew very fond of each other. Wherever Kay went, Catkin went too. If Kay was in the garden, Catkin followed. If Kay was in the kitchen, Catkin sat there too. When Kay was reading, Catkin would play with a bit of string at her feet. In the evenings they cuddled together on the sofa and watched TV. Kay fed Catkin healthy food, but soon Catkin grew even plumper.
  Then, one afternoon, Kay came home and found the house empty.
  "Where's Catkin?" she wondered.

TTYP: Where do you think Catkin could be?

Red Rhythms – Spelling Red Words See *Get Writing! Yellow*, p.23.

DAY 2

Day 2 timetable	a. Daily Speed Sounds Lesson	f. Second Read – Children
See guidance below for activities in **bold**. See pp.58–60 for other Day 2 activities.	b. Speedy Green Words (online file 5.6b)	**g. Fred Fingers – Spelling Green Words**
	c. Red Word Cards	h. Red Rhythms
	d. Partner Practice	**i. Hold a Sentence – 1 and 2**
	e. Jump-in	j. Handwriting

Fred Fingers – Spelling Green Words See *Get Writing!* Book, p.23.

Hold a Sentence – 1 and 2

> **1** Will you let the kittens stay with me when you go on holiday?

> **2** He is very happy and playful.

See *Get Writing!* Book, p. 22.

Day 3 timetable	a. Daily Speed Sounds Lesson	e. Questions to Talk About
See guidance below for activities in **bold**. See pp.60–61 for other Day 3 activities.	b. Partner Practice	f. Questions to Read and Answer
	c. Think About the Story	**g. Build a Sentence**
	d. Third Read – Children	h. Handwriting

 Think About the Story

p.9 TOL about who has put up the 'Lost' notice and why, and where she might have pinned it up.
Freeze Frame Kay's expression as she puts up the notice.
TTYP: How is she feeling, and why? *Frantic/Worried because Catkin might be in danger or lost.*

pp.10–11 TOL about how Ray finds Catkin in his shed – what he sees in bed with Catkin.
TTYP: How does Ray feel? *Surprised to find the kittens and pleased to find Catkin.*
Freeze Frame Kay's expression.
TTYP: How is she feeling? *Relieved/Happy.*

MTYT (with feeling): **Hooray**! Today is **such** a happy day! Thank you **so much** for finding my Catkin! It's what I was praying for!

p.12 TOL about what Ray is asking Kay in his letter.

p.13 TOL about what Kay wants to know about Catkin and the kittens, and where she posts the postcard from.

p.14 TOL about why Ray thinks the grey kitten should stay with him.

p.15 TOL about what Kay says she will do to help Ray.

  Build a Sentence

Tell children that tomorrow they will write a letter (in the role of Ray) telling a friend about his new kitten. Explain that today you are going to help them build up a sentence describing a new kitten.

1. Display the picture of the kitten (online file 5.6d). **MTYT:** *I've got a kitten.*

2. **TTYP:** What does it look like? Ask children to describe kittens, drawing out responses such as *grey/tabby/white/black/brown eyes/tiny/long-haired.* Demonstrate how to build some of the children's responses into the original sentence, e.g. *I've got a black kitten with big eyes.*

3. **TTYP:** What does it feel like? For example, *soft/cuddly/silky/smooth/spiky claws.* Expand the original sentence further, e.g. *I've got a silky black kitten with big eyes.*

4. Ask partners to decide on their own sentence and to practise saying it until they can remember it. Select a few partners to say their sentences to the group.

5. Ask children to write their own sentence on p.22 of their *Get Writing!* Book. Encourage children to spell new words using their phonic knowledge. Accept phonically-plausible spellings.

Day 4 timetable	a. Daily Speed Sounds Lesson	e. Proofread – Spelling
See guidance below for activities in **bold**. See pp.61–63 for other Day 4 activities.	b. Spell Check	f. Proofread – Grammar
	c. Grammar	**g. Write About the New Kitten**
	d. Vocabulary	h. Handwriting

GW **Grammar**

1. Tell (or remind) children that *singular* means one of something, and *plural* means more than one of something.

2. On the board, write *singular* and *plural* at the top of two columns. Use **MTYT** to say these words. Write the word *dog* in the singular column and ask children to **TTYP** to say what the plural of *dog* is (*dogs*). Remind them that to make a plural we usually add -s or -es to the end of a word. If a word ends in *s* or *x* in the singular, it usually ends -es in the plural. Add these examples to the board: *fox, foxes; bus, buses*.

3. Ask children to complete the Grammar activity on p.23 of their *Get Writing!* Book.

4. Ask children to **TTYP** to check if they have written the same words and if not, to discuss which answers are correct and why.

5. Tell children the correct responses and explain any difficult points. Support children if necessary with the final answer, pointing out that it's an irregular plural which doesn't follow the usual rules. (They should have written: *cats, kittens, boxes, sheds, kisses, mice.*)

GW **Vocabulary**

1. Explain that good writers try to develop a wide vocabulary and use a variety of words to make their writing more interesting for the reader.

2. Write *contact* on the board. Use **MTYT** to say the word. Give the context of the word in the story: *If you find her, contact Kay West.* Write three more words next to *contact* (e.g. *shout, tell, buy*). Ask children to **TTYP** to say which word means the same as *contact (tell).*

3. Ask children to turn to the Vocabulary activity on p.23 of their *Get Writing!* Book. Talk through the activity, explaining any words that they are unsure of. Then ask children to complete the activity.

4. Ask children to **TTYP** to check if they have circled the same words and if not, to discuss which answers are correct and why.

5. Tell children the correct responses and explain any difficult points. (They should have circled: *fat, happy, dry grass, lost*.)

 GW **Write About the New Kitten**

Note that this activity should be started on Day 4 and completed on Day 5.

1. **TOL** about when you (or someone you know) got a new kitten. Recall how pleased you were but also how nervous you were in case it got lost or came to any harm. Remember the things you had to buy for it, e.g. a cat flap, cat food and a special saucer. Tell children how you used to creep down at night when you thought it might be lonely. **TTYP:** Have you ever held a kitten? What did it feel like? (Draw on the ideas covered in the Build a Sentence activity.)

2. Use online file 5.6 (tab g onwards) for this activity. Explain to children that they are going to write a letter in role as Ray to his friend Fred, telling him all about the new kitten. Ask children to turn to p.24 of their *Get Writing!* Book.

3. Ask children (who are in role as Ray) the first question: Where did you find the kitten? Draw out responses that range beyond the Storybook, e.g. *I found the kitten... on my doorstep/in a cupboard/shivering in the snow/hiding in some bushes in my garden.* Use **MTYT** to build children's ideas into a full sentence. Ask children the rest of the questions and gather their responses.

4. Return to the first sentence and use the online file (tab g) to model how to complete it, e.g. *I found the kitten shivering in the snow.* **TOL** as you write, and keep re-reading to make sure it makes sense.

5. Hide your writing. Ask children to practise their own first sentence aloud with their partner until they can remember it. Select a few partners to say their sentences to the group. Then children can write their own sentence on p.24 of their *Get Writing!* Book. Point out the Useful words in their *Get Writing!* Book. Encourage children to spell new words using their phonic knowledge. Accept phonically-plausible spellings.

6. Repeat Steps 4 and 5 (demonstrate how you write, then ask children to write) with all the questions, so that children complete their letter.

DAY 5

Day 5 timetable	a. Daily Speed Sounds Lesson	d. Partner Proofread
See Day 4 for guidance on the activity in **bold**. See pp.63–64 for other Day 5 activities.	b. Spell Test	e. Words to Keep
	c. Write About the New Kitten (continued)	f. Linked Text

GW **Write About the New Kitten (continued)**

On Day 5, children continue the writing activity that they began on Day 4.

Do we have to keep it?

Teacher's Preparation

Prepare as for p.56. Print out and display the Story Green Words (see online file '5.7 Do we have to keep it?', starting with tab a): *Dan Reed, heels, eel, dumps, combats, guess*, both*, wash*, insect, settee, seconds, greedy, carrot, sloppy, pretend*, almost*, sister*, every*, wheels.*
Note that Challenge Words are marked with an asterisk.
Display these Red Word Cards in your pocket chart: *want, all, one, to, do, you, I'm, I've, baby.*

DAY 1

Day 1 timetable	a. Daily Speed Sounds Lesson	g. Story Introduction
See guidance below for activities in **bold**. See pp.56–58 for other Day 1 activities.	b. Speed Sounds from the Storybook	h. First Read – Children
	c. Story Green Words	i. Read Aloud – Teacher
	d. Speedy Green Words (online file 5.7b)	j. **Red Rhythms – Spelling Red Words**
	e. Red Word Cards	k. Handwriting
	f. Partner Practice	

Story Introduction

Dan Reed lives with his mum, dad and big sister at 15 Fleetwood Street. Before Mum had a new baby, Dan did things with his family all the time. He learnt to cook with Dad and went to football matches with Mum. Best of all, he always got to choose what was on TV. But now, everyone is too busy doing things with the baby.

"Can we take the baby back to the shop?" he asks Mum.

"No!" she shouts.

Every day is the same. The baby sits on Mum's lap and twists and wriggles its body like an eel. It always needs feeding, because it's so greedy. Dan is hungry too, but he has to wait until dinnertime!

The worst part is when Mum dumps the baby on Dan's knee, because it's sick on its bib, or it wees on Dan's best combats.

When the baby is finally put in its cot to sleep, Dan thinks they can all have a bit of a rest, until he hears, "Eeeeee! Wheeee!"

TTYP: What could it be this time?

Red Rhythms – Spelling Red Words See *Get Writing! Yellow*, p.27.

DAY 2

Day 2 timetable	a. Daily Speed Sounds Lesson	f. Second Read – Children
See guidance below for activities in **bold**. See pp.58–60 for other Day 2 activities.	b. Speedy Green Words (online file 5.7b)	g. **Fred Fingers – Spelling Green Words**
	c. Red Word Cards	h. Red Rhythms
	d. Partner Practice	i. **Hold a Sentence – 1 and 2**
	e. Jump-in	j. Handwriting

Fred Fingers – Spelling Green Words See *Get Writing!* Book, p.27.

Hold a Sentence – 1 and 2

1 Mum dumps the baby on my knee.

2 I have got a funny feeling that I will miss him.

See *Get Writing!* Book, p.26.

DAY 3

Day 3 timetable	a. Daily Speed Sounds Lesson	e. Questions to Talk About
See guidance below for activities in **bold**. See pp.60–61 for other Day 3 activities.	b. Partner Practice	f. Questions to Read and Answer
	c. Think About the Story	**g. Build a Sentence**
	d. Third Read – Children	h. Handwriting

 Think About the Story

p.9 **TOL** about who is telling the story. Freeze Frame Dan's expression.
TTYP: How is he feeling, and why? *Unhappy because there is a new baby in the family.*
MTYT (with feeling): *I **did** tell Mum that I wanted a **stick insect**, but no, **she** went and got a **baby**.*

p.10 **TOL** about how Dan describes the way the baby moves.

p.11 **TOL** about what Dan thinks about how the baby eats.

p.12 **TOL** about why the baby annoys him and why he thinks his sister Sheena is a creep.

p.14 **TOL** about how Mum gets the baby to sleep – and how Dan feels when the baby wakes up.

p.15 Freeze Frame Dan's expression as he gets ready to go out.
TTYP: What does he feel and why? *Mixed feelings because he's pleased to be having time with Dad, but is actually starting to like the baby.*
TOL about what Dan has a funny feeling about in the end.

 Build a Sentence

Tell children that tomorrow they will write an email (in role as Dan) to his friend, about the new baby. Explain that today you are going to help them build up a few sentences about the new baby.

1. Display the picture of the baby (online file 5.7d). **MTYT:** *Everyone thinks babies are cute.* **TTYP:** What things do people say to babies? *Coochy coo/Who's a lovely, jubbly, bubbly baby…*

2. Display the picture of Dan. **TTYP:** What does Dan think of the baby? *He thinks it's annoying/ noisy/messy/leaky.* **TTYP:** Would Dan agree that babies are cute? *(No.)* Encourage children to respond in role as Dan, e.g. *I don't think babies are cute.*

3. **TTYP:** Why aren't babies cute? Draw out children's opinions about what annoying things babies do, e.g. *They… wee on the carpet/are sick on favourite clothes/dribble on everything/drop food everywhere/scream all night/won't sit still.* Use children's responses to build up the sentences, e.g. *I don't think babies are cute. They wee on the carpet and scream all night.*

4. Ask partners to decide on their own sentences and to practise saying them until they can remember them. Select a few partners to say their sentences to the group.

5. Ask children to write their own sentences on p.26 of their *Get Writing!* Book. Encourage children to spell new words using their phonic knowledge. Accept phonically-plausible spellings.

DAY 4	**Day 4 timetable**	a. Daily Speed Sounds Lesson	e. Proofread – Spelling
See guidance below for activities in **bold**. See pp.61–63 for other Day 4 activities.		b. Spell Check	f. Proofread – Grammar
		c. Grammar	**g. Write About the New Baby**
		d. Vocabulary	h. Handwriting

 Grammar

1. Tell (or remind) children that two sentences can be joined together using the word *and*. (Use the term 'conjunction' if appropriate to the year group.) On the board write two sentences: *I'm almost ten. I live at fifteen, Fleetwood Street.* Use **MTYT** to say both sentences. Demonstrate how to delete the full stop and add the word *and* to join the two clauses, making one longer sentence.

2. Ask children to complete the Grammar activity on p.27 of their *Get Writing!* Book. Remind them to delete the full stop, add the word *and* and that the word after *and* should begin with a small letter, unless it is the word *I* or a proper noun (the name of a person or place).

3. Ask children to **TTYP** to check if they have the same answers and if not, to discuss which answers are correct and why.

 Vocabulary

1. Explain that good writers try to develop a wide vocabulary and use a variety of words to make their writing more interesting for the reader.

2. Explain that some words have similar meanings, such as *big* and *huge*, but other words can mean the opposite of each other, such as *big* and *little*. If appropriate to the year group, use the terms 'antonyms' (words that mean the opposite of each other) and 'synonyms' (words that mean the same as each other).

3. On the board write the word *hard*. Use **MTYT** to say the word. Ask children to **TTYP** and think of a word that means the opposite. Draw out suggestions such as *soft/squashy/bouncy*.

4. Ask children to turn to the Vocabulary activity on p.27 of their *Get Writing!* Book. Talk through the activity, explaining any words that they are unsure of. Then ask children to complete the activity.

5. Ask children to **TTYP** to check if they have written the same words and if not, to discuss which are correct and why.

6. Tell children the correct responses and explain any difficult points. (They should have written: *hard, sad, last, small*.)

 Write About the New Baby

Note that this activity should be started on Day 4 and completed on Day 5.

1. **TOL** about how you (or someone else) felt about having a new baby in the house when you were young. Recall how everyone focused on the new baby and how you felt left out. **TTYP:** Do you know anyone who has a new baby in the house? How do things change when a new baby arrives?

2. Use online file 5.7 (tab g onwards) for this activity. Explain to children that they are going to write an email in role as Dan to his friend Rajeev about the new baby. Ask children to turn to p.28 of their *Get Writing!* Book.

3. Ask children (who are in role as Dan) all the questions. Encourage them to build upon the ideas in the story and to draw on their own experiences. Make this into a conversation and use **MTYT** to develop their ideas into full sentences.

   TTYP: How are you feeling and why? *I feel... grumpy/annoyed/irritable because the baby is getting all the attention.*

   TTYP: What does the baby do to annoy you? *The baby gets on my nerves. It... screams/dribbles/drops food everywhere/wees on my trousers.*

   Repeat with all the questions.

4. Return to the first question and use the online file (tab g) to model how to write the response. **TOL** as you write, and keep re-reading to make sure it makes sense.

5. Hide your writing. Ask children to practise their own first sentences aloud with their partner until they can remember them. Select a few partners to say their sentences to the group. Then children can write their own sentences on p.28 of their *Get Writing!* Book. Point out the Useful words on p.28 of their *Get Writing!* Book. Encourage children to spell new words using their phonic knowledge. Accept phonically-plausible spellings.

6. Repeat Steps 4 and 5 (demonstrate how you write, then ask children to write) with all the questions, so that children complete their email.

Day 5 timetable	a. Daily Speed Sounds Lesson	d. Partner Proofread
See Day 4 for guidance on the activity in **bold**. See pp.63–64 for other Day 5 activities.	b. Spell Test	e. Words to Keep
	c. Write About the New Baby (continued)	f. Linked Text

GW **Write About the New Baby (continued)**

On Day 5, children continue the writing activity that they began on Day 4.

Danny and the Bump-a-lump

Teacher's Preparation

Prepare as for p.56. Print out and display the Story Green Words (see online file '5.8 Danny and the Bump-a-lump', starting with tab a): *flung, knight, fluff, kind, eyes*, Danny, midnight, moonlight, settee, nightlight, daylight, supper*, under*, between, frightened, rushed, spots, cooking.*
Note that Challenge Words are marked with an asterisk.
Display these Red Word Cards in your pocket chart: *there, watch, small, what, some, of, was, to, you, I've, I'm, all.*

DAY 1

Day 1 timetable	a. Daily Speed Sounds Lesson	g. Story Introduction
See guidance below for activities in **bold**. See pp.56–58 for other Day 1 activities.	b. Speed Sounds from the Storybook	h. First Read – Children
	c. Story Green Words	i. Read Aloud – Teacher
	d. Speedy Green Words (online file 5.8b)	j. Red Rhythms – Spelling Red Words
	e. Red Word Cards	k. Handwriting
	f. Partner Practice	

Story Introduction

Danny couldn't sleep. Midnight came and he was still awake, staring into the bright moonlight. He was scared that there was something hiding under his bed. He flung back the sheet and rushed downstairs.

Mum was sitting on the sofa, watching her favourite TV programme and sipping a cup of tea. "Please go back to bed, right away!" she said angrily.

"But I've got a thing under my bed," he whined. "It's a Bump-a-lump."

Mum sighed and turned off the TV. "Is it there in the daylight," she asked, "or just in the night time?"

"Just at night," he told her, nervously. He had never seen the Bump-a-lump, but he knew it was there.

"I'm frightened of it!" he said. "Tell it to go away!"

The next night, as Danny lay in his bed, he was sure the Bump-a-lump was there again...

"Aaaaah! Help!" he screamed. He flung back the sheet and rushed off to find Mum again. She was downstairs making her supper. But this time, she gave him a way to get rid of the Bump-a-lump...

TTYP: How do you think Mum helped Danny to get rid of the Bump-a-lump?

Red Rhythms – Spelling Red Words See *Get Writing! Yellow*, p.31.

DAY 2

Day 2 timetable	a. Daily Speed Sounds Lesson	f. Second Read – Children
See guidance below for activities in **bold**. See pp.58–60 for other Day 2 activities.	b. Speedy Green Words (online file 5.8b)	g. Fred Fingers – Spelling Green Words
	c. Red Word Cards	h. Red Rhythms
	d. Partner Practice	i. Hold a Sentence – 1 and 2
	e. Jump-in	j. Handwriting

Fred Fingers – Spelling Green Words See *Get Writing!* Book, p.31.

Hold a Sentence – 1 and 2

1 Is it there in the daylight, or just in the night?

2 Tell it to go away!

See *Get Writing!* Book, p.30.

Day 3 timetable	a. Daily Speed Sounds Lesson	e. Questions to Talk About
See guidance below for activities in **bold**. See pp.60–61 for other Day 3 activities.	b. Partner Practice	f. Questions to Read and Answer
	c. Think About the Story	**g. Build a Sentence**
	d. Third Read – Children	h. Handwriting

Think About the Story

p.9 **TOL** about what Danny has under his bed.
Freeze Frame Danny's expression.
TTYP: How is he feeling, and why?

p.10 **TOL** about why Danny doesn't know what the Bump-a-lump looks like.

p.11 **TOL** about why his mum thinks he's being silly.

p.12 **TOL** about why Danny's mum tells him to go away again.

p.13 **TOL** about what Danny says the Bump-a-lump *might* look like.
MTYT (with feeling): *"But, **Mum**, I've got a **thing** under my bed! It's a **Bump-a-lump**!"*

p.14 **TOL** about what his mum does to get rid of the Bump-a-lump.

p.15 **TOL** about what is actually under Danny's bed.
Freeze Frame Mum's expression.
TTYP: How is she feeling, and why?

  Build a Sentence

Tell children that tomorrow they will write a play about being scared at night. Explain that today you are going to help them build up a sentence about something scary under the bed.

1. Display the picture of Danny thinking about what the Bump-a-lump might look like (online file 5.8d). **MTYT:** *There's a thing under my bed.*

2. **TTYP:** What size is this thing? Draw out responses, encouraging comparisons, e.g. *as big as my teddy/a tiger/as small as a mouse/cat.* Model how to build the children's ideas into the sentence, e.g. *There's a thing under my bed that's as big as a tiger.*

3. Continue to build the sentence using other questions as prompts about the colour and other features of the monster. Show how to build up the sentence using different ideas, e.g. *There's a red and blue thing under my bed that's as big as a tiger.*

4. Ask partners to decide on their own sentence and to practise saying it until they can remember it. Select a few partners to say their sentences to the group.

5. Ask children to write their own sentence on p.30 of their *Get Writing!* Book. Encourage children to spell new words using their phonic knowledge. Accept phonically-plausible spellings.

Day 4 timetable	a. Daily Speed Sounds Lesson	e. Proofread – Spelling
See guidance below for activities in **bold**. See pp.61–63 for other Day 4 activities.	b. Spell Check	f. Proofread – Grammar
	c. Grammar	**g. Write About Something Under the Bed**
	d. Vocabulary	h. Handwriting

Grammar

1. Remind children that we use full stops to show the end of a sentence.

2. On the board write this sentence, omitting the full stops: *I found Mum She was cooking supper.* Use **MTYT** to say the sentences. Explain that there are two sentences in this writing, but the full stops are missing. Ask children to use punctuation mimes (see p.20) to show you where the full stops should go (after *Mum* and *supper*). For another example, write *I slid between the sheets I shut my eyes tight.* Full stops should go after *sheets* and *tight*.

3. Ask children to complete the Grammar activity on p.31 of their *Get Writing!* Book.

4. Ask children to **TTYP** to check if they have put the full stops in the same places and if not, to discuss which places are correct.

5. Tell children the correct responses and explain any difficult points. (Full stops come after the words: *bed* and *lump*; *Danny* and *bed*; *bed* and *fluff*; *bed* and *head*.)

 Vocabulary

1. Explain that good writers try to develop a wide vocabulary and use a variety of words to make their writing more interesting for the reader.

2. Explain that sometimes we can put two words together to make another word. Write on the board: *super* and *man*. Use **MTYT** to say both words. Ask children to **TTYP** to say what word is made when we join these two words together *(superman)*. Use the term 'compound word' if appropriate to the year group.

3. Ask children to turn to the Vocabulary activity on p.31 of their *Get Writing!* Book. Talk through the activity, explaining any words that they are unsure of. Then ask children to complete the activity.

4. Ask children to **TTYP** to check if they have made any of the same compound words. (Note that there are more than four possibilities, so they may differ and still be correct.)

5. Tell children the correct responses and explain any difficult points. (Children could make the following words: *nightlight, something, daylight, someday, tonight, today.*)

 Write About Something Under the Bed

Note that this activity should be started on Day 4 and completed on Day 5.

1. **TOL** about a time when you – or someone you know – imagined that there was something living under your bed. Recall how your family didn't believe you. **TTYP:** Do you know anyone who thinks that there is a creature living under their bed?

2. Use online file 5.8 (tab g onwards) for this activity. Explain to children that they are going to write a play – like the one in the story. Remind them that in a play script, the name of the person speaking comes first, then a colon (:) and then the words that they say. Ask children to turn to p.32 of their *Get Writing!* Book.

3. Ask children the questions. You play the role of Mum, while they take on the role of Danny. Encourage children to build upon the ideas in the story and to draw on their own experiences. Make the exchanges into a conversation and use **MTYT** to develop their ideas into full sentences.

4. Go back to the first question and use the online file (tab g) to model how to write one of the children's responses on the board, e.g. *Danny: There is a monster under my bed.* **TOL** as you write, and keep re-reading to make sure it makes sense.

5. Hide your writing. Ask children to practise their own sentence aloud with their partner until they can remember it. Select a few partners to say their sentences to the group. Then children can write their own sentence on p.32 of their *Get Writing!* Book. Point out the Useful words in their *Get Writing!* Book. Encourage children to spell new words using their phonic knowledge. Accept phonically-plausible spellings.

6. Repeat Steps 4 and 5 (demonstrate how you write, then ask children to write) with the rest of the questions so that children complete their play.

DAY 5

Day 5 timetable	a. Daily Speed Sounds Lesson	d. Partner Proofread
See Day 4 for guidance on the activity in **bold**. See pp.63–64 for other Day 5 activities.	b. Spell Test	e. Words to Keep
	c. Write About Something Under the Bed (continued)	f. Linked Text

 Write About Something Under the Bed (continued)

On Day 5, children continue the writing activity that they began on Day 4.

97

Grow your own radishes

Teacher's Preparation

Prepare as for p.56. Print out and display the Story Green Words (see online file '5.9 Grow your own radishes', starting with tab a): *crop, sow, seeds, batch, sill, damp, weeds, length*, wash*, packet, shallow, compost, level, seedling, fantastic, every*, radishes, pecking, slowly, shallots, potting.* Note that Challenge Words are marked with an asterisk.

Display these Red Word Cards in your pocket chart: *their, you, your, want, some, they, are, small, of, fall*, call, any, to.*

Red Words for this book only are marked with an asterisk.

If possible, bring in some raw fruit and vegetables to make a salad, e.g. apples, cabbage, courgettes, tomatoes, carrots, peas, radishes, onions. Bring in a dressing or dip, e.g. yoghurt mixed with mayonnaise. If it is spring, you may wish to buy some radish seeds and sow them following the instructions in the book.

DAY 1	**Day 1 timetable**	a. Daily Speed Sounds Lesson	**g. Story Introduction**
	See guidance below for activities in **bold**. See pp.56–58 for other Day 1 activities.	b. Speed Sounds from the Storybook	h. First Read – Children
		c. Story Green Words	i. Read Aloud – Teacher
		d. Speedy Green Words (online file 5.9b)	**j. Red Rhythms – Spelling Red Words**
		e. Red Word Cards	k. Handwriting
		f. Partner Practice	

Story Introduction

At the start of Spring, Mel went to the garden centre to buy some seeds with her mum. Together, they looked at all the vegetables they could grow: cauliflowers, cabbages and tomatoes.

"Let's buy some radish seeds – they should be easy to grow," suggested Mel's mum. Mel liked the radish seeds: they were small, round and light brown.

When they got home, they filled a shallow plant pot with compost and sand. Then Mel started to sow the seeds. She pushed the seeds down through the soft sand, to the level of the compost. She put a sheet from a black bin bag on top to stop the birds from coming near the radishes.

Mel placed the plant pot on the windowsill in the sun. As the weeks went by, she took off the bin bag and kept watering the compost to keep it damp. She pulled out any weeds and checked the radish plants as often as she could.

The leaves grew big and bright green. After three weeks, it was time to pull the radishes out. Mel grabbed the fresh leaves and pulled until the juicy red radishes popped up. Then Mel and her mum chose what dish to make with the radishes!

This book will show you how to grow your own radishes.

TTYP: What vegetables would you like to grow?

Red Rhythms – Spelling Red Words See *Get Writing! Yellow*, p.35.

Day 2 timetable	a. Daily Speed Sounds Lesson	f. Second Read – Children
See guidance below for activities in **bold**. See pp.58–60 for other Day 2 activities.	b. Speedy Green Words (online file 5.9b)	**g. Fred Fingers – Spelling Green Words**
	c. Red Word Cards	h. Red Rhythms
	d. Partner Practice	**i. Hold a Sentence – 1 and 2**
	e. Jump-in	j. Handwriting

Fred Fingers – Spelling Green Words See *Get Writing!* Book, p.35.

 Hold a Sentence – 1 and 2

> **1** Plant the seeds in a narrow window box and put them in the sun.

> **2** Keep the compost damp and watch the seeds grow.

See *Get Writing!* Book, p.34.

Day 3 timetable	a. Daily Speed Sounds Lesson	e. Questions to Talk About
See guidance below for activities in **bold**. See pp.60–61 for other Day 3 activities.	b. Partner Practice	f. Questions to Read and Answer
	c. Think About the Story	**g. Build a Sentence**
	d. Third Read – Children	h. Handwriting

 Think About the Story

`p.9` **TOL** about how long it takes to grow your own radishes.

`p.10` **TOL** about what you need to grow your radishes.

`p.11` **TOL** about how to prepare your plant pot or window box for the radishes.

`p.12` **TOL** about the best way to plant your seeds.

`p13` **TOL** about the best place to put the radishes.

`p.15` **TOL** about what you can do with your fresh radishes.

  Build a Sentence

Tell children that tomorrow they will write some adverts for salad lunches. Explain that today you are going to help them build up a sentence about a delicious salad.

1. Display the pictures of different colourful salads (online file 5.9d). Say the simple sentence: *Have you tasted our salad?*

2. **TTYP:** What is in our salad? Draw out responses such as *cucumber/tomato/carrot/radishes/onion/lettuce/cabbage/nuts/fruit.* Demonstrate how to use some of the children's ideas to build up the sentence, e.g. *Have you tasted our cucumber and tomato salad?*

3. **TTYP:** What does it taste like? Remind children that we use **adjectives** to describe things, and display the list of adjectives. Read out the list, but encourage children to think of their own too. Demonstrate how to choose some adjectives to build into the sentence, e.g. *Have you tasted our delicious cucumber and tomato salad?*

4. Ask partners to decide on their own sentence and to practise saying it until they can remember it. Select a few partners to say their sentences to the group.

5. Ask children to write their own sentence on p.34 of their *Get Writing!* Book. Encourage children to spell new words using their phonic knowledge. Accept phonically-plausible spellings.

Day 4 timetable	a. Daily Speed Sounds Lesson	e. Proofread – Spelling
See guidance below for activities in **bold**. See pp.61–63 for other Day 4 activities.	b. Spell Check	f. Proofread – Grammar
	c. Grammar	**g. Write Adverts for Salad Lunches**
	d. Vocabulary	h. Handwriting

GW Grammar

1. Tell (or remind) children that **adjectives** can be used to describe people, places or things (nouns). Write on the board *the pink radish*. Use **MTYT** to say the phrase. Ask children to **TTYP** and point out the noun *(radish)*, and the adjective *(pink)* used to describe it.

2. Ask children to complete the Grammar activity on p.35 of their *Get Writing!* Book.

3. Ask children to **TTYP** to check if they have underlined the same words and if not, to discuss which answers are correct and why.

4. Tell children the correct responses and explain any difficult points. (They should have underlined: *shallow, damp, sunny, crunchy* and *fresh*.)

GW Vocabulary

1. Explain that good writers try to develop a wide vocabulary and use a variety of words to make their writing more interesting for the reader.

2. Write *pull* on the board. Use **MTYT** to say the word. Give the context of the word in the story: *Pull up the radishes when they are 2–3 cm long*. Write three more words next to *pull* (e.g. *tug, squash, push*). Ask children to **TTYP** to say which one means the same as *pull (tug)*.

3. Ask children to turn to the Vocabulary activity on p.35 of their *Get Writing!* Book. Talk through the activity, explaining any words that they are unsure of. Then ask children to complete the activity.

4. Ask children to **TTYP** to check if they have circled the same words and if not, to discuss which answers are correct and why.

5. Tell children the correct responses and explain any difficult points. (They should have circled: *plant, thin, small plants* and *watching*.)

GW Write Adverts for Salad Lunches

Note that this activity should be started on Day 4 and completed on Day 5.

1. Use online file 5.9 (tab g onwards) for this activity. **TOL** about how healthy school meals are now, compared to when you went to school. Talk about how there are delicious salads for children and staff every day. Tell them about your favourite salads. Display the pictures of fresh vegetables (including radishes) and fruit (tab g).

2. Explain that some children need to be persuaded to try out salads. Tell them that they are going to write some adverts to encourage children to choose a salad lunch. Remind them how important it is to eat fruit and vegetables to stay healthy. If possible, invite the school cook to talk about the salads they are going to make next week. Ask children to turn to p.36 of their *Get Writing!* Book.

3. Navigate to the next tab and show the list of adjectives. If possible, give children small pieces of raw vegetables and fruit to try, dipping them into the dressing. **TTYP:** Which two words describe the [apple]? Repeat with the names of fruit and vegetables that you have brought in.

Tell the children that they will need to use adjectives to describe the salads, as well as the names of the ingredients (vegetables and fruit). Draw out some of their ideas and use **MTYT** to develop them into full sentences, e.g. *Come and try our scrummy apple and cabbage salad with a yoghurt dressing*.

4. Navigate to the next tab and model how you write down a sentence for Monday, using the lists of sentence starters, adjectives and ingredients on p.36 of the *Get Writing!* Book.

5. Hide your writing. Ask children to practise their own sentence aloud with their partner until they can remember it. Select a few partners to say their sentences to the group. Then children can write their own sentence on p.37 of their *Get Writing!* Book. Remind them to use words from the lists on p.36 of the *Get Writing!* Book. Encourage children to spell new words using their phonic knowledge. Accept phonically-plausible spellings.

6. Repeat Steps 4 and 5 (demonstrate how you write, then ask children to write) until children have written an advert for each day.

DAY 5	**Day 5 timetable**	a. Daily Speed Sounds Lesson	d. Partner Proofread
	See Day 4 for guidance on the activity in **bold**. See pp.63–64 for other Day 5 activities.	b. Spell Test	e. Word to Keep
		c. Write Adverts for Salad Lunches (continued)	f. Linked Text

GW **Write Adverts for Salad Lunches (continued)**

On Day 5, children continue the writing activity that they began on Day 4.

The foolish witch

Teacher's Preparation

Prepare as for p.56. Print out and display the Story Green Words (see online file '5.10 The foolish witch', starting with tab a): *Hansel, Gretel, munch, crumbs, goose, thumb, quick as a flash, wrist, path, salt*, cabin, gooey, satin, broomstick, gloomy, clumpy, oven*, supper*, sobbing, scooping, screeched, stooped.*

Note that Challenge Words are marked with an asterisk.

Display these Red Word Cards in your pocket chart: *where, some, they, was, you, said, to, were, there, are, tall, call, wall*, of.* Red Words in this book only are marked with an asterisk.

DAY 1	**Day 1 timetable**	a. Daily Speed Sounds Lesson	**g. Story Introduction**
	See guidance below for activities in **bold**. See pp.56–58 for other Day 1 activities.	b. Speed Sounds from the Storybook	h. First Read – Children
		c. Story Green Words	i. Read Aloud – Teacher
		d. Speedy Green Words (online file 5.10b)	**j. Red Rhythms – Spelling Red Words**
		e. Red Word Cards	k. Handwriting
		f. Partner Practice	

Story Introduction

Hansel and Gretel had been left in the forest by their father and wicked stepmother. This was the second time they had done this to them. Last time, Hansel and Gretel had left a trail of stones so they could find their way back home. But this time, birds had eaten all the breadcrumbs they dropped on the way.

They were lost and alone in the gloomy wood, without any food. Sobbing, they set off along a narrow path, until they came to a log cabin.

As they got closer, they saw the walls were not made out of logs but thick, gooey toffee, and the windows were not made of glass but sugary sweets. Hungrily, they began to munch on the roof. Gretel bent down to scoop up the crumbs, and a head popped out of the bathroom window.

It was a witch!

She invited the children in to have supper. With empty tummies and tired eyes, they said yes. She fed them a fat goose with fresh mushrooms and beetroot and gave them a room with soft beds and smooth satin sheets.

'She must be a good witch!' they thought, and they fell asleep in the moonlight.

But the next day, the witch was in a very bad mood. She dragged Hansel into a gloomy hut and left him there.

"Stay there until you are good and fat!" she screeched.

TTYP: How do you think Hansel might escape?

Red Rhythms – Spelling Red Words See *Get Writing! Yellow*, p.39.

DAY 2	**Day 2 timetable**	a. Daily Speed Sounds Lesson	f. Second Read – Children
	See guidance below for activities in **bold**. See pp.58–60 for other Day 2 activities.	b. Speedy Green Words (online file 5.10b)	**g. Fred Fingers – Spelling Green Words**
		c. Red Word Cards	h. Red Rhythms
		d. Partner Practice	**i. Hold a Sentence – 1 and 2**
		e. Jump-in	j. Handwriting

Fred Fingers – Spelling Green Words See *Get Writing!* Book, p.39.

 Hold a Sentence – 1 and 2

> **1** They slept on soft beds with smooth satin sheets.

> **2** Stay there until you are good and fat.

See *Get Writing!* Book, p.38.

DAY 3

Day 3 timetable	a. Daily Speed Sounds Lesson	e. Questions to Talk About
See guidance below for activities in **bold**. See pp.60–61 for other Day 3 activities.	b. Partner Practice	f. Questions to Read and Answer
	c. Think About the Story	**g. Build a Sentence**
	d. Third Read – Children	h. Handwriting

Think About the Story

p.9 TOL about why Hansel and Gretel might have got lost in the wood.
TOL about why the log cabin was surprising.

p.10 Freeze Frame the children's expression when they saw and heard the witch.
TTYP: What were they feeling and thinking? *Scared but also tempted to accept the witch's offer of food and a bed.*
MTYT (with feeling): *"You look hungry, my poppets!" she screeched. "Let me give you some food."*

p.11 TOL about why Hansel and Gretel thought she must be a good witch.

p.12 TOL about how wrong they had been about the witch.
TOL about what the witch intended to do with Hansel.
MTYT (in a screechy voice): *"Stay there until you are good and fat!"*
TTYP: How were Hansel and Gretel feeling then?

p.13 TOL about how Hansel tricked the witch.

p.14 TOL about how Gretel tricked the witch.

p.15 TOL about how they escaped.
Freeze Frame their expressions.
TTYP: How did they feel as they ran away?

 Build a Sentence

Tell children that tomorrow they will write the end of the story from Hansel's point of view. (So they will tell the story as if they *are* Hansel, showing what he is feeling and thinking.) Explain that today you are going to help them build up some sentences for Hansel and Gretel to say to their father and stepmother when they get home.

1. Using **MTYT**, say the question: *Why did you abandon us?* Check children understand the word *abandon* (leave behind).

2. **TTYP**: Where did they abandon you? Draw out responses such as *deep in the forest/in the middle of the woods/in the darkest, deepest part of the forest*. Demonstrate how to build the children's suggestions into the sentence, e.g. *Why did you abandon us deep in the dark forest?*

3. **TTYP**: What did they leave you with? *No food/Nothing to drink/No shelter*. Again, model how to build ideas into the sentence, e.g. *Why did you abandon us deep in the dark forest with nowhere to sleep and nothing to eat?*

4. **TTYP**: How did you feel? *Scared/Frightened/Terrified*. **TTYP**: What were you scared of? *Being alone/Wild animals that might attack us/Strange noises in the dark*. Model how to build up the sentences further, e.g. *Why did you abandon us deep in the dark forest with nowhere to sleep and nothing to eat? We were scared of the noises, the dark and being alone.*

5. Ask partners to decide on their own sentences and to practise saying them until they can remember them. Select a few partners to say their sentences to the group.

6. Ask children to write their own sentences on p.38 of their *Get Writing!* Book. Encourage children to spell new words using their phonic knowledge. Accept phonically-plausible spellings.

Day 4 timetable	a. Daily Speed Sounds Lesson	e. Proofread – Spelling
See guidance below for activities in **bold**. See pp.61–63 for other Day 4 activities.	b. Spell Check	f. Proofread – Grammar
	c. Grammar	**g. Write Hansel's Story**
	d. Vocabulary	h. Handwriting

GW Grammar

1. Tell (or remind) children that a **noun** names people, places or things, e.g. *Hansel, wood, cabin, toffee*. **TTYP:** What must we remember about writing a *proper* noun, for example, someone's name? *(It starts with a capital letter.)*

2. On the board, write *Gretel sat on a stool and cooked bread.* **TTYP:** Which are the nouns in this sentence? *Gretel, stool* and *bread*. **TTYP:** Why does *Gretel* start with a capital letter? *(It's a proper noun.)*

3. Ask children to complete the Grammar activity on p.39 of their *Get Writing!* Book.

4. Ask children to **TTYP** to check if they have underlined the same words and if not, to discuss which answers are correct and why.

5. Tell children the correct responses and explain any difficult points. (They should have underlined: 1 – *witch, hat, chin*; 2 – *goose, mushrooms, beetroot*; 3 – *Hansel, witch*; 4 – *Hansel, Gretel, cabin, woods*.)

GW Vocabulary

1. Explain that good writers try to develop a wide vocabulary and use a variety of words to make their writing more interesting for the reader.

2. Write *called* on the board. Use **MTYT** to say the word. Give the context of the word in the story: *Soon, Hansel called, "Look, Gretel! A log cabin!"* Write three more words next to *called* (e.g. *shouted, whispered, giggled*.) Ask children to **TTYP** to say which one means the same as *called* *(shouted)*.

3. Ask children to turn to the Vocabulary activity on p.39 of their *Get Writing!* Book. Talk through the activity, explaining any words that they are unsure of. Then ask children to complete the activity.

4. Ask children to **TTYP** to check if they have circled the same words and if not, to discuss which answers are correct and why.

5. Tell children the correct responses and explain any difficult points. (They should have circled: *trick, evil, screamed, pushing, chucked*.)

Write Hansel's Story

Note that this activity should be started on Day 4 and completed on Day 5.

1. **TOL** about when you read the story of Hansel and Gretel as a child. Recall who read it to you and how you puzzled over why the father and stepmother abandoned Hansel and Gretel in the forest. Not just once, but twice! **TTYP:** Why do you think Hansel and Gretel were abandoned?

2. Use online file 5.10 (tab g onwards) for this activity. Ask children to imagine that they are Hansel and explain that they are going to write the end of the story from his point of view. Ask children to turn to p.40 in the *Get Writing!* Book. Draw attention to the possible sentence starters.

3. **TTYP:** What did Hansel think about when he was in the hut? *How he could escape/Why his father had abandoned them/What the witch was doing to Gretel.*

   TTYP: What different ideas did Hansel think of to escape? *Break down the door/Call to Gretel to push the key under the door/Dig a hole in the ground to escape.*

   Use **MTYT** to build up children's ideas into full sentences, e.g. *When I was in the gloomy hut, I thought about escaping. Maybe I could kick the door and break it down.*

4. Use the online file (tab g) to model how to write the first paragraph on the board, using the children's response. **TOL** as you write, and keep re-reading to make sure it makes sense.

5. Hide your writing. Ask children to practise their own first sentences aloud with their partner until they can remember them. Select a few partners to say their sentences to the group. Then children can write their own sentences on p.40 of their *Get Writing!* Book, using the Useful words if necessary. Encourage children to spell new words using their phonic knowledge. Accept phonically-plausible spellings.

6. Repeat Steps 3, 4 and 5 (ask the questions, demonstrate how you write, then ask children to write) with each paragraph, so that children complete writing the story.

DAY 5

Day 5 timetable	a. Daily Speed Sounds Lesson	d. Partner Proofread
See Day 4 for guidance on the activity in **bold**. See pp.63–64 for other Day 5 activities.	b. Spell Test	e. Words to Keep
	c. Write Hansel's Story (continued)	f. Linked Text

 Write Hansel's Story (continued)

On Day 5, children continue the writing activity that they began on Day 4.

In the park

For ease, we have continued to refer to 'Story' Green Words in the non-fiction lessons.

Teacher's Preparation

Prepare as for p.56. Print out and display the Story Green Words (see online file 'NF5.1 In the park', starting with tab a): *park, large, grass, bench, count, pond, part, dig, fetch, garden, cricket, picnic, lolly, carton, playground, roundabout, exploring, bushes, flying, swings, sticks.*
Display these Red Word Cards in your pocket chart: *of, you, there, are, to, do, watch, above, they, love, ball.*
Collect together some leaflets showing information about a range of places.

DAY 1	**Day 1 timetable**	a. Daily Speed Sounds Lesson	**g. Book Introduction**
	See guidance below for activities in **bold**. See pp.56–58 for other Day 1 activities.	b. Speed Sounds from the Storybook	h. First Read – Children
		c. Story Green Words	i. Read Aloud – Teacher
		d. Speedy Green Words (online file NF5.1b)	**j. Red Rhythms – Spelling Red Words**
		e. Red Word Cards	k. Handwriting
		f. Partner Practice	

Book Introduction

Reminisce about your childhood experiences of playing in the park. For example:
    When I was a child, there was nothing I enjoyed more than going to the park on a Sunday afternoon. The park was full of lawns, paths, plants and tall trees – like a huge garden. There was so much space to run around in.
    We played cricket and football, or sometimes we just threw a ball or frisbee around. We would ride up and down the long paths on our scooters, or race each other on our bikes or roller-skates.
    In the playground we'd build castles in the sand pit, zoom down the slide, go high on the swing. Mum would always tell us not to go *too* high.
    When the weather was good, we'd take a picnic and, after we've finished eating our sandwiches, we'd go exploring in the bushes and trees or count the fish in the pond. Sometimes we'd just lie back and watch the birds flying above.
    On a really hot day we would get a lolly from the ice-cream van. Yummy!
    Sometimes my friend would come along with her dog and we'd throw big sticks for it to catch. This book tells us about all the things you can do at the park.

TTYP: What do you like doing at the park?

Red Rhythms – Spelling Red Words See *Get Writing! Yellow,* p.43.

DAY 2	**Day 2 timetable**	a. Daily Speed Sounds Lesson	f. Second Read – Children
	See guidance below for activities in **bold**. See pp.58–60 for other Day 2 activities.	b. Speedy Green Words (online file NF5.1b)	**g. Fred Fingers – Spelling Green Words**
		c. Red Word Cards	h. Red Rhythms
		d. Partner Practice	**i. Hold a Sentence – 1 and 2**
		e. Jump-in	j. Handwriting

Fred Fingers – Spelling Green Words See *Get Writing!* Book, p.43.

Hold a Sentence – 1 and 2

> **1** You can have fun exploring in the trees and bushes.

> **2** Throw a stick for your dog to fetch.

See *Get Writing!* Book, p.42.

Day 3 timetable	a. Daily Speed Sounds Lesson	e. Questions to Talk About
See guidance below for activities in **bold**. See pp.60–61 for other Day 3 activities.	b. Partner Practice	f. Questions to Read and Answer
	c. Think About the Information	**g. Build a Sentence**
	d. Third Read – Children	h. Handwriting

 Think About the Information

p.9 TOL about how a park is like a big garden.

pp.10–11 TOL about the games and activities you can do in a park.
MTYT (with feeling): *You can go **exploring** in the trees and bushes.*

p.13 TOL about your favourite lolly or ice cream.

pp.14–15 TOL about different equipment in playgrounds, e.g. slides, swings, climbing frames, poles, roundabouts, ladders.
TTYP: What do you like best in the playground?
TOL about playing in the sandpit – what you need and what you can make.

p.16 TOL about how your dog (or one that you know) loves the park.

 Build a Sentence

Tell children that tomorrow they will write a leaflet about a local park. Explain that today you are going to help them build up a sentence describing some activities that people can enjoy in the park.

1. Display the pictures of the park, showing different features and activities (online files NF5.1d). **MTYT:** *You can have fun in the park.*

2. **TTYP:** What can you do in the park? Draw out responses such as *cycling/rollerskating/playing in the sandpit/climbing on the frame/going down the slide/having a picnic.* Model how to build some of the children's ideas into a sentence, starting *You can...,* e.g. *You can ride your bike in the park.*

3. **TTYP:** What else can you do in the park? Encourage children to think of another activity and show how to add it to their sentence, e.g. *You can ride your bike in the park and you can have a picnic.*

4. Ask partners to decide on their own sentence and to practise saying it until they can remember it. Select a few partners to say their sentences to the group.

5. Ask children to write their own sentence on p.42 of their *Get Writing!* Book. Encourage children to spell new words using their phonic knowledge. Accept phonically-plausible spellings.

Day 4 timetable	a. Daily Speed Sounds Lesson	e. Proofread – Spelling
See guidance below for activities in **bold**. See pp.61–63 for other Day 4 activities.	b. Spell Check	f. Proofread – Grammar
	c. Grammar	**g. Write a Leaflet about the Park**
	d. Vocabulary	h. Handwriting

 Grammar

1. Remind children that non-fiction texts are written to give people information. Explain that leaflets

107

are a type of non-fiction text that usually give information about places or events, encouraging people to visit and enjoy them. (If possible, show children some leaflets that you have collected.) Point out that core information is usually given in sentences which are **statements** (as opposed to questions, exclamations or commands).

2. Ask children to complete the Grammar activity on p.43 of their *Get Writing!* Book. Remind them that statements always start with a capital letter and end with a full stop. (They are sometimes confused with commands (instructions), which can also end in a full stop, but commands always start with a verb that gives an order. You can use the term 'imperative' if appropriate to the year group.)

3. Ask children to **TTYP** to check if they have ticked the same sentences and if not, to discuss which answers are correct and why.

4. Tell children the correct responses and explain any difficult points. (The statements are: *You can have fun in the park. Dogs love to run and play in the park.* and *The sandpit is full of soft sand.*)

GW Vocabulary

1. Explain that good writers try to develop a wide vocabulary and use a variety of words to make their writing more interesting. Point out that it can sound repetitive to use the same words again and again, e.g. *I went on the slide, then I went on the swing, then I went on the roundabout.* It's more interesting to say *I whizzed down the slide, then I kicked high up on the swing, then I spun round on the roundabout until I was dizzy.*

2. On the board write the word *said* in the centre. Use **MTYT** to say the word. Explain that this word is often used too much and there are more interesting words that could be used instead. Ask children to **TTYP** to say other words that mean something similar but are more interesting. Draw out suggestions such as *shouted/whispered/yelled/cried/called/mumbled* and add them to the board, making a spider diagram.

3. Ask children to turn to the Vocabulary activity on p.43 of their *Get Writing!* Book. Ask them to complete a spider diagram for the words *looked* and *ran*. If necessary, give children example sentences containing these words, such as: *I looked at the old house*, or *Amid and Jemma ran in the park.*

4. Ask children to **TTYP** to check if they have written some of the same words. Note that there are many correct alternatives, so any differences do not necessarily mean they are wrong.

5. Take feedback from children and explain any difficult points. (Responses might include the following vocabulary for *looked*: *glared/watched/peered/gazed/peeped/glanced/stared*; *ran*: *jogged, raced, scampered, sprinted, dashed.*)

GW Write a Leaflet about the Park

Note that this activity should be started on Day 4 and completed on Day 5.

1. **TOL** about some of the things that you like doing in the park and how you want to encourage other people to enjoy the park too.

2. Use online file NF5.1 (tab g onwards) for this activity. Say that you have agreed to help write a leaflet about the park which will be printed and given out to local people. Explain that the children will be helping you to write this leaflet.

Ask children to turn to pp.44–45 in their *Get Writing!* Book. Display the outline of the leaflet on the online file and point out that it is divided into two sections. The first section will tell people what they can do in the park. The second section will tell people what they cannot do and what they should do in the park. **TOL** about how important it is that people look after places to keep them safe and clean for everyone to enjoy.

3. **TTYP:** What can you do in the park? Encourage children to draw on information from the book. They can also add their own ideas if they wish. Draw out responses such as *ride a bike or scooter/ play football/have a picnic/look at trees and bushes/run races/play in the sandpit.* Remind children of the ideas they had in the Build a Sentence activity on Day 3. Use **MTYT** to build one of the responses into a full sentence, e.g. *You can ride a bike or have a picnic.*

Now ask children to think about rules of the park and how everyone should try to keep it safe and clean. **TTYP:** What are the rules of the park? Draw out responses such as *Put your litter in the bin/Pick up your dog's mess/Do not pick the flowers/Take turns on the swings/Keep off the flower beds.* Using the children's ideas, develop a full sentence, using **MTYT**, e.g. *Pick up your litter and put it in the bin.* Encourage children to phrase these rules as instructions (commands), starting with an imperative verb.

4. Go back to the ideas about what you can do in the park. Drawing on some of the children's ideas, use the online file (tab g) to model how to write the first bullet point, starting *You can…* Keep re-reading as you write to check that it makes sense.

5. Hide your writing. Ask children to practise their own sentences aloud with their partner until they can remember them. Select a few partners to say their sentences to the group. Then children can write their own sentences on pp.44–45 of their *Get Writing!* Book, using the Useful words if necessary. Encourage children to spell new words using their phonic knowledge. Accept phonically-plausible spellings.

6. Repeat Steps 4 and 5 (demonstrate how you write, then ask children to write) for both sections of the leaflet, providing as much support as children need to complete writing their leaflets.

DAY 5

Day 5 timetable	a. Daily Speed Sounds Lesson	d. Partner Proofread
See Day 4 for guidance on the activity in **bold**. See pp.63–64 for other Day 5 activities.	b. Spell Test	e. Words to Keep
	c. Write a Leaflet about the Park (continued)	f. Linked Text

 Write a Leaflet about the Park (continued)

On Day 5, children continue the writing activity that they began on Day 4.

A mouse in the house

DAY 1

Day 1 timetable	a. Daily Speed Sounds Lesson	**g. Book Introduction**
See guidance below for activities in **bold**. See pp.56–58 for other Day 1 activities.	b. Speed Sounds from the Storybook	h. First Read – Children
	c. Story Green Words	i. Read Aloud – Teacher
	d. Speedy Green Words (online file NF5.5b)	**j. Red Rhythms – Spelling Red Words**
	e. Red Word Cards	k. Handwriting
	f. Partner Practice	

Book Introduction

Mice make great pets. They are lively, friendly animals that love to be held and stroked. However, keeping any pet takes a lot of care and attention.

To keep a mouse you need a big cage with lots of hay on the floor. The mouse also needs bedding to curl up in, so that it feels warm and cosy when it sleeps. It is important to keep your mouse house clean. It should be washed out once a week and the bedding should be changed – otherwise it gets dirty and smelly.

Do you know what a mouse likes to eat and drink? It needs a water feeder in its cage so it can have a sip of fresh water whenever it gets thirsty. It also needs a food bowl topped up with special mouse food. Did you know that mice should never eat cheese? Lots of people think mice like cheese, but it makes them very sick!

A mouse that is well looked after will have lots of energy and will love to play and run about. You can watch it run on its wheel and feel its tickly little feet as it runs over your hand and up your arm. Make sure you keep a close eye on your mouse if it runs on the ground. People might step on it by accident, or a cat could pounce on it!

If your mouse becomes ill or injured, you must take it to the vet.

TTYP: Do you or any of your friends own a pet? What sort of pet is it?

Red Rhythms – Spelling Red Words See *Get Writing! Yellow*, p.47.

DAY 2

Day 2 timetable	a. Daily Speed Sounds Lesson	f. Second Read – Children
See guidance below for activities in **bold**. See pp.58–60 for other Day 2 activities.	b. Speedy Green Words (online file NF5.5b)	**g. Fred Fingers – Spelling Green Words**
	c. Red Word Cards	h. Red Rhythms
	d. Partner Practice	**i. Hold a Sentence – 1 and 2**
	e. Jump-in	j. Handwriting

Fred Fingers – Spelling Green Words See *Get Writing! Book*, p.47.

GW **Hold a Sentence – 1 and 2**

1 Fill the mouse house with lots of soft bedding.

2 Your mouse will be happy playing in a mouse wheel.

See *Get Writing!* Book, p.46.

DAY 3

Day 3 timetable	a. Daily Speed Sounds Lesson	e. Questions to Talk About
See guidance below for activities in **bold**. See pp.60–61 for other Day 3 activities.	b. Partner Practice	f. Questions to Read and Answer
	c. Think About the Information	**g. Build a Sentence**
	d. Third Read – Children	h. Handwriting

Think About the Information

p.9 TOL about what makes a good house for a mouse.

p.10 TOL about what you need to put in the cage.

p11 TOL about how to keep the cage clean.

pp.12–13 TOL about what a mouse needs to eat and drink.
MTYT: *Cheese is bad for your mouse!*

p.14 TOL about what exercise a mouse likes.

p.15 TTYP: Why is it dangerous for a mouse to be on the floor?

p.16 TOL about the importance of taking pets to the vet if they are unwell.
TTYP: What can a vet do for a pet that is unwell? e.g. *Look at it carefully to find out what is wrong/Give advice on changing its food or giving it more exercise/Give it pills or an injection/Tell you how to look after it until it gets better.*

  GW **Build a Sentence**

Tell children that tomorrow they will write some instructions for a friend who will be looking after your pet mouse while you are on holiday. Explain that today you are going to help them build up a sentence about how to look after a mouse.

1. Display the picture of the mouse (online file NF5.5d).

2. **TTYP:** How do you look after a mouse? Encourage children to use information from the book, drawing out responses about housing, feeding and playing with your mouse. Model how to use one of the children's ideas and build it into an instruction, e.g. *Keep its cage clean.* Point out that the sentence starts with a word that gives an order (imperative verb): *keep.* Remind children that instructions are also called commands.

3. **TTYP:** How do you keep its cage clean? (Or ask another question to draw out a more detailed response, building on their first sentence.) Encourage children to develop their ideas and model how to build up the sentence, such as *Keep its cage clean by washing it out every week.*

4. Ask partners to decide on their own instruction and to practise saying it until they can remember it. (It doesn't have to be the same as the one modelled. Encourage children to think of their own ideas.) Select a few partners to say their sentence to the group.

5. Ask children to write their sentence on p.46 of their *Get Writing!* Book. Encourage children to spell new words using their phonic knowledge. Accept phonically-plausible spellings.

Day 4 timetable	a. Daily Speed Sounds Lesson	e. Proofread – Grammar
See guidance below for activities in **bold**. See pp.61–63 for other Day 4 activities.	b. Spell Check	**f. Write About Looking After a Mouse**
	c. Grammar	g. Handwriting
	d. Vocabulary	

GW Grammar

1. Remind children of some of the different sentence types:

   – questions (which end with a question mark, e.g. *Are you ready?*)

   – exclamations (which end with an exclamation mark, e.g. *How scary he is!*)

   – statements (which tell us something and end with a full stop, e.g. *I like dogs.*)

   – commands (which tell us to do, or not do, something. They usually start with a verb that gives an order, e.g. *Tidy your room.*)

2. Ask children to complete the Grammar activity on p.47 of their *Get Writing!* Book.

3. Ask them to **TTYP** to check if they have ticked the same sentence types and if not, to discuss which answers are correct and why.

4. Tell children the correct responses and explain any difficult points. (They should have ticked: *Exclamation, Statement, Question, Command.*)

GW Vocabulary

1. Remind children that some words mean the opposite of each other, e.g. *hot* is the opposite of *cold*; *wet* is the opposite of *dry*. Use **MTYT** to repeat these words. If appropriate to the year group, use the word 'antonyms' to describe words that mean the opposite of each other.

2. Ask children to turn to the Vocabulary activity on p.47 of their *Get Writing!* Book. Talk through the activity, explaining any words that they are unsure of. Then ask children to complete the activity.

3. Ask children to **TTYP** to check if they have linked up the same words and if not, to discuss which answers are correct and why.

4. Tell children the correct responses and explain any difficult points. (They should have linked up the following pairs: *good/bad; smelly/fresh; full/empty; ill/well; small/large; up/down.*)

GW Write About Looking After a Mouse

Note that this activity should be started on Day 4 and completed on Day 5.

1. **TOL** about how you (or someone you know) always look after your friend's pets when they go away on holiday. Talk about all the different things you have to do, such as feed the cat and fish, walk the dog, fill up the hamster's water bottle, give flies to the lizard. Comment on how tricky it is to remember to do everything, so you are glad that they always leave you a list of instructions. Explain that when you go away, you leave instructions for your friend to care for your mouse. **TTYP:** Do you ever look after someone's pet? What do you have to do?

2. Use online file NF5.5 (tab g onwards) for this activity. Display the (incomplete) list of instructions. Read out *How to look after my mouse*. Explain that you want children to help you write the instructions, using information from the book. Remind them they will need to start each instruction with a word that gives an order (imperative verb), because instructions are a type of command.

3. **TTYP:** What do we need to do with the mouse's house? Draw out responses such as *Put sawdust on the floor/Scoop out the dirty bedding/Wash the house.* Ask children to turn to pp.48–49 of their *Get Writing!* Book.

   TTYP: What do we need to do for the mouse's food and water? *Give it food in a bowl/Give it fresh water/Do not give it cheese!*

   TTYP: How do we play with the mouse? *Let it run on its wheel/Let it run up and down your arm/on the floor.*

   Use **MTYT** to build up children's ideas into full sentences.

4. Go back to the first ideas about the mouse house. Use the online file (tab g) to model how to write the first instruction. Point out the word that gives an order (imperative verb) *Wash* and remind children that an instruction or command always starts with a word like this. **TOL** as you write, and keep re-reading to make sure the sentence makes sense.

5. Hide your writing. Ask children to practise their own instructions aloud with their partner until they can remember them. Select a few partners to say their sentences to the group. Then children can write their own sentences on p.48 of their *Get Writing!* Book. Point out the Useful words on p.48 of their *Get Writing!* Book. Encourage children to spell new words using their phonic knowledge. Accept phonically-plausible spellings.

6. Repeat Steps 4 and 5 (demonstrate how you write, then ask children to write) for the mouse's food, exercise and play, until children complete their list of instructions.

DAY 5

Day 5 timetable	a. Daily Speed Sounds Lesson	d. Partner Proofread
See Day 4 for guidance on the activity in **bold**. See pp.63–64 for other Day 5 activities.	b. Spell Test	e. Words to Keep
	c. Write About Looking After a Mouse (continued)	f. Linked Text

 Write About Looking After a Mouse (continued)

On Day 5, children continue the writing activity that they began on Day 4.

Barker

Teacher's Preparation

1. Print out the Story Green Words (see online file '6.1 Barker', starting with tab a) and stack them into your pocket chart: *darts match, pinch, shelf, keen, chunk, arm, scar, guard dog*, grey*, paw*, postman, sandwiches, carton, cartoon, postcard, barks, ripped, knocked, charged, washed*.*

   Note that Challenge Words are marked with an asterisk.

2. Display these Red Word Cards in your pocket chart: *does, were, all, one, said, of, to, they.* These are the Red Words in the Storybook text.

3. Practise reading the Storybook Introduction (below and printable online file 6.1a) and the whole story with expression, for reading aloud to children.

4. Prepare sticky notes you may need for activities such as Think About the Story, Build a Sentence and Write a Newspaper Report. Ideas are provided but you may wish to add your own.

DAY 1

Daily Speed Sounds Lesson

1. Review one Set 3 Speed Sound with a particular focus on spelling. See pp.40–51.

2. Review Set 2 and 3 Speed Sounds. See pp.33–51.

Speed Sounds from the Storybook

Find the circled focus graphemes on pp.4–5 of the Storybook. Point to each focus grapheme on the Complex Speed Sounds poster and use **MTYT (My turn Your turn)** to say them: *kn, ge, tch, ar.*

Story Green Words

Follow the steps below to read the Story Green Words (printed from online) with the children. After they have read each Story Green Word, explain the meaning of any new words. Definitions for some of the words can be found in the Vocabulary Check on p.7 of the Storybook.

Names and single-syllable words

1. Hold up the first card, e.g. 'pinch' and ask children to tell you the 'special friends' (digraph – *ch*) or shake their heads if there aren't any. If children have difficulty spotting the 'special friends', show them the side of the card with the dots and dashes to give them a quick reminder.

2. Ask them to say the sounds *p-i-n-ch* and then say *pinch.*

3. Say the word *pinch* with exaggerated pronunciation. Ask children to repeat it.

4. Repeat for the other words.

Multi-syllabic words

1. Fold the card 'postman' and hold it up so only the first syllable is showing. Ask children to read the syllable – only using Fred Talk if necessary.

2. Repeat with the next syllable.

3. Unfold the card and ask children to read the whole word, tweaking the pronunciation if necessary.

4. Repeat for the other words.

Root words and suffixes

1. Fold the card 'barks' so you can only see the root word ('bark') and hold it up. Ask children to read it without Fred Talk.

2. Repeat with the suffix (-s).

3. Unfold the card and ask children to read the whole word, tweaking the pronunciation if necessary.

4. Repeat for the other words.

Challenge Words

Follow the steps as for the Red Word Cards, below.

 Speedy Green Words

1. Display the first Speedy Green Word (online file 6.1b).

2. Tell children to first read the sounds silently using 'Fred in your head'. Then ask them to say the word aloud when the word animates, or when you push the word towards them if you have printed out the words.

3. Repeat Steps 1 and 2 with the other Speedy Green Words, increasing the pace as children become more confident.

4. Review Speedy Green Words from a previous Storybook that need further practice.

Red Word Cards

1. Hold up the first card, e.g. 'does'.

2. Say the word *does* and ask children to repeat it.

3. Point to the card and say the sounds you can hear: *d-u-z* and say *does*. Ask children to repeat.

4. Help children to spot any tricky letters that aren't on the Speed Sounds poster ('oe').

5. Say the word again. Ask children to repeat it.

6. Repeat for the other Red Words.

S B **Partner Practice**

Children practise the Speed Sounds and Story Green Words on pp.4–6. Ensure partners sit at the table with one Storybook between them and one lolly stick for pointing.

1. Ask one partner to teach the sounds out of order using **MTYT**. Ensure that children point accurately underneath the sounds.

2. Ask the other partner to teach the words out of order using **MTYT**.

3. During the activity, note any sounds/words that need further practice and review together at the end of the activity.

On subsequent books, ask a different partner to start teaching the sounds.

Next, children practise the Red Words on p.8. Note that the grid contains Red Words from the Storybook text, plus some revision Red Words.

1. Ask partners to take turns reading the words across the rows or down the columns. Ensure that children point accurately underneath the words. (Partners help each other if stuck.)

2. Repeat until they can read all of the Red Words at speed.

 Story Introduction

Read the introduction (below and printable online file 6.1a) to children using expression. Explain the meaning of any words children are unsure of. Ask children to **TTYP (Turn to your partner)** to discuss the question and then select two pairs to feed back (Choose two – see p.18).

> George has a very naughty best friend. He's very big, he's very hairy and he's called Barker.
> George thinks Barker is the best, but the rest of his family don't always agree.

It took a long time for George to persuade his dad, Mr Black, to buy him a dog. Every day, he would beg him – and every day, his dad would just say no, until one day, he said: "If I get you a dog, you will need to look after it yourself."

"I will, Dad!" promised George.

"And I don't want one of those dogs that are always chewing things up. I don't want to find anyone's slippers ripped into shreds."

"I'll train him very well," said George.

"You'll need to feed him very well, too," said Dad. "Otherwise he'll be eating food off the kitchen tops and out of the bins. That'll make him sick."

Dad went on and on with his demands. He even made George promise that he wouldn't let the dog go into his bedroom and leave muddy footprints on the sheets. George promised his dad that he would train him so well that he wouldn't even bother the postman. But when Barker arrived, things didn't turn out as well as George had hoped.

TTYP: Do you think George will ever be able to convince Dad that getting Barker was a good idea?

S B **First Read – Children**

Ensure partners sit at the table with one Storybook between them and one lolly stick for pointing.

1. Ask Partner 1s to:

   – point to the words while their partner reads the first page of the story.

   – prompt their partner to Fred Talk words they read incorrectly.

2. Swap roles on the second page. Continue to swap roles page by page.

3. Remind children who finish quickly to re-read the story.

4. Note any words that need further practice and review these when children have finished reading.

Read Aloud – Teacher

1. Ask children to close their Storybooks.

2. Read the whole story to children with expression.

TTYP: Do you think the family will forgive Barker if he chews Grandad's slippers or bites the postman in future?

Red Rhythms – Spelling Red Words

The children should keep their *Get Writing! Blue* Book closed. However, you will need to use the Red Words in the panel on p.3 of the *Get Writing!* Book: *does, were, one, said, they.*

1. Write the first word on the board or flipchart.

2. Say the word and ask children to repeat it.

3. Point to each sound as you say it, then say the whole word. Ask children to repeat.

4. Help children to spot any tricky letters that aren't on the Speed Sounds Chart and circle these.

5. Point as you say the letter names in a rhythm (exaggerating the tricky letters) and then say the word.

6. Repeat with all the Red Words in the panel on p.3 of the *Get Writing!* Book.

7. Hide the words that are on the board or flipchart. Say the first Red Word again. Ask children to say the letter names as they write the word in their exercise book. Write the word on the board and ask children to tick/correct the spelling of each sound. Repeat with the other Red Words.

Handwriting

Follow the handwriting lesson plan on pp.25–28 to review Stage 2/3 handwriting.

Daily Speed Sounds Lesson

1. Review one Set 3 Speed Sound with a particular focus on spelling. See pp.40–51.

2. Review Set 2 and 3 Speed Sounds. See pp.33–51.

 ### Speedy Green Words

Repeat as for Day 1. Increase the speed children read these words by reducing the 'Fred in your head' time. To do this, display them at a faster speed or, if using the cards, push the card forward sooner each time until children can read them almost immediately.

Red Word Cards

Repeat the Red Word Cards activity from Day 1, increasing the speed.

S B Partner Practice

Ensure partners sit at the table with one Storybook between them and one lolly stick for pointing. Children practise the Speedy Green Words on p.18 and the Red Words on p.8.

1. Ask partners to take turns reading the words across the rows or down the columns. Ensure that children point accurately underneath the words.

2. Repeat until they can read all the Speedy Green Words correctly without Fred Talk and the Red Words at speed.

S B Jump-in

1. Ask one partner to track under the words with a lolly stick as you read the story aloud, but ask both partners to 'Jump-in' and read the word when you hesitate on four/five words per page.

2. Ask partners to swap roles after each page.

S B Second Read – Children

Ask partners to read the whole story again, taking turns to read alternate pages. (See Day 1 First Read.) Ask Partner 2s to point on the first page this time.

Fred Fingers – Spelling Green Words

Children keep their *Get Writing!* Book closed. However, you will need to use the Green Words in the panel on p.3 of the *Get Writing!* Book. Ask children to write the spellings in their exercise books.

Single-syllable words

night

1. Say the word *night* and ask children to repeat it.

2. Ask children to:

   – Hide their fingers as they count the sounds on them.

   – Show their fingers when you say *fingers*.

   – Repeat the word, then pinch their fingers as they say the sounds.

   – Write the word as they say the sounds, underlining any 'special friends'.

3. Write the word on the board and ask children to tick/correct the spelling of each sound in their own work.

Multi-syllabic words

between, kitchen

1. Say the whole word *between*, and ask children to repeat it.

2. Say the word in syllables: *be-tween*, and ask children to repeat it.

3. Say the first syllable and ask children to repeat it, then hide their fingers as they count the sounds in the syllable. When you say *fingers*, they show their fingers. Then ask them to write the syllable and underline any 'special friends'.

4. Repeat with each syllable.

5. Write the word on the board and ask children to tick/correct the spelling of each sound in their own work.

6. Repeat for the next word.

Root words with a suffix

beginning, started

1. Say the whole word *beginning* and ask children to say the root *begin*.

2. Ask children to:
    – Hide their fingers as they count the sounds in the root word until you say *fingers*.
    – Repeat the root word and pinch their fingers as they say the sounds.

3. Ask children to write the root word, underlining any special friends.

4. Write the root on the board and **TOL (Think out loud)** about how you would add the suffix -ing noting any letters that need doubling.

5. Ask children to write the suffix.

6. Ask children to tick/correct the spelling of each sound in their own work.

7. Repeat for the other word.

Red Rhythms

Repeat the Red Rhythms activity in Day 1, with the same Red Words.

[GW] **Hold a Sentence – 1 and 2**

(1) He picked up the food and started running away.

1. Say the sentence above and ask children to repeat it.

2. Use **MTYT** until children can remember the whole sentence, and then add punctuation mimes (see p.20).

3. Write the sentence on the board and ask children to help you:
    – Use Fred Fingers to spell Green Words.
    – **TOL** about how to spell any Red Words.
    – Use punctuation and finger spaces.
    – Re-read the sentence to check it makes sense.

4. Hide the sentence and ask children to write it in their *Get Writing!* Book, p.2.

5. Display the sentence again and help children to mark each word of their own work.

6. Repeat Steps 1 to 5 with the sentence below.

(2) He started barking when we were all asleep one night.

Handwriting

Follow the handwriting lesson plan on pp.25–28 to review Stage 2/3 handwriting.

> **Daily Speed Sounds Lesson**
>
> 1. Review one Set 3 Speed Sound with a particular focus on spelling. See pp.40–51.
>
> 2. Review Set 2 and 3 Speed Sounds. See pp.33–51.

S B Partner Practice

Ensure partners sit at the table with one Storybook between them and one lolly stick for pointing. Repeat as for Day 2, practising the Speedy Green Words on p.18 and the Red Words on p.8.

Think About the Story

Children do not need their Storybooks. Display the Storybook pictures (online file 6.1c) as you read the story aloud from your Storybook. Use your prepared notes for **TOL, MTYT, TTYP** and Freeze Frames to reinforce children's understanding. For example:

p.9 Freeze Frame the boy's expression when he thinks about Barker.
TTYP: How is he feeling? *Pleased/Proud of his dog.*
MTYT with feeling: *He's the **best**!*
TOL about what the rest of the family think about Barker.

p.10 **TOL** about why Grandad is cross.
MTYT with feeling: *"**No**, Barker." And Barker just barked.* (Repeat each time the refrain occurs.)

p.11 **TOL** about how we know that Barker isn't fussy.
TOL about how Barker looked like a cartoon dog.

p.12 **TOL** about why Mum is cross.

p.13 **TOL** about why the postman is cross.

p.14 **TOL** about why Barker was sick.

p.15 **TOL** about why everyone loves Barker now.
MTYT with feeling: *"Smart dog, Barker! You're a star!"*
Freeze Frame the expression on the family's faces.
TTYP: How has the family's opinion of Barker changed from the beginning of the story, and why?

S B Third Read – Children

Ask partners to read the whole story again, taking turns to read each page. (See Day 1 First Read.) Ask Partner 1s to point on the first page this time.

S B Questions to Talk About

Read out the questions on p.16 of the Storybook. For each question, direct children to the correct page to find the answer. Ask them to **TTYP** and to respond using 'Fastest finger first' (FF) where they find the answer in the text or 'Have a think' (HaT) where they have to justify their answer/opinion.

S B Questions to Read and Answer

Ask children to turn to p.17 in the Storybook.

1. Show partners how to take turns to read the questions and find the answers in the text. They should swap roles after each question.

2. After children have completed the questions with their partner, take feedback.

Build a Sentence

Tell children that tomorrow they are going to write a newspaper report about Barker. Explain that today you are going to help them build up some sentences to explain why Dad was angry.

1. Display the pictures of Barker (online file 6.1d). Say the simple sentence: *Dad was angry.*

2. Use **MTYT** each time you expand the sentence using the children's ideas. **TTYP:** Why was Dad angry? Draw out responses such as *Dad was angry because Barker chewed Grandad's slippers/ snatched the cold meat/slept on the bed.*

3. **TTYP:** What might Dad have said when Barker chewed Grandad's slippers? For example, *How many times have I told you that you must not let Barker near Grandad's slippers?/I won't let Barker go in the living room if he does that again.*

4. **TOL** as you build the sentences. *"Don't let Barker go in the living room," he said.*

   TTYP: How did he say this? Draw out verbs such as *shouted, yelled, frowned, bellowed.*

5. Build the sentence into: *Dad was angry because Barker chewed Grandad's slippers. "Don't let Barker go in the living room," he shouted.*

6. Ask partners to decide on their own sentences and to practise saying them until they can remember them. Select a few partners to say their sentences to the group.

7. Ask children to write their own sentences on p.2 of their *Get Writing!* Book. Encourage children to spell new words using their phonic knowledge. Accept phonically-plausible spellings.

Handwriting

Follow the handwriting lesson plan on pp.25–28 to review Stage 2/3 handwriting.

> **Daily Speed Sounds Lesson**
>
> 1. Review one Set 3 Speed Sound with a particular focus on spelling. See pp.40–51.
>
> 2. Review Set 2 and 3 Speed Sounds. See pp.33–51.

GW **Spell Check**

Ask children to turn to the panels of Red and Green Words on p.3 in the *Get Writing!* Book.

1. Ask Partner 1s to:

   – choose and say one of the Red or Green Words, then cover it up

   – help their partner to write the word in their exercise book

   – look back at the listed word and help their partner tick/correct the spelling of each sound.

2. Ask partners to swap after each word, so that each partner writes at least five words.

GW **Grammar**

1. Tell (or remind) children that a **noun phrase** is a group of words that has a noun as its main word, with other words telling us more about that noun.

2. On the board write *He is a bad dog.* Use **MTYT** to say the sentence. Point out the underlined noun phrase. Ask children to **TTYP** to say which word is the noun *(dog).* Explain that the other words in the noun phrase (*a* and *bad*) tell us more about the dog. (Grammatically speaking, they are the article and adjective.) Other examples of noun phrases are: *I had a cheese sandwich; We ate some jam tarts.*

3. Ask children to complete the Grammar activity on p.3 of their *Get Writing!* Book.

4. Ask children to **TTYP** to check they have underlined and circled the same words and if not, to discuss which answers are correct and why.

120

5. Tell children the correct responses and explain any difficult points. (They should have identified these noun phrases and nouns: *some cold **beef**; a cartoon **dog**; the muddy **marks**; the kitchen **window**.*)

GW **Vocabulary**

1. Explain that good writers use many different words to help the reader see pictures in their minds (not all Storybooks have pictures). It is important that a writer chooses words carefully, so the reader builds up a clear picture. As readers, it is important to understand as many words as possible.

2. Write *grabbed* on the board. Use **MTYT** to say the word. Say the word in the context of a sentence, e.g. *He grabbed the bone.* Write three more words next to *grabbed* (e.g. *ran, snatched, barked*). Ask children to **TTYP** to say which one means the same as *grabbed (snatched)*. Model how to select and check the correct answer by inserting it into the example sentence: *He snatched the bone.*

3. Ask children to turn to the Vocabulary activity on p.3 of their *Get Writing!* Book. Talk through the activity, explaining any words that they are unsure of. Then ask children to complete the activity.

4. Ask children to **TTYP** to check if they have circled the same words and if not, to discuss which answers are correct and why.

5. Tell children the correct responses and explain any difficult points. (They should have circled: *broken, tore, annoyed, clever.*)

 GW **Proofread – Spelling**

1. Display the sentences on screen (online file 6.1e) and read them aloud.

2. Ask partners to spot the errors.

3. Take feedback and show how to correct the errors.

4. Hide the sentences and ask children to correct the sentences on p.4 of their *Get Writing!* Book.

5. Display the sentences written correctly and help children check their own corrections.

 GW **Proofread – Grammar**

Use online file 6.1f. Follow as for the Proofread – Spelling activity.

 GW **Write a Newspaper Report**

Note that this activity should be started on Day 4 and completed on Day 5.

1. **TOL** about a pet that you have had. You might have started off not having strong feelings about it, but gradually grown to love it. **TOL** about how the dad in the story, Mr Black, changes his mind about Barker.

2. Use online file 6.1 (tab g onwards) for this activity. Explain to children that they are going to write a newspaper report about how Barker saved the family from being burgled. Ask children to turn to pp.4–5 of their *Get Writing!* Book. Display the start of the newspaper report (tab g). Read out the headline, explaining that it tells the reader what the report is about. Read the introduction and draw attention to how it sets the scene for the report. Ask children to copy the headline into their exercise book.

3. **TTYP:** What did Mr Black feel about Barker at first? *He would be smelly/messy/noisy/hard to look after/expensive.*

   Use **MTYT** to create full sentences out of some of their responses, e.g. *When he first got Barker, Mr Black thought that he would be nothing but trouble because he would be smelly and messy.*

4. **TOL** as you use the online file (tab g) to complete the first sentence on the board. Model how you keep re-reading to make sure it makes sense.

121

5. Hide your writing. Ask partners to decide on their own sentences and to practise saying them until they can remember them. Select a few partners to say their sentences to the group. Then they should write their own first sentence. Draw their attention to the Useful words on p.4 of the *Get Writing!* Book. They can also make notes on p.5. Encourage children to spell new words using their phonic knowledge. Accept phonically-plausible spellings.

6. Repeat Steps 3, 4 and 5 (ask each question, demonstrate how you write, then ask children to write) so that children complete their report.

Handwriting

Follow the handwriting lesson plan on pp.25–28 to review Stage 2/3 handwriting.

> **Daily Speed Sounds Lesson**
>
> 1. Review one Set 3 Speed Sound with a particular focus on spelling. See pp.40–51.
>
> 2. Review Set 2 and 3 Speed Sounds. See pp.33–51.

Spell Test

1. Choose one of the Red or Green Words listed on p.3 of the *Get Writing!* Book. Say it aloud and ask children to write it in their exercise book. Remind them to use Fred Fingers if necessary.

2. Write the word on the board.

3. Ask children to tick/correct the spelling of each sound.

4. Repeat with the other nine listed words.

 ### Write a Newspaper Report (continued)

Complete the writing activity started on Day 4.

Partner Proofread

1. Remind children of the proofreading activity they did on Day 4. **TTYP:** What sort of things do we check when we proofread our work?

2. Share responses and note features to check on the board. These may include:
   - spaces between words
   - capital letters (**TOL** – at the start of a sentence, for proper nouns and the pronoun *I*)
   - full stops (**TOL** – at the end of a sentence)
   - question marks or exclamation marks (**TOL** – to show a question or exclamation)
   - spelling.

3. If necessary, model how to correct a sentence that contains common errors made by the class. Do not use any of the children's work, but create your own sentence to correct.

4. Ask Partner 1s to place their exercise book on top of Partner 2's. Tell partners they have three minutes to proofread Partner 1's writing, together. Encourage Partner 1s to mark any corrections in their own exercise book.

5. Repeat for Partner 2's work.

 ### Words to Keep

Ask children to re-read their writing and select the words they are most proud of, or words they might want to use again. Then ask them to write these in the Words to keep section on p.5 of their *Get Writing!* Book.

Linked Text

Read the linked text for the next Storybook.

The poor goose

Teacher's Preparation

1. Print out the Story Green Words (see online file '6.2 The poor goose', starting with tab a) and stack them into your pocket chart: *goose, sport, know, dash, moor, hitch, store, tore, thorn, guess*, popcorn, insult, farmyard, transports, after*, ever*, farmer*, chatting, bored, snorted, ignored, scornfully, honked.*

   Note that Challenge Words are marked with an asterisk.

2. Display these Red Word Cards in your pocket chart: *any, other, two, one, all, her, there, said, were, I'm, to.* These are the Red Words in the Storybook text.

3. Practise reading the Storybook Introduction (below and printable online file 6.2a) and the whole story with expression, for reading aloud to the children.

4. Prepare sticky notes you may need for activities such as Think About the Story, Build a Sentence and Write About Winning. Ideas are provided but you may wish to add your own.

DAY 1

Daily Speed Sounds Lesson

1. Review one Set 3 Speed Sound with a particular focus on spelling. See pp.40–51.

2. Review Set 2 and 3 Speed Sounds. See pp.33–51.

Speed Sounds from the Storybook

Find the circled focus graphemes on pp.4–5 of the Storybook. Point to each focus grapheme on the Complex Speed Sounds poster and use **MTYT** to say them: *kn, se, ce, or, oor, ore.*

Story Green Words

Follow the steps below to read the Story Green Words (printed from online) with the children. After they have read each Story Green Word, explain the meaning of any new words. Definitions for some of the words can be found in the Vocabulary Check on p.7 of the Storybook.

Names and single-syllable words

1. Hold up the first card, e.g. 'sport' and ask children to tell you the 'special friends' (*or*) or shake their heads if there aren't any. If children have difficulty spotting the 'special friends', show them the side of the card with the dots and dashes to give them a quick reminder.

2. Ask them to say the sounds *sp-or-t* and then say *sport*.

3. Say the word *sport* with exaggerated pronunciation. Ask children to repeat it.

4. Repeat for the other words.

Multi-syllabic words

1. Fold the card 'insult' and hold it up so only the first syllable is showing. Ask children to read the syllable – only using Fred Talk if necessary.

2. Repeat with the next syllable.

3. Unfold the card and ask children to read the whole word, tweaking the pronunciation if necessary.

4. Repeat for the other words.

Root words and suffixes

1. Fold the card 'snorted' so you can only see the root word ('snort') and hold it up. Ask children to read it without Fred Talk.
2. Repeat with the suffix (-ed).
3. Unfold the card and ask children to read the whole word, tweaking the pronunciation if necessary.
4. Repeat for the other words.

Challenge Words

Follow the steps as for the Red Word Cards, below.

Speedy Green Words

1. Display each Speedy Green Word (online file 6.2b).
2. Tell children to first read the sounds silently using 'Fred in your head'. Then ask them to say the word aloud when the word animates, or when you push the word towards them if you have printed out the words.
3. Repeat Steps 1 and 2 with the other Speedy Green Words, increasing the pace as children become more confident.
4. Review Speedy Green Words from a previous Storybook that need further practice.

Red Word Cards

1. Hold up the first card, e.g. 'other'.
2. Say the word *other* and ask children to repeat it.
3. Point to the card and say the sounds you can hear, *u-th-er* and say *other*. Ask children to repeat.
4. Help children to spot the tricky letter ('o').
5. Say the word again. Ask children to repeat it.
6. Repeat for the other Red Words.

S B Partner Practice

Children practise the Speed Sounds and Story Green Words on pp.4–6. Ensure partners sit at the table with one Storybook between them and one lolly stick for pointing.

1. Ask one partner to teach the sounds out of order using **MTYT**. Ensure that children point accurately underneath the sounds.
2. Ask the other partner to teach the words out of order using **MTYT**.
3. During the activity, note any sounds/words that need further practice and review together at the end of the activity.

On subsequent books, ask a different partner to start teaching the sounds.

Next, children practise the Red Words on p.8. Note that the grid contains Red Words from the Storybook text, plus some revision Red Words.

1. Ask partners to take turns reading the words across the rows or down the columns. Ensure that children point accurately underneath the words. (Partners help each other if stuck.)
2. Repeat until they can read all of the Red Words at speed.

Story Introduction

Read the introduction (on the following page and printable online file 6.2a) to children using expression. Explain the meaning of any words children are unsure of. Ask children to **TTYP** to discuss the question and then select two pairs to feed back (Choose two – see p.18).

There was once a goose who lived on Farmer Popcorn's farm with a horse and a sheepdog. The horse and the sheepdog thought she was short, fat and silly. But one day, she showed them she wasn't so silly after all.

It was a sunny morning. The horse, sheepdog and goose were chatting in the farmyard.

"I'm bored!" snorted the horse. "Let's have a race from the farmyard to the barn at the end of the track. I'll get there before you two!" he boasted. The horse had long, strong legs. He thought he was the fastest animal ever born. And he knew a secret shortcut across the moor.

The sheepdog thought he could win too. He was crafty. He would hitch a lift on the back of Farmer Popcorn's cart. So as soon as Farmer Popcorn left to take his sacks of corn to the corn store, the sheepdog jumped on board. He knew it was cheating – but he didn't care as long as he won.

The goose didn't seem very worried. She had something that could get her to the barn quicker than both of them.

TTYP: Can you guess what the goose was thinking of?

S B **First Read – Children**

Ensure partners sit at the table with one Storybook between them and one lolly stick for pointing.

1. Ask Partner 1s to:

   – point to the words while their partner reads the first page of the story.

   – prompt their partner to Fred Talk words they read incorrectly.

2. Swap roles on the second page. Continue to swap roles page by page.

3. Remind children who finish quickly to re-read the story.

4. Note any words that need further practice and review these when children have finished reading.

Read Aloud – Teacher

1. Ask children to close their Storybooks.

2. Read the whole story to the children with expression.

TTYP: How did the goose win the race?

Red Rhythms – Spelling Red Words

The children should keep their *Get Writing! Blue* Book closed. However, you will need to use the Red Words in the panel on p.7 of the *Get Writing!* Book: *any, other, one, there, were.*

1. Write the first word on the board or flipchart.

2. Say the word and ask children to repeat it.

3. Point to each sound as you say it, then say the whole word. Ask children to repeat.

4. Help children to spot any tricky letters that aren't on the Speed Sounds Chart and circle these.

5. Point as you say the letter names in a rhythm (exaggerating the tricky letters) and then say the word.

6. Repeat with all the Red Words in the panel on p.7 of the *Get Writing!* Book.

7. Hide the words that are on the board or flipchart. Say the first Red Word again. Ask children to say the letter names as they write the word in their exercise book. Write the word on the board and ask children to tick/correct the spelling of each sound. Repeat with the other Red Words.

Handwriting

Follow the handwriting lesson plan on pp.25–28 to review Stage 2/3 handwriting.

DAY 2 **Daily Speed Sounds Lesson**

1. Review one Set 3 Speed Sound with a particular focus on spelling. See pp.40–51.

2. Review Set 2 and 3 Speed Sounds. See pp.33–51.

 Speedy Green Words

Repeat as for Day 1. Increase the speed children read these words by reducing the 'Fred in your head' time. To do this, display them at a faster speed or, if using the cards, push the card forward sooner each time until children can read them almost immediately.

Red Word Cards

Repeat the Red Word Cards activity from Day 1, increasing the speed.

S B **Partner Practice**

Ensure partners sit at the table with one Storybook between them and one lolly stick for pointing. Children practise the Speedy Green Words on p.18 and the Red Words on p.8:

1. Ask partners to take turns reading the words across the rows or down the columns. Ensure that children point accurately underneath the words.

2. Repeat until they can read all the Speedy Green Words correctly without Fred Talk and the Red Words at speed.

S B **Jump-in**

1. Ask one partner to track under the words with a lolly stick as you read the story aloud, but ask both partners to 'Jump-in' and read the word when you hesitate on four/five words per page.

2. Ask partners to swap roles after each page.

S B **Second Read – Children**

Ask partners to read the whole story again, taking turns to read alternate pages. (See Day 1 First Read.) Ask Partner 2s to point on the first page this time.

Fred Fingers – Spelling Green Words

The children should keep their *Get Writing!* Book closed. However, you will need to use the Green Words in the panel on p.7 of the *Get Writing!* Book. Ask children to write the spellings in their exercise books.

Single-syllable words

horse, chance

1. Say the word *horse* and ask children to repeat it.

2. Ask children to:

   – Hide their fingers as they count the sounds on them.

   – Show their fingers when you say *fingers*.

   – Repeat the word, then pinch their fingers as they say the sounds.

   – Write the word as they say the sounds, underlining any 'special friends'.

3. Write the word on the board and ask children to tick/correct the spelling of each sound in their own work.

4. Repeat for the next word.

Multi-syllabic words

animal, across, morning

1. Say the whole word *animal* and ask children to repeat it.

2. Say the word in syllables: *an-i-mal* and ask children to repeat it.

3. Say the first syllable and ask children to repeat it, then hide their fingers as they count the sounds in the syllable. When you say *fingers*, they show their fingers. Then ask them to write the syllable and underline any 'special friends'.

4. Repeat with each syllable.

5. Write the word on the board and ask children to tick/correct the spelling of each sound in their own work.

6. Repeat for the other words.

Red Rhythms – Spelling Red Words

Repeat the Red Rhythms activity in Day 1, with the same Red Words.

GW Hold a Sentence – 1 and 2

(**1**) Run from the farmyard to the barn.

1. Say the sentence above and ask children to repeat it.

2. Use **MTYT** until children can remember the whole sentence, and then add punctuation mimes (see p.20).

3. Write the sentence on the board and ask children to help you:

   – Use Fred Fingers to spell Green Words.

   – **TOL** about how to spell any Red Words.

   – Use punctuation and finger spaces.

   – Re-read the sentence to check it makes sense.

4. Hide the sentence and ask children to write it in their *Get Writing!* Book, p.6.

5. Display the sentence again and help children to mark each word of their own work.

6. Repeat Steps 1 to 5 with the sentence below.

(**2**) "I am the smartest animal," said the dog.

Handwriting

Follow the handwriting lesson plan on pp.25–28 to review Stage 2/3 handwriting.

Daily Speed Sounds Lesson

1. Review one Set 3 Speed Sound with a particular focus on spelling. See pp.40–51.

2. Review Set 2 and 3 Speed Sounds. See pp.33–51.

S B Partner Practice

Ensure partners sit at the table with one Storybook between them and one lolly stick for pointing. Repeat as for Day 2, practising the Speedy Green Words on p.18 and the Red Words on p.8.

127

Think About the Story

Children do not need their Storybooks. Display the Storybook pictures (online file 6.2c) as you read the story aloud from your Storybook. Use your prepared notes for **TOL, MTYT, TTYP** and Freeze Frames to reinforce children's understanding. For example:

p.9 **TOL** about why the horse suggested they had a race.

p.10 **TOL** about why the horse thought he could win.

p.11 **TOL** about why the dog thought he could win.
MTYT (with feeling): *"I'm the **smartest** sort of animal."*
TTYP: What do you think of the dog's behaviour?

p.12 **TOL** about what the goose was thinking and why she didn't say anything.

p.14 **TOL** about how the dog cheated.
Freeze Frame the expression on the dog's face as he sat in the cart.
TTYP: How was he feeling? *Pleased with himself.*

p.15 **TOL** about why the others didn't guess that the goose would win.
TTYP: Why do you think the dog and horse didn't insult the goose any more?
TTYP: How do you think the dog felt at the end? *Sorry/Red-faced/Ashamed.*

SB **Third Read – Children**

Ask partners to read the whole story again, taking turns to read each page. (See Day 1 First Read.) Ask Partner 1s to point on the first page this time.

SB **Questions to Talk About**

Read out the questions on p.16 of the Storybook. For each question, direct children to the correct page to find the answer. Ask them to **TTYP** and to respond using 'Fastest finger first' (FF) where they find evidence in the text or 'Have a think' (HaT) where they have to justify their answer/opinion.

SB **Questions to Read and Answer**

Ask children to turn to p.17 in the Storybook.

1. Show partners how to take turns to read the questions and find the answers in the text. They should swap roles after each question.

2. After children have completed the questions with their partner, take feedback.

GW **Build a Sentence**

Tell children that tomorrow they will re-write the story. Explain that today you are going to help them build a few sentences to describe the cart ride from the dog's point of view. (So they will describe the cart ride as if they *are* the dog, showing what he is feeling and thinking.) Note that they will be giving a more detailed description than is actually in the Storybook.

1. **MTYT**: *I sat on the cart.* Point out that the *I* in the story is the dog speaking. **TTYP**: Where did you sit? Encourage children to give as much detail as they can, e.g. *on top of a sack of corn.* Model how to incorporate the children's response into the sentence, e.g. *I sat on top of a sack of corn on the cart.*

2. **TTYP**: How did you sit? *Perched/Balanced/Wobbled.* Incorporate the response into the sentence, using **MTYT**, e.g. *I wobbled on top of a sack of corn on the cart.*

3. **TTYP**: What did you see? *Tall trees/stones on the track/flowers/puddles/fences/walls.* Encourage children to build another sentence to follow on from the first, e.g. *I wobbled on top of a sack of corn on the cart. I could see tall trees and stones on the track.*

4. Ask partners to decide on their own sentences and to practise saying them until they can remember them. Select a few partners to say their sentences to the group.

5. Ask children to write their own sentences on p.6 of their *Get Writing!* Book. Encourage children to spell new words using their phonic knowledge. Accept phonically-plausible spellings.

Handwriting

Follow the handwriting lesson plan on pp.25–28 to review Stage 2/3 handwriting.

> **Daily Speed Sounds Lesson**
>
> 1. Review one Set 3 Speed Sound with a particular focus on spelling. See pp.40–51.
>
> 2. Review Set 2 and 3 Speed Sounds. See pp.33–51.

GW Spell Check

Ask children to turn to the panels of Red and Green Words p.7 in the *Get Writing!* Book.

1. Ask Partner 1s to:

   – choose and say one of the Red or Green Words, then cover it up

   – help their partner to write the word in their exercise book

   – look back at the listed word and help their partner tick/correct the spelling of each sound.

2. Ask partners to swap after each word, so that each partner writes at least five words.

GW Grammar

1. Tell (or remind) children that a **verb** tells us what someone or something is doing. It is an 'action' word. On the board, write *I walked to the barn.* Use **MTYT** to say the sentence. Ask children to **TTYP** to say which word is the verb in the sentence *(walked).* Point out the -ed ending and remind children that a lot of verbs end with -ed in the past tense (when things have already happened). Other examples are: *The dog hitched a lift* and *He barked loudly.*

2. Ask children to complete the Grammar activity on p.7 of their *Get Writing!* Book.

3. Ask children to **TTYP** to check they have underlined the same words and if not, to discuss which answers are correct and why.

4. Tell children the correct responses and explain any difficult points. (They should have underlined: *agreed, looked, bumped, snorted, ignored, sat.* You may need to point out that *sat* is the past tense of the verb *sit* even though it does not have the -ed ending.)

GW Vocabulary

1. Explain that some words mean the opposite of each other, e.g. *hot* and *cold* are opposites. On the board, write the word *bad.* Use **MTYT** to say the word. Ask children to **TTYP** to say a word that means the opposite *(good).* If appropriate to the year group, tell children that words that mean the opposite of each other are called 'antonyms'.

2. Ask children to turn to the Vocabulary activity on p.7 of their *Get Writing!* Book. Talk through the activity, explaining any words that they are unsure of. Then ask children to complete the activity.

3. Ask children to **TTYP** to check they have linked up the same words and if not, to discuss which are correct and why.

4. Tell children the correct responses and explain any difficult points. (Children should have linked up the following pairs: *fast/slow; smart/silly; agree/disagree; dash/plod; short/tall; fat/thin.*)

Proofread – Spelling

1. Display the sentences on screen (online file 6.2e) and read them aloud.

2. Ask partners to spot the errors.

3. Take feedback and show how to correct the errors.

4. Hide the sentences and ask children to correct the sentences in their *Get Writing!* Book on p.8.

5. Display the sentences written correctly and help children check their own corrections.

 Proofread – Grammar

Use online file 6.2f. Follow as for the Proofread – Spelling activity.

 Write About Winning

Note that this activity should be started on Day 4 and completed on Day 5.

1. **TOL** about a race that you have entered; how keen you were to win; how you looked at the other people in the race and wondered who would beat you. **TTYP:** Have you ever been in a race? How did you feel? *Worried/Anxious/Excited/Nervous.*

2. Use online file 6.2 (tab g onwards) for this activity. Explain to children that they are going to re-write the story about the horse, sheepdog and goose, but they will be the sheepdog, re-telling the tale. Remind them that they will need to use the pronoun *I*. Tell them that before they start writing, they will talk about what happened with a partner. They should build up a 'conversation' through questions.

3. **TTYP:** Where were you? Who were you chatting to? In their responses, encourage children to draw on their own experiences as well as to use ideas from the Storybook. Use **MTYT** to model how to turn some of the children's responses into full sentences, e.g. *I was in the farmyard. I was chatting to the farmer when the horse said, "I'm bored!"*

4. Focus on the first paragraph and use the online file (tab g) to model how to write your first few sentences. **TOL** as you write and keep re-reading to make sure your writing makes sense.

5. Hide your writing. Ask children to practise their own first sentences aloud with their partners until they can remember them. Select a few partners to say their sentences to the group. Children can make notes in their *Get Writing!* Book if necessary, then they should write their own sentences in their exercise books. Point out the Useful words on p.8 in their *Get Writing!* Book, and also the questions and sentence starters on p.9. Encourage children to use their own sentences if they don't need the structured support. Encourage children to spell new words using their phonic knowledge. Accept phonically-plausible spellings.

6. Repeat Steps 3, 4 and 5 (ask each question, demonstrate how you write, then ask children to write) for all the paragraphs. At the end, encourage children to draw out the moral of the story: that you shouldn't cheat, or judge people by their looks.

Handwriting

Follow the handwriting lesson plan on pp.25–28 to review Stage 2/3 handwriting.

 Daily Speed Sounds Lesson

1. Review one Set 3 Speed Sound with a particular focus on spelling. See pp.40–51.

2. Review Set 2 and 3 Speed Sounds. See pp.33–51.

GW **Spell Test**

1. Choose one of the Red or Green Words listed in the panels on p.7 of the *Get Writing!* Book. Say it aloud and ask children to write it in their exercise book. Remind them to use Fred Fingers if necessary.

2. Write the word on the board.

3. Ask children to tick/correct the spelling of each sound.

4. Repeat with the other nine listed words.

GW **Write About Winning (continued)**

Complete the writing activity started on Day 4.

Partner Proofread

1. Remind children of the proofreading activity they did on Day 4. **TTYP:** What sort of things do we check when we proofread our work?

2. Share responses and note features to check on the board. These may include:

   - spaces between words

   - capital letters (**TOL** – at the start of a sentence, for proper nouns and the pronoun *I*)

   - full stops (**TOL** – at the end of a sentence)

   - question marks or exclamation marks (**TOL** – to show a question or exclamation)

   - spelling.

3. If necessary, model how to correct a sentence that contains common errors made by the class. Do not use any of the children's work, but create your own sentence to correct.

4. Ask Partner 1s to place their exercise book on top of Partner 2's. Tell partners they have three minutes to proofread Partner 1's writing, together. Encourage Partner 1s to mark any corrections in their own exercise book.

5. Repeat for Partner 2's work.

GW **Words to Keep**

Ask children to re-read their writing and select the words they are most proud of, or words they might want to use again. Then ask them to write these in the Words to keep section on p.9 of their *Get Writing!* Book.

Linked Text

Read the linked text for the next Storybook.

Hairy fairy

Teacher's Preparation

Prepare as for p.114. Print out and display the Story Green Words (see online file '6.3 Hairy fairy', starting with tab a): *Mrs Blair, whisk, sack, nips, ball*, wand*, frilly, millionaire, tinsel, hairdresser, despair, honest* money*, magic*, Father Christmas*, wrapping, swaps*.*
Note that Challenge Words are marked with an asterisk.
Display these Red Word Cards in your pocket chart: *could, there, all, they, any, I'm, I've, to, what, do, ball.*

DAY 1 Day 1 timetable	a. Daily Speed Sounds Lesson	g. **Story Introduction**
See guidance below for activities in **bold**. See pp.114–116 for other Day 1 activities.	b. Speed Sounds from the Storybook	h. First Read – Children
	c. Story Green Words	i. Read Aloud – Teacher
	d. Speedy Green Words (online file 6.3b)	j. **Red Rhythms – Spelling Red Words**
	e. Red Word Cards	k. Handwriting
	f. Partner Practice	

Story Introduction

The hairy fairy isn't like any other fairy. He has all the things a fairy needs, such as a magic wand, fairy dust, and sparkly wings, but he's unhappy. Actually, he's more than unhappy – he's in despair. What he wants is a job. A job like all the other fairies.

At first, the Fairy Queen sent him to work as a tooth fairy. He worked very hard. At night time he crept quietly and swapped the teeth children had put under their pillows for money. But the Fairy Queen gave him the sack. He was so hairy she thought he might frighten the children.

Then he became a Christmas tree fairy at Mr and Mrs Blair's house. He stood very still on top of the tree, looking down on the glass balls and tinsel. But Mrs Blair shook her head and said, "He looks all wrong."

No matter how hard he tried, things did not go well for the hairy fairy. He was fed up, and so was the Fairy Queen.

"That's it," she told him. "You're going to get a haircut." The hairdresser snipped all day, but the hairy fairy's hair soon grew back – even thicker than before!

The Fairy Queen was in despair! What was she going to do with him now?

TTYP: Do you think the hairy fairy will ever find a job? What kind of job?

Red Rhythms – Spelling Red Words See *Get Writing! Blue*, p.11.

DAY 2 Day 2 timetable	a. Daily Speed Sounds Lesson	f. Second Read – Children
See guidance below for activities in **bold**. See pp.117–119 for other Day 2 activities.	b. Speedy Green Words (online file 6.3b)	g. **Fred Fingers – Spelling Green Words**
	c. Red Word Cards	h. Red Rhythms
	d. Partner Practice	i. **Hold a Sentence – 1 and 2**
	e. Jump-in	j. Handwriting

Fred Fingers – Spelling Green Words See *Get Writing!* Book, p.11.

GW **Hold a Sentence – 1 and 2**

1 How can I be a good fairy when I'm so hairy?

2 "Stop frightening the children," she said.

See *Get Writing!* Book, p.10.

DAY 3	**Day 3 timetable**	a. Daily Speed Sounds Lesson	e. Questions to Talk About
	See guidance below for activities in **bold**. See pp.119–120 for other Day 3 activities.	b. Partner Practice	f. Questions to Read and Answer
		c. Think About the Story	**g. Build a Sentence**
		d. Third Read – Children	h. Handwriting

Think About the Story

p.9 TOL about how the fairy has everything a fairy needs. There's just one problem... MTYT (with feeling): **But** – *and it's a **big** but – I'm **hairy**! **Very** hairy indeed.* Freeze Frame his expression. TTYP: How is he feeling? *Miserable/Sad/ Despairing.*

p.10 TOL about why the fairy thinks life is so unfair.

p.11 Explain the job of a tooth fairy. TOL about why the Fairy Queen thought he might frighten the children.

p.12 TOL about what a Christmas tree fairy should look like and do, and why the hairy fairy lost his job.

p.13 TOL about why the trip to the hairdresser wasn't successful.

p.14 TOL about why fairies don't want to work with Father Christmas, but why it's the perfect job for the hairy fairy.

p.15 TOL about the best thing about working for Father Christmas. MTYT (with feeling): ***Not bad**, for a hairy fairy.* Freeze Frame his expression. TTYP: How is the hairy fairy feeling now? *Happy/Full of hope/Optimistic/ Successful.*

GW **Build a Sentence**

Tell children that tomorrow they will imagine that they are the hairy fairy and write a letter to the Fairy Queen about getting a new job. Explain that today you are going to help them build up a sentence, in role as the hairy fairy, explaining one of the jobs that he has had.

1. Start with the simple sentence, using **MTYT**: *I had a job.*

   TTYP: What sort of job did you have? Encourage children either to use ideas from the Storybook or to think up their own, e.g. *tooth fairy/Christmas tree fairy/make-a-cake fairy/tidy-your-bedroom fairy/book fairy.* Demonstrate how to build some of the children's ideas into the sentence, e.g. *I had a job as a tooth fairy.*

2. **TTYP:** What did you do? Encourage children to explain the job in more detail, e.g. *swapping teeth for money/sitting on a Christmas tree/making cakes for people who were sad/helping good children to keep their room clean and tidy.* Show how to build the ideas into the sentence, e.g. *I had a job as a tooth fairy, swapping teeth for money.*

3. **TTYP:** Why did you stop doing your job? *I frightened the children/Mrs Blair said I looked all wrong/I kept eating the cakes/I was better at making a mess than tidying.* Model how to expand the sentence, e.g. *I had a job as a tooth fairy, swapping teeth for money, but I frightened the children so I lost my job.*

4. Ask partners to decide on their own sentence and to practise saying it until they can remember it. Select a few partners to say their sentences to the group.

5. Ask children to write their own sentence on p.10 of their *Get Writing!* Book. Encourage children to spell new words using their phonic knowledge. Accept phonically-plausible spellings.

Day 4 timetable	a. Daily Speed Sounds Lesson	e. Proofread – Spelling
See guidance below for activities in **bold**. See pp.120–122 for other Day 4 activities.	b. Spell Check	f. Proofread – Grammar
	c. Grammar	**g. Write a Letter**
	d. Vocabulary	h. Handwriting

GW **Grammar**

1. Tell (or remind) children that an **adjective** can tell us more about a noun. Write *the fairy* on the board and use **MTYT** to say it. Point out that *fairy* is a noun (a word that names a person or thing). Ask children to **TTYP** and think of a word to describe a fairy (any fairy). Choose one of the adjectives and add it to the board, e.g. *the hairy fairy*. Point out that the adjective usually comes *before* the noun that it is describing. Discuss alternatives, e.g. *the sad fairy/happy fairy/tall fairy/ blue fairy/cross fairy.*

2. Ask children to complete the Grammar activity on p.11 of their *Get Writing!* Book. If necessary, remind them to look for a word that describes something or someone.

3. Ask children to **TTYP** to check they have underlined the same words and if not, to discuss which answers are correct and why.

4. Tell children the correct responses and explain any difficult points. (They should have underlined: *pink, sparkly, gold, magic, big, rich.*)

GW **Vocabulary**

1. Remind children that a good story uses words that help the reader to see pictures in their minds (not all storybooks have pictures). It is important that the writer chooses words carefully, so the reader builds up a clear picture. Point out that adjectives are very useful describing words. They can describe what things look like and also how people feel.

2. On the board write the incomplete sentence *"I am _____"* and pull a grumpy face. Ask children to **TTYP** and think of a word (an adjective) to describe how they think you are feeling to complete the sentence. Draw out responses such as *grumpy/cross/fed-up*. Demonstrate how to insert the word to complete the sentence, then use **MTYT** to say it in full.

3. Ask children to turn to the Vocabulary activity on p.11 of their *Get Writing!* Book. Talk through the activity, explaining any words that they are unsure of. Then ask children to complete the activity.

4. Ask children to **TTYP** to check they have written the same words and if not, to discuss which answers are correct and why.

5. Tell children the correct responses and explain any difficult points. (The adjectives should be: *chilly, upset, sleepy, delighted.*)

 GW **Write a Letter**

Note that this activity should be started on Day 4 and completed on Day 5.

1. **TOL** about all the things you and your friends dreamed of doing when you were children, e.g. being an astronaut, an acrobat in a circus, a singer or dancer on TV, becoming a vet. Explain that as you all got older, you tried out different hobbies and jobs until you found something that you really wanted to do and that really suited you.

2. Use online file 6.3 (tab g onwards) for this activity. Explain that children are going to imagine they are the hairy fairy. He has heard that Father Christmas is looking for help and wants to write to the Fairy Queen asking for the job. Tell children to turn to p.13 in their *Get Writing!* Book. Point out the start of the letter and the different paragraphs for children to write. Ask children to copy the first two lines of the letter into their exercise book.

3. **TTYP:** Why do you want this job? Draw out responses such as *I am a hairy fairy so... I don't feel the cold/I enjoy the frost and don't mind being in the snow/I think Father Christmas is wonderful and he would be fun to work with/I want to visit the far north/I love reindeer.* Use **MTYT** to model how to put some of the children's ideas into full sentences, e.g. *I am a hairy fairy so I don't feel the cold at all. I enjoy the frost and snow.* Encourage children to develop their own ideas and to add more detail to their sentences.

   TTYP: What other jobs have you had? *I was a tooth fairy/cake-making fairy/book fairy/tidying-your-bedroom fairy.* Model how to build full sentences from the children's ideas, adding detail about what these jobs involved. Again, encourage children to draw on their own ideas, as well as those featured in the Storybook.

   TTYP: Why would you be good at this job? *I am good at... working hard/fixing sledges/working with elves and reindeer.*

4. Go back to the first question/paragraph. Decide on a full sentence and **TOL** as you use the online file (tab g) to model how to write it on the board. Keep re-reading as you write to make sure it makes sense.

5. Hide your writing. Tell children to practise their own first sentences aloud with their partners until they can remember them. Select a few partners to say their sentences to the group. Children should then write their own sentences in their exercise book. Point out the Useful words on p.12 of their *Get Writing!* Book. Encourage children to use the sentence starters on p.13 and make notes here, if they wish. Encourage children to spell new words using their phonic knowledge. Accept phonically-plausible spellings.

6. Repeat Steps 4 and 5 (demonstrate how you write, then ask children to write) for the other questions. Encourage children to use their own ideas as they complete the letter.

DAY 5	**Day 5 timetable**	a. Daily Speed Sounds Lesson	d. Partner Proofread
	See Day 4 for guidance on the activity in **bold**. See p.122 for other Day 5 activities.	b. Spell Test	e. Words to Keep
		c. **Write a Letter (continued)**	f. Linked Text

 Write a Letter (continued)

On Day 5, children continue the writing activity that they began on Day 4.

King of the birds

Teacher's Preparation

Prepare as for p.114. Print out and display the Story Green Words (see online file '6.4 King of the birds', starting with tab a): *Jay, Crow, grand, dull, chance, front*, Parrot, Hummingbird, Cockatoo, quarrel, elephant, handsome, display, splendid, amidst, terrific, firmly, squirted, whirled, twirled, whirring, pranced, squirmed, admitted, feathers*.*

Note that Challenge Words are marked with an asterisk.

Display these Red Word Cards in your pocket chart: *would, want, their, watch, some, there, said, all, water, were, they, are, to, was, one, wash*, you.*

Note that Red Words in this book only are marked with an asterisk.

DAY 1

Day 1 timetable	a. Daily Speed Sounds Lesson	g. **Story Introduction**
See guidance below for activities in **bold**. See pp.114–116 for other Day 1 activities.	b. Speed Sounds from the Storybook	h. First Read – Children
	c. Story Green Words	i. Read Aloud – Teacher
	d. Speedy Green Words (online file 6.4b)	j. **Red Rhythms – Spelling Red Words**
	e. Red Word Cards	k. Handwriting
	f. Partner Practice	

Story Introduction

One day, two birds – Parrot and Jay – were having a quarrel in the branches of a dark fir tree.

"We need a king," they decided, "to make sure we play fair." So they arranged an important meeting where all the birds could come to choose their king.

"I wonder if I could be king," Crow said to himself when he heard about these plans. "But maybe everyone will think I'm too dull-looking." He thought about Cockatoo's lovely yellow feathers and Hummingbird's bright blue chest and elegant long beak.

"Cockatoo looks fantastic," he chirped sadly, looking at his plain black feathers, "and look at little Hummingbird! I've got no chance."

On the day of the meeting, all the birds tried to look as good as possible. The elephants squirted and sprayed water to clean the birds, and the crocs used their teeth to brush off all the dirt from their feathers.

Crow stood watching sadly from the side of the pond.

"Crow looks so plain," Cockatoo whispered to Hummingbird as they got ready.

"He's got no chance!" Hummingbird chirped back.

All the birds flew off to the meeting – except Crow, who stood miserably by the side of the pond. Then he spotted some bright feathers lying on the grass and he had an idea.

"Maybe they can help me win…"

TTYP: How do you think the bright feathers might help Crow become king?

Red Rhythms – Spelling Red Words See *Get Writing! Blue*, p.15.

Day 2 timetable	a. Daily Speed Sounds Lesson	f. Second Read – Children
See guidance below for activities in **bold**. See pp.117–119 for other Day 2 activities.	b. Speedy Green Words (online file 6.4b)	**g. Fred Fingers – Spelling Green Words**
	c. Red Word Cards	h. Red Rhythms
	d. Partner Practice	**i. Hold a Sentence – 1 and 2**
	e. Jump-in	j. Handwriting

Fred Fingers – Spelling Green Words See *Get Writing!* Book, p.15.

GW **Hold a Sentence – 1 and 2**

1 The wild birds whirled off to their important meeting.

2 Who will they choose to be king of the birds?

See *Get Writing!* Book, p.14.

Day 3 timetable	a. Daily Speed Sounds Lesson	e. Questions to Talk About
See guidance below for activities in **bold**. See pp.119–120 for other Day 3 activities.	b. Partner Practice	f. Questions to Read and Answer
	c. Think About the Story	**g. Build a Sentence**
	d. Third Read – Children	h. Handwriting

Think About the Story

p.9 **TOL** about why the birds thought they needed a king.

p.10 **TOL** about why Crow thought no one would choose him to be king.
MTYT (with feeling): *"As for **me** – I've got no chance."*
Freeze Frame Crow's expression.
TTYP: How was Crow feeling? *Downcast/ Sad/Fed-up/Miserable.*

p.11 **TOL** about why the birds gathered at the pond.

p.12 **TOL** about why Crow stuck the feathers on to his back.
MTYT (with feeling): *"What a **handsome** bird!"*
Freeze Frame Crow's expression.
TTYP: How was he feeling? *Pleased with himself/Proud/Vain.*

p.13 **TOL** about what the birds might have said to each other.

p.14 **TOL** about what happened to the feathers.
TTYP: Why did Crow squirm? *He felt ashamed/embarrassed/silly.*
MTYT (with feeling): *"You have **tricked** us, sir!" said Cockatoo.*
TTYP: How did the other birds feel, and why? *Let down/Angry/Cross because they didn't like being lied to.*

p.15 **TOL** about how Crow persuaded the other birds to choose him to be king.

  GW **Build a Sentence**

Tell children that tomorrow they will write a story about a boy who told a fib, because he wanted his friends to like him more. Explain that today you are going to help them build up some sentences about what Crow did when the birds discovered his trick.

1. Display the picture of Crow with Cockatoo (online file 6.4d). Use **MTYT** to say the sentence *Crow hung his head*. Check that children understand that this posture shows that someone is ashamed.

2. **TTYP:** How did Crow feel and why? *Ashamed/Embarrassed because he had been found out.* Model how to incorporate the children's responses into the sentence, e.g. *Crow hung his head in shame because he knew he had done wrong.*

3. **TTYP:** What did he say to the other birds? *I'm so sorry/I'll never trick you again/I know I shouldn't lie to you.* Demonstrate how to build up the sentence, e.g. *Crow hung his head in shame because he knew he had done wrong. "I'm so sorry. I'll never try to trick you again."*

4. Ask partners to decide on their own sentences and to practise saying them until they can remember them. Select a few partners to say their sentences to the group.

5. Ask children to write their own sentences on p.14 of their *Get Writing!* Book. Encourage children to spell new words using their phonic knowledge. Accept phonically-plausible spellings.

DAY 4	**Day 4 timetable**	a. Daily Speed Sounds Lesson	e. Proofread – Spelling
	See guidance below for activities in **bold**.See pp.120–122 for other Day 4 activities.	b. Spell Check	f. Proofread – Grammar
		c. Grammar	**g. Write About a Lie**
		d. Vocabulary	h. Handwriting

 Grammar

1. Tell (or remind) children that an **adverb** can give us more information about a verb (an action word). On the board write *Cockatoo nodded slowly.* Use **MTYT** to say the sentence. Ask children to **TTYP** to say which word is the verb *(nodded)*. Point out that 'slowly' is the adverb. It tells us more about the verb – it tells us *how* the bird nodded. Remind children that adverbs often (but not always) end in -ly. Other examples of adverbs are: *The birds washed <u>quickly</u>* and *Parrot spoke <u>kindly</u>.*

2. Ask children to complete the Grammar activity on p.15 of their *Get Writing!* Book.

3. Ask children to **TTYP** to check they have ticked the same words and if not, to discuss which answers are correct and why.

4. Tell children the correct responses and explain any difficult points. (Children should have identified the following: *sadly* = adverb, *squirted* = verb, *firmly* = adverb, *wore* = verb.)

Vocabulary

1. Remind children that when they are reading they may come across words that they don't understand. They can sometimes work out the meaning of a word from the sentence it is in.

2. On the board write *He <u>spotted</u> some bright red feathers.* Use **MTYT** to say the sentence. Underline the word *spotted* and ask children to **TTYP** and say what it means. Draw out that it doesn't mean that something had spots on, but it means *saw*. Emphasise that they can work out the meaning by looking at how it works in the sentence.

3. Ask children to turn to the Vocabulary activity on p.15 of their *Get Writing!* Book. Talk through the activity, explaining any words that they are unsure of. Remind children that they may be able to use their knowledge of the events and characters in the story to work out the meanings of the words. Then ask children to complete the activity.

4. Ask children to **TTYP** to check they have circled the same words and if not, to discuss which answers are correct and why.

5. Tell children the correct responses and explain any difficult points. (They should have circled: *show off, handsome, agreed, squabble.*)

Write About a Fib

Note that this activity should be started on Day 4 and completed on Day 5.

1. **TOL** about how Crow tried to trick the birds so that they would like him more and choose him to be their king. Explain that sometimes people tell lies, hoping that they will make people like them more. They may claim to have the latest trainers, or games, or a new bike, or that they go on the best holidays. **TTYP:** What might people say to make others like them more?

2. Use online file 6.4 (tab g onwards) for this activity. Explain to children that they are going to write a story about a child called Otto who told a fib about himself to get his friends to like him more. Ask them to turn to p.17 in their *Get Writing!* Book. Explain that they can use the questions to help plan their story. First, tell children to choose a title for their story and to think of names for Otto's three friends. Ask children to write their chosen title in their exercise book.

3. **TTYP:** Who are the characters in the story? Then **TTYP:** What was the fib that Otto told? Encourage children to think up a fib, such as *Otto said,… "My dad is going to buy me a new bike."/"I've got the latest game for my games console."/"We are going on holiday all round the world."/"I scored six goals when I played football last weekend."*

Focus on ideas for the other paragraphs, encouraging children to develop the story so that the friends challenge Otto and the truth comes out. Ensure children think carefully about the friends' reactions. Perhaps one forgives him but the others don't. Draw out Otto's response and feelings. Use **MTYT** to develop children's ideas into some full sentences.

4. Go back to the first question. Drawing on children's ideas, decide on the first few sentences and use the online file (tab g) to model how to write them on the board. **TOL** as you write, and keep re-reading to make sure your writing makes sense.

5. Hide your writing. Tell children to practise their own first sentences aloud with their partners until they can remember them. Select a few partners to say their sentences to the group. Then children can write their own sentences in their exercise book. Point out the Useful words in the panel on p.16 of their *Get Writing!* Book. Encourage children to use the sentence starters on p.17 and make notes here if they wish. Encourage children to spell new words using their phonic knowledge. Accept phonically-plausible spellings.

6. Repeat Steps 4 and 5 (demonstrate how you write, then ask children to write) for the other paragraphs.

Day 5 timetable	a. Daily Speed Sounds Lesson	d. Partner Proofread
See Day 4 for guidance on the activity in **bold**. See p.122 for other Day 5 activities.	b. Spell Test	e. Words to Keep
	c. Write About a Fib (continued)	f. Linked Text

 Write About a Fib (continued)

On Day 5, children continue the writing activity that they began on Day 4.

139

Our house

Prepare as for p.114. Print out and display the Story Green Words (see online file '6.5 Our house', starting with tab a): *Carl, shout, couch, flour, pound, snout, proud, our, doubt*, guess*, Bounder, bouncy, grouchy, shampoo, knockout, greyhound*, pounced, devoured, washing*, hours*.*
Note that Challenge Words are marked with an asterisk.
Display these Red Word Cards in your pocket chart: *anyone, over, who, all, one, watch, does, they, school, you, to, were, was, said, wasn't.*

DAY 1

Day 1 timetable	a. Daily Speed Sounds Lesson	g. **Story Introduction**
See guidance below for activities in **bold**. See pp.114–116 for other Day 1 activities.	b. Speed Sounds from the Storybook	h. First Read – Children
	c. Story Green Words	i. Read Aloud – Teacher
	d. Speedy Green Words (online file 6.5b)	j. **Red Rhythms – Spelling Red Words**
	e. Red Word Cards	k. Handwriting
	f. Partner Practice	

Story Introduction

Alex lives on Mount Street with his mum, his grandad, his brother Carl and Grandad's greyhound, Bounder.

Their house isn't much to look at. It's sort of pink, with a small red door and a little garden all around it. The garden has lots of weeds, and holes made by Bounder's digging.

Alex shares a bedroom with his brother Carl. Carl plays CDs for hours. The music is so loud that Alex's head starts to pound. His mum shouts up the stairs, "Stop that!" She can get a bit grouchy sometimes.

Alex doesn't seem to like Bounder very much. Last week, when Alex was eating dinner with his grandad, Bounder ate a bit of egg sandwich he found on the floor next to Grandad's chair. 'Yuck,' thought Alex.

Every time Bounder has his bath, Grandad spills the shampoo and leaves dog hairs all over the floor! It's always Alex who has to mop up.

But as Alex thinks more and more about his house and family, he realises something surprising.

TTYP: What do you think Alex might have realised about his house and family?

Red Rhythms – Spelling Red Words See *Get Writing! Blue,* p.19.

DAY 2

Day 2 timetable	a. Daily Speed Sounds Lesson	f. Second Read – Children
See guidance below for activities in **bold**. See pp.117–119 for other Day 2 activities.	b. Speedy Green Words (online file 6.5b)	g. **Fred Fingers – Spelling Green Words**
	c. Red Word Cards	h. Red Rhythms
	d. Partner Practice	i. **Hold a Sentence – 1 and 2**
	e. Jump-in	j. Handwriting

Fred Fingers – Spelling Green Words See *Get Writing!* Book, p.19.

Hold a Sentence – 1 and 2

> **1** Bounder pounced on the sandwich when it fell to the ground.

> **2** I stuffed most of the little sweets into my mouth.

See *Get Writing!* Book, p.18.

Day 3 timetable	a. Daily Speed Sounds Lesson	e. Questions to Talk About
See guidance below for activities in **bold**. See pp.119–120 for other Day 3 activities.	b. Partner Practice	f. Questions to Read and Answer
	c. Think About the Story	**g. Build a Sentence**
	d. Third Read – Children	h. Handwriting

 Think About the Story

p.9 TOL about how the boy describes his house and why he thinks you wouldn't stop to look at it.

p.10 Freeze Frame Mum's and the boy's expression when Carl plays his music. **TTYP:** How do they feel? *Irritated/Cross because it is too loud.*

p.11 TOL about how we know it's not a very clean or tidy house.

p.12 TOL about why the boy might clean up after Bounder's bath.

p.13 Freeze Frame the boy's expression as he sits in bed.
TTYP: How does he feel and why? *Contented/Happy/Satisfied because he knows things aren't perfect but there are good things too – even Bounder isn't too bad.*

p.14 TOL about the boy's relationship with Carl and Grandad.

p.15 MTYT (with feeling): *Our house is – well, it's **all right**.*

Build a Sentence

Tell children that tomorrow they will write about their own bedroom, describing it to a friend or relative who is coming to stay. Explain that today you are going to help them build up a few sentences to describe Alex's bedroom.

1. Use **MTYT** to say the simple sentence: *Alex sits in his bedroom.*

   TTYP: What size bedroom is it? Draw out responses such as *small/tiny/huge/enormous.* Show how to build the children's responses into the sentence, e.g. *Alex sits in his tiny bedroom.*

   TTYP: Who shares the room with Alex? *His brother, Carl.* Expand the sentence with more detail, e.g. *Alex sits in his tiny bedroom that he shares with his brother, Carl.*

2. What does he keep in his room? For example, *clothes/comics/games/books/toys/shoes.* **TTYP:** Where does he keep his things? *In the cupboard/In drawers/Under his bed/In boxes/On the floor.* Demonstrate how to build the detail into a sentence, e.g. *Alex sits in his tiny bedroom that he shares with his brother, Carl. His toys are in boxes under his bed and his clothes are in the drawers.*

3. **TTYP:** How tidy does he keep his room? *Scruffy/Cluttered/Messy/Clean.* Encourage children to describe the state of Alex's room, building ideas in a full sentence, e.g. *Alex sits in his tiny bedroom that he shares with his brother, Carl. His toys are shoved under his bed in a mess and his clothes spill out of the drawers.*

4. Ask partners to decide on their own two sentences and to practise saying them until they can remember them. Select a few partners to say their sentences to the group.

5. Ask children to write their sentences on p.18 of their *Get Writing!* Book. Encourage children to spell new words using their phonic knowledge. Accept phonically-plausible spellings.

DAY 4	Day 4 timetable	a. Daily Speed Sounds Lesson	e. Proofread – Spelling
	See guidance below for activities in **bold**. See pp.120–122 for other Day 4 activities.	b. Spell Check	f. Proofread – Grammar
		c. Grammar	**g. Write About Your Bedroom**
		d. Vocabulary	h. Handwriting

 Grammar

1. Tell (or remind) children that a **noun phrase** is a group of words that has a noun as its main word, with other words telling us more about that noun.

2. On the board write *Bounder is always looking for his bouncy ball.* Use **MTYT** to say the sentence. Point out the underlined noun phrase. Ask children to **TTYP** to say which word is the noun *(ball)*. Explain that the other two words tell us more about the ball (i.e. it is *bouncy*, and it is *his* – it belongs to Bounder). Other examples are: *We have a red door* and *Grandad sat in his chair*.

3. Ask children to complete the Grammar activity on p.19 of their *Get Writing!* Book.

4. Ask children to **TTYP** to check they have underlined and circled the same words and if not, to discuss which answers are correct and why.

5. Tell children the correct responses and explain any difficult points. (They should have identified these noun phrases and nouns: *an egg **sandwich**; some **flour**; one small **bathroom**; a little **garden**.*)

 Vocabulary

1. Explain that good writers try to develop a wide vocabulary and use a variety of words to make their writing more interesting for the reader. They do not always use the most obvious, common words. Write the word *devoured* on the board. Using **MTYT**, say the sentence *Bounder devoured the egg sandwich at top speed.* Point out that the writer could have just said *Bounder ate the egg sandwich*... but *devoured* makes Bounder sound more greedy and hungry. It creates a much more interesting picture in the reader's mind.

2. Ask children to turn to the Vocabulary activity on p.19 of their *Get Writing!* Book. Talk through the activity first. Invite children to practise their sentences aloud with a partner before writing them down. Encourage children to use the word *because* in their sentences, to demonstrate a clear understanding of the context for each word. For example, *The cat pounced on the mouse because he wanted to catch it before it ran away.*

3. Give feedback on the children's sentences, checking that they have demonstrated their understanding of these words.

 Write About Your Bedroom

Note that this activity should be started on Day 4 and completed on Day 5.

1. **TOL** about having friends or relatives to stay when you were a child. Recall how you looked forward to them coming, the games you played and the things you talked about. **TTYP:** Which friends or relatives come to stay at your house? What games do you play? What do you talk about?

2. Use online file 6.5 (tab g onwards) for this activity. Explain to children that they are going to write to a friend or cousin who they haven't seen for a long time. They are coming to stay, so children need to tell them all about their room and where they will sleep. Ask children to turn to pp.20–21 of their *Get Writing!* Book. Ask them to decide on the name of their friend or cousin and write it after the word 'Dear' in their exercise book. Then ask them to copy the first sentence of the letter.

3. Ask children to think about their first paragraph. **TTYP:** What things do you have in your bedroom and where do you keep them? Draw out responses, using **MTYT** to demonstrate how to build them into a full sentence, e.g. *In my bedroom I have... my clothes in a wardrobe and my books on a shelf.* Encourage children to give more details about cupboards, shelves, bookcases, drawers, boxes, etc.

TTYP: Does your bedroom look tidy or messy*? My bedroom is... very messy, with things all over the floor/tidy, with everything put away neatly.* Remind children of their ideas for the Build a Sentence activity and encourage them to incorporate them.

TTYP: What colour are the curtains/blinds/duvet/carpets/walls? Draw out descriptions about colour and designs, e.g. *My bedroom is decorated with... green patterned wallpaper/a stripy red and white rug/a flowery duvet cover/plain blue walls/brightly coloured posters/pictures.*

Go through the other questions, using **MTYT** to model how to build the children's ideas into full, detailed sentences.

4. Go back to the first paragraph. Decide on the first few sentences and **TOL** as you use the online file (tab g) to model how to write them on the board. Keep re-reading as you write to make sure that your writing makes sense.

5. Hide your writing. Tell children to practise their own first sentences aloud with their partners until they can remember them. Select a few partners to say their sentences to the group. Then children can write their own sentences in their exercise book. Point out the Useful words on p.20 of their *Get Writing!* Book. Encourage children to use the sentence starters on p.21 and make notes here if they wish. Encourage children to spell new words using their phonic knowledge. Accept phonically-plausible spellings.

6. Repeat Steps 4 and 5 (demonstrate how you write, then ask children to write) for the remaining questions. Encourage children to use their own ideas as they complete their letter.

Day 5 timetable	a. Daily Speed Sounds Lesson	d. Partner Proofread
See Day 4 for guidance on the activity in **bold**. See p.122 for other Day 5 activities.	b. Spell Test	e. Words to Keep
	c. Write About Your Bedroom (continued)	f. Linked Text

GW **Write About Your Bedroom (continued)**

On Day 5, children continue the writing activity that they began on Day 4.

The jar of oil

Teacher's Preparation

Prepare as for p.114. Print out and display the Story Green Words (see online file '6.6 The jar of oil', starting with tab a): *prince, oil, coins, joint, lamb, grill, grand, spoil, soil, royal, highness, princess, palace, splendid, appoint, handsome, employed, toiled, hoisted, oysters, embroidered, destroyed, scented**.

Note that Challenge Words are marked with an asterisk.

Display these Red Word Cards in your pocket chart: *through, once, there, son, who, your, her, was, to, you, of, one, all.*

DAY 1

Day 1 timetable	a. Daily Speed Sounds Lesson	g. **Story Introduction**
See guidance below for activities in **bold**. See pp.114–116 for other Day 1 activities.	b. Speed Sounds from the Storybook	h. First Read – Children
	c. Story Green Words	i. Read Aloud – Teacher
	d. Speedy Green Words (online file 6.6b)	j. **Red Rhythms – Spelling Red Words**
	e. Red Word Cards	k. Handwriting
	f. Partner Practice	

Story Introduction

Once, there was a poor man who worked in a very grand palace. The prince employed him to do odd jobs there, and every day he toiled away in the royal gardens. One day, the prince presented him with a big jar of scented oil, to thank him for all his hard work.

The poor man carried the jar back to his little one-room house, where he placed it carefully on a shelf. Sitting down on his three-legged stool, he thought about the gold coins he could get if he sold the precious oil.

He imagined what life would be like if he were a rich man: the delicious food he would eat – the oysters, the sweet milk puddings, the big joints of lamb and the hot fresh bread.

'I will ask a rich girl to marry me,' he thought. 'We can live together in a grand house like the prince's and have a strong and handsome son. We will play with pointed swords and sticks.' The man swung a stick around as he imagined playing with his son.

TTYP: Can you guess what happened as the man swished his stick through the air?

Red Rhythms – Spelling Red Words See *Get Writing! Blue*, p.23.

DAY 2

Day 2 timetable	a. Daily Speed Sounds Lesson	f. Second Read – Children
See guidance below for activities in **bold**. See pp.117–119 for other Day 2 activities.	b. Speedy Green Words (online file 6.6b)	g. **Fred Fingers – Spelling Green Words**
	c. Red Word Cards	h. Red Rhythms
	d. Partner Practice	i. **Hold a Sentence – 1 and 2**
	e. Jump-in	j. Handwriting

Fred Fingers – Spelling Green Words See *Get Writing!* Book, p.23.

Hold a Sentence – 1 and 2

1 "I will sell it," the man said to his little yellow dog.

2 We will marry and live together in a grand house.

See *Get Writing!* Book, p.22.

 DAY 3

Day 3 timetable	a. Daily Speed Sounds Lesson	e. Questions to Talk About
See guidance below for activities in **bold**. See pp.119–120 for other Day 3 activities.	b. Partner Practice	f. Questions to Read and Answer
	c. Think About the Story	**g. Build a Sentence**
	d. Third Read – Children	h. Handwriting

 Think About the Story

p.9 TOL about why the prince gave the poor man a jar of oil.
Freeze Frame the poor man's expression. **TTYP:** How did he feel? *Grateful/Happy/Thrilled/Delighted.*

p.10 TOL about what we know about how the poor man lived.

p.11 TOL about why the poor man wanted to sell the jar of oil.

p.12 TOL about what he hoped his future would be like.

pp.13–14 TOL about what he would give his son and how he would treat him.

p.15 Freeze Frame the poor man's expression as the jar crashed to the floor (e.g. eyes wide open, mouth screaming, arms stretched out, then hands covering his face, head bent into his hands).
TTYP: How did he feel? *Shocked/Horrified/In despair.*
TOL about how breaking the jar of oil would destroy his plans.
MTYT (with feeling): *A **poor** man – and a **foolish** one.*

 Build a Sentence

Tell children that tomorrow they will write a letter (in role as the poor man) to the prince, asking him to give you another jar of oil. Explain that today you are going to help them build up some sentences about the moment when the poor man realised that the jar of oil had smashed.

1. Use **MTYT** to say the simple sentence: *The jar of oil crashed to the floor*.

2. Ask children to Freeze Frame the moment when the poor man saw the jar crash to the ground. (They did this in the previous activity, but encourage them to describe it orally as well.) **TTYP:** What did the poor man do? Draw out responses such as *stood with his eyes wide open/shouted/stretched out his arms/groaned/covered his face with his hands/stood in silence*. **MTYT:** *The poor man stood with his eyes wide open in horror as the jar of oil crashed to the floor.*

3. **TTYP:** What did he say? *"All my hopes are gone."/"I shall be poor forever."/"What will I do now?"* Demonstrate how to build up the sentences, e.g. *The poor man stood with his eyes wide open in horror as the jar of oil crashed to the floor. Then he said, "Now I shall be poor forever."*

4. **TTYP:** How did he say this? *He wailed/cried/shrieked in despair/He said... miserably/gloomily/in a heartbroken voice.* Use some of the children's responses to expand the sentence, e.g. *The poor man stood with his eyes wide open in horror as the jar of oil crashed to the floor. "Now I shall be poor forever," he wailed in despair.*

5. Ask partners to decide on their own sentences and to practise saying them until they can remember them. Select a few partners to say their sentences to the group.

6. Ask children to write their own sentences on p.22 of their *Get Writing!* Book. Encourage children to spell new words using their phonic knowledge. Accept phonically-plausible spellings.

Day 4 timetable	a. Daily Speed Sounds Lesson	e. Proofread – Spelling
See guidance below for activities in **bold**. See pp.120–122 for other Day 4 activities.	b. Spell Check	f. Proofread – Grammar
	c. Grammar	**g. Write a Letter to the Prince**
	d. Vocabulary	h. Handwriting

GW Grammar

1. Remind children that we use the **past tense** of verbs to describe things that have happened earlier (in the past). Write on the board *A poor man lived near a palace.* Use **MTYT** to say the sentence. Ask children to **TTYP** to identify the verb *(lived)*. Draw attention to the past-tense ending -ed.

2. Point out that although many past tense verbs end with -ed, there are many that don't. For example, write on the board *He runs to the palace.* Use **MTYT** to say the sentence. Ask children to **TTYP** to change this sentence into the past tense, as if describing something that has already happened. *(He ran to the palace.)* Check children have correctly changed *runs* to *ran*. Other examples are: *I have/had a jar of oil* and *I am/was a poor man.*

3. Ask children to complete the Grammar activity on p.23 of their *Get Writing!* Book.

4. Ask children to **TTYP** to check they have written the same words and if not, to discuss which answers are correct and why.

5. Tell children the correct responses and explain any difficult points. (They should have written: *said, took, had.*)

GW Vocabulary

1. Explain that we are very lucky to have so many words in the English language because it means that, as writers, we have a lot of choice. When we want to write or say something, there are usually many different ways that we can write it.

2. Write three words on the board: *smashed, prized, destroyed.* Use **MTYT** to say all three words. Ask children to **TTYP** and say which word is the odd one out, because it means something different *(prized).*

3. Ask children to turn to the Vocabulary activity on p.23 of their *Get Writing!* Book. Talk through the activity, explaining any words that they are unsure of. Then ask children to complete the activity.

4. Ask children to **TTYP** to check they have ticked the same words and if not, to discuss which answers are correct and why.

5. Tell children the correct responses and explain any difficult points. (They should have ticked: *slept, swished, dropped.*)

GW Write a Letter to the Prince

Note that this activity should be started on Day 4 and completed on Day 5.

1. **TOL** about how awful you felt when you broke something that was precious to you – or someone else that you know. It could be a vase, a mirror, a glass sculpture or a precious ornament. **TTYP:** Have you ever broken something that was precious to you?

2. Use online file 6.6 (tab g onwards) for this activity. Explain to children that they are going to write a letter (in role as the poor man) to the prince, begging for another jar of oil. Ask them to turn to p.25 in their *Get Writing!* Book. Draw attention to the outline of the letter. Read the letter opening and then ask children to copy the first two lines of the letter into their exercise books.

3. Ask children questions and encourage them to respond in the role of the poor man. Ask children to **TTYP** and then draw out their responses and use **MTYT** to model how to turn them into full sentences.

   – How did you feel when the prince gave it to you? *I felt... delighted to have such a fabulous jar of oil/amazed at his kindness/pleased to have such a fine jar of oil.*

   – How did you break the jar of oil? *I broke the jar of oil when... I knocked it off the shelf/I caught it with a stick/I was play fighting.*

   – What had you hoped to do with the oil? *I wanted to... sell it for gold coins/make expensive perfume/become rich/find a wife/have a son/live in a grand house.*

   – How will you make sure the next jar of oil is safe? *I will keep it safe by... putting it in a cupboard/never playing with sticks again/taking it straight to the market/keeping it behind my bed.*

   – What will you do if the prince gives you another jar of oil? *I promise to... work extra hard/work for you for 10 years/make you a wonderful perfume.*

4. Go back to the first question and use the online file (tab g) to model how to answer it. **TOL** as you write, and keep re-reading to check that it all makes sense.

5. Hide your writing. Ask children to practise their own first sentence aloud with their partners until they can remember them. Select a few partners to say their sentences to the group. Then children can write their own sentence in their exercise book. Point out the Useful words on p.24 of their *Get Writing!* Book. They can also make notes on p.25. Encourage children to spell new words using their phonic knowledge. Accept phonically-plausible spellings.

6. Repeat Steps 4 and 5 (demonstrate how you write, then ask children to write) for the other paragraphs.

DAY 5

Day 5 timetable	a. Daily Speed Sounds Lesson	d. Partner Proofread
See Day 4 for guidance on the activity in **bold**. See p.122 for other Day 5 activities.	b. Spell Test	e. Words to Keep
	c. **Write a Letter to the Prince (continued)**	f. Linked Text

 Write a Letter to the Prince (continued)

On Day 5, children continue the writing activity that they began on Day 4.

Jade's party

Teacher's Preparation

Prepare as for p.114. Print out and display the Story Green Words (see online file '6.7 Jade's party', starting with tab a): *Jade, cake, group, stale, pale, blame, shame, chocolate, lemonade, teenage, trolley, currant, behave, pavement, fishcake, sparklers, music*, shopping, plates, raced.*
Note that Challenge Words are marked with an asterisk.
Display these Red Word Cards in your pocket chart: *brother, all, where, said, one, was, you, of.*

DAY 1

Day 1 timetable	a. Daily Speed Sounds Lesson	g. **Story Introduction**
See guidance below for activities in **bold**. See pp.114–116 for other Day 1 activities.	b. Speed Sounds from the Storybook	h. First Read – Children
	c. Story Green Words	i. Read Aloud – Teacher
	d. Speedy Green Words (online file 6.7b)	j. **Red Rhythms – Spelling Red Words**
	e. Red Word Cards	k. Handwriting
	f. Partner Practice	

Story Introduction

On Sunday, it was Jade's birthday.
   "Let's plan a party!" said her dad. "We'll start by making a shopping list." They made a long list with lots of yummy things on it, like lemonade, crisps and a big chocolate cake.
   "Don't forget the plates, balloons and party music," said Jade.
   Dad asked Jade's teenage brother, Dave, to take her to the shops.
   "Let's get a trolley," Dave said when they got there. "I'll get the bread rolls and cheese; you get the crisps and milk shakes."
   The trolley started to fill up. They found the napkins and plates, a big packet of balloons, and a CD by a new music group.
   Most importantly, they got a huge chocolate cake, the biggest one in the shop. It said 'Happy Birthday' on top in swirly pink letters.
   "Enjoy your party!" said the checkout girl as she packed all the stuff into plastic bags.
   Jade raced all the way to the bus stop, making up party games with Dave on the way.
   But when Dad unpacked the shopping, his face went white with shock.
   "What's wrong, Dad?" asked Jade.

TTYP: Why do you think Dad's face was white with shock?

Red Rhythms – Spelling Red Words See *Get Writing! Blue*, p.27.

DAY 2

Day 2 timetable	a. Daily Speed Sounds Lesson	f. Second Read – Children
See guidance below for activities in **bold**. See pp.117–119 for other Day 2 activities.	b. Speedy Green Words (online file 6.7b)	g. **Fred Fingers – Spelling Green Words**
	c. Red Word Cards	h. Red Rhythms
	d. Partner Practice	i. **Hold a Sentence – 1 and 2**
	e. Jump-in	j. Handwriting

Fred Fingers – Spelling Green Words See *Get Writing!* Book, p.27.

Hold a Sentence – 1 and 2

1. We raced along the pavement to the place where the bus stopped.

2. Take this shopping back to the shop and pick up the right bag.

See *Get Writing!* Book, p.26

Day 3 timetable	a. Daily Speed Sounds Lesson	e. Questions to Talk About
See guidance below for activities in **bold**. See pp.119–120 for other Day 3 activities.	b. Partner Practice	f. Questions to Read and Answer
	c. Think About the Story	**g. Build a Sentence**
	d. Third Read – Children	h. Handwriting

 Think About the Story

p.9 **TOL** about who the party was for.
MTYT (with feeling): *But the party **almost** didn't happen!*

p.10 **TOL** about how lots of food meant that there were lots of people coming to the party.

pp.11–12 **TOL** about Jade and Dave's excitement as they bought everything on their list.

p.13 **TOL** about what they talked about as they hurried home.

p.14 Freeze Frame Jade and Dave's expressions as they unpacked the shopping.
TTYP: How do they feel, and why?

Confused/Disappointed/Embarrassed/ Couldn't understand how they picked up the wrong bags.
Freeze Frame Dad's expression.
TTYP: How was he feeling, and why?
Annoyed/Cross because he thought he could trust Dave to shop without him.

p.15 **TOL** about how Dad made everything okay in the end.
Freeze Frame Jade's expression.
TTYP: How was she feeling now? *Happy/ Relieved.*
MTYT (with feeling): *Then out came a man with a **birthday** cake!*

 Build a Sentence

Tell children that tomorrow they will write a birthday party invitation. Explain that today you are going to help them build up a sentence about the sort of cake you will have at your party.

1. Use **MTYT** to say *We will have a cake.*

   TTYP: What sort of cake will you have? Draw out responses such as *chocolate/lemon/orange/ coffee/plain*. Demonstrate how to build one of the children's ideas into the sentence, e.g. *We will have a chocolate cake.*

2. **TTYP:** What will you have inside the cake? For example, *fruit/butter cream/thick oozy cream/ chocolate spread/sticky raspberry jam*. Use some ideas to expand the sentence, e.g. *We will have a chocolate cake with jam and cream in the middle.*

3. **TTYP:** What will you put on top of your cake? For example, *hard crackly icing/rainbow candles/ pink flowers/chocolate buttons*. Demonstrate how to build the sentence further, e.g. *We will have a chocolate cake with jam and cream in the middle and chocolate buttons on the top.*

4. Ask partners to decide on their own sentence and to practise saying it until they can remember it. Select a few partners to say their sentences to the group.

5. Ask children to write their own sentence on p.26 of their *Get Writing!* Book. Encourage children to spell new words using their phonic knowledge. Accept phonically-plausible spellings.

DAY 4	**Day 4 timetable**	a. Daily Speed Sounds Lesson	e. Proofread – Spelling
	See guidance below for activities in **bold**. See pp.120–122 for other Day 4 activities.	b. Spell Check	f. Proofread – Grammar
		c. Grammar	**g. Write a Party Invitation**
		d. Vocabulary	h. Handwriting

 Grammar

1. Remind children that a **comma** can show a pause in a sentence. It can also be used in a list to separate things. Write on the board *We bought party napkins, plates and a packet of balloons.* Use **MTYT** to say the sentence. Point out the comma and draw attention to the fact that there is no comma before the final *and* in the sentence. Another example is: *I took a packed lunch to school on Monday, Wednesday and Friday.*

2. Ask children to complete the Grammar activity on p.27 of their *Get Writing!* Book.

3. Ask children to **TTYP** to check they have inserted the commas in the same places and if not, to discuss where they should be and why.

4. Tell children the correct responses and explain any difficult points. (1. Place comma after 'rolls'; 2. Place comma after 'crisps'; 3. Place commas after 'grapes' and 'nappies'; 4. Place commas after 'pizza' and 'chips'. Ensure that children do not add a comma before the final *and* in each list.)

 Vocabulary

1. Explain how important it is to try to use a variety of words in writing so that we can build up an interesting picture in the reader's mind.

2. On the board write the sentence *Jade had a big birthday cake.* Underline the word *big*. **TTYP:** How else could we describe a cake? What other words could we use? For example, *fruity/delicious/ fabulous/sparkly/special/colourful.* Model how to re-read the sentence, replacing *big* with one of the children's suggestions, e.g. *Jade had a **delicious** birthday cake.*

3. Ask children to turn to the Vocabulary activity on p.27 of their *Get Writing!* Book. Talk through the activity, discussing possible words with them. Encourage children to be imaginative. For example: 1: *hot, spicy, crunchy, yummy*; 2: *noisy, funny, energetic, silly*; 3: *spotty, soft, stripy, flowery.* Then ask children to complete the activity.

4. Ask children to **TTYP** to discuss their choices.

Write a Party Invitation

Note that this activity should be started on Day 4 and completed on Day 5.

1. **TOL** about a party you have planned. Recall all the things you had to do to make sure it went well, e.g. thinking up a theme, inviting people, organising the food and drinks, buying balloons, thinking up games to play. **TTYP:** What kind of parties have you been to? What did you eat? What games did you play?

2. Use online file 6.7 (tab g onwards) for this activity. Explain to children that they are going to write a birthday party invitation. Ask them to turn to p.29 in their *Get Writing!* Book. Tell children to copy the first two lines of the invitation into their exercise book, inserting the name of the person they want to invite.

3. Use **TTYP** to draw out responses.

   – Where will the party take place? *My house/The hall/The pizza place.*

   – What date and time will it be on?

   – What games will we play? *We will play... Treasure hunt/Pass the parcel/Sleeping lions/Musical chairs.*

   Go through all the questions, drawing out suggestions from children and using **MTYT** to model how to turn them into full sentences, e.g. *It will be at my house.*

4. Go back to the first heading and use the online file (tab g) to model how to write a sentence. **TOL** as you write, and keep re-reading to check that it all makes sense.

5. Hide your writing. Ask children to practise their own first sentence aloud with their partners until they can remember it. Select a few partners to say their sentences to the group. Then children can write their own sentence in their exercise book. Point out the Useful words and sentence starters on pp.28–29 of their *Get Writing!* Book, where they can make notes. Encourage children to spell new words using their phonic knowledge. Accept phonically-plausible spellings.

6. Repeat Steps 4 and 5 (demonstrate how you write, then ask children to write) for the other headings.

Day 5 timetable	a. Daily Speed Sounds Lesson	d. Partner Proofread
See Day 4 for guidance on the activity in **bold**. See p.122 for other Day 5 activities.	b. Spell Test	e. Words to Keep
	c. Write a Party Invitation (continued)	f. Linked Text

GW **Write a Party Invitation (continued)**

On Day 5, children continue the writing activity that they began on Day 4.

Jellybean

Teacher's Preparation

Prepare as for p.114. Print out and display the Story Green Words (see online file '6.8 Jellybean', starting with tab a): *seal, beast, hay, cream, leave, mouse, cage, cheap, noise, wolf*, Jellybean, weasel, greedy, afford, goldfish, creased, freaked, teased, bleated, squeaked, screamed, frighten.* Note that Challenge Words are marked with an asterisk.

Display these Red Word Cards in your pocket chart: *any, what, one, was, want, does, could, said, some, of.*

DAY 1

Day 1 timetable	a. Daily Speed Sounds Lesson	g. **Story Introduction**
See guidance below for activities in **bold**. See pp.114–116 for other Day 1 activities.	b. Speed Sounds from the Storybook	h. First Read – Children
	c. Story Green Words	i. Read Aloud – Teacher
	d. Speedy Green Words (online file 6.8b)	j. **Red Rhythms – Spelling Red Words**
	e. Red Word Cards	k. Handwriting
	f. Partner Practice	

Story Introduction

Explain to the children that you are going to take on the role of the girl in the book, who tells her story.

My name is Annabelle and I love animals! I've had lots of pets, but every time I get one, something always goes wrong. First, I asked Mum for an elephant.

"Please, please, please, Mum," I begged her, "let me have a pet!"

To begin with Mum was unsure, but then she got me an elephant! It lived in the garden and I fed it three sacks of hay each morning. Then one day, Mum said, "We can't afford it. The elephant has to leave." So I asked her for a sheep.

"Please, please, please, Mum," I begged her again, "let me have a pet!"

The sheep lived in the kitchen. But it bleated and bleated and no one could get any sleep. So one day, Mum said, "The sheep has to leave."

After that, I asked her for a mouse. And she did get me one, but something happened and I don't think Mum will let me get another pet...

TTYP: What do you think the mouse did?

Red Rhythms – Spelling Red Words See *Get Writing! Blue*, p.31.

DAY 2

Day 2 timetable	a. Daily Speed Sounds Lesson	f. Second Read – Children
See guidance below for activities in **bold**. See pp.117–119 for other Day 2 activities.	b. Speedy Green Words (online file 6.8b)	g. **Fred Fingers – Spelling Green Words**
	c. Red Word Cards	h. Red Rhythms
	d. Partner Practice	i. **Hold a Sentence – 1 and 2**
	e. Jump-in	j. Handwriting

Fred Fingers – Spelling Green Words See *Get Writing! Book*, p.31.

GW **Hold a Sentence – 1 and 2**

1 Please can I have a horse for a pet?

2 The sheep bleated all night so it had to leave.

See *Get Writing! Book*, p.30.

Day 3 timetable	a. Daily Speed Sounds Lesson	e. Questions to Talk About
See guidance below for activities in **bold**. See pp.119–120 for other Day 3 activities.	b. Partner Practice	f. Questions to Read and Answer
	c. Think About the Story	**g. Build a Sentence**
	d. Third Read – Children	h. Handwriting

Think About the Story

p.9 TOL about Annabelle and the first pet animal she hopes to get.
Freeze Frame her expression.
TTYP: How does she feel? *Hopeful/Keen/Enthusiastic.*
MTYT (with feeling, each time the refrain occurs): *"Please, please, **please**, Mum, let me have a **pet**!"*

p.10 TOL about how they looked after the elephant, and why they had to let it go.

p.11 TOL about what animal she hopes for next.

p.12 TOL about why the sheep had to go.

p.13 TOL about what animal she hopes for next.

p.14 TOL about why the mouse had to go.

p.15 TOL about why a goldfish is the perfect pet.
Freeze Frame Annabelle's expression
TTYP: How does she feel? *Relieved/Contented/Happy/Satisfied.*

GW **Build a Sentence**

Tell children that tomorrow they will write a poem about different animals who don't want to be kept in a garden. Explain that today you are going to help them build up some sentences that a grumpy animal might say if you tried to keep it in your garden.

1. Tell children to imagine they are Annabelle's elephant. (They need to talk in role.) Explain that the elephant is grumpy because it doesn't want to be in a garden. **MTYT:** *"I won't be your pet," said the elephant.*

2. **TTYP:** What would you do? For example, *swing my trunk/knock down your fence/eat your flowers/trample on your lawn/drink from your pond/knock over your bins.* Use some of the children's ideas to demonstrate how to build up the sentences, e.g. *"I won't be your pet," said the elephant. "If I were, I would swing my trunk and knock down your fence."*

3. Build the sentence further using more of the ideas. *"I won't be your pet," said the elephant. "If I were, I would swing my trunk, knock down your fence and knock over your bins."*

4. Ask partners to decide on their own sentences and to practise saying them until they can remember them. Select a few partners to say their sentences to the group.

5. Ask children to write their own sentences on p.30 of their *Get Writing!* Book. Encourage children to spell new words using their phonic knowledge. Accept phonically-plausible spellings.

Day 4 timetable	a. Daily Speed Sounds Lesson	e. Proofread – Spelling
See guidance below for activities in **bold**. See pp.120–122 for other Day 4 activities.	b. Spell Check	f. Proofread – Grammar
	c. Grammar	**g. Write a Poem**
	d. Vocabulary	h. Handwriting

GW Grammar

1. Tell (or remind) children that we use **joining words** (conjunctions) to link ideas together in a sentence. On the board, write *I would like a horse or bee.* Use **MTYT** to say the sentence. **TTYP:** Which is the joining word? *(or)* Point out that *or* joins together the words *horse* and *bee.*

2. Tell children that some other useful joining words are *and* and *but.* For example: *I have a pet cat and dog* and *I wanted a wolf but now I am happy with Jellybean.*

3. Write this incomplete sentence on the board: *Mum freaked out at first _____ she got me one.* Ask children which joining word would best complete the sentence: *and, or, but (but).*

4. Ask children to complete the Grammar activity on p.31 of their *Get Writing!* Book.

5. Ask children to **TTYP** to check they have chosen the same words and if not, to discuss which answers are correct and why.

6. Tell children the correct responses and explain any difficult points. (They should have written: *and, or, but, and.*)

GW Vocabulary

1. Explain how important it is in our writing to use words that bring a story alive for a reader. Good vocabulary can make a story more fun and interesting. On the board write *An elephant with creased grey skin.* Use **MTYT** to repeat the sentence. Underline *creased grey skin* and **TOL** about what a lovely picture this creates for the reader. It makes us think of crinkled paper or material.

2. Draw attention to the noun *(skin)* and the adjectives *(creased, grey).* Tell the children that these three words make up a **noun phrase**. The word *skin* is the noun in the phrase, and the adjectives describe it. Use **MTYT** to say *noun phrase.*

3. Explain to the children that they are going to write a noun phrase to complete a sentence about a duck. Write *I am a duck. I have…* Ask children for suggestions, such as *an orange beak/a shiny green head/webbed feet/soft feathers/beady eyes/a loud quack.* Model how to complete the sentence with some of the children's ideas, e.g. *I am a duck. I have a shiny green head.* Draw attention to the adjectives and nouns that make up the noun phrase, i.e. *shiny green head.*

4. Ask children to turn to the Vocabulary activity on p.31 of their *Get Writing!* Book. Talk through the activity, discussing possible ideas for each animal before children decide on their own, e.g. tiger: *long sharp teeth/vicious claws/strong fast legs/powerful stripy body*; gorilla: *huge hairy body/massive chunky shoulders/dark grumpy face*; kangaroo: *neat little pouch/long strong tail/powerful jumping legs*; panda: *black and white patches/soft round ears, big heavy paws.*)

Write a Poem

Note that this activity should be started on Day 4 and completed on Day 5.

1. **TOL** about how much space animals need to live happily, how they need room to roam in the wild. Recall how you felt sorry for some animals when you went to a zoo and you wondered what they were thinking. **TTYP:** Have you ever been to a zoo or seen animals kept in small places? Which animals did you see?

2. Use online file 6.8 (tab g onwards) for this activity. Explain to children that they are going to write a poem about what different animals might say to the little girl who wants to keep them as a pet. Ask children to turn to p.33 in their *Get Writing!* Book. Draw attention to the outline of a poem, called "I won't live in your garden". Ask children to copy the title into their exercise book (or choose their own). Ensure children understand that they will take on the role of each animal, using different verses to focus on a different animal. Note that children can draw on some of their ideas from the Vocabulary activity that they completed earlier.

3. Display the image of a tiger (tab g). **TTYP:** What do you look like? *I am... strong/stripy/large/ powerful/orange/black.* **MTYT:** *I am a strong, stripy tiger.*

   TTYP: What do you have? *I have... vicious claws/huge yellow eyes/long, sharp teeth.* **MTYT:** *I have vicious claws and long, sharp teeth.*

   TTYP: What would you do if you lived in a garden? *If I did, I would... roar all night/tear down the fence/trample all the flowers.* **MTYT:** *If I did, I would roar all night.*

4. Model how to complete the first verse on the board, using the online file (tab g). **TOL** as you write, and keep re-reading to check that it all makes sense.

5. Hide your writing. Tell children to practise their own first line aloud with their partners until they can remember it. Select a few partners to say their lines to the group. Then children can write their own line in their exercise book. Point out the Useful words and line starters on pp.32–33 of their *Get Writing!* Book, where they can also jot down ideas. Encourage children to spell new words using their phonic knowledge. Accept phonically-plausible spellings.

6. Repeat Steps 3, 4 and 5 (ask each question, demonstrate how you write, then ask children to write) for the other animals.

DAY 5	**Day 5 timetable**	a. Daily Speed Sounds Lesson	d. Partner Proofread
	See Day 4 for guidance on the activity in **bold**. See p.122 for other Day 5 activities.	b. Spell Test	e. Words to Keep
		c. Write a Poem (continued)	f. Linked Text

 Write a Poem (continued)

On Day 5, children continue the writing activity that they began on Day 4.

A box full of light

Teacher's Preparation

Prepare as for p.114. Print out and display the Story Green Words (see online file '6.9 A box full of light', starting with tab a): *Kite, rice, pile, pine, chink, prize, lie, miles, shine, steal, bolt, Kestrel, beside, untied, lightning, whined, decided, humans, gliding, trotted, guided, wives, spicy.*
Display these Red Word Cards in your pocket chart: *all, who, there, their, could, some, of, was, they, to, said, saw, what.*

DAY 1	Day 1 timetable	a. Daily Speed Sounds Lesson	**g. Story Introduction**
	See guidance below for activities in **bold**. See pp.114–116 for other Day 1 activities.	b. Speed Sounds from the Storybook	h. First Read – Children
		c. Story Green Words	i. Read Aloud – Teacher
		d. Speedy Green Words (online file 6.9b)	**j. Red Rhythms – Spelling Red Words**
		e. Red Word Cards	k. Handwriting
		f. Partner Practice	

Story Introduction

This story is a myth, which means it might not be true but it was told long ago, to explain how the whole world came to have light. (The people didn't understand about the sun, as we do today.)

This myth begins in the Land of Animals, where it was always dark. There was no light to find food, and the animals were always bumping into each other.

One particularly hungry day, Fox had had enough. He decided that something must be done.

'I need a good pal to help me, but who would that be?' he wondered. 'Kestrel has strong wings and very good sight. She will see much farther than me in the darkness. She'll do just fine.'

So Fox and Kestrel made their way to the Land of Humans, where Kestrel had heard there was a very bright light.

Soon they saw flashes of lightning up ahead. Fox couldn't believe his eyes. "That must be the light!" he said with a smile.

They followed the light to a little camp with five brightly lit tents. As they got closer, they saw men and women sitting around a fire, cooking delicious food.

'This is a fine sight,' thought Kestrel and Fox, watching the men and women as they ate thick slices of rabbit pie.

Then, out of the corner of his eye, Fox noticed a box buried beside a pile of pine logs. It had a little chink of light in one of its sides...

TTYP: What do you think was inside the box?

Red Rhythms – Spelling Red Words See *Get Writing! Blue*, p.35.

DAY 2	Day 2 timetable	a. Daily Speed Sounds Lesson	f. Second Read – Children
	See guidance below for activities in **bold**. See pp.117–119 for other Day 2 activities.	b. Speedy Green Words (online file 6.9b)	**g. Fred Fingers – Spelling Green Words**
		c. Red Word Cards	h. Red Rhythms
		d. Partner Practice	**i. Hold a Sentence – 1 and 2**
		e. Jump-in	j. Handwriting

Fred Fingers – Spelling Green Words See *Get Writing!* Book, p.35.

 Hold a Sentence – 1 and 2

> **1** What do you think is inside the box?

> **2** "Let's hide behind this for a while," said Fox with a smile.

See *Get Writing!* Book, p.34.

DAY 3	**Day 3 timetable**	a. Daily Speed Sounds Lesson	e. Questions to Talk About
	See guidance below for activities in **bold**. See pp.119–120 for other Day 3 activities.	b. Partner Practice	f. Questions to Read and Answer
		c. Think About the Story	**g. Build a Sentence**
		d. Third Read – Children	h. Handwriting

Think About the Story

p.9 **TOL** about why Fox didn't like living in the dark.
MTYT (with feeling): "*I don't like this at all!*"

p.10 **TOL** about why Fox chose Kestrel to help him.

p.11 **TOL** about what they decided to do and why they were pleased to see the lightning.

p.12 **TOL** about why they thought they were now in the Land of Humans.

p.13 **TOL** about how they stole the box of light.

p.14 Freeze Frame Fox's face when the light shot up out of the box.
TTYP: How did Fox feel? *Frightened/ Startled/Terrified/Panicky.*
MTYT (with feeling): "*Fetch the **light** back!*" he said.

p.15 **TOL** about what Kestrel tried to do.
TOL about how the story had a happy ending.

  ### Build a Sentence

Tell children that tomorrow they will write about Fox's journey. Explain that today you are going to help them build up some sentences to describe Fox's journey.

1. Display the picture of Fox (online file 6.9d). Tell children to think of themselves as Fox. Use **MTYT** for the first sentence: *I travelled for days.*

2. **TTYP:** How did you find your way in the dark? Draw out responses such as *stumbled through brambles/tripped over rocks/felt my way round bushes.* Show how to incorporate the children's ideas into the sentence using the correct verb forms, e.g. *I travelled for days, stumbling through brambles and tripping over rocks.*

3. **TTYP:** What could you hear? For example, *tweeting/roaring/thundering/squeaking.* Build the ideas into the sentence, e.g. *I travelled for days, stumbling through brambles and tripping over rocks, not knowing what the tweeting and roaring could be.*

4. **TTYP:** What was the weather like? For example, *stormy/wild/windy/wet/cold.* Show how to build up the detail of the sentences, e.g. *I travelled for days and weeks, stumbling through brambles and tripping over rocks. I walked through windy wet weather, not knowing what the tweeting and roaring could be.*

5. Ask partners to decide on their own sentences and to practise saying them until they can remember them. Select a few partners to say their sentences to the group.

6. Ask children to write their own sentences on p.34 of their *Get Writing!* Book. Encourage children to spell new words using their phonic knowledge. Accept phonically-plausible spellings.

DAY 4	**Day 4 timetable**	a. Daily Speed Sounds Lesson	e. Proofread – Spelling
	See guidance below for activities in **bold**. See pp.120–122 for other Day 4 activities.	b. Spell Check	f. Proofread – Grammar
		c. Grammar	**g. Write About a Journey**
		d. Vocabulary	h. Handwriting

GW Grammar

1. Tell (or remind) children that sometimes we shorten words, pushing two together, using an apostrophe to show which letters we are leaving out. (Use the term 'apostrophe of omission' or 'contractions', if appropriate for your year group.)

2. On the board write *didn't*. Use **MTYT** to say the word. Ask children to **TTYP** and say which two words make up this contraction (*did not*). Point out that the *o* in *not* has been left out, and that the apostrophe shows this.

3. Write *what is* on the board. Ask children to **TTYP** and say *what is* as one word (*what's*). Demonstrate how to write the contraction on the board.

4. Ask children to complete the Grammar activity on p.35 of their *Get Writing!* Book.

5. Ask children to **TTYP** to check they have linked up the same words and if not, to discuss which are correct and why.

6. Tell children the correct responses and explain any difficult points. (They should have linked up the following pairs: *could not/couldn't, we will/we'll, what is/what's, did not/didn't, can not, can't.*)

GW Vocabulary

1. Explain that good writers try to develop a wide vocabulary and use a variety of words to make their writing more interesting for the reader.

2. Write *whined* on the board. Use **MTYT** to say the word. Give the context of the word in the story: *"I don't like this at all!" whined Fox.* Write three words next to *whined* (e.g. *whistled, whispered, moaned*). Ask children to **TTYP** and say which one has a similar meaning to *whined (moaned)*.

3. Ask children to turn to the Vocabulary activity on p.35 of their *Get Writing!* Book. Talk through the activity, explaining any words that they are unsure of. Then ask children to complete the activity.

4. Ask children to **TTYP** to check they have circled the same words and if not, to discuss which answers are correct and why.

5. Tell children the correct responses and explain any difficult points. (They should have circled: *difficult, flying, friend, slid.*)

GW Write About a Journey

Note that this activity should be started on Day 4 and completed on Day 5.

1. **TOL** about a journey or walk you have been on that was a bit scary. Maybe you got lost, or the weather was very bad. **TTYP:** Have you ever been caught in a storm? What was it like?

2. Use online file 6.9 (tab g onwards) for this activity. Explain to children that they are going to write down the story Fox told the animals about his journey to the Land of Humans. (Children will be in role as Fox.) Say that the animals will ask lots of questions. Tell children that Fox loves to tell stories and wants all the animals to think he was very brave. Ask children to turn to pp.36–37 in their *Get Writing!* Book. Draw attention to the Useful words and questions. Explain that they will help children when they are writing. Ask children to write their chosen title in their exercise book.

3. Look at p.37 in the *Get Writing!* Book and ask the questions one by one. Use **TTYP** to draw out responses, reminding children to respond in role as Fox and use **MTYT** to develop their ideas into full sentences.

   – Why did you go on the journey? *I went on the journey because... I wanted to find some light/ it was always dark/we kept bumping into things.*

   – Why did you choose Kestrel to go on your journey? *I chose Kestrel because... she's a good pal/ she has strong wings/she has good eyesight.*

   – How long was your journey? *Our journey took... days/weeks/months/years.*

   – What did you see on your journey? *On the way, we saw... rivers/mountains/cliffs/woods/forests/ lakes.*

   – What was the weather like? *The weather was... stormy/windy/rainy/thundery/showery/blustery/ freezing cold.*

   – What were your scariest moments? *I was frightened when... I fell into a river/I was swept out to sea/I heard the howls in the woods/I was chased by a lion/I saw a tree falling nearby/I saw strange shadows.*

   Continue through all the questions, encouraging children to be imaginative in their responses and to use interesting, adventurous vocabulary.

4. Use online file (tab g) to model how to write the opening sentences, using some of the children's ideas, e.g. *I went on a journey because I was fed up that it was always night. I kept bumping into things. I chose Kestrel because she's a good pal and has strong wings.* **TOL** as you write, focusing on the word *I* as you are talking in role as Fox. Keep re-reading your writing to check that it makes sense.

5. Hide your writing. Tell children to practise their own first sentences aloud with their partners until they can remember them. Select a few partners to say their sentences to the group. Then children can write their own sentences in their exercise book. They can also make notes in their *Get Writing!* Book. Encourage children to spell new words using their phonic knowledge. Accept phonically-plausible spellings.

6. Repeat Steps 4 and 5 (demonstrate how you write, then ask children to write) for the other questions, possibly grouping some together, depending on how much support your group needs.

DAY 5	**Day 5 timetable**	a. Daily Speed Sounds Lesson	d. Partner Proofread
	See Day 4 for guidance on the activity in **bold**. See p.122 for other Day 5 activities.	b. Spell Test	e. Words to Keep
		c. **Write About a Journey (continued)**	f. Linked Text

 Write About a Journey (continued)

On Day 5, children continue the writing activity that they began on Day 4.

The hole in the hill

Prepare as for p.114. Print out and display the Story Green Words (see online file '6.10 The hole in the hill', starting with tab a): *stone, broke, stole, thrown, strange, pipe, rose, throne, holes, spoke, strode, barns, Hamelin, Pied Piper, crimson, meadow, suppose, quarrel, robes, notes, bellowed, toes*.*
Note that Challenge Words are marked with an asterisk.
Display these Red Word Cards in your pocket chart: *whole, want, your, any, could, their, was, small, tall, all, of, to, you, were, people.*

DAY 1

Day 1 timetable	a. Daily Speed Sounds Lesson	g. **Story Introduction**
See guidance below for activities in **bold**. See pp.114–116 for other Day 1 activities.	b. Speed Sounds from the Storybook	h. First Read – Children
	c. Story Green Words	i. Read Aloud – Teacher
	d. Speedy Green Words (online file 6.10b)	j. **Red Rhythms – Spelling Red Words**
	e. Red Word Cards	k. Handwriting
	f. Partner Practice	

Story Introduction

This is a story about the people from a little town called Hamelin, who were punished because their King broke a promise.

The story starts when the people were happy. They lived in large stone houses and their barns were full of yellow corn stored ready for the winter. Things began to go wrong when the barns were invaded by rats. There were big rats, small rats, short rats and tall rats. They broke into the barns and stole the corn. The people did everything they could to get rid of the rats, but nothing worked.

One day a strange fellow entered the town. He wore a long cloak, had bells on his toes and he carried a pipe – like a recorder. He was called the Pied Piper. He convinced the King that he could rid Hamelin of all the rats. The King, wearing his long crimson robes, rose from his throne and offered to pay the Pied Piper five bags of gold if he were successful.

The Pied Piper was as good as his word. When the rats heard his pipe, they followed the sweet notes down to the river where they ran straight into the water and drowned.

The people were thrilled, but when the Pied Piper went to collect his five bags of gold, the King only gave him one bag. They started to quarrel. The Pied Piper said words they would never forget, "You chose the wrong man to quarrel with."

He strode out of the King's palace. No one guessed the dreadful thing he was about to do...

TTYP: How do you think the Pied Piper felt? What do you think the Pied Piper did next?

Red Rhythms – Spelling Red Words See *Get Writing! Blue*, p.39.

DAY 2

Day 2 timetable	a. Daily Speed Sounds Lesson	f. Second Read – Children
See guidance below for activities in **bold**. See pp.117–119 for other Day 2 activities.	b. Speedy Green Words (online file 6.10b)	g. **Fred Fingers – Spelling Green Words**
	c. Red Word Cards	h. Red Rhythms
	d. Partner Practice	i. **Hold a Sentence – 1 and 2**
	e. Jump-in	j. Handwriting

Fred Fingers – Spelling Green Words See *Get Writing!* Book, p.39.

GW **Hold a Sentence – 1 and 2**

(1) Give me five bags of gold!

(2) Everybody wrote a note asking for the children to come home.

See *Get Writing!* Book, p.38.

DAY 3

Day 3 timetable	a. Daily Speed Sounds Lesson	e. Questions to Talk About
See guidance below for activities in **bold**. See pp.119–120 for other Day 3 activities.	b. Partner Practice	f. Questions to Read and Answer
	c. Think About the Story	**g. Build a Sentence**
	d. Third Read – Children	h. Handwriting

Think About the Story

p.9 TOL about what life in Hamelin was like before the rats came.
TOL about what life in Hamelin was like after the rats came.
MTYT: *Big rats...lots of rats.*

p.10 TOL about how the Pied Piper said he would help and the deal he made with the King. Read each section of dialogue with expression. Ask children to copy.

p.11 TOL about what happened to the rats when they went into the river.

p.12 TOL about how the Pied Piper felt when the King broke his promise.
MTYT: *And he poked the Pied Piper in the chest.*

p.13 MTYT: *"You chose the wrong man to quarrel with."*
TOL about how the children followed the Pied Piper in the same way as the rats... and what might happen to them?

p.14 TOL about what happened to the King when he fell in the river.

p.15 Freeze Frame the expression on the villagers' faces as their children returned.
TTYP: How did the villagers feel? *Relieved/Happy/Grateful.*

GW **Build a Sentence**

Tell children that tomorrow they will write about what happened when the children were taken by the Pied Piper. Explain that today you are going to help them build up some sentences that the people might have said to the King, when they discovered he had broken his promise to the Piper.

1. Use **MTYT** to repeat the sentence *"We are cross," said the people to the King.*

2. **TTYP:** How did the people feel? For example, *furious/mad/angry/upset/full of rage.* Demonstrate how to use some of the children's ideas to build up the sentence, e.g. *"We are furious," said the people to the King.*

3. **TTYP:** Why were they so furious? *The King broke his promise/He let us down/He put our children at risk/He tricked the Piper/The King lied.* Incorporate some of the ideas into the sentence, e.g. *"We are furious. You broke your promise," said the people to the King.*

4. **TTYP:** What word could we use instead of *said*? We need to show how cross the people were. For example, *yelled/screamed/shouted/roared/shrieked/bellowed.* Build up the sentences further, e.g. *"We are furious. You broke your promise," shouted the people to the King.*

5. Ask partners to decide on their own sentences and to practise saying them until they can remember them. Select a few partners to say their sentences to the group.

6. Ask children to write their own sentences on p.38 of their *Get Writing!* Book. Encourage children to spell new words using their phonic knowledge. Accept phonically-plausible spellings.

Day 4 timetable	a. Daily Speed Sounds Lesson	e. Proofread – Spelling
See guidance below for activities in **bold**. See pp.120–122 for other Day 4 activities.	b. Spell Check	f. Proofread – Grammar
	c. Grammar	**g. Write About the Child Who Was Left Behind**
	d. Vocabulary	h. Handwriting

Grammar

1. On the board, write the sentence *The Pied Piper spoke slowly*. Use **MTYT** to say the sentence, with particular emphasis on the word *slowly*. Check children understand its meaning (if necessary, saying the word very slowly to demonstrate). Point out that it is an **adverb** and gives more information about the verb *spoke*. It tells us *how* the Pied Piper spoke. Other examples are: *The people wrote to the Pied Piper sadly* and *The rats scampered madly across the meadow.*

2. Draw attention to the -ly ending of *slowly*. Explain that many adverbs end in -ly (but not all).

3. Ask children to complete the Grammar activity on p.39 of their *Get Writing!* Book.

4. Ask children to **TTYP** to check they have underlined the same words and if not, to discuss which answers are correct and why.

5. Tell children the correct responses and explain any difficult points. (They should have underlined: *sweetly, quickly, badly, crossly, happily.*)

Vocabulary

1. Explain how important it is to try to use a variety of words in writing so that we can build up an interesting picture in the reader's mind.

2. On the board write the sentence *The King looked grand in his crimson robes*. Underline the word *grand*. Ask what other words we could use to describe how the King looked. For example, *important/wealthy/powerful/magnificent*. Model how to re-read the sentence, replacing the word *grand* with one of the children's suggestions, e.g. *The King looked magnificent in his crimson robes.*

3. Ask children to turn to the Vocabulary activity on p.39 in their *Get Writing!* Book. Go through the sentences with them, encouraging them to think of alternative words. For example: 1: *furious, angry, enraged*; 2: *tossed, hurled, threw*; 3: *shouted, roared, yelled*.

4. Ask children to complete the Vocabulary activity on their own. Encourage them to be adventurous with their vocabulary, even if they are unsure of spelling. They do not have to use the words that you modelled previously.

Write About the Child Who Was Left Behind

Note that this activity should be started on Day 4 and completed on Day 5.

1. **TOL** about how terrible it must have been for the mums and dads when the children followed the Pied Piper. Explain that this is a very old story and that there are many different versions. In one story that you heard, one child was left behind, because he couldn't walk as fast as the other children.

2. Use online file 6.10 (tab g onwards) for this activity. Tell children that they are going to write a story in role as the child who was left behind. Explain that you will ask them some questions, and they should respond to them with their partners. This 'conversation' will help them prepare for their writing. Ask children to turn to p.41 in their *Get Writing!* Book. Draw attention to the different questions. Ask children to write their chosen title in their exercise book.

3. Ask the questions one by one. Use **TTYP** to draw out responses from children and use **MTYT** to develop their ideas into full sentences.

   – What was life like in Hamelin before the rats came*? Before the rats came, Hamelin was... busy/friendly/normal/people worked hard/people had fun.* Ask children what they used to do together and whether people felt happy.

   – What changed when the rats came? *When the rats came... they ate all the corn/they made everyone cross and unhappy/the people didn't have enough to eat.* Encourage children to say why the Pied Piper took the other children away.

   – How did you feel after the Pied Piper took the other children? *I felt... sad/lonely/confused.*

   Continue with the other questions.

4. Explain that you are going to show children how to write the first paragraph, then they will write their own. Choose some of the children's ideas and use the online file (tab g) to model how to write the first few sentences. **TOL** as you write and keep re-reading to make sure your writing makes sense.

5. Hide your writing. Then ask children to decide on their own sentences and practise them with their partners until they can remember them. Select a few partners to say their sentences to the group. Then children can write the first paragraph of their story in their exercise book. Point out the Useful words on p.40 of the *Get Writing!* Book, and the space on p.41, where they can make notes if they wish. Encourage children to spell new words using their phonic knowledge. Accept phonically-plausible spellings.

6. Repeat Steps 4 and 5 (demonstrate how you write, then ask children to write) for the other paragraphs. Some children may be able to complete the remaining paragraphs without teacher support.

Day 5 timetable	a. Daily Speed Sounds Lesson	d. Partner Proofread
See Day 4 for guidance on the activity in **bold**. See p.122 for other Day 5 activities.	b. Spell Test	e. Words to Keep
	c. Write About the Child Who Was Left Behind (continued)	f. Linked Text

GW **Write About the Child Who Was Left Behind (continued)**

On Day 5, children continue the writing activity that they began On Day 4.

163

On your bike

For ease, we have continued to refer to 'Story' Green Words in the non-fiction lessons.

Teacher's Preparation

Prepare as for p.114. Print out and display the Story Green Words (see online file 'NF6.3 On your bike', starting with tab a): *book, read, ride, bike, safe, size, small, bell, switch, white, wide, price, each, side, slip, slide, ice, fine, safe, front*, guidelines, helmet, pavement, traffic, forget, trousers, brakes, shorts, skirts, trapped, wheels, fits.*

Note that Challenge Words are marked with an asterisk.

Display these Red Word Cards in your pocket chart: *your, you, small, how, they, do.*

If possible, bring a child's bike into the classroom.

DAY 1			
Day 1 timetable	a. Daily Speed Sounds Lesson	**g. Book Introduction**	
See guidance below for activities in **bold**. See pp.114–116 for other Day 1 activities.	b. Speed Sounds from the Storybook	h. First Read – Children	
	c. Story Green Words	i. Read Aloud – Teacher	
	d. Speedy Green Words (online file NF6.3b)	**j. Red Rhythms – Spelling Red Words**	
	e. Red Word Cards	k. Handwriting	
	f. Partner Practice		

Book Introduction

Riding a bike is a great thing to do! It's a good way to keep fit. It gets you to places quickly and it can be fun.

To get the most out of riding your bike you need to be safe. Having the right equipment is very important. The first thing you should do is to make sure your bike is the right size – your feet should be able to touch the ground. Don't wear any loose clothes that could trail on the ground or get caught in the wheels, and *always* wear a helmet.

Check that your bike has good brakes and a bell and front and back lights that work: a bright white light at the front and a red one at the back. Put on your lights as soon as it starts to get dark so that people crossing the road or driving a car can see you coming.

Practise riding your bike in a park or on a quiet road. If you are cycling on streets where there are cars, make sure you stay near the pavement. Don't cycle on busy roads or in bad weather; ice or snow on the ground can make you slip.

Be safe when you ride your bike and have lots of fun!

TTYP: Who do you know who rides a bike? Where do they cycle?

Red Rhythms – Spelling Red Words See *Get Writing! Blue,* p.43.

DAY 2			
Day 2 timetable	a. Daily Speed Sounds Lesson	f. Second Read – Children	
See guidance below for activities in **bold**. See pp.117–119 for other Day 2 activities.	b. Speedy Green Words (online file NF6.3b)	**g. Fred Fingers – Spelling Green Words**	
	c. Red Word Cards	h. Red Rhythms	
	d. Partner Practice	**i. Hold a Sentence – 1 and 2**	
	e. Jump-in	j. Handwriting	

Fred Fingers – Spelling Green Words See *Get Writing!* Book, p.43.

Hold a Sentence – 1 and 2

1 Check your lights and brakes before you ride.

2 Do not ride your bike in ice and snow.

See *Get Writing!* Book, p.42.

Day 3 timetable	a. Daily Speed Sounds Lesson	e. Questions to Talk About
See guidance below for activities in **bold**. See pp.119–120 for other Day 3 activities.	b. Partner Practice	f. Questions to Read and Answer
	c. Think About the Information	**g. Build a Sentence**
	d. Third Read – Children	h. Handwriting

 Think About the Information

p.9 **TOL** about what this book is about: *How to be safe while riding your bike.* **TOL** about red triangle road signs. *They are warnings for people using the roads.* **TTYP:** Why is some information in this book in red triangles? *It shows the reader that this information is a warning or an alert – it is important.*

pp.10–11 **TOL** about the different parts of a bike and what you use them for. *The lights are so that people can see you in the dark; the bell is to warn people that you are there; the brakes are for when you want to slow down or stop.*

p.12 **TOL** about suitable clothing for riding a bike.

p.13 **TOL** about how important it is that your helmet fits well.

pp.14–15 **TOL** about things to do and not do on a bike.

p.16 **TTYP:** What must you always remember when you ride your bike? *To be safe.*

 Build a Sentence

Tell children that tomorrow they will write some instructions (commands) about how to be safe on a bike. Explain that today you are going to help them build up an instruction about wearing a helmet.

1. Display the picture of the boy wearing a helmet (online file NF6.3d). Use **MTYT** to say the sentence: *Put on your helmet.* Point out that this sentence starts with a word that gives an order (imperative verb) *Put*, which shows that this is an instruction (command).

2. **TTYP:** When should you put on your helmet? Draw out responses such as *before you get on your bike/every time you ride your bike.* Incorporate the children's suggestion into the main sentence, e.g. *Put on your helmet before you get on your bike.*

3. **TTYP:** What must you check? *That it fits well/That the straps are tight/That it is secure.* Model how to expand the original sentence further, e.g. *Put on your helmet before you get on your bike and check that the straps are tight.*

4. Ask partners to decide on their own sentence and to practise saying it until they can remember it. Select a few partners to say their sentences to the group.

5. Ask children to write their own sentences on p.42 of their *Get Writing!* Book. Encourage children to spell new words using their phonic knowledge. Accept phonically-plausible spellings.

Day 4 timetable	a. Daily Speed Sounds Lesson	e. Proofread – Spelling
See guidance below for activities in **bold**. See pp.120–122 for other Day 4 activities.	b. Spell Check	f. Proofread – Grammar
	c. Grammar	**g. Write About How to Ride a Bike Safely**
	d. Vocabulary	h. Handwriting

GW Grammar

1. Remind children that there are four different types of sentences: questions, exclamations, statements and commands (instructions). If necessary, give them an example of each, e.g. *Can I help you?* (question); *What a beautiful day it is!* (exclamation); *I like riding my bike.* (statement); *Get on your bike.* (command). Challenge some children to come up with examples of each type of sentence on their own.

2. Focus in particular on commands. Remind children that these are instructions: they are telling someone to *do* something. They often start with verbs that give an order (imperatives) such as *Go, Put, Take, Get, Look, Give, Be, Do not, Ask.*

3. Ask children to complete the Grammar activity on p.43 of their *Get Writing!* Book.

4. Ask children to **TTYP** to check they have ticked the same sentences and if not, to discuss which answers are correct and why.

5. Tell children the correct responses and explain any difficult points. (They should have ticked: *Check your bike before you ride it; Switch on your lights; Put on shorts or tight trousers; Wear a helmet when you ride a bike.*)

GW Vocabulary

1. Remind children that commands (instructions) often start with a verb that gives an order. Remind them that commands tell someone to do or be something.

2. On the board write three imperatives*: Put, Paint, Run.* Use **MTYT** to say the words. Then write the incomplete sentence: _____ *on your helmet before you ride your bike.* Ask children to **TTYP** and say which word should complete the sentence *(Put).*

3. Ask children to turn to the Vocabulary activity on p.43 of their *Get Writing!* Book. Talk through the activity, explaining any words that they are unsure of. Then ask children to complete the activity.

4. Ask children to **TTYP** to check they have written the same words and if not, to discuss which answers are correct and why.

5. Tell children the correct responses and explain any difficult points. (The correct words are: *Choose, Switch, Wear, Practise.*)

GW Write About How to Ride a Bike Safely

Note that this activity should be started on Day 4 and completed on Day 5.

1. **TOL** about how you (or someone you know) loves riding their bike. Explain where you ride to, how it gets you there more quickly than walking, and how it keeps you fit and healthy. Say that you love feeling the air moving past quickly and your feet whizzing round on the pedals. **TTYP:** What do you (or people you know) like about riding a bike?

   If possible, bring in a child's bike and ask how you would tell a child who has never ridden before how to ride a bike. Encourage them to use the imperative form of verbs, e.g. *Sit on the seat/Put your hands on the handlebars/Put your feet on the pedals/Push down with your legs to turn the pedals/Steer with the handlebars/Balance on your bike/Pull on the brakes to stop/Put your feet down when you stop.*

166

2. Use online file NF6.3 (tab g onwards) for this activity. Tell children that they are going to write down some instructions about how to ride a bike safely. Ask children to turn to p.45 in their *Get Writing!* Book. Draw attention to the questions that will help them think about what instructions to write. Ask children to copy the title into their exercise books (or choose their own).

3. Ask the questions one by one. Use **TTYP** to draw out responses from children and use **MTYT** to develop their ideas into full sentences.

   – What sort of bike should you choose? *Choose a bike that is... not too big/not too small/the right size.*

   – What must you do as it gets dark? *Switch on... your lights/Put a white light... at the front. Put a red light... at the back.*

   – How should you dress? *Wear... shorts or tight trousers/nothing long or flared that could get trapped in the wheels. Check that your helmet fits well/helmet has a tight strap.*

   – Where should you ride your bike? *Ride your bike on quiet streets/in the park/beside the pavement. Do not ride your bike in traffic.*

   – When should you not ride your bike? *Do not ride your bike in snow or ice, or in heavy rain.*

4. Use the online file (tab g) to model how to write the first instruction down as a full sentence, e.g. *Choose a bike that is not too big or too small.* **TOL** as you write and keep re-reading to make sure that it makes sense.

5. Hide your writing. Ask children to discuss the first instruction with their partner and practise it until they can remember it. Select a few partners to say their instructions to the group. Then children can write their own first instruction in their exercise book. Point out the Useful words on p.44 in the *Get Writing!* Book. Encourage children to spell new words using their phonic knowledge. Accept phonically-plausible spellings.

6. Repeat Steps 4 and 5 (demonstrate how you write, then ask children to write) with the next questions, supporting children as necessary as they complete their instructions. They can draft phrases or sentences in their *Get Writing!* Book.

DAY 5

Day 5 timetable	a. Daily Speed Sounds Lesson	d. Partner Proofread
See Day 4 for guidance on the activity in **bold**. See p.122 for other Day 5 activities.	b. Spell Test	e. Words to Keep
	c. Write About How to Ride a Bike Safely (continued)	f. Linked Text

 Write About How to Ride a Bike Safely (continued)

On Day 5, children continue the writing activity that they began on Day 4.

At the seaside

Teacher's Preparation

Prepare as for p.114. Print out and display the Story Green Words (see online file 'NF6.5 At the seaside', starting with tab a): *read, book, spade, sea, mask, line, kite, lie, shade, close, beach, harm, skin, cream, eat, clean, seaside, bucket, snorkel, explore, adult, seahorses, seaweed, driftwood, starfish, collect, forget, T-shirt, picnic, rubbish, lemonade, games, pools, caves, crabs, shells, stones, cones.*

Note that Challenge Words are marked with an asterisk.

Display these Red Word Cards in your pocket chart: *you, water, some, your, of, all, ball.*

DAY 1	**Day 1 timetable**	a. Daily Speed Sounds Lesson	**g. Book Introduction**
	See guidance below for activities in **bold**. See pp.114–116 for other Day 1 activities.	b. Speed Sounds from the Storybook	h. First Read – Children
		c. Story Green Words	i. Read Aloud – Teacher
		d. Speedy Green Words (online file NF6.5b)	**j. Red Rhythms – Spelling Red Words**
		e. Red Word Cards	k. Handwriting
		f. Partner Practice	

Book Introduction

I love going to the seaside, especially on a hot, sunny day. There are so many things you can do by the sea. You can take a bucket and spade to dig up sand or bury your friend right up to their shoulders! You can play ball games, fly kites, explore caves or even go fishing with a net.

If you feel like exploring, take a look in the rock pools – there's a lot to see, from pretty shells and floating seaweed to tiny starfish and scuttling crabs. You can collect them in your bucket.

If you get too hot, you can cool off in the sea, splash about near the shore in your armbands or go swimming or snorkelling with an adult. Remember to top up your sun cream when you come out of the sea or you might get burnt.

Then you can lie back in the shade with a good book. You can read, listening to the sound of the waves and feel the heat of the sun through the sunshade.

The best thing is eating fish and chips at the end of the day or having an ice cream.

Always make sure you take your rubbish with you when you leave so the beach is clean and tidy when you come back tomorrow.

TTYP: What do you think you would enjoy most at the seaside?

Red Rhythms – Spelling Red Words See *Get Writing! Blue*, p.47.

DAY 2	**Day 2 timetable**	a. Daily Speed Sounds Lesson	f. Second Read – Children
	See guidance below for activities in **bold**. See pp.117–119 for other Day 2 activities.	b. Speedy Green Words (online file NF6.5b)	**g. Fred Fingers – Spelling Green Words**
		c. Red Word Cards	h. Red Rhythms
		d. Partner Practice	**i. Hold a Sentence – 1 and 2**
		e. Jump-in	j. Handwriting

Fred Fingers – Spelling Green Words See *Get Writing! Book*, p.47.

GW **Hold a Sentence – 1 and 2**

1 Don't forget your sun cream when you play on the beach.

2 Drink lots of water when you are in the sun.

See *Get Writing!* Book, p.46.

DAY 3

Day 3 timetable	a. Daily Speed Sounds Lesson	e. Questions to Talk About
See guidance below for activities in **bold**. See pp.119–120 for other Day 3 activities.	b. Partner Practice	f. Questions to Read and Answer
	c. Think About the Information	**g. Build a Sentence**
	d. Third Read – Children	h. Handwriting

Think About the Information

p.9 **TOL** about when you might go to the seaside: *for a holiday or day out.*

pp.10–11 **TOL** about the heading: 'Things you can do [at the seaside]'.
TOL about the layout – the bulleted points introduced by a colon.
TOL about the red triangles which act like warning signs.
MTYT: *Always swim with an adult!*

pp.12–13 **TOL** about the heading: 'Things you can see on the beach'.
MTYT: *Hot sun can harm your skin!*

pp.14–15 **TOL** about what you can eat and drink at the seaside.
MTYT: *Keep our beaches clean!*

p.16 **TTYP:** What do you think the boys in the photograph are doing?
Freeze Frame the children's expressions as they have fun at the seaside.

GW **Build a Sentence**

Tell children that tomorrow they will write a poster to advertise a beach holiday in a place called Southpool, or your own town if it is a seaside town. Explain that today you are going to help them write a heading for that poster.

1. Use **MTYT** to say the simple sentence: *Come to Southpool.* Point out that this sentence is a command – it starts with a word that gives an order (imperative): *Come.* Tell children that adverts often use commands, because they are telling people what they should do or buy.

2. **TOL** about how you need to make Southpool sound as lovely as you can. **TTYP:** What adjective could we use to describe Southpool? Draw out responses such as *sunny/super/fantastic/ wonderful.* Try the words in the sentence, commenting on how you like *sunny Southpool* because of the alliteration (same sounds at the start of words). Model how to expand the sentence, e.g. *Come to sunny Southpool.*

3. **TTYP:** What is at Southpool? *Sandy beach/Seaside/Cliffs/Pier.* Show how to incorporate some of the children's ideas, e.g. *Come to the seaside at sunny Southpool.* Note that this sentence could be expanded further, but point out that the heading for a poster should be short and snappy, to attract people's attention. The detail can come later on in the poster.

4. Ask partners to decide on their own sentence and to practise saying it until they can remember it. Select a few partners to say their sentences to the group.

5. Ask children to write their own sentence on p.46 of their *Get Writing!* Book. Encourage children to spell new words using their phonic knowledge. Accept phonically-plausible spellings.

Day 4 timetable	a. Daily Speed Sounds Lesson	e. Proofread – Spelling
See guidance below for activities in **bold**. See pp.120–122 for other Day 4 activities.	b. Spell Check	f. Proofread – Grammar
	c. Grammar	**g. Write a Poster**
	d. Vocabulary	h. Handwriting

Grammar

1. Remind children what a **verb** is (a word that tells us what someone or something is doing, e.g. *sing, write, walk, hop, play).* **TOL** about how verbs can be in different forms and tenses, e.g. the verb *look* can change to *looks, looking, looked.*

2. On the board, write *Yesterday, we explored the rock pools.* Use **MTYT** to say the sentence. Ask children to **TTYP** to say which word is the verb *(explored).* Encourage children to explain how they recognised it. (For example, because of the -ed past tense ending, or simply because it is a *doing word.* If necessary, remind children that not all verbs in the past tense end in -ed, such as *went* or *saw*.)

3. Ask children to complete the Grammar activity on p.47 of their *Get Writing!* Book.

4. Ask children to **TTYP** to check they have underlined the same words and if not, to discuss which answers are correct and why.

5. Tell children the correct responses and explain any difficult points. (They should have underlined: *dug, take, played, fishes, collected, Use.*)

Vocabulary

1. On the board write the word *starfish.* Use **MTYT** to say the word. Ask children to **TTYP** and say what this is. Clarify any misunderstandings. Tell the children that this word is made up of two shorter words. Ask children to **TTYP** to say which two words make up the word *starfish* (*star* and *fish*). Remind children that we call this a **compound** word.

2. Ask children to turn to the Vocabulary activity on p.47 of their *Get Writing!* Book. Talk through the activity, explaining any words that they are unsure of. Then ask children to complete the activity.

3. Ask children to **TTYP** to check they agree on the new words.

4. Tell children the correct responses and explain any difficult points. (Children should make the following words: *seahorse, seaweed, seaside, driftwood, sunhat.*)

Write a Poster

Note that this activity should be started on Day 4 and completed on Day 5.

1. Use online file NF6.5 (tab g onwards) for this activity. **TOL** about the posters you see advertising things, such as films, holidays and days out. Describe a poster that you saw recently, e.g. for a day at a wildlife park, talking about the pictures and how the words made you want to go and see the animals for yourself. Explain that the poster gave you information about what there was to see at the park, what food was sold and reminded you not to feed the animals. Display the example posters (tab g onwards).

   TTYP: What posters have you seen advertising places to go or see?

2. Explain to children that they are going to write a poster advertising a day out at the seaside. Remind them of the heading that they wrote in the Build a Sentence activity. Ask children to turn to p.49 in their *Get Writing!* Book. Draw attention to the questions that will help them think about what to write on their poster.

3. Ask the questions one by one. Use **TTYP** to draw out responses from children and use **MTYT** to develop their ideas into full sentences..

   – What can you do at the seaside? *You can: play in the sand/make sandcastles/explore rock pools/swim in the sea/use a snorkel and mask to watch the fish/play with a kite/lie on the sand and read a book/go fishing.*

   – What can you collect at the seaside? *You can collect... shells/stones/driftwood/cuttlefish bones.*

   – What can you play? *You can play... rounders/cricket/football/volleyball/Frisbee.*

   – What can you see at the seaside? *You can see: driftwood/seaweed/crabs/starfish.*

   – What can you hear at the seaside? *You can hear... waves crashing/seagulls squawking/children splashing/feet crunching on pebbles/music from the ice cream van/the wind whistling.*

   – What can you eat and drink at the seaside? *You can: eat fish and chips/eat ice creams and lollies/eat a picnic/drink lemonade/drink milk shakes.*

   – What must you remember to do at the seaside? *Use sun cream/Take your rubbish home/Wear arm bands and a sun hat/Swim with an adult.*

4. Use the online file (tab i) to model how to write the first point as a bulleted list. Start *You can:* then bullet some of the children's ideas. **TOL** as you write and keep re-reading to make sure that your writing makes sense.

5. Hide your writing. Ask children to discuss their own ideas for the first section with their partner and practise them until they can remember them. Note that they do not have to be the same as yours and they do not have to be in a bulleted list if children prefer to write in full sentences. Select a few partners to say their ideas to the group. Then children can write their own ideas in their exercise book. Point out the Useful words on p.48 of the *Get Writing!* Book and the space on p.49 for noting ideas before they write. Encourage children to spell new words using their phonic knowledge. Accept phonically-plausible spellings.

6. Repeat Steps 4 and 5 (demonstrate how you write, then ask children to write) with the next questions, supporting children as necessary as they complete their poster. They may wish to decorate their poster with pictures and designs inspired by the seaside.

DAY 5	**Day 5 timetable**	a. Daily Speed Sounds Lesson	d. Partner Proofread
	See Day 4 for guidance on the activity in **bold**. See p.122 for other Day 5 activities.	b. Spell Test	e. Words to Keep
		c. Write a Poster (continued)	f. Linked Text

 Write a Poster (continued)

On Day 5, children continue the writing activity that they began on Day 4.

Rex to the rescue

Teacher's Preparation

1. Print out the Story Green Words (see online file '7.1 Rex to the rescue', starting with tab a) and stack them into your pocket chart: *Luke, Bruce, Sue, Duke, cute, lead, brute, rage, growl, snarl, mule, stroke, truce, tattoo, velvet, collar, minute, maroon, accuse, stubborn, pounced, choking, escaped, refused, chased.*

2. Display these Red Word Cards in your pocket chart: *should, were, there, call, want, come, could, one, through, was, you, to, said, all, of, through.* These are the Red Words in the Storybook text.

3. Practise reading the Storybook Introduction (below and printable online file 7.1a) and the whole story with expression, for reading aloud to children.

4. Prepare sticky notes you may need for activities such as Think About the Story, Build a Sentence and Write a Poster. Ideas are provided but you may wish to add your own.

DAY 1

Daily Speed Sounds Lesson

1. Review one Set 3 Speed Sound with a particular focus on spelling. See pp.40–51.

2. Review Set 2 and 3 Speed Sounds. See pp.33–51.

Speed Sounds from the Storybook

Find the circled focus graphemes on pp.4–5 of the Storybook. Point to each focus grapheme on the Complex Speed Sounds poster and use **MTYT (My turn Your turn)** to say them: *le, ce, oo, u-e, ue.*

Story Green Words

Follow the steps below to read the Story Green Words (printed from online) with children. After they have read each Story Green Word, explain the meaning of any new words that are unfamiliar. Definitions for some of the words can be found in the Vocabulary Check on p.7 of the Storybook.

Names and single-syllable words

1. Hold up the first card, e.g. 'snarl' and ask children to tell you the 'special friends' (digraph – *ar*) or shake their heads if there aren't any. If children have difficulty spotting the 'special friends', show them the side of the card with the dots and dashes to give them a quick reminder.

2. Ask them to say the sounds *s-n-ar-l* and say *snarl*.

3. Say the word *snarl* with exaggerated pronunciation. Ask children to repeat it.

4. Repeat for the other words.

Multi-syllabic words

1. Fold the card 'velvet' and hold it up so only the first syllable is showing. Ask children to read the syllable – only using Fred Talk if necessary.

2. Repeat with the next syllable.

3. Unfold the card and ask children to read the whole word, tweaking the pronunciation if necessary.

4. Repeat for the other words.

Root words and suffixes

1. Fold the card 'pounced' so you can only see the root word ('pounce') and hold it up. Ask children to read it without Fred Talk.

2. Repeat with the suffix (-ed).

3. Unfold the card and point out that the final *e* on the root word 'pounce' has been replaced by the ending -ed. Ask children to read the whole word, tweaking the pronunciation if necessary.

4. Repeat for the other words.

Speedy Green Words

1. Display the first Speedy Green Word (online file 7.1b).

2. Tell children to first read the sounds silently using 'Fred in your head'. Then ask them to say the word aloud when the word animates, or when you push the word towards them if you have printed out the words.

3. Repeat Steps 1 and 2 with the other Speedy Green Words, increasing the pace as children become more confident.

4. Review Speedy Green Words from a previous Storybook that need further practice.

Red Word Cards

1. Hold up the first card, e.g. 'was'.

2. Say the word *was* and ask children to repeat it.

3. Point to the card and say the sounds you can hear, *w-o-z* and say *was*. Ask children to repeat.

4. Help children to spot the tricky letter ('a').

5. Say the word again. Ask children to repeat it.

6. Repeat for the other Red Words.

S B Partner Practice

Children practise the Speed Sounds and Story Green Words on pp.4–6. Ensure partners sit at the table with one Storybook between them and one lolly stick for pointing.

1. Ask one partner to teach the sounds out of order using **MTYT**. Ensure that children point accurately underneath the sounds.

2. Ask the other partner to teach the words out of order using **MTYT**.

3. During the activity, note any sounds/words that need further practice and review together at the end of the activity.

On subsequent books, ask a different partner to start teaching the sounds.

Next, children practise the Red Words on p.8. Note that the grid contains Red Words from the Storybook text, plus some revision Red Words.

1. Ask partners to take turns reading the words across the rows or down the columns. Ensure that children point accurately underneath the words. (Partners help each other if stuck.)

2. Repeat until they can read all of the Red Words at speed.

Story Introduction

Read the introduction (on the following page and printable online file 7.1a) to children using expression. Explain the meaning of any words children may be unsure of. Ask children to **TTYP (Turn to your partner)** to discuss the question and then select two pairs to feed back (Choose two – see p.18).

Note that children may need extra help in remembering who is who, as many of the names have similar sounds in them. If necessary, display the images of the dogs and their owners to help clarify this (online file 7.1c).

Luke is a big man with a shaved head and lots of tattoos. He enjoys sniffing red roses in the park, reading 'Gardening Today' and humming little tunes. But the thing he likes best is his *tiny pug dog*, little Bruce.

Sue is a small lady in a smart maroon skirt, carrying a blue handbag. She likes to go to the park too, with her very *large brute of a dog*, big Duke.

One day, little Bruce was at the park chasing twigs. Big Duke was at the park too – and he was looking for a fight. Big Duke sniffed the ground and smelt dog. He zoomed across the grass, running past the slide, the roundabout and the swings. He leapt through a rose bush and came nose to nose with little Bruce.

Luke was choked with rage. "Shoo, you horrid brute!" he shouted. But big Duke just growled and snarled at him. Then he pounced on poor little Bruce.

Sue came running up, but instead of telling Duke off, she said: "Kiss Mummy, Dukey darling!"

"Bruce isn't used to fighting," Luke told her. "He's only had one fight in his life – and that was with a hamster. Bruce lost!"

"Hmmph!" said Sue, and wandered off.

The very next day, the same thing happened.

TTYP: How do you think Luke stopped big Duke from bullying little Bruce?

SB **First Read – Children**

Ensure partners sit at the table with one Storybook between them and one lolly stick for pointing.

1. Ask Partner 1s to:

– point to the words while their partner reads the first page of the story.

– prompt their partner to Fred Talk words they read incorrectly.

2. Swap roles on the second page. Continue to swap roles page by page.

3. Remind children who finish quickly to re-read the story.

4. Note any words that need further practice and review these when children have finished reading.

Read Aloud – Teacher

1. Ask children to close their Storybooks.

2. Read the whole story aloud with expression.

TTYP: What happened to Duke at the end of the story?

Red Rhythms – Spelling Red Words

Children should keep their *Get Writing! Grey* Book closed. However, you will need to use the Red Words in the panel on p.3 of the *Get Writing!* Book: *should, were, call, want, through*.

1. Write the first word on the board or flipchart.

2. Say the word and ask children to repeat it.

3. Point to each sound as you say it, then say the whole word. Ask children to repeat.

4. Help children to spot any tricky letters that aren't on the Speed Sounds Chart and circle these.

5. Point as you say the letter names in a rhythm (exaggerating the tricky letters) and then say the word.

6. Repeat with all the Red Words in the panel on p.3 of the *Get Writing!* Book.

7. Hide the words that are on the board or flipchart. Say the first Red Word again. Ask children to say the letter names as they write the word in their exercise book. Write the word on the board and ask children to tick/correct the spelling of each sound. Repeat with the other Red Words.

Handwriting

Follow the handwriting lesson plan on pp.25–28 to review Stage 2/3 handwriting.

DAY 2

> **Daily Speed Sounds Lesson**
>
> 1. Review one Set 3 Speed Sound with a particular focus on spelling. See pp.40–51.
>
> 2. Review Set 2 and 3 Speed Sounds. See pp.33–51.

Speedy Green Words

Repeat as for Day 1. Increase the speed children read these words by reducing the 'Fred in your head' time. To do this, display them at a faster speed or, if using the cards, push the card forward sooner each time until children can read them almost immediately.

Red Word Cards

Repeat the Red Word Cards activity from Day 1, increasing the speed.

S B Partner Practice

Ensure partners sit at the table with one Storybook between them and one lolly stick for pointing. Children practise the Speedy Green Words on p.18 and the Red Words on p.8.

1. Ask partners to take turns reading the words across the rows or down the columns. Ensure that children point accurately underneath the words.

2. Repeat until they can read all the Speedy Green Words correctly without Fred Talk and the Red Words at speed.

S B Jump-in

1. Ask one partner to track under the words with a lolly stick as you read the story aloud, but ask both partners to 'Jump-in' and read the word when you hesitate on four/five words per page.

2. Ask partners to swap roles after each page.

S B Second Read – Children

Ask partners to read the whole story again, taking turns to read alternate pages. (See Day 1 First Read.) Ask Partner 2s to point on the first page this time.

Fred Fingers – Spelling Green Words

Children keep their *Get Writing!* Book closed. However, you will need to use the Green Words in the panel on p.3 of the *Get Writing!* Book. Ask children to write the spellings in their exercise books.

Single-syllable words

tune, nose

1. Say the word *tune* and ask children to repeat it.

2. Ask children to:

   – Hide their fingers as they count the sounds on them.

   – Show their fingers when you say *fingers*.

   – Repeat the word, then pinch their fingers as they say the sounds.

   – Write the word as they say the sounds, underlining any 'special friends'.

3. Write the word on the board and ask children to tick/correct the spelling of each sound in their own work.

4. Repeat for the next word.

Multi-syllabic words

listen, little

1. Say the whole word *listen* and ask children to repeat it.
2. Say the word in syllables *li-sten* and ask children to repeat it.
3. Say the first syllable and ask children to repeat it, then hide their fingers as they count the sounds in the syllable. When you say *fingers*, they show their fingers. Then ask them to write the syllable and underline any `special friends'.
4. Repeat with each syllable.
5. Write the word on the board and ask children to tick/correct the spelling of each sound in their own work.
6. Repeat for the next word.

Root words with a suffix

likes

1. Say the whole word *likes* and ask children to say the root (*like*).
2. Ask children to:
   - Hide their fingers as they count the sounds in the root word until you say *fingers*.
   - Repeat the root word and pinch their fingers as they say the sounds.
3. Ask children to write the root word, underlining any special friends.
4. Write the root on the board and **TOL (Think out loud)** about how you would add the suffix -s.
5. Ask children to write the suffix.
6. Ask children to tick/correct the spelling of each sound in their own work.

Red Rhythms – Spelling Red Words

Repeat the Red Rhythms activity in Day 1, with the same Red Words.

GW **Hold a Sentence – 1 and 2**

(**1**) "Put that dog on a lead before he bites someone!" said Luke.

1. Say the sentence above and ask children to repeat it.
2. Use **MTYT** until children can remember the whole sentence, and then add punctuation mimes (see p.20).
3. Write the sentence on the board and ask children to help you:
   - Use Fred Fingers to spell Green Words.
   - **TOL** about how to spell any Red Words.
   - Use punctuation and finger spaces.
   - Re-read the sentence to check it makes sense.
4. Hide the sentence and ask children to write it in their *Get Writing! Book*, p.2.
5. Display the sentence again and help children to mark each word of their own work.
6. Repeat Steps 1 to 5 with the sentence below.

(**2**) Sue thought Luke was being rude and didn't listen to him.

Handwriting

Follow the handwriting lesson plan on pp.25–28 to review Stage 2/3 handwriting.

DAY 3 | **Daily Speed Sounds Lesson**

1. Review one Set 3 Speed Sound with a particular focus on spelling. See pp.40–51.

2. Review Set 2 and 3 Speed Sounds. See pp.33–51.

S B **Partner Practice**

Ensure partners sit at the table with one Storybook between them and one lolly stick for pointing. Repeat as for Day 2, practising the Speedy Green Words on p.18 and the Red Words on p.8.

 Think About the Story

Children do not need their Storybooks. Display the Storybook pictures (online file 7.1c) as you read the story aloud from your Storybook. Use your prepared notes for **TOL**, **MTYT**, **TTYP** and Freeze Frames to reinforce children's understanding. For example:

p.9 **TOL** about the things Luke and Bruce like to do at the park.
TOL about what is surprising about Luke and little Bruce.

p.10 **TOL** about what is surprising about Sue and big Duke.

p.11 Freeze Frame Luke's expression when big Duke chases little Bruce.
MTYT (with feeling): *"Shoo, you **horrid** brute!"*
TTYP: Why is Luke so angry?

p.12 **TOL** about why Sue's behaviour was wrong. *She didn't tell Duke off.*

p.13 **TOL** about what Luke suggested Sue should do and what Sue did in response.

p.14 **TOL** about what Rex did to Duke.

p.15 **TOL** about how Duke learnt his lesson.
MTYT (with feeling): *"I want all the dogs to call a truce. No more fighting! **Okay**?"*
TTYP: What can we learn from this story? *Don't treat others in a way that you wouldn't like to be treated yourself.*

S B **Third Read – Children**

Ask partners to read the whole story again, taking turns to read each page. (See Day 1 First Read.) Ask Partner 1s to point on the first page this time.

S B **Questions to Talk About**

Read out the questions on p.16 of the Storybook. For each question, direct children to the correct page to find the answer. Ask them to **TTYP** and to respond using 'Fastest finger first' (FF) where they find the answer in the text or 'Have a think' (HaT) where they have to justify their answer/opinion.

S B **Questions to Read and Answer**

Ask children to turn to p.17 in the Storybook.

1. Show partners how to take turns to read the questions and find the answers in the text. They should swap roles after each question.

2. After children have completed the questions with their partner, take feedback.

G W **Build a Sentence**

Tell children that tomorrow they will write a poster called 'Stop bullying'. Explain that today you are going to help them build up a sentence that a bullied child might say.

1. Ask children to imagine that they are being bullied. Use **MTYT** to say the sentence: *There's a bully in our school.*

2. **TTYP:** What does he or she say? Draw out responses such as *Do as I tell you/Don't talk to my friends/You are stupid/You are ugly.* Demonstrate how to extend the basic sentence to incorporate the children's responses, e.g. *There's a bully in our school who says, "Do as I tell you."*

3. **TTYP:** What does the bully do if you don't do what he or she wants? *He/She hits/kicks/pushes/steals/calls people names.* Model how to expand the basic sentence further, e.g. *There's a bully in our school who says, "Do as I tell you or I will push you."*

4. Ask partners to decide on their own sentence and to practise saying it until they can remember it. Select a few partners to say their sentences to the group.

5. Ask children to write their own sentence on p.2 of their *Get Writing!* Book.

Handwriting

Follow the handwriting lesson plan on pp.25–28 to review Stage 2/3 handwriting.

> **Daily Speed Sounds Lesson**
>
> 1. Review one Set 3 Speed Sound with a particular focus on spelling. See pp.40–51.
>
> 2. Review Set 2 and 3 Speed Sounds. See pp.33–51.

GW Spell Check

Ask children to turn to the panels of Red and Green Words on p.3 in the *Get Writing!* Book.

1. Ask Partner 1s to:

   – choose and say one of the Red or Green Words, then cover it up

   – help their partner to write the word in their exercise book

   – look back at the listed word and help their partner tick/correct the spelling of each sound.

2. Ask partners to swap after each word, so that each partner writes at least five words.

GW Grammar

1. Tell (or remind) children that we use **joining words** (conjunctions) to link ideas together in a sentence. On the board, write *Bruce chases sticks and barks at the ducks.* **TTYP:** Which is the joining word? *(and)* Point out that *and* joins together the two parts of sentence: the first part tells us that Bruce chases sticks, the second part tells us that Bruce barks at the ducks.

2. Use the term 'clause' if appropriate for the year group. Emphasise that a joining word can join two longer parts of a sentence (clauses) as in the above example, or it can just join two words, e.g. *I like apples and oranges.*

3. Tell the children that some other useful joining words are *or* and *but*.

4. Write this incomplete sentence on the board: *Luke looks scary _____ he is a quiet, gentle man.* Ask children which joining word could complete the sentence *(but)*.

5. Write this incomplete sentence on the board: *You must choose one colour: pink _____ purple.* Ask children which joining word could complete the sentence *(or)*.

6. Ask children to complete the Grammar activity on p.3 of their *Get Writing!* Book.

7. Tell children to **TTYP** to check if they have written the same words and if not, to discuss which answers are correct and why.

8. Tell children the correct responses and explain any difficult points. (They should have written: *or, and, or, but*.)

GW Vocabulary

1. Explain that good writers try to develop a wide vocabulary and use a variety of words to make their writing more interesting for the reader. Tell children that it is important to check that they understand all words that they read.

2. On the board, write *Rex is as stubborn as a mule.* Use **MTYT** to say the sentence. Check children's understanding of a mule *(a donkey crossed with a horse, well known for refusing to do what it doesn't want to)*. Underline the word *stubborn*. Write three words next to it: *strong, short, determined*. **TTYP**: Which word means the same as *stubborn*? *(determined)*

3. Ask children to turn to the Vocabulary activity on p.3 of their *Get Writing!* Book. Talk through the activity, explaining any words that they are unsure of. Then ask children to complete the activity.

4. Ask children to **TTYP** to check if they have circled the same words and if not, to discuss which answers are correct and why.

5. Tell children the correct responses and explain any difficult points. (They should have circled: *end to fighting*; *bent down*; *flower*; *say that someone did something wrong*.)

 Proofread – Spelling

1. Display the sentences on screen (online file 7.1e) and read them aloud.

2. Ask partners to spot the errors.

3. Take feedback and show how to correct the errors. ◤

4. Hide the sentences and ask children to correct the sentences on p.4. of their *Get Writing!* Book.

5. Display the sentences written correctly and help children check their own corrections.

 Proofread – Grammar

Use online file 7.1f. Follow as for the Proofread – Spelling activity.

 Write a Poster

Note that this activity should be started on Day 4 and completed on Day 5.

1. **TOL** about a time when you were unhappy at school because someone had bullied you – or talk about someone you know who suffered from bullying. Explain how bad it can make you feel, even though it's not your fault.

2. Use online file 7.1 (tab g onwards) for this activity. Tell children that they are going to write a poster called 'Stop bullying'. Ask children to turn to p.5 of their *Get Writing!* Book. Point out that the poster is split into two parts. Explain that before children write the poster, you are going to talk about bullying: who bullies are, what they do, and how you should deal with bullies.

3. Use **TTYP** to draw out responses from children, and use **MTYT** to develop their ideas into full sentences.

   – What does a bully look like*?* Draw out children's responses, and then conclude that bullies come in all shapes and sizes – you can only recognise them by what they say and do.

   – What does a bully do? *A bully makes people feel lonely/sad/afraid/bad about themselves; might push/punch/kick; might say mean things and start rumours; might tell people not to be your friend.*

   – What does a bully say? *"Give me that"/"You are silly"/"I am better than you"/"You can't join in".*

   – What sort of children do bullies pick on? *Sometimes quiet, shy children/Sometimes children they are jealous of/Sometimes anyone they think is different.*

   – What should you do if you are being bullied? *You should tell an adult/walk away/ignore the bully/find friends who are kind.*

   – What should you do if you see someone else being bullied? *You should tell an adult/be a friend to the person being bullied.*

4. Use the online file (tab g) to model how to write some of the children's ideas about what a bully looks like. **TOL** as you write and keep re-reading to make sure it makes sense.

5. Hide your writing. Ask children to decide on their own sentences and to practise them aloud with a partner until they can remember them. Select a few partners to say their ideas to the group. Then children can write their own sentences in their exercise book. Point out the Useful words on p.4 of the *Get Writing!* Book and the questions on p.5 that should help prompt ideas. They can also write notes here if they wish.

6. Repeat Steps 4 and 5 (demonstrate how you write, then ask children to write) for the rest of the questions.

Handwriting

Follow the handwriting lesson plan on pp.25–28 to review Stage 2/3 handwriting.

Daily Speed Sounds Lesson

1. Review one Set 3 Speed Sound with a particular focus on spelling. See pp.40–51.

2. Review Set 2 and 3 Speed Sounds. See pp.33–51.

Spell Test

1. Choose one of the Red or Green Words listed in the panels on p.3 of the *Get Writing!* Book. Say it aloud and ask children to write it in their exercise book. Remind them to use Fred Fingers if necessary.

2. Write the word on the board.

3. Ask children to tick/correct the spelling of each sound.

4. Repeat with the other nine listed words.

 ## Write a Poster (continued)

Complete the writing activity started on Day 4.

Partner Proofread

1. Remind children of the proofreading activity they did on Day 4. **TTYP:** What sort of things do we check when we proofread our work?

2. Share responses and note features to check on the board. These may include:
   – spaces between words
   – capital letters (**TOL** – at the start of a sentence, for proper nouns and the pronoun *I*)
   – full stops (**TOL** – at the end of a sentence)
   – question marks or exclamation marks (**TOL** – to show a question or exclamation)
   – spelling.

3. If necessary, model how to correct a sentence that contains common errors made by the class. Do not use any of the children's work, but create your own sentence to correct.

4. Ask Partner 1s to place their exercise book on top of Partner 2's. Tell partners they have three minutes to proofread Partner 1's writing, together. Encourage Partner 1s to mark any corrections in their own exercise book.

5. Repeat for Partner 2's work.

 ## Words to Keep

Ask children to re-read their writing and select the words they are most proud of, or words they might want to use again. Then ask them to write these in the Words to keep section on p.5 of their *Get Writing!* Book.

Linked Text

Read the linked text for the next Storybook.

The lion's paw

Teacher's Preparation

1. Print out the Story Green Words (see online file '7.2 The lion's paw', starting with tab a) and stack them into your pocket chart: *den, paw, thorn, sore, dawn, raw, straw, slops, jaws, sword*, Roman, circus, mighty, loyal, Androcles*, crawled, gnashing, yawned, peacefully, feasting, gnawing, scornfully, jeering.*

   Note that Challenge Words are marked with an asterisk.

2. Display these Red Word Cards in your pocket chart: *many, could, one, are, were, other, through, was, call, to, there, they, said.* These are the Red Words in the Storybook text.

3. Practise reading the Storybook Introduction (below and printable online file 7.2a) and the whole story with expression, for reading aloud to children.

4. Prepare sticky notes you may need for activities such as Think About the Story, Build a Sentence and Write About Androcles and the Lion. Ideas are provided but you may wish to add your own.

DAY 1

Daily Speed Sounds Lesson

1. Review one Set 3 Speed Sound with a particular focus on spelling. See pp.40–51.

2. Review Set 2 and 3 Speed Sounds. See pp.33–51.

Speed Sounds from the Storybook

Find the circled focus graphemes on pp.4–5 of the Storybook. Point to each focus grapheme on the Complex Speed Sounds poster and use **MTYT** to say them: *gn, ce, ge, or, oor, ore, aw.*

Story Green Words

Follow the steps below to read the Story Green Words (printed from online) with children. After they have read each Story Green Word, explain the meaning of any new words. Definitions for some of the words can be found in the Vocabulary Check on p.7 of the Storybook.

Single-syllable words

1. Hold up the first card, e.g. 'dawn', and ask children to tell you the 'special friends' (*aw*) or shake their heads if there aren't any. If children have difficulty spotting the 'special friends', show them the side of the card with the dots and dashes to give them a quick reminder.

2. Ask them to say the sounds *d-aw-n* and then say *dawn.*

3. Say the word *dawn* with exaggerated pronunciation. Ask children to repeat it.

4. Repeat for the other words.

Multi-syllabic words

1. Fold the card 'Roman' and hold it up so only the first syllable is showing. Ask children to read the syllable – only using Fred Talk if necessary.

2. Repeat with the next syllable.

3. Unfold the card and ask children to read the whole word, tweaking the pronunciation if necessary.

4. Repeat for the other words.

Root words and suffixes

1. Fold the card 'feasting' so you can only see the root word ('feast') and hold it up. Ask children to read it without Fred Talk.

2. Show and say the suffix (-ing).

3. Unfold the card and ask children to read the whole word, tweaking the pronunciation if necessary.

4. Repeat for the other words.

Challenge Words

Follow the steps as for the Red Word Cards, below.

Speedy Green Words

1. Display the first Speedy Green Word (online file 7.2b).

2. Tell children to first read the sounds silently using 'Fred in your head'. Then ask them to say the word aloud when the word animates, or when you push the word towards them if you have printed out the words.

3. Repeat Steps 1 and 2 with the other Speedy Green Words, increasing the pace as children become more confident.

4. Review Speedy Green Words from a previous Storybook that need further practice.

Red Word Cards

1. Hold up the first card, e.g. 'many'.

2. Say the word *many* and ask children to repeat it.

3. Point to the card and say the sounds you can hear, *m-e-n-ee* and say *many*. Ask children to repeat.

4. Help children to spot the tricky letter ('a').

5. Say the word again. Ask children to repeat it.

6. Repeat for the other Red Words.

S B Partner Practice

Children practise the Speed Sounds and Story Green Words on pp.4–6. Ensure partners sit at the table with one Storybook between them and one lolly stick for pointing.

1. Ask one partner to teach the sounds out of order using **MTYT**. Ensure that children point accurately underneath the sounds.

2. Ask the other partner to teach the words out of order using **MTYT**.

3. During the activity, note any sounds/words that need further practice and review together at the end of the activity.

On subsequent books, ask a different partner to start teaching the sounds.

Next, children practise the Red Words on p.8. Note that the grid contains Red Words from the Storybook text, plus some revision Red Words.

1. Ask partners to take turns reading the words across the rows or down the columns. Ensure that children point accurately underneath the words. (Partners help each other if stuck.)

2. Repeat until they can read all of the Red Words at speed.

Story Introduction

Read the introduction (on the following page and printable online file 7.2a) to children using expression. Explain the meaning of any words children may be unsure of. Ask children to **TTYP** to discuss the question and then select two pairs to feed back (Choose two – see p.18).

There was once a Roman slave called Androcles, whose master treated him so badly that he ran away. Looking for shelter, Androcles crawled into a cave that had been dug out of the hillside. He didn't realise it was a lion's den!

Soon a shadow fell across the floor. Androcles began to tremble as a lion approached, but then it just stretched out on the dusty floor and held out its paw – which had a sharp thorn stuck in it.

"Poor beast," said Androcles, taking the lion's sore paw in his hands and pulling out the thorn.

After that, Androcles lived happily with the lion for many months, but he began to miss the company of other men. So one day, he shook the lion by the paw and set off back to Rome.

His wicked master spotted him in the street. "You have broken the law and you must be punished!" he shouted scornfully. Androcles was flung into prison. He soon learnt that he was to be thrown to the lions.

One morning, he was given a sword and a helmet and was pushed through a wooden door. He found himself in a huge circus-like ring, with thousands of people shouting insults and jeering from the stands. He stood there, frozen, as he looked around.

TTYP: What else do you think Androcles saw in the ring?

S B First Read – Children

Ensure partners sit at the table with one Storybook between them and one lolly stick for pointing.

1. Ask Partner 1s to:

   – point to the words while their partner reads the first page of the story.

   – prompt their partner to Fred Talk words they read incorrectly.

2. Swap roles on the second page. Continue to swap roles page by page.

3. Remind children who finish quickly to re-read the story.

4. Note any words that need further practice and review these when children have finished reading.

Read Aloud – Teacher

1. Ask children to close their Storybooks.

2. Read the whole story aloud with expression.

TTYP: Why was Androcles set free?

Red Rhythms – Spelling Red Words

The children should keep their *Get Writing! Grey* Book closed. However, you will need to use the Red Words in the panel on p.7 of the *Get Writing!* Book: *many, could, through, are, said.*

1. Write the first word on the board or flipchart.

2. Say the word and ask children to repeat it.

3. Point to each sound as you say it, then say the whole word. Ask children to repeat.

4. Help children to spot any tricky letters that aren't on the Speed Sounds Chart and circle these.

5. Point as you say the letter names in a rhythm (exaggerating the tricky letters) and then say the word.

6. Repeat with all the Red Words in the panel on p.7 of the *Get Writing!* Book.

7. Hide the words that are on the board or flipchart. Say the first Red Word again. Ask children to say the letter names as they write the word in their exercise book. Write the word on the board and ask children to tick/correct the spelling of each sound. Repeat with the other Red Words.

Handwriting

Follow the handwriting lesson plan on pp.25–28 to review Stage 2/3 handwriting.

DAY 2

Daily Speed Sounds Lesson

1. Review one Set 3 Speed Sound with a particular focus on spelling. See pp.40–51.

2. Review Set 2 and 3 Speed Sounds. See pp.33–51.

Speedy Green Words

Repeat as for Day 1. Increase the speed children read these words by reducing the 'Fred in your head' time. To do this, display them at a faster speed or, if using the cards, push the card forward sooner each time until children can read them almost immediately.

Red Word Cards

Repeat the Red Word Cards activity from Day 1, increasing the speed.

S B Partner Practice

Ensure partners sit at the table with one Storybook between them and one lolly stick for pointing. Children practise the Speedy Green Words on p.18 and the Red Words on p.8.

1. Ask partners to take turns reading the words across the rows or down the columns. Ensure that children point accurately underneath the words.

2. Repeat until they can read all the Speedy Green Words correctly without Fred Talk and the Red Words at speed.

S B Jump-in

1. Ask one partner to track under the words with a lolly stick as you read the story aloud, but ask both partners to 'Jump-in' and read the word when you hesitate on four/five words per page.

2. Ask partners to swap roles after each page.

S B Second Read – Children

Ask partners to read the whole story again, taking turns to read alternate pages. (See Day 1 First Read.) Ask Partner 2s to point on the first page this time.

Fred Fingers – Spelling Green Words

Children keep their *Get Writing!* Book closed. However, you will need to use the Green Words in the panel on p.7 of the *Get Writing!* Book. Ask children to write the spellings in their exercise books.

Single-syllable words

saw, strange, teeth

1. Say the word and ask children to repeat it.

2. Ask children to:

    –   Hide their fingers as they count the sounds on them.

    –   Show their fingers when you say *fingers*.

    –   Repeat the word, then pinch their fingers as they say the sounds.

    –   Write the word as they say the sounds, underlining any 'special friends'.

3. Write the word on the board and ask children to tick/correct the spelling of each sound in their own work.

4. Repeat for the other words.

Multi-syllabic words

shadow, angry

1. Say the whole word *shadow* and ask children to repeat it.

2. Say the word in syllables *sha-dow* and ask children to repeat it.

184

3. Say the first syllable and ask children to repeat it, then hide their fingers as they count the sounds in the syllable. When you say *fingers*, they show their fingers. Then ask them to write the syllable and underline any `special friends'.

4. Repeat with each syllable.

5. Write the word on the board and ask children to tick/correct the spelling of each sound in their own work.

6. Repeat for the next word.

Red Rhythms – Spelling Red Words

Repeat the Red Rhythms activity in Day 1, with the same Red Words.

GW **Hold a Sentence – 1 and 2**

(1) Inside he saw a pile of bones and a golden hair on the floor.

1. Say the sentence above and ask children to repeat it.

2. Use **MTYT** until children can remember the whole sentence, and then add punctuation mimes (see p.20).

3. Write the sentence on the board and ask children to help you:
   – Use Fred Fingers to spell Green Words.
   – **TOL** about how to spell any Red Words.
   – Use punctuation and finger spaces.
   – Re-read the sentence to check it makes sense.

4. Hide the sentence and ask children to write it in their *Get Writing!* Book, p.6.

5. Display the sentence again and help children to mark each word of their own work.

6. Repeat Steps 1 to 5 with the sentence below.

(2) Do you think it is strange that the lion held out his paw?

Handwriting

Follow the handwriting lesson plan on pp.25–28 to review Stage 2/3 handwriting.

DAY 3 | **Daily Speed Sounds Lesson**

   1. Review one Set 3 Speed Sound with a particular focus on spelling. See pp.40–51.

   2. Review Set 2 and 3 Speed Sounds. See pp.33–51.

S B **Partner Practice**

Ensure partners sit at the table with one Storybook between them and one lolly stick for pointing. Repeat as for Day 2, practising the Speedy Green Words on p.18 and the Red Words on p.8.

 Think About the Story

Children do not need their Storybooks. Display the Storybook pictures (file 7.2c) as you read the story aloud from your Storybook. Use your prepared notes for **TOL, MTYT, TTYP** and Freeze Frames to reinforce children's understanding. For example:

p.9   **TOL** about why Androcles crawled inside a cave.

p.10   Freeze Frame his expression when he realised he was in a lion's den.
      TTYP: What did he feel? *Fear/terror/horror.*
      MTYT (with feeling): *The lion was back!*

185

p.12   **TOL** about how Androcles and the lion lived happily together.

p.13   **TOL** about what happened when Androcles returned to Rome.

p.14   **MTYT** (with feeling): *"You are going to be thrown to the **lions**."*
Freeze Frame the moment Androcles entered the ring.
TTYP: What could he hear? Who did he see? *Shouting crowds, a growling lion.*
TTYP: What did he feel? *Terror.*

p.15   **MTYT** (with feeling): *The lion opened his mighty jaws, Gnashing his teeth, and flashing his claws, And then he stretched out on the dusty floor, Looked up at Androcles, held out his paw.*
TOL about what happened when Androcles and the lion saw each other again.
TTYP: What did the crowds think and feel?
MTYT (with feeling): *"Set them free! Set them free!"*

`S B` Third Read – Children

Ask partners to read the whole story again, taking turns to read each page. (See Day 1 First Read.) Ask Partner 1s to point on the first page this time.

`S B` Questions to Talk About

Read out the questions on p.16 of the Storybook. For each question, direct children to the correct page to find the answer. Ask them to **TTYP** and to respond using 'Fastest finger first' (FF) where they find the answer in the text or 'Have a think' (HaT) where they have to justify their answer/opinion.

`S B` Questions to Read and Answer

Ask children to turn to p.17 in the Storybook.

1. Show partners how to take turns to read the questions and find the answers in the text. They should swap roles after each question.

2. After children have completed the questions with their partner, take feedback.

`GW` Build a Sentence

Tell children that tomorrow they will write the story of Androcles and the lion. Explain that today you are going to help them build up some sentences to describe what happened when Androcles kissed the lion's paw.

1. Display the picture of Androcles kissing the lion's paw (online file 7.2d). Use **MTYT** to say the sentence: *Androcles kissed the lion's paw.*

2. **TTYP:** What did the crowd do? Draw out responses, such as *shouted/cheered/roared/clapped/ jumped up and down.* Model how to incorporate the ideas into the basic sentence, e.g. *The crowd shouted and clapped when Androcles kissed the lion's paw.*

3. **TTYP:** What did the crowd say? *"Set them free"/"Give them their freedom"/"This is amazing".* Model how to add another sentence, following on from the first, e.g. *The crowd shouted and clapped when Androcles kissed the lion's paw. "Give them their freedom," they said.*

   Model how to rearrange the words to make one longer sentence, e.g. *"Give them their freedom," shouted the crowd when Androcles kissed the lion's paw.*

4. Ask partners to decide on their own sentence and to practise saying it until they can remember it. Select a few partners to say their sentences to the group.

5. Ask children to write their own sentence on p.6 of their *Get Writing!* Book.

Handwriting

Follow the handwriting lesson plan on pp.25–28 to review Stage 2/3 handwriting.

DAY 4

Daily Speed Sounds Lesson

1. Review one Set 3 Speed Sound with a particular focus on spelling. See pp.40–51.

2. Review Set 2 and 3 Speed Sounds. See pp.33–51.

GW **Spell Check**

Ask children to turn to the panels of Red and Green Words on p.7 in the *Get Writing!* Book.

1. Ask Partner 1s to:

   – choose and say one of the Red or Green Words, then cover it up

   – help their partner to write the word in their exercise book

   – look back at the listed word and help their partner tick/correct the spelling of each sound.

2. Ask partners to swap after each word, so that each partner writes at least five words.

GW **Grammar**

1. Tell (or remind) children that when we are talking about things that are happening now we use the **present tense**. On the board write *The lion opens his mighty jaws*. Point to the verb *opens* and emphasise that this verb is in the present tense. Explain that we can also say *The lion is opening his mighty jaws*. This is also the present tense, telling us that the lion is still opening his jaws. (It is called the progressive present tense, but children don't need to know this term.) More examples of present tense verbs in sentences are: *The lion gnashes his teeth* and *The lion is gnashing his teeth*.

2. Point out that if we were talking about what happened yesterday, we would use the **past tense**. We would say *The lion opened his mighty jaws* or *The lion was opening his mighty jaws*. (The latter is an example of the progressive past tense.) More examples of past tense verbs in sentences are: *The lion looked at Androcles* and *The lion was looking at Androcles*.

3. Ask children to complete the Grammar activity on p.7 of their *Get Writing!* Book.

4. Tell children to **TTYP** to check if they have the same answers and if not, to discuss which are correct and why. (They should have ticked: *Past tense, Past tense, Present tense, Past tense, Present tense*.)

GW **Vocabulary**

1. Remind children that when they are reading, they may come across words that they don't understand. They can usually work out the meaning of the word from the sentence it is in.

2. On the board write *They began to chant: "Set them free!"*. Use **MTYT** to say the sentences. Underline the word *chant*, then write three different explanations under it, e.g. *clap their hands; call out in a rhythm; eat food*. Ask children to choose the correct meaning (*call out in a rhythm*).

3. Ask children to turn to the Vocabulary activity on p.7 of their *Get Writing!* Book. Talk through the activity, then ask them to complete it independently.

4. Ask children to **TTYP** to check if they have circled the same words and if not, to discuss which answers are correct and why.

5. Tell children the correct responses and explain any difficult points. (They should have circled: *grinding, faithful, chewing, watery soup*.)

GW **Proofread – Spelling**

1. Display the sentences on screen (online file 7.2e) and read them aloud.

2. Ask partners to spot the errors.

3. Take feedback and show how to correct the errors.

4. Hide the sentences and ask children to correct the sentences on p.8 of their *Get Writing!* Book.

5. Display the sentences written correctly and help children check their own corrections.

Proofread – Grammar

Use online file 7.2f. Follow as for the Proofread – Spelling activity.

 Write About Androcles and the Lion

Note that this activity should be started on Day 4 and continued on Day 5. If necessary, allow another writing session on another day for children to complete their work.

1. **TOL** about how you love hearing stories about your grandparents' lives. Give an example of something they told you that you will always remember, e.g. when they first watched a colour TV or bought their first computer.

2. Use online file 7.2 (tab g onwards) for this activity. Tell children to imagine that they are Androcles, now an old man, telling his grandchildren what happened to him with the lion. Explain that you are going to be in role as one of his grandchildren, asking lots of questions, and they should answer in role as Androcles. The 'conversation' should draw out ideas and vocabulary that children can then use in their writing.

   Ask children to turn to p.9 in their *Get Writing!* Book. Draw attention to some possible story titles and the different questions that can help children divide their writing into paragraphs. Ask children to choose a title or write their own in their exercise book.

3. Go through all the questions orally with children. Use **TTYP** and encourage children to create their own responses, but give guidance using **MTYT** where necessary. For example, questions and responses for the first paragraph might be:

   – What was life like when you were a slave? Encourage children to describe the jobs they did. *When I was a slave… I had to work in the fields/cook and clean/look after the animals.* They should also describe how they felt. *I felt very unhappy/sad/exhausted.* They could detail where they slept and what they ate. *I slept in the kitchens on some old rags/I was just given scraps of food.*

   Questions and responses for the second paragraph might be:

   – How did you escape? *I escaped by… running away early one morning before anyone got up/ creeping out of the house at night/running into the mountains where no one would find me.*

   – What was your journey like? *The journey was… long and exhausting. I kept running for as long as I could/I begged a ride in a cart/I ate berries and wild mushrooms and drank from a stream/ I ran until my legs ached and my feet were sore.*

   Repeat for the rest of the questions.

4. Explain that you are going to show children how to write the first paragraph, then they will write their own. Remind children of the first question, 'What was life like when you were a slave?' Choose some of the children's ideas and use the online file (tab g) to model how to write the first few sentences of the first paragraph. **TOL** as you write and keep re-reading to make sure your writing makes sense.

5. Hide your writing. Ask children to decide on their own sentences and practise them aloud with a partner until they can remember them. Select a few partners to say their sentences to the group. Then children can write the first sentences of their story in their exercise book. Point out the Useful words on p.8 in their *Get Writing!* Book and the space for making notes on p.9.

6. Repeat Steps 4 and 5 (demonstrate how you write, then ask children to write) for the other paragraphs. Some children may be able to complete the remaining paragraphs without teacher support. Encourage children to think carefully about the last line of their story. It should show the moral of the story, e.g. *I have learnt that one good deed deserves another/I have learnt if you are good to people, they will be good to you.*

Handwriting

Follow the handwriting lesson plan on pp.25–28 to review Stage 2/3 handwriting.

Daily Speed Sounds Lesson

1. Review one Set 3 Speed Sound with a particular focus on spelling. See pp.40–51.

2. Review Set 2 and 3 Speed Sounds. See pp.33–51.

Spell Test

1. Choose one of the Red or Green Words listed in the panels on p.7 of the *Get Writing!* Book. Say it aloud and ask children to write it in their exercise book. Remind them to use Fred Fingers if necessary.

2. Write the word on the board.

3. Ask children to tick/correct the spelling of each sound.

4. Repeat with the other nine listed words.

 ### Write About Androcles and the Lion (continued)

Complete the writing activity started on Day 4. If necessary, allow another writing session on another day for children to complete their work.

Partner Proofread

1. Remind children of the proofreading activity they did on Day 4.

TTYP: What sort of things do we check when we proofread our work?

2. Share responses and note features to check on the board. These may include:

   – spaces between words

   – capital letters (**TOL** – at the start of a sentence, for proper nouns and the pronoun *I*)

   – full stops (**TOL** – at the end of a sentence)

   – question marks or exclamation marks

   – speech marks (**TOL** – at the beginning and end of speech)

   – spelling.

3. If necessary, model how to correct a sentence that contains common errors made by the class. Do not use any of the children's work, but create your own sentence to correct.

4. Ask Partner 1s to place their exercise book on top of Partner 2's. Tell partners they have three minutes to proofread Partner 1's writing, together. Encourage Partner 1s to mark any corrections in their own exercise book.

5. Repeat for Partner 2's work.

 ### Words to Keep

Ask children to re-read their writing and select the words they are most proud of, or words they might want to use again. Then ask them to write these in the Words to keep section on p.9 of their *Get Writing!* Book.

Linked Text

Read the linked text for the next Storybook.

I dare you

Teacher's Preparation

Prepare as for p.172. Print out and display the Story Green Words (see online file '7.3 I dare you', starting with tab a): *Radar Rob, Cosmic Clare, spare, dare, bare, huge, eyes*, compare, chicken, fanfare, crater, notice, nostrils, reprogram, software, repair, scared, sprinted, declared, bulging, flared, peeped, glared.*

Note that Challenge Words are marked with an asterisk.

Display the Red Word Cards: *two, there, who, were, you, said, your, one, could, what, was, school, to, of, all.*

DAY 1	Day 1 timetable	a. Daily Speed Sounds Lesson	g. **Story Introduction**
	See guidance below for activities in **bold**. See pp.172–175 for other Day 1 activities.	b. Speed Sounds from the Storybook	h. First Read – Children
		c. Story Green Words	i. Read Aloud – Teacher
		d. Speedy Green Words (online file 7.3b)	j. **Red Rhythms – Spelling Red Words**
		e. Red Word Cards	k. Handwriting
		f. Partner Practice	

Story Introduction

Radar Rob and Cosmic Clare are both spacekids – and they are also best friends. Rob has a square blue body, six yellow legs and a pointed head. Clare has a small, green, round body. They live together on planet Zox, where there isn't much to do.

One day, they were kicking a spaceball on the stairs before astroschool when Cosmic Clare suggested they play 'I dare you'.

"Prepare to be very, very scared, Clare," said Radar Rob, daring her to peel off her green skin and run around the astroschool – bare.

Clare shouted, "I'm not scared!" And off she sprinted.

When Clare came back, she dared Rob to put on some moonboots and climb right to the top of the radar mast.

"That's not fair!" said Rob.

"Chicken!" shouted Clare.

"I'll get you back for that, Clare!" Rob said on his way down. He dared her to play a fanfare on her rocket-boosted trumpet, while throwing her space hat in the air – all at the same time.

'Now it's my turn,' thought Clare. 'I'm going to give you the scariest dare of all – to go to the crater where the robodog lives!'

TTYP: Why do you think this might be the scariest dare of all?

Red Rhythms – Spelling Red Words See *Get Writing! Grey*, p.11.

DAY 2	Day 2 timetable	a. Daily Speed Sounds Lesson	f. Second Read – Children
	See guidance below for activities in **bold**. See pp.175–176 for other Day 2 activities.	b. Speedy Green Words (online file 7.3b)	g. **Fred Fingers – Spelling Green Words**
		c. Red Word Cards	h. Red Rhythms
		d. Partner Practice	i. **Hold a Sentence – 1 and 2**
		e. Jump-in	j. Handwriting

Fred Fingers – Spelling Green Words See *Get Writing!* Book, p.11.

GW **Hold a Sentence – 1 and 2**

1 There is a lot of spare time in space.

2 "Prepare to be very, very scared," said Rob.

See *Get Writing!* Book, p.10.

DAY 3

Day 3 timetable	a. Daily Speed Sounds Lesson	e. Questions to Talk About
See guidance below for activities in **bold**. See pp.177–178 for other Day 3 activities.	b. Partner Practice	f. Questions to Read and Answer
	c. Think About the Story	g. Build a Sentence
	d. Third Read – Children	h. Handwriting

Think About the Story

p. 9 TOL about why kids who live in space often get bored.

p.10 TOL about what Rob dared Clare to do. MTYT (with feeling): *"Prepare to be **very, very** scared."* TTYP: How did Clare feel? *Not scared/ Excited/Boastful.*

p.11 TOL about what Clare dared Rob to do. Freeze Frame Rob's expression. TTYP: How did he feel? *Things weren't fair/Grumpy/Indignant.*

p.12 TOL about how Rob got Clare back. Freeze Frame Clare's expression TTYP: How did she feel? *Surprised/ Shocked.*

p.13 TOL about what Rob had to do next. Freeze Frame Clare's expression. TTYP: How did she feel? *Worried for Rob.*

p.14 TOL about what happened to Radar Rob.

p.15 TOL about why they decided to stop playing 'I dare you'. MTYT (with feeling): *"That **seems** fair. Just one more thing – no more games of '**I dare you**'!"*

GW **Build a Sentence**

Tell children that tomorrow they will write some instructions about how to play some of their favourite games. Explain that today you are going to help them build some sentences that tell people how to prepare for some games.

1. Use **MTYT** to say the sentence: *Prepare to be very, very scared when you play 'I dare you'.*

2. **TTYP:** How do we need to prepare when we play Hide and Seek? Draw out responses such as *be quiet/silent/still.* Model how to build it into the sentence, e.g. *Prepare to be very, very quiet when you play Hide and Seek.*

   TTYP: How do we need to prepare when we play football? *Be quick/watchful/speedy.* Build this into a sentence, e.g. *Prepare to be very, very quick when we play football.*

   TTYP: How do we need to prepare when we play Musical Chairs? *Be watchful/quick/speedy.* e.g. *Prepare to be very, very watchful when we play Musical Chairs.*

3. Ask partners to decide on their own game and sentence and to practise saying the sentence until they can remember it. Select a few partners to say their sentences to the group.

4. Ask children to write their own sentence on p.10 of their *Get Writing!* Book.

DAY 4	**Day 4 timetable**	a. Daily Speed Sounds Lesson	e. Proofread – Spelling
	See guidance below for activities in **bold**. See pp.178–180 for other Day 4 activities.	b. Spell Check	f. Proofread – Grammar
		c. Grammar	**g. Write About Games**
		d. Vocabulary	h. Handwriting

GW **Grammar**

1. Remind children that a command (instruction) tells someone to do something. It usually starts with a verb that gives an order (an imperative). For example: _Stand_ up; _Go_ away; _Take_ this to your mum. Use **MTYT** to say these example sentences.

2. On the board write _Mix, Peel, Slice_. Point out that these words can be three verbs which give orders. (They can also be used as nouns in some contexts.) Now write the incomplete command/instruction: _____ _the orange and throw away the skin._ Ask children which is the most suitable verb to complete the command _(Peel)._

3. Ask children to complete the Grammar activity on p.11 of their _Get Writing!_ Book.

4. Tell children to **TTYP** to check if they have written the same words and if not, to discuss which answers are correct and why.

5. Tell children the correct responses and explain any difficult points. (They should have written the words in this order: _Climb, Put, Shout, Sit._)

GW **Vocabulary**

1. Explain that good writers use interesting descriptions to build up pictures in the reader's mind. Comment on how important this is when a book doesn't have any pictures to look at, particularly if they are describing something that the reader hasn't seen before – like an alien spacekid!

2. Remind children of the descriptions of Rob _(square blue body, six yellow legs, pointed head)_ and Clare _(small, green, round)_. Point out that the writer has chosen her vocabulary very carefully, picking out the most important things about the way these spacekids look.

3. Tell children to complete the Vocabulary activity on p.11 of their _Get Writing!_ Book. Remind them to think carefully about numbers (of limbs and features), colours and shapes.

4. Encourage partners to describe their characters to each other and to discuss which other words they could have used.

U GW **Write About Games**

Note that this activity should be started on Day 4 and completed on Day 5.

1. **TOL** about the games you liked playing when you were at school, e.g.

   – party games such as Musical Chairs, Pass the Parcel, Musical Statues

   – playground games such as ball games, skipping games, clapping games, Follow my Leader, Hopscotch

   – home games such as Hide and Seek, Sardines, Simon Says, What's the Time, Mr Wolf?

     TTYP: What games do you like playing at home and at school?

2. Use online file 7.3 (tab g onwards) for this activity. Explain to children that they are going to write about some games for Radar Rob and Cosmic Clare to play, so they don't get bored, but don't get hurt either! Ask children to turn to p.13 of their _Get Writing!_ Book.

3. Decide together on the first game that children will write about, e.g. Hide and Seek. Use **TTYP** to gather responses and **MTYT** to develop these responses into full sentences.

   TTYP: Instead of saying 'Prepare to be very, very scared', what shall we say? *Prepare to be... very, very quiet/still.*

   TTYP: What's the first instruction for the game? *First, choose someone to be 'it'.*

   TTYP: What is the second instruction? *Then the others go and hide in secret places.*

   TTYP: What is the third instruction? *Next, the person who is 'it' should count to 20 then look for the others.*

   TTYP: How do you win? *The last person to be found is the winner.*

4. Use the online file (tab g onwards) to model how to write the first instructions for this game on the board. **TOL** as you write your first sentences. Keep re-reading to make sure they make sense.

5. Hide your writing. Ask children to decide on their own first sentences and to practise them aloud with a partner until they can remember them. Select a few partners to say their sentences to the group. Then children can write their own sentences in their exercise book. Point out the Useful words on p.12 of the *Get Writing!* Book and the questions on p.13 that should help prompt the children's ideas. They can also make notes here.

6. Repeat Steps 4 and 5 (demonstrate how you write, then ask children to write) for the rest of the instructions. Then ask children to choose another game and repeat the process.

Day 5 timetable	a. Daily Speed Sounds Lesson	d. Partner Proofread
See Day 4 for guidance on the activity in **bold**. See p.180 for other Day 5 activities.	b. Spell Test	e. Words to Keep
	c. Write About Games (continued)	f. Linked Text

GW **Write About Games (continued)**

On Day 5, children continue the writing activity that they began on Day 4.

193

Looking after a hamster

Teacher's Preparation

Prepare as for p.172. Print out and display the Story Green Words (see online file '7.4 Looking after a hamster', starting with tab a): *cute, peat, curl, cage, tube, squeeze, chew, stale, eyes*, hamster, ginger, animal, shelter, litter, scatter, corner, electric, whiskers, scamper, discovering, sipper, pouches, climbers.*

Note that Challenge Words are marked with an asterisk.

Display the Red Word cards: *mother, are, you, want, to, one, your, they, come, other, of, water.*

DAY 1	**Day 1 timetable**	a. Daily Speed Sounds Lesson	**g. Story Introduction**
	See guidance below for activities in **bold**. See pp.172–175 for other Day 1 activities.	b. Speed Sounds from the Storybook	h. First Read – Children
		c. Story Green Words	i. Read Aloud – Teacher
		d. Speedy Green Words (online file 7.4b)	**j. Red Rhythms – Spelling Red Words**
		e. Red Word Cards	k. Handwriting
		f. Partner Practice	

Story Introduction

Ashley has got a hamster from the animal shelter. The hamster has clean, sleek fur and bright eyes. She's cute and small, with ginger hair and long, twitchy whiskers.

'I'll call her Fluffy!' Ashley decides.

She buys a big cage for Fluffy to scamper around in. To make her comfortable, Ashley puts a layer of peat on the floor and scatters shredded paper and wood shavings on top.

As soon as Ashley puts Fluffy in her new cage, the hamster curls up in the corner under the wood chippings and falls asleep. She must be very tired!

Ashley feeds Fluffy some cereal and food pellets, which she bought from the pet shop. As a treat, she gives her currants, nuts and bits of cheese. Fluffy stuffs the food into her cheek pouches for later.

When Ashley goes to school, she makes sure there are lots of toys for Fluffy to play with. There's a hamster wheel for her to run in and tunnels made from old loo roll tubes that she can scamper through.

TTYP: Would you like a hamster? Would you look after it as well as Ashley does?

Red Rhythms – Spelling Red Words See *Get Writing! Grey*, p.15.

DAY 2	**Day 2 timetable**	a. Daily Speed Sounds Lesson	f. Second Read – Children
	See guidance below for activities in **bold**. See pp.175–176 for other Day 2 activities.	b. Speedy Green Words (online file 7.4b)	**g. Fred Fingers – Spelling Green Words**
		c. Red Word Cards	h. Red Rhythms
		d. Partner Practice	**i. Hold a Sentence – 1 and 2**
		e. Jump-in	j. Handwriting

Fred Fingers – Spelling Green Words See *Get Writing!* Book, p.15.

Hold a Sentence – 1 and 2

> (**1**) Your hamster will like to come out of its cage each day to play.

> (**2**) What do you need to feed your hamster?

See *Get Writing!* Book, p.14.

DAY 3

Day 3 timetable	a. Daily Speed Sounds Lesson	e. Questions to Talk About
See guidance below for activities in **bold**. See pp.177–178 for other Day 3 activities.	b. Partner Practice	f. Questions to Read and Answer
	c. Think About the Story	**g. Build a Sentence**
	d. Third Read – Children	h. Handwriting

Think About the Story

> p.9 **TOL** about the sort of people who make a good hamster owner *(animal lovers).*

> p.10 **TOL** about how to make sure your hamster is old enough and healthy enough to take home.

> p.11 **TOL** about how to prepare your cage.

> p.12 **TOL** about the best toys to give your hamster.

> p.13 **TOL** about how to play with your hamster.

> p.14 **TOL** about what to feed your hamster.

> p.15 **TOL** about how to check that your hamster is well.
> **MTYT** (with feeling): ***Remember! Never let an animal suffer.***

 Build a Sentence

Talk about how children need looking after. Mums and dads make sure they are safe, clean, eat well, exercise, play, learn to read and, above all, that they are happy! Tell children that tomorrow they will write about how they need to be looked after while their parents are away. (It could be for an older sibling, their grandparents, or another relative.) Explain that today you are going to help them build up a sentence explaining what happens at bedtime.

1. Use **MTYT** to say the sentence starter *I can't go to sleep until...*

2. **TTYP:** What happens before you go to sleep? Draw out responses such as *I listen to a story/switch on a night light/keep the door open a little/snuggle the duvet round me/cuddle my favourite toy/ kiss my mum and dad goodnight.*

3. Using one of the children's responses, model how to build it into the sentence, e.g. *I can't go to sleep until I've listened to a story.*

4. **TTYP:** What else do you do before you go to sleep? Incorporate more ideas into the sentence, e.g. *I can't go to sleep until I've listened to a story, cuddled my teddy and kissed my mum.*

5. Ask partners to decide on their own sentence and to practise saying it until they can remember it. Select a few partners to say their sentences to the group.

6. Ask children to write their own sentence on p.14 of their *Get Writing!* Book.

DAY 4	**Day 4 timetable**	a. Daily Speed Sounds Lesson	e. Proofread – Spelling
	See guidance below for activities in **bold**. See pp.178–180 for other Day 4 activities.	b. Spell Check	f. Proofread – Grammar
		c. Grammar	**g. Write About Looking After Me**
		d. Vocabulary	h. Handwriting

GW **Grammar**

1. Tell (or remind) children that a **noun** names people, places or things, e.g. *Ashley, hamster, shop, water*. **TTYP:** What must we remember about writing a *proper* noun, for example, someone's name? *(It starts with a capital letter.)*

2. On the board, write *Fluffy needs toys to play with.* **TTYP:** Which are the nouns in this sentence? (*Fluffy* and *toys*) **TTYP:** Why does *Fluffy* start with a capital letter? *(It's a proper noun.)*

3. Ask children to complete the Grammar activity on p.15 of their *Get Writing!* Book.

4. Tell children to **TTYP** to check if they have underlined the same words and if not, to discuss which answers are correct and why.

5. Tell children the correct responses and explain any difficult points. (They should have underlined: 1: *Ashley, hamster*; 2: *Fluffy, fur, eyes*; 3: *toys, cage*; 4: *Fluffy, pellets, nuts, currants*; 5: *hamster, whiskers*.)

GW **Vocabulary**

1. Explain that good writers use many different words to help the reader see pictures in their minds (not all books have pictures). It is important that a writer chooses words carefully, so the reader builds up a clear picture. As readers, it is important to understand as many words as possible.

2. Write *scooped* on the board. Use **MTYT** to say the word. Say the word in the context of a sentence, e.g. *She scooped up her hamster in both hands.* Write three more words next to *scooped* (e.g. *stroked, tapped, picked*). Ask children to **TTYP** to say which one means the same as *scooped* (*picked*). Model how to select and check the correct answer by inserting it into the example sentence, i.e. *She picked up her hamster in both hands.* **TOL** about how the word 'scooped' gives a nice idea of picking something up smoothly, from underneath – like a spoon scooping up soup.

3. Ask children to turn to the Vocabulary activity on p.15 of their *Get Writing!* Book. Talk through the activity, explaining any words that they are unsure of. Then ask children to complete the activity.

4. Tell children to **TTYP** to check if they have circled the same words and if not, to discuss which answers are correct and why.

5. Tell children the correct responses and explain any difficult points. (They should have circled: *run, finding, hairs on their faces, feel pain, orange.*)

 GW **Write About Looking After Me**

Note that this activity should be started on Day 4 and completed on Day 5.

1. **TOL** about a time when your grandparents came to look after you when you were young. Tell children about the things that you loved doing together, like reading books, going for walks, making cakes. Recall that they could be a bit forgetful and sometimes you went to bed without cleaning your teeth, or went to school without your reading book. **TTYP:** Has anyone ever come to look after you while your parents were out or away? What was it like?

2. Use online file 7.4 (tab g onwards) for this activity. Tell children to imagine that a rather scatty (but very caring) older brother is going to look after them for a few days. Explain that children are going to write a list of things to remind them what to do. First they are going to talk through some ideas, then write them down. Ask children to turn to p.17 of their *Get Writing!* Book.

3. Go through the questions, focusing on what happens before and after school. Use **TTYP** to draw out responses from children and **MTYT** to develop their ideas into full sentences.

   – What time do you have to be woken up?

   – What do you have for breakfast?

   – What do you need to wear?

   – What do you need to pack for school?

   – What do you like for tea?

   – What do you like to watch on TV?

   – What do you do before you go to bed?

   – What do you do before you go to sleep?

4. Use the online file (tab g) to model how to start writing the list on the board. Use some of the ideas that children suggested as a basis for your sentences. **TOL** as you write. Keep re-reading as you write, to make sure your sentences make sense.

5. Hide your writing. Ask children to decide on their own first sentences and to practise them aloud with a partner until they can remember them. Select a few partners to say their sentences to the group. Then children can write their own sentences in their exercise book. Point out the Useful words on p.16 of the *Get Writing!* Book and the questions on p.17 that should help prompt their ideas. Point out the sentence starters which children may want to use, but emphasise that they don't have to if they prefer to think up their own. They can also write notes here before they write their sentences.

6. Repeat Steps 4 and 5 (demonstrate how you write, then ask children to write) with the rest of the questions, giving as much support as children need, until they complete their list.

<table>
<tr><td rowspan="2">**DAY 5**</td><td>**Day 5 timetable**</td><td>a. Daily Speed Sounds Lesson</td><td>d. Partner Proofread</td></tr>
<tr><td rowspan="2">See Day 4 for guidance on the activity in **bold**. See p.180 for other Day 5 activities.</td><td>b. Spell Test</td><td>e. Words to Keep</td></tr>
<tr><td></td><td>**c. Write About Looking After Me (continued)**</td><td>f. Linked Text</td></tr>
</table>

 Write About Looking After Me (continued)

On Day 5, children continue the writing activity that they began on Day 4.

How silly!

Teacher's Preparation

Prepare as for p.172. Print out and display the Story Green Words (see online file '7.5 How silly!', starting with tab a): *Barbara, Howard, beam, howl, inn, drown, cellar, hopeless, farmhouse, nightgown, stockings, cauliflower*, crouched, silliest, bowed, politely, frowned, shared, clouds, parted, gathered.*

Note that Challenge Words are marked with an asterisk.

Display the Red Word cards: *above, father, son, mother, some, here, who, there, people, water, was, to, you, all, what, come, they, were, one.*

DAY 1

Day 1 timetable	a. Daily Speed Sounds Lesson	**g. Story Introduction**
See guidance below for activities in **bold**. See pp.172–175 for other Day 1 activities.	b. Speed Sounds from the Storybook	h. First Read – Children
	c. Story Green Words	i. Read Aloud – Teacher
	d. Speedy Green Words (online file 7.5b)	**j. Red Rhythms – Spelling Red Words**
	e. Red Word Cards	k. Handwriting
	f. Partner Practice	

Story Introduction

I'm going to tell you a very silly story! It all began at Hopeless Howard's house, when Bossy Barbara – who was thinking of marrying Howard – was helping his mother to make cauliflower cheese.

Howard went down to the cellar to fetch some flour for the dish. He noticed a big cooking pot hanging from a beam above his head and suddenly had a very strange thought: 'What if I marry Barbara and our son grows up and I send him down here for flour and that cooking pot falls down and knocks him out?'

Howard started to cry. He told his mother and father what was wrong. They started to cry, too. Soon, they were all howling so loudly that Barbara came down to find out what all the fuss was about.

"Worrying about something that might never happen is very silly!" she cried. "I can't marry the silliest man in the land!"

Then Bossy Barbara said a very strange thing: "Before I agree to marry you, Howard, I must find three sillies even sillier than you."

TTYP: Why does Barbara think she needs to find sillier people than Howard?

Red Rhythms – Spelling Red Words See *Get Writing! Grey*, p.19.

DAY 2

Day 2 timetable	a. Daily Speed Sounds Lesson	f. Second Read – Children
See guidance below for activities in **bold**. See pp.175–176 for other Day 2 activities.	b. Speedy Green Words (online file 7.5b)	**g. Fred Fingers – Spelling Green Words**
	c. Red Word Cards	h. Red Rhythms
	d. Partner Practice	**i. Hold a Sentence – 1 and 2**
	e. Jump-in	j. Handwriting

Fred Fingers – Spelling Green Words See *Get Writing! Book*, p.19.

Hold a Sentence – 1 and 2

1 "Go down to the cellar and fetch me some flour," shouted Barbara.

2 Where can I find a very silly man?

See *Get Writing!* Book, p.18.

 DAY 3

Day 3 timetable	a. Daily Speed Sounds Lesson	e. Questions to Talk About
See guidance below for activities in **bold**. See pp.177–178 for other Day 3 activities.	b. Partner Practice	f. Questions to Read and Answer
	c. Think About the Story	**g. Build a Sentence**
	d. Third Read – Children	h. Handwriting

 Think About the Story

p.9 TOL about why Howard is in the cellar and what he sees.

p.10 TOL about why Howard is suddenly so upset.

p.11 Freeze Frame Barbara's expression when she hears why they are crying.
TTYP: How does she feel, and why? *Shocked that they could worry over something so silly.*
MTYT (with feeling): *"How silly you all sound! I can't marry the **silliest** man in the land!"*
TOL about why Barbara wants to find three people sillier than Howard.

pp.12–14 TOL about how each character is sillier than Howard.

p.14 Freeze Frame Barbara's expression when she hears the boy saying that the sun has fallen into the pond.

p.15 Freeze Frame Howard's expression when the cooking pot does fall down.
TTYP: What does he say? *It can happen after all/Maybe I wasn't silly!/I was silly to worry because it didn't hurt anyone.*

 Build a Sentence

Tell children that tomorrow they will write about a friend and why they like them. Explain that today you are going to help them write some sentences about why Barbara likes Howard, even though he is so silly sometimes.

1. Use **MTYT** to say the sentence starter: *Although Howard is silly, he is also…* **TTYP:** What qualities does Howard have? Draw out ideas that give a positive impression of Howard, e.g. *kind/thoughtful/cheerful/funny.* Show how to complete the sentence with some of the children's suggestions, e.g. *Although Howard is silly, he is also kind and thoughtful.*

2. **TTYP:** What sort of things does he do? Encourage children to think about how he might demonstrate these positive qualities, e.g. *He might be kind when Barbara is upset/good at cooking/happy to help with chores/always polite and good at listening to people/cheerful/quick to laugh.* Demonstrate how to put some ideas into full sentences, e.g. *Although Howard is silly, he is also kind and thoughtful. He is always happy to help with chores and is very good at listening to people.*

3. Ask partners to decide on their own sentences and to practise saying them until they can remember them. Select a few partners to say their sentences to the group.

4. Ask children to write their own sentences on p.18 of their *Get Writing!* Book.

199

Day 4 timetable	a. Daily Speed Sounds Lesson	e. Proofread – Spelling
See guidance below for activities in **bold**. See pp.178–180 for other Day 4 activities.	b. Spell Check	f. Proofread – Grammar
	c. Grammar	**g. Write About Your Friend**
	d. Vocabulary	h. Handwriting

Grammar

1. Tell (or remind) children that an **apostrophe** can show that something belongs to someone. (You may also want to remind them that an apostrophe can show that some letters are missing in a word – so there are two different ways it can be used.) On the board write *Howard's mother*. Use **MTYT** to repeat the sentence from the Storybook: *She was helping Howard's mother make cauliflower cheese.* **TTYP:** Who does the mother belong to? *(Howard)* Other examples are *Barbara's son fetched some flour* and *Howard's cooking pot fell down*.

2. Ask children to complete the Grammar activity on p.19 of their *Get Writing!* Book.

3. Ask children to **TTYP** to check they have written the same answers and if not, to discuss which answers are correct and why.

4. Tell children the correct answers and explain any difficult points. (They should have written: *Rose's stockings; Barbara's nightgown; Howard's son; the boy's net.*)

Vocabulary

1. Remind children that when they are reading, they may come across words that they don't understand. They can often work out the meaning of the word from the sentence it is in.

2. On the board write *Barbara stopped at an inn for the night*. Use **MTYT** to say the sentence. Underline the word *inn* and ask children to **TTYP** and say what it means *(a hotel)*. Emphasise that they can often work out the meaning of a word by looking at how it works in the sentence.

3. Ask children to turn to the Vocabulary activity on p.19 of their *Get Writing!* Book. Talk through the activity, explaining any words that they are unsure of. Then ask children to complete the activity.

4. Ask children to **TTYP** to check they have circled the same words and if not, to discuss which answers are correct and why.

5. Tell children the correct responses and explain any difficult points. (They should have circled: *room under the house; cried; small lake; squatted.*)

Write About Your Friend

Note that this activity should be started on Day 4 and completed on Day 5.

1. **TOL** about how, although family and friends can irritate us sometimes (such as when Howard irritated Barbara when he was silly), there is usually a stronger reason why we like them and want to spend time with them. Reflect on particular friends and why you like them (e.g. *I like Andrew because he listens well and is always there when I have a problem. I like Maggie because we enjoy shopping together and cooking.*) Emphasise that not everyone has the same good qualities, but everyone has something that we like about them.

   TTYP: What do you like about your friends and family? *I like people who are kind/can listen/you can have fun with/make you laugh/you can talk to.*

2. Use online file 7.5 (tab g onwards) for this activity. Explain to children that they are going to write about a friend. Ask children to turn to p.21 of their *Get Writing!* Book. Explain that the questions will help them to build up a conversation about their friend.

3. Ask Partner 1s to start by telling their partner about their friend. Ask one question at a time and take feedback from Partner 1s as a group after each question. Partners then swap roles. Use **MTYT** to build children's ideas into full sentences.

TTYP: When did you first meet? Encourage children to try to remember the exact moment – who was with them, where they were.

TTYP: How did you feel when you first met them? Ask children if they knew they would be friends or did their friendship develop later?

TTYP: How often do you see each other? Where?

TTYP: What sort of things do you chat about?

TTYP: What do you do together?

TTYP: What is your friend good at?

TTYP: What is the best thing about your friend? e.g. *He/She is kind/funny/serious/thoughtful/ trustworthy/a good listener.*

4. Go back to the first question and the children's responses. Use the online file (tab g) to model how to write the first sentences about a friend. **TOL** as you write. Keep re-reading to make sure your writing makes sense.

5. Hide your writing. Ask children to decide on their own first sentences and to say them aloud with a partner until they can remember them. Select a few partners to say their sentences to the group. Then children can write their own sentences in their exercise book. Point out the Useful words on p.20 of the *Get Writing!* Book and the questions on p.21 that should help prompt ideas. They can also make notes here.

6. Repeat Steps 4 and 5 (demonstrate how you write, then ask children to write) for all of the questions. If any children have time, ask them to repeat the process, using the same questions to write about more friends.

Day 5 timetable	a. Daily Speed Sounds Lesson	d. Partner Proofread
See Day 4 for guidance on the activity in **bold**. See p.180 for other Day 5 activities.	b. Spell Test	e. Words to Keep
	c. Write About Your Friend (continued)	f. Linked Text

DAY 5

 Write About Your Friend (continued)

On Day 5, children continue the writing activity that they began on Day 4.

Wailing Winny's car boot sale

> ## Teacher's Preparation
>
> Prepare as for p.172. Print out and display the Story Green Words (see online file '7.6 Wailing Winny's car boot sale', starting with tab a): *Spain, sale, crate, slime, pale, drain, chain, faint, bargain, fingernails, trainers, peabrain, exclaimed, straightening, peered, containing, complained, revving, nailed, trailed, raised, demonstrating, ghostly*.*
> Note that Challenge Words are marked with an asterisk.
> Display the Red Word cards: *buy, bought, do, some, to, of, said, you.*
> Gather together some treasured old books and toys for young children, e.g. *Each Peach Pear Plum* by Janet and Allan Ahlberg.

DAY 1

Day 1 timetable	a. Daily Speed Sounds Lesson	**g. Story Introduction**
See guidance below for activities in **bold**. See pp.172–175 for other Day 1 activities.	b. Speed Sounds from the Storybook	h. First Read – Children
	c. Story Green Words	i. Read Aloud – Teacher
	d. Speedy Green Words (online file 7.6b)	**j. Red Rhythms – Spelling Red Words**
	e. Red Word Cards	k. Handwriting
	f. Partner Practice	

Story Introduction

> Winny is a witch. Like lots of witches, she wears a big pointy hat, has a warty green face and flies a dusty old broomstick. But Winny is not like other witches – she is a friendly witch.
>
> One day, Winny decided to have a car boot sale. She collected all the things she didn't use anymore and packed everything in the boot of her witchmobile: a book of out-of-date spells, a set of second-hand chains, a crate of old toenail clippings, six cans of snail slime, a rat's tail and a lovely pair of smelly old trainers!
>
> She stuck posters to the wall in her cave with blobs of bat spit to let visitors know all about her sale. Everything was ready.
>
> The car boot sale was a great success. Winny's friends snapped up every last item – even the smelly old trainers. But that evening, when Winny's husband, Phantom Phil, offered to take the cash to the Banshee Bank, he noticed his trainers were missing.
>
> "Have you seen my trainers?" he asked Winny.
>
> Winny gulped.
>
> **TTYP:** How do you think Winny will get the trainers back?

Red Rhythms – Spelling Red Words   See *Get Writing! Grey*, p.23.

DAY 2

Day 2 timetable	a. Daily Speed Sounds Lesson	f. Second Read – Children
See guidance below for activities in **bold**. See pp.175–176 for other Day 2 activities.	b. Speedy Green Words (online file 7.6b)	**g. Fred Fingers – Spelling Green Words**
	c. Red Word Cards	h. Red Rhythms
	d. Partner Practice	**i. Hold a Sentence – 1 and 2**
	e. Jump-in	j. Handwriting

Fred Fingers – Spelling Green Words   See *Get Writing!* Book, p.23.

Hold a Sentence – 1 and 2

1 "Go and find my best trainers straight away," said Phil.

2 Winny was afraid she wouldn't find the trainers again.

See *Get Writing!* Book, p.22.

Day 3 timetable	a. Daily Speed Sounds Lesson	e. Questions to Talk About
See guidance below for activities in **bold**. See pp.177–178 for other Day 3 activities.	b. Partner Practice	f. Questions to Read and Answer
	c. Think About the Story	**g. Build a Sentence**
	d. Third Read – Children	h. Handwriting

 Think About the Story

p.9 TOL about the event Winny planned.

p.10 TOL about the disgusting things Winny planned to sell.

p.11 Freeze Frame Winny's expression when she realised she had sold Phil's trainers.
TTYP: How did she feel? *Anxious/ Worried/Embarrassed.*
Freeze Frame Phil's expression when he realised Winny had sold his trainers.
TTYP: How did he feel? *Furious/Angry/ Outraged.*
MTYT (with feeling): *"You've sold my best trainers!"*

pp.12–14 TOL about how Winny searched for the trainers.
MTYT on each page (with feeling): *"Did you buy a pair of smelly old trainers at the boot sale?" wailed Winny.*

p.15 TOL about how Nelly transformed the trainers.
TTYP: Do you think Phil will want Nelly's dusty lace-up boots?

Build a Sentence

Tell children that tomorrow they will write about some of their old toys and books. Explain that today you are going to help them build up a sentence explaining how special something was to you when you were younger.

1. Hold up *Each Peach Pear Plum* (or choose a book that children know well from their nursery/ reception days). Use **MTYT** to say: *This book has always been special to me.*

2. **TTYP:** What other words mean the same as *special*? (Use the term 'synonyms' if appropriate for your year group.) Draw out responses such as *precious/valued/important/treasured.* Model how to incorporate alternative words into the sentence, e.g. *This book has always been precious to me.*

3. **TTYP:** Why have you always treasured this book? *I loved the pictures/I liked to say it off by heart/I like the way it rhymes/My nan always used to read it to me/I like spotting the characters.* Demonstrate how to expand the sentence, altering it to make it as fluent as possible, e.g. *I have always treasured this book because I loved saying the rhymes aloud.*

4. Ask partners to decide on their own sentence and to practise saying it until they can remember it. Select a few partners to say their sentences to the group.

5. Ask children to write their own sentence on p.22 of their *Get Writing!* Book.

Day 4 timetable	a. Daily Speed Sounds Lesson	e. Proofread – Spelling
See guidance below for activities in **bold**. See pp.178–180 for other Day 4 activities.	b Spell Check	f. Proofread – Grammar
	c. Grammar	**g. Write About Your Toys and Books**
	d. Vocabulary	h. Handwriting

 Grammar

1. Tell (or remind) children that sentences can be in the **present tense** (happening now) or the **past tense** (happened earlier).

2. On the board, write *I am playing a game.* Use **MTYT** to say the sentence. **TTYP:** Is this sentence in the present tense or past tense? *(present)* Point out that we know this from looking at the verbs *am playing*. If appropriate for the year group, tell children that this is an example of the present progressive tense.

3. Then write *I was playing a game.* Use **MTYT** to say the sentence. **TTYP:** Is this sentence in the present tense or past tense? *(past)* Point out the verbs *was playing*, which indicate the past tense. If appropriate for the year group, use the term 'past progressive tense'.

4. Ask children to turn to the Grammar activity on p.23 of their *Get Writing!* Book. Talk through the activity, then ask them to complete it.

5. Ask children to **TTYP** to check if they have ticked the same tenses and if not, to discuss which answers are correct and why.

6. Tell children the correct responses and explain any difficult points. (They should have ticked: *Present tense, Past tense, Present tense, Past tense.*)

GW **Vocabulary**

1. Explain that good writers use many different words to help the reader see pictures in their minds (not all books have pictures). It is important that a writer chooses words carefully, so the reader builds up a clear picture. As readers, it is important to understand as many words as possible.

2. Write *witchmobile* on the board. Use **MTYT** to say the word. Say the word in the context of a sentence, e.g. *Winny peered into the boot of her witchmobile.* Write three more words next to *witchmobile* (e.g. *phone, house, car*). Ask children to **TTYP** to say which one means the same as *witchmobile (car)*. Model how to select and check the correct answer by inserting it into the example sentence, i.e. *Winny peered into the boot of her car.* **TOL** about how the word *witchmobile* gives the idea of a car designed specifically for a witch.

3. Ask children to turn to the Vocabulary activity on p.23 of their *Get Writing!* Book. Talk through the activity, explaining any words that they are unsure of. Then ask children to complete the activity.

4. Tell children to **TTYP** to check if they have cirlced the same words and if not, to discuss which answers are correct and why.

5. Tell children the correct responses and explain any difficult points. (They should have circled: *lifted, swept, showing, shiny.*)

GW **Write About Your Toys and Books**

Note that this activity should be started on Day 4 and completed on Day 5.

1. Use online file 7.6 (tab g onwards) for this activity. **TOL** about Winny and all the things she cleared out from her cave. Comment that even witches have to have a clear out now and again! Display the old toys that you have brought in or the pictures of old toys (tabs g and h). **TOL** about when your mum and dad asked you to sort out your old toys. You had to put all the broken toys in one pile and all the ones that were in good condition in another. The broken toys were thrown away, but the toys in good condition were given to a charity shop, so they could go to younger children who would enjoy them. **TTYP:** Have you ever sorted out your old toys? What did you give away?

2. Say that you felt sad to give away your old toys but your mum suggested you put a tag on your favourite toys to tell the new owner why you liked it. That made you feel a lot better. Explain to children that they will write tags for some imaginary toys that they give away. Ask children to turn to p.25 in their *Get Writing!* Book.

3. Show children your first toy (or display the pictures on screen – tabs g and h). Use **TTYP** to gather children's suggestions and model building them into full sentences using **MTYT**.

   TTYP: Which words do you remember mean the same as *special*? For example, *precious/ treasured/loved/favourite/dearest/most valued.*

   TTYP: What are you giving away? *I am giving away my... precious doll/treasured train set/much loved teddy bear.*

   TTYP: Why was it special to you? *It was special because... Mum gave it to me/I got it for my birthday.*

   TTYP: How did you play with it? *I pretended.../I made it into.../I went on adventures.../ I took it to...*

   TTYP: What else would you like to say to the new owner? *Please take care of my toy/I hope you enjoy it/Look after it/Have fun with it.*

4. Use the online file (tab i) to model how you write the first tag. Use some of the ideas that children suggested as a basis for your sentences. **TOL** as you write, considering different ways of introducing ideas, such as *Please take care of this... It was very special to me because...* Keep re-reading as you write, to make sure your sentences make sense.

5. Hide your writing. Ask children to decide on their own sentences for their first tag and to practise them aloud with a partner until they can remember them. Select a few partners to say their sentences to the group. Then children can write their own sentences in their exercise book. Point out the Useful words on p.24 in the *Get Writing!* Book and the questions on p.25 that should help prompt ideas, which they can note here.

6. Repeat Steps 4 and 5 (demonstrate how you write, then ask children to write) with as many tags for toys as the children have time for, giving as much support as they need. They may also want to repeat the process with favourite books they have read, using the question prompts on p.25.

Day 5 timetable	a. Daily Speed Sounds Lesson	d. Partner Proofread
See Day 4 for guidance on the activity in **bold**. See p.180 for other Day 5 activities.	b. Spell Test	e. Words to Keep
	c. Write About Your Toys and Books (continued)	f. Linked Text

 GW **Write About Your Toys and Books (continued)**

On Day 5, children continue the writing activity that they began on Day 4.

205

Toad

Teacher's Preparation

Prepare as for p.172. Print out and display the Story Green Words (see online file '7.7 Toad', starting with tab a): *Joan, toad, cloak, throat, gnome, palace, amongst, shadowy, afloat, petticoat, knobbly, slowcoach, wicked, loathsome*, boasted, roaming, bouncing, croaky, moaning, groaning, jeered, foaming, bellowed.*
Note that Challenge Words are marked with an asterisk.
Display the Red Word cards: *father, one, watch, should, there, come, said, who, anyone, whole, water, was, ball, of, what, your, could, you, were.*

DAY 1

Day 1 timetable	a. Daily Speed Sounds Lesson	**g. Story Introduction**
See guidance below for activities in **bold**. See pp.172–175 for other Day 1 activities.	b. Speed Sounds from the Storybook	h. First Read – Children
	c. Story Green Words	i. Read Aloud – Teacher
	d. Speedy Green Words (online file 7.7b)	**j. Red Rhythms – Spelling Red Words**
	e. Red Word Cards	k. Handwriting
	f. Partner Practice	

Story Introduction

Princess Joan lived in a grand palace by a lake.

One beautiful summer's day, she was bouncing her ball amongst the oak trees as she roamed the palace grounds. She was beginning to make her way down the narrow road to the lake, when her ball fell into the water. As she watched it sink below the shadowy surface, she burst into tears.

"What's wrong, Princess Joan?" asked a croaky voice.

She looked up and saw a loathsome, yellow-brown toad afloat on a piece of wood.

"I've lost my ball," she explained through muffled sobs.

"I will get your ball back," he croaked. "But what will you give *me* in return?"

"My clothes, my cloak, my petticoat, the bows in my hair...?" she offered.

The toad told her he didn't want any of those things. "But if you let me eat from your bowl, drink from your mug and sleep on your pillow – I will be the happiest toad alive!"

TTYP: Do you think the princess will agree?

Red Rhythms – Spelling Red Words See *Get Writing! Grey*, p.27.

DAY 2

Day 2 timetable	a. Daily Speed Sounds Lesson	f. Second Read – Children
See guidance below for activities in **bold**. See pp.175–176 for other Day 2 activities.	b. Speedy Green Words (online file 7.7b)	**g. Fred Fingers – Spelling Green Words**
	c. Red Word Cards	h. Red Rhythms
	d. Partner Practice	**i. Hold a Sentence – 1 and 2**
	e. Jump-in	j. Handwriting

Fred Fingers – Spelling Green Words See *Get Writing!* Book, p.27.

Hold a Sentence – 1 and 2

1 Why should a pretty princess agree to live with an ugly toad?

2 "Keep your promise," the King said to his beautiful child.

See *Get Writing!* Book, p.26.

 DAY 3

Day 3 timetable	a. Daily Speed Sounds Lesson	e. Questions to Talk About
See guidance below for activities in **bold**. See pp.177–178 for other Day 3 activities.	b. Partner Practice	f. Questions to Read and Answer
	c. Think About the Story	**g. Build a Sentence**
	d. Third Read – Children	h. Handwriting

 Think About the Story

p.9 **TOL** about what Joan is doing in the palace grounds.

p.10 **TOL** about what happens to her ball. Freeze Frame Joan's expression when she sees the toad.
TTYP: How does she feel about the toad, and why?

p.11 **TOL** about what the toad wants from Joan in return for the ball.

p.12 **TOL** about how Joan avoids the toad.

p.13 **TOL** about what Joan must do to keep her promise to the toad.
Freeze Frame Joan's expression when her father says she must keep her promise.
TTYP: What does she feel, and why?
She feels it isn't fair/She knows she is in the wrong, but doesn't want to be close to the toad.

p.14 **TOL** about why Joan has to put the toad on her pillow.
Freeze Frame Joan's expression when she has to put the toad on her pillow.
TTYP: How does she feel, and why?

p.15 **TOL** about why the toad turns into a handsome prince.
Freeze Frame Joan's expression when she sees the prince.
Freeze Frame the prince's expression.
TTYP: What does he feel, and why?
MTYT (with feeling): *"I was turned into a toad by a **wicked** gnome. **You** have set me free, Joan. And **now** I hope you will be my wife!"*
TTYP: Do you think the prince should have asked Joan to marry him?

 Build a Sentence

Point out that, so far, children have heard the story from Joan's point of view (she told the story). Tell them that tomorrow they will write what the toad might have thought about what happened. Explain that today you are going to help children build up a sentence to describe the toad, as he first appeared to Princess Joan.

1. Display the image of the toad (online file 7.7d). Use **MTYT** to say the simple sentence: *You are a toad.* Point out that *a toad* is a noun phrase, which you are going to build up into a more detailed description. **TTYP:** How might Joan have described the toad at first? *Loathsome/Horrible/ Repulsive/Revolting/Ugly.* Model how to build some of the children's ideas into the sentence, e.g. *You are a repulsive, ugly toad.*

2. **TTYP:** What is its skin like? *Knobbly/Green/Brown/Slimy/Lumpy.* Build up the description further, e.g. *You are a repulsive, ugly toad with green lumpy skin.*

207

3. **TTYP:** What are its eyes like? *Bulging/Scary/Watery.* Model how to incorporate ideas into the sentence, e.g. *You are a repulsive, ugly toad with green lumpy skin and bulging eyes.*

4. Ask partners to decide on their own sentence and to practise saying it until they can remember it. Select a few partners to say their sentences to the group.

5. Ask children to write their own sentence on p.26 of their *Get Writing!* Book.

Day 4 timetable	a. Daily Speed Sounds Lesson	e. Proofread – Spelling
See guidance below for activities in **bold**. See pp.178–180 for other Day 4 activities.	b. Spell Check	f. Proofread – Grammar
	c. **Grammar**	g. **Write about the Toad's Thoughts**
	d. **Vocabulary**	h. Handwriting

[GW] **Grammar**

1. Tell (or remind) children that an **adverb** can tell us more about a verb (an action word). On the board write *The ball sank slowly.* Use **MTYT** to say the sentence. Ask children to **TTYP** to say which word is the main verb *(sank).* Point out that *slowly* is the adverb. It tells us more about the verb – it tells us *how* the ball sank. Remind children that adverbs often (but do not always) end in -ly.

2. Ask children to complete the Grammar activity on p.27 of their *Get Writing!* Book.

3. Ask children to **TTYP** to check they have underlined the same words and if not, to discuss which answers are correct and why.

4. Tell children the correct responses and explain any difficult points. (Children should have underlined: *quickly, unkindly, angrily, hungrily.*)

[GW] **Vocabulary**

1. Remind children that when they are reading, they may come across words that they don't understand. They can often work out the meaning of the word from the sentence it is in.

2. On the board write *I was roaming round the palace grounds.* Use **MTYT** to say the sentence. Underline the word *roaming* and ask children to **TTYP** and say what it means. Draw out that it means *wandering.* Emphasise that they can work out the meaning by looking at how it works in the sentence.

3. Ask children to turn to the Vocabulary activity on p.27 of their *Get Writing!* Book. Talk through the activity, explaining any words that they are unsure of. Then ask children to complete the activity.

4. Ask children to **TTYP** to check they have circled the same words and if not, to discuss which answers are correct and why.

5. Tell children the correct responses and explain any difficult points. (They should have circled: *showed off, dark, scratchy, shouted.*)

 Write About the Toad's Thoughts

Note that this activity should be started on Day 4 and completed on Day 5.

1. **TOL** about how we often think things that we wouldn't say aloud. People would think we were very rude if we did! For example, if someone bumped into you, you shouldn't say, "You clumsy, silly person. How dare you bump into me!" Instead you would hope that they would just apologise and you would smile and forgive them.

2. Use online file 7.7 (tab g onwards) for this activity. Tell children that we know what Princess Joan is thinking right through the story (because she is telling it). Point out that we don't know what the toad is thinking. Explain to children that they are going to write down what they think the toad might be thinking at different points in the story. Ask children to open their *Get Writing!* Book at p.29.

3. Display the first scene at the pond, where the toad is offering to get Joan's ball back (tab g). **TTYP:** What is the toad thinking when he offers to get the ball back? *Here's my chance to become a prince/The princess is very pretty/She is making a big fuss about a little ball/I wonder if she'll let me come to the palace.*

Repeat with the rest of the scenes (tabs h–k), using **TTYP** to ask the questions and **MTYT** to show children how to create full sentences from their answers. Thoughts for some of these might include:

Scene 2 – when the princess runs back to the palace: *I can't believe she is jeering at me/Goodness me – she broke her promise so quickly!/What an unkind young lady!/She might be pretty but she is behaving in a very ugly way/I can't keep up with her.*

Scene 3 – when the toad knocks on the door: *I wonder if someone will answer the door/I hope the king isn't as mean as his daughter/I wonder if I'm doing the right thing/I can't let her get away with this.*

Scene 4 – when the toad eats from the princess's plate: *I wish she wasn't pulling that face while I eat/Oh, this sweet, foaming cocoa is delicious!/I am enjoying this loaf of bread.*

4. Return to the first scene (tab g) and model how you would write what the toad is thinking, using the first person, starting *I…* **TOL** as you write and keep re-reading to check that it makes sense.

5. Hide your writing. Encourage children to think of their own sentences and say them aloud to a partner until they can remember them. Select a few partners to say their sentences to the group. Then ask children to write the toad's thoughts in their exercise book. They can use the Useful words on p.28 and make notes on p.29 of their *Get Writing!* Book.

6. Repeat Steps 4 and 5 (demonstrate how you write, then ask children to write) to help children complete the thoughts for the rest of the scenes. They may be able to do the final scene (when the toad turns into a handsome prince) independently. It might contain thoughts such as: *I hope she will be my wife/I don't think she'll be unkind again/I think she's learnt her lesson.*

Day 5 timetable	a. Daily Speed Sounds Lesson	d. Partner Proofread
See Day 4 for guidance on the activity in **bold**. See p.180 for other Day 5 activities.	b. Spell Test	e. Words to Keep
	c. **Write About the Toad's Thoughts (continued)**	f. Linked Text

 Write About the Toad's Thoughts (continued)

On Day 5, children continue the writing activity that they began on Day 4.

Andrew

Teacher's Preparation

Prepare as for p.172. Print out and display the Story Green Words (see online file '7.8 Andrew', starting with tab a): *view, shore, phew, crew, threw, newt, deck, stew, eye*, Tuesday, Stewart, newspaper, amuse, lifeboat, wetsuit*, dunes, bobbed, listening, confused, rescued, brewed, unscrewed, gently.*

Note that Challenge Words are marked with an asterisk.

Display the Red Word cards: *great, brother, above, where, could, was, what, here, someone, through, another, there, school, water, of, were, to, all, one.*

<table>
<tr><td rowspan="6">DAY 1

Day 1 timetable
See guidance below for activities in bold. See pp.172–175 for other Day 1 activities.</td><td>a. Daily Speed Sounds Lesson</td><td>g. Story Introduction</td></tr>
<tr><td>b. Speed Sounds from the Storybook</td><td>h. First Read – Children</td></tr>
<tr><td>c. Story Green Words</td><td>i. Read Aloud – Teacher</td></tr>
<tr><td>d. Speedy Green Words (online file 7.8b)</td><td>j. Red Rhythms – Spelling Red Words</td></tr>
<tr><td>e. Red Word Cards</td><td>k. Handwriting</td></tr>
<tr><td>f. Partner Practice</td><td></td></tr>
</table>

Story Introduction

On the first day of the school holidays, Andrew went to the beach with his older brother Stewart. They packed a picnic in a cool bag and found a nice spot on the sand dunes where they sat looking out at the calm blue sea, eating tasty cucumber sandwiches and scoffing salt and vinegar crisps.

"I want to read my newspaper now," said Stewart. "Can you amuse yourself?"

Andrew sifted the soft sand through his fingers until he got bored, then he took his new blow-up boat down to the sea.

He climbed in, steadying the little red boat as it bobbed gently up and down. He lay down on his back, listening to the sound of the waves and the noisy seagulls flying above his head and swooping down to catch fish. Soon he drifted off to sleep...

While he was sleeping, the wind grew strong and the waves became big and choppy, slopping into the little boat. Suddenly, Andrew's legs felt wet and cold – he woke up with a start. He looked for the shore but it was now far, far away.

TTYP: What do you think happened next?

Red Rhythms – Spelling Red Words See *Get Writing! Grey*, p.31.

<table>
<tr><td rowspan="5">DAY 2

Day 2 timetable
See guidance below for activities in bold. See pp.175–176 for other Day 2 activities.</td><td>a. Daily Speed Sounds Lesson</td><td>f. Second Read – Children</td></tr>
<tr><td>b. Speedy Green Words (online file 7.8b)</td><td>g. Fred Fingers – Spelling Green Words</td></tr>
<tr><td>c. Red Word Cards</td><td>h. Red Rhythms</td></tr>
<tr><td>d. Partner Practice</td><td>i. Hold a Sentence – 1 and 2</td></tr>
<tr><td>e. Jump-in</td><td>j. Handwriting</td></tr>
</table>

Fred Fingers – Spelling Green Words See *Get Writing!* Book, p.31.

Hold a Sentence – 1 and 2

> **1** Why was Andrew confused about where he was?

> **2** I knew I was safe when I saw the red, white and blue boat.

See *Get Writing!* Book, p.30.

Day 3 timetable	a. Daily Speed Sounds Lesson	e. Questions to Talk About
See guidance below for activities in **bold**. See pp.177–178 for other Day 3 activities.	b. Partner Practice	f. Questions to Read and Answer
	c. Think About the Story	**g. Build a Sentence**
	d. Third Read – Children	h. Handwriting

 Think About the Story

p.9 TOL about what Stewart and Andrew did on the first day of the school holidays.

p.10 TOL about what Andrew could see and hear while he was in the boat.
MTYT (with feeling): *My boat bobbed gently up and down, up and down.*
TTYP: How was he feeling? *Calm/relaxed/Glad he was on holiday.*

p.11 TOL about what happened while Andrew was asleep.
Freeze Frame Andrew's expression when he woke up.
TTYP: What could he see? What could he hear? What was he feeling?
MTYT (with feeling): *When I woke up, I felt confused. Where was I?*

p.12 TOL about what Andrew was thinking. Freeze Frame his expression when he heard someone shouting.
TTYP: What might he have shouted back?
TOL about how Andrew knew he was going to be rescued.

p.13 TOL about how they rescued Andrew.

p.14 TOL about why Stewart was being told off. Freeze Frame Stewart's expression.
TTYP: How did he feel, and why? *Embarrassed/Ashamed/Sorry.*

p.15 TOL about why rules are important.

 Build a Sentence

Tell children that tomorrow they will write about how Stewart answered his parents' questions after Andrew had been rescued. Explain that today you are going to help them build up some sentences that Stewart might have said to describe what happened when he first realised that Andrew was missing.

1. Ask children to take on the role of Stewart. Remind them that he had been reading his newspaper and forgotten all about his younger brother. When he'd finished reading, he remembered Andrew and tried to find him. Use **MTYT** to say: *I looked everywhere.*

TTYP: Where did you look? For example, *along the shore/in the sand dunes/by the ice-cream van/among groups of children playing by the sea.* Model how to incorporate the children's ideas into full sentences, e.g. *I looked everywhere. I searched all along the shore and in the sand dunes.*

TTYP: How did you feel? *I was in a panic/anxious/scared/worried/frantic/desperate.* Model how to expand the sentences further, e.g. *I looked everywhere. I searched all along the shore and in the sand dunes. My mind was racing and I was in a panic.*

TTYP: What did you say to yourself? *I'm so stupid/I can't believe I forgot him/Why didn't I look after him better?* Build up the sentences further, e.g. *I looked everywhere. I searched all along the shore and in the sand dunes. My mind was racing and I was in a panic. 'I'm so stupid!' I kept saying to myself.*

2. Ask partners to decide on their own sentences and to practise saying them until they can remember them. Select a few partners to say their sentences to the group.

3. Ask children to write their own sentences on p.30 of their *Get Writing!* Book.

Day 4 timetable	a. Daily Speed Sounds Lesson	e. Proofread – Spelling
See guidance below for activities in **bold**. See pp.178–180 for other Day 4 activities.	b. Spell Check	f. Proofread – Grammar
	c. Grammar	**g. Write About What Stewart Said**
	d. Vocabulary	h. Handwriting

GW **Grammar**

1. Remind children that a command (instruction) tells someone to do, or not to do, something. It usually starts with a verb that gives an order (an imperative). For example: *Do not...; Keep away...; Pick up...* Remind children of the rules that Andrew wrote – they were all commands.

2. On the board write the incomplete command: _____ *for help if you are in trouble.* Then write these three words: *Shout, Whisper, Dig.* Point out that, in the context of this sentence, these words are verbs, telling someone to do something. Ask children which is the most suitable verb to complete the command in the context of swimming *(Shout).*

3. Ask children to complete the Grammar activity on p.31 of their *Get Writing!* Book.

4. Tell children to **TTYP** to check if they have written the same words and if not, to discuss which answers are correct and why.

5. Tell children the correct responses and explain any difficult points. (They should have written the words in this order: *Wear, Pick, Swim, Look.*)

GW **Vocabulary**

1. Explain that good writers try to develop a wide vocabulary and use a variety of words to make their writing more interesting for the reader.

2. Write *cold, sandy* and *chilly* on the board. Tell children that two of these words have quite similar meanings, but the other one doesn't. Ask them to **TTYP** to decide which is the odd one out *(sandy).*

3. Ask children to turn to the Vocabulary activity on p.31 of their *Get Writing!* Book. Talk through the activity, explaining any words that they are unsure of. Then ask children to complete the activity.

4. Ask children to **TTYP** to check if they have underlined the same words and if not, to discuss which answers are correct and why.

5. Tell children the correct responses and explain any difficult points. (They should have underlined: *warm, amused, bumpy, sea, further, called, soft, hotter.*)

 GW **Write About What Stewart Said**

Note that this activity should be started on Day 4 and completed on Day 5.

1. **TOL** about a time when you lost a younger child when you were out for the day, e.g. in a supermarket or at a beach. Explain the horror you felt when you couldn't see the child, how you searched for them and eventually found them, feeling hugely relieved. **TTYP:** Have you ever been lost? What did your mum or dad say to you when they found you?

2. Use online file 7.8 (tab g onwards) for this activity. Explain to children that they are going to be Stewart, Andrew's older brother. His parents are very cross with him and are asking lots of questions. You are going to be Stewart's parents, ask the questions, and children will respond orally, to their partners, as Stewart. After all the questions have been talked through, children will then write down what Stewart said. Ask children to turn to p.33 of their *Get Writing!* Book. Point out the questions that Stewart's parents are going to ask.

212

3. In role as Stewart's parents, ask children the questions. Use **TTYP** to draw out responses and **MTYT** to develop children's ideas into full sentences.

   – Why did you take the boat to the beach? *I took the boat to the beach because ... Andrew wanted to/we thought we'd try it out/it seemed like a good idea/we've had fun with the boat before.*

   – Why didn't you play with Andrew at the beach? *I didn't play with Andrew because ... I wanted to read the newspaper and relax/I thought Andrew was happy to play on his own.*

   – How did you feel when you noticed that Andrew was missing? *When I noticed Andrew was missing, I felt... horrified/panicked/angry at myself/worried/scared.*

   – What did you do when you saw he was gone? *When I saw Andrew was gone, I ... leapt to my feet/raced along the beach/asked at the ice-cream van/looked all over the dunes/called his name/told the lifeguard.*

   – How did you feel when Andrew was found safe and sound? *When Andrew was found, I felt ... so relieved/happy to see he was OK.*

   – What have you learnt from this? *I have learnt ... to take better care of Andrew/to be more responsible/to think about other people/to remember Andrew is still young and I need to look out for him.*

4. Go back to the first question and use the online file (tab g) to model how you would write Stewart's response. **TOL** as you write, remembering to use the first person as you are now in role as Stewart. Keep re-reading your writing as you develop the sentences to ensure they make sense. Note that this piece of writing should develop into a recount, told by Stewart, rather than just a list of answers.

5. Hide your writing. Ask children to recall their response to the first question and to practise it aloud with a partner until they can remember it. Select a few partners to say their sentences to the group. Then children can write their own sentences in their exercise book. Point out the space to make notes on p.33 of their *Get Writing!* Book, and the Useful words on p.32.

6. Repeat Steps 4 and 5 (demonstrate how you write, then ask children to write) with the next questions, providing as much support as children need to complete their writing. If possible, children should work independently for the final part of the recount.

DAY 5 **Day 5 timetable**	a. Daily Speed Sounds Lesson	d. Partner Proofread
See Day 4 for guidance on the activity in **bold**. See p.180 for other Day 5 activities.	b. Spell Test	e. Words to Keep
	c. **Write About What Stewart Said (continued)**	f. Linked Text

 Write About What Stewart Said (continued)

On Day 5, children continue the writing activity that they began on Day 4.

Dear Vampire

Teacher's Preparation

Prepare as for p.172. Print out and display the Story Green Words (see online file '7.9 Dear Vampire', starting with tab a): *hire, fangs, smear, fear, eyes*, firework, entire, computer, require, vampire, bonfire, enquire, dentist, tiresome, appear, wired, dancing, retired, perched, drooped, fainted, disappeared, hopeless, scary.*

Note that Challenge Words are marked with an asterisk.

Display the Red Word cards: *walk, said, they, were, was, what, small, are, any, here, son, who, would, there, to, you, all.*

DAY 1	**Day 1 timetable**	a. Daily Speed Sounds Lesson	**g. Story Introduction**
	See guidance below for activities in **bold**. See pp.172–175 for other Day 1 activities.	b. Speed Sounds from the Storybook	h. First Read – Children
		c. Story Green Words	i. Read Aloud – Teacher
		d. Speedy Green Words (online file 7.9b)	**j. Red Rhythms – Spelling Red Words**
		e. Red Word Cards	k. Handwriting
		f. Partner Practice	

Story Introduction

Do you remember Wailing Winny and her car boot sale? In this story, Winny is planning a bonfire party. Before the big day, Winny and her husband, Phantom Phil, went shopping to get the best fireworks they could find.

"This year's bonfire party will be brill!" wailed Winny excitedly, as she dropped the last firework into her shopping bag.

As they walked home, Winny spotted a poster with a huge bat on it. 'Vampire for hire!' it read. 'Lots of fun for the entire family.'

When she got back home to Snailtrail Cave, Winny wired up her computer, plugged in the mouse (I mean rat), and sent an email to www.fang.con. She requested a very scary vampire with sharp fangs for the big bonfire party.

The big day came and the party began. Sam Spook and Smelly Nelly danced to their favourite band, The Night Whisperers. Dustbin Dave played along, clanging his dustbin lids loudly.

Phantom Phil was busy lighting the fireworks when Winny heard a quiet knock at the door.

'It must be the vampire!' she thought. But when she went to open it, the vampire wasn't quite what she had expected...

TTYP: How do you think the vampire might be different from what Winny expected?

Red Rhythms – Spelling Red Words See *Get Writing! Grey*, p.35.

DAY 2	**Day 2 timetable**	a. Daily Speed Sounds Lesson	f. Second Read – Children
	See guidance below for activities in **bold**. See pp.175–176 for other Day 2 activities.	b. Speedy Green Words (online file 7.9b)	**g. Fred Fingers – Spelling Green Words**
		c. Red Word Cards	h. Red Rhythms
		d. Partner Practice	**i. Hold a Sentence – 1 and 2**
		e. Jump-in	j. Handwriting

Fred Fingers – Spelling Green Words See *Get Writing!* Book, p.35.

Hold a Sentence – 1 and 2

1 "Is it nearly time for this year's bonfire party?" asked Winny.

2 "Oh, dear!" wailed Winny. "I wanted a scary vampire."

See *Get Writing!* Book, p.34.

Day 3 timetable	a. Daily Speed Sounds Lesson	e. Questions to Talk About
See guidance below for activities in **bold**. See pp.177–178 for other Day 3 activities.	b. Partner Practice	f. Questions to Read and Answer
	c. Think About the Story	**g. Build a Sentence**
	d. Third Read – Children	h. Handwriting

 Think About the Story

p.9 **TOL** about how we know that Winny was getting ready for her party.

p.10 **TOL** about why Winny thought a vampire was just what they needed for the party.

p.11 **TOL** about who Winny expected to see at the door.

p.12 Freeze Frame Winny's expression when she saw the vampire bat.
TTYP: How did she feel? *Disappointed/Confused/Surprised.*
MTYT (with feeling): *"I wanted a **scary** vampire, and I wanted **sharp** fangs – but you haven't got any fangs **at all**!"*

p.13 **TOL** about how the vampire bat tried to scare the guests.

p.14 **TOL** about what the vampire bat was afraid of.

p.15 Freeze Frame Winny's expression.
TTYP: How did Winny feel? *Frustrated/ Exasperated/Impatient/Cross.*
TOL about why Winny wanted the vampire to go away.

 Build a Sentence

Tell children that tomorrow they will write about a boy who goes to a fun fair or theme park for his birthday treat and enjoys lots of scary rides. Explain that today you are going to help them build up a sentence about going on a scary ride.

1. Ask children to imagine being on a ride with a relative or friend. Talk about how scary it is, even though they know they are safely buckled in. Use **MTYT** to say the sentence: *I gripped Dad's arm.*

2. **TTYP:** Which ride are you on? *The roller coaster/helter skelter/bumper cars/waltzer.* Show how to build the response into the sentence, e.g. *I gripped Dad's arm on the roller coaster.*

3. **TTYP:** What is happening? *It's about to… go downhill very quickly/go faster/go higher.* Expand the sentence using one of the children's responses, e.g. *I gripped Dad's arm as the roller coaster tipped over the top of the hill.*

4. **TTYP:** How do you feel? *Terrified/Scared/Excited/Thrilled.* Build up the sentence further, e.g. *Terrified, I gripped Dad's arm as the roller coaster tipped over the top of the hill.*

5. Ask partners to decide on their own sentence and to practise saying it until they can remember it. Select a few partners to say their sentences to the group.

6. Ask children to write their own sentence on p.34 of their *Get Writing!* Book.

215

Day 4 timetable	a. Daily Speed Sounds Lesson	e. Proofread – Spelling
See guidance below for activities in **bold**. See pp.178–180 for other Day 4 activities.	b. Spell Check	f. Proofread – Grammar
	c. Grammar	**g. Write About Sam's Birthday**
	d. Vocabulary	h. Handwriting

GW Grammar

1. Tell (or remind) children that a **suffix** is added to the end of a word to change its meaning. On the board write *toothless*. Use **MTYT** to say *You toothless twit!* (which is what Winny says to the vampire bat). **TTYP:** What does the word *toothless* mean? *(Without teeth)* **TTYP:** What is the root word *(tooth)* and what is the suffix (-less)? Write the word *helpful*. **TTYP:** What does the word *helpful* mean? *(Full of help/happy to help)* **TTYP:** Which is the root word *(help)* and which is the suffix (-ful)?

2. Ask children to turn to the Grammar activity on p.35 of their *Get Writing!* Book. Talk through the activity to check children understand it, before they start to complete it on their own.

3. Ask children to **TTYP** to check if they have written the same suffixes and if not, to discuss which answers are correct and why.

4. Tell children the correct responses and explain any difficult points. (Children should have formed these words: *hopeless, careful, brainless, forgetful, useless*.)

GW Vocabulary

1. Remind children that when they are reading, they may come across words that they don't understand. They can often work out the meaning of a word from the sentence it is in.

2. On the board write *The vampire perched on Dustbin Dave's ear.* Use **MTYT** to say the sentence. Underline the word *perched* and ask children to **TTYP** and say what it means. Draw out that it means *sat*. Emphasise that they can work out the meaning by looking at how it works in the sentence.

3. Ask children to turn to the Vocabulary activity on p.35 of their *Get Writing!* Book. Talk through the activity, explaining any words that they are unsure of. Then ask children to complete the activity.

4. Ask children to **TTYP** to check they have circled the same words and if not, to discuss which answers are correct and why.

5. Tell children the correct responses and explain any difficult points. (They should have circled: *need, floating, whole, ask, annoying*.)

GW Write About Sam's Birthday Trip

Note that this activity should be started on Day 4 and completed on Day 5.

1. Use online file 7.9 (tab g onwards) for this activity. **TOL** about how lots of people enjoy feeling scared – the sort of scared feeling you get when you are really very safe – like watching a scary film or going down a slide at the park very quickly, or going on a big wheel at a funfair. **TOL** about a time when you went to a funfair and were very, very scared, perhaps on a roller coaster or big wheel, or waltzer. Display the pictures of scary rides (tab g).

   TTYP: Which rides do you think are the scariest? Or do you prefer to watch people being scared? Show the film clip of people riding a roller coaster (tab h).

2. Explain to children that they are going to write about a child, Sam, going to a fun fair or a theme park for a birthday treat. Explain that you are going to talk through what happened, asking lots of questions, so that they can think up their own ideas. Ask children to open their *Get Writing!* Book at p.37. Point out the story outline and questions that they should use to prompt their writing.

3. Read the questions, asking children to **TTYP** to give their responses. If necessary, show children how to build their responses into full sentences using **MTYT**.

- Which rides did Sam want to go on for his birthday? *Sam wanted to go on... the big wheel/the roller coaster/the bumper cars.*

- What did Sam do or feel before his birthday? *Before his birthday, Sam... felt excited/saved his pocket money/invited a friend.*

- When did Sam wake up on his birthday and how did he feel? *On his birthday, Sam woke up ... early, as he was so excited he could hardly sleep/so early that his mum told him to go back to bed.*

- Where did Sam and his dad go first when they arrived? *When they arrived, they went on the bumper cars/big wheel/waltzer.*

- What happened on the ride? *On the ride, Sam's car wouldn't move/he was bumped from behind.*

- How did Sam feel as it got faster and faster? *When the ride got faster and faster, Sam's heart started to race/Sam felt a big thrill/Sam was so excited.*

- How did Sam feel at the end of the ride? *After the ride, Sam felt thrilled/happy/a bit shaky.*

- Where did Sam and his dad go next? *Next, Sam and his dad... went on the roller coaster/the waltzer/had a toffee apple before going on the roller coaster.*

4. Go back to the first question and use the online file (tab i) to model how you would write about Sam choosing the rides. **TOL** as you write, and keep re-reading your writing as you develop your sentence to make sure it makes sense.

5. Hide your writing. Ask children to recall their response to the first question and to practise it aloud with a partner until they can remember it. Select a few partners to say their sentences to the group. Then children can write their own sentences in their exercise book. Point out the space to make notes on p.37 of their *Get Writing!* Book, and the Useful words on p.36.

6. Repeat Steps 4 and 5 (demonstrate how you write, then ask children to write) with the next questions, providing as much support as children need to complete their writing. If possible children should work independently towards the end of the writing.

Day 5 timetable	a. Daily Speed Sounds Lesson	d. Partner Proofread
See Day 4 for guidance on the activity in **bold**. See p.180 for other Day 5 activities.	b. Spell Test	e. Words to Keep
	c. Write About Sam's Birthday Trip (continued)	f. Linked Text

DAY 5

 Write About Sam's Birthday Trip (continued)

On Day 5, children continue the writing activity that they began on Day 4.

Vulture culture

Teacher's Preparation

Prepare as for p.172. Print out and display the Story Green Words (see online file '7.10 Vulture culture', starting with tab a): *Andean condor, South America, glide, bald, rare, ledge of rock, weigh*, metre*, height*, vulture, nature, feature, capture, temperature, extinct, future, creature, pleasure, feathers.*

Note that Challenge Words are marked with an asterisk.

Display the Red Word cards: *one, some, their, where, they, many, are, were, come, two, of, above.*

Find a map to show children where the Andes Mountains are in South America.

Day 1 timetable	a. Daily Speed Sounds Lesson	g. **Story Introduction**
See guidance below for activities in **bold**. See pp.172–175 for other Day 1 activities.	b. Speed Sounds from the Storybook	h. First Read – Children
	c. Story Green Words	i. Read Aloud – Teacher
	d. Speedy Green Words (online file 7.10b)	j. **Red Rhythms – Spelling Red Words**
	e. Red Word Cards	k. Handwriting
	f. Partner Practice	

DAY 1

Story Introduction

Have you ever seen a vulture? Yesterday, Billy saw one at the zoo. It had black feathers on its body and a ruff of white feathers around its neck. It was completely bald – even balder than Billy's dad!

"This vulture is an Andean condor," said the zookeeper. "These condors live in the mountain ranges of South America and are the largest of all flying birds."

"What do they eat?" asked Billy, excitedly.

"That's a very good question," said the zookeeper. "Condors eat all kinds of animals, but it's very rare for them to kill their own food. They glide high above the mountains to spot animals which have already died."

Next, the zookeeper explained how condors lay eggs every two years. "When the chicks have hatched," he said, "they can't fly for about 6 months, so the parents have to feed them. Condors can live for as long as 50 years."

'Wow,' thought Billy.

When the zookeeper had told them everything he could about the Andean condors, Billy bought a vulture sticker and a colouring book.

"Can we come again tomorrow, Dad?" he asked on the way home.

Do you want to find out more about vultures? This book will tell you everything you need to know!

TTYP: What else would you like to know about vultures?

Red Rhythms – Spelling Red Words See *Get Writing! Grey*, p.39.

DAY 2

Day 2 timetable	a. Daily Speed Sounds Lesson	f. Second Read – Children
See guidance below for activities in **bold**. See pp.175–176 for other Day 2 activities.	b. Speedy Green Words (online file 7.10b)	g. **Fred Fingers – Spelling Green Words**
	c. Red Word Cards	h. Red Rhythms
	d. Partner Practice	i. **Hold a Sentence – 1 and 2**
	e. Jump-in	j. Handwriting

Fred Fingers – Spelling Green Words See *Get Writing!* Book, p.39.

GW **Hold a Sentence – 1 and 2**

(1) A condor is an amazing animal because it is the largest flying bird.

(2) A condor has a mixture of black and white feathers.

See *Get Writing!* Book, p.38.

DAY 3

Day 3 timetable	a. Daily Speed Sounds Lesson	e. Questions to Talk About
See guidance below for activities in **bold**. See pp.177–178 for other Day 3 activities.	b. Partner Practice	f. Questions to Read and Answer
	c. Think About the Story	**g. Build a Sentence**
	d. Third Read – Children	h. Handwriting

Think About the Story

TOL about the questions that act as headings in this text. Point out that they help to divide up the information, helping the reader to find out facts that they are looking for. Ask children to find the other headings in the text: *Where do they live?/What do they look like?/What do they eat?/How do they breed?/The future.*

p.9 **TOL** about where these vultures live. Display a map of South America which shows the Andes Mountains running down the west coast.

p.10 **TOL** about the size of the bird. Use two children's arm spans and height to compare.

p.11 **TOL** about what condors look like.

p.12 **TOL** about how condors find their food.

p.13 **TOL** about how condors breed.

p.14 **TOL** about the maximum life span of a condor.

p.15 **TOL** about the future of condors.

GW **Build a Sentence**

Tell children that tomorrow they will write some notes about another huge bird, the Marabou stork, and then compare it with the Andean condor. Explain that today you are going to help them build up some sentences about how the Andean condor finds food.

1. Use **MTYT** to say the sentence: *The condor searches for food.*

2. **TOL** about the word *scavenge*. **TTYP:** What does *scavenge* mean? *To search for something among rubbish or dead things.* **MTYT:** *The condor scavenges for food.* **TTYP:** What type of food? *Dead animals.* Demonstrate how to build up the sentence: *The condor scavenges for dead animals.*

3. **TTYP:** How does it do this? *It flies high above the mountains/spots dead animals with its good eyesight/dives down/pulls the flesh apart with its sharp claws and beak.*

4. Build the information into sentences, such as *The condor scavenges for dead animals. When it spots an animal, it dives down and claws the flesh apart.*

5. Ask partners to decide on their own sentences and to practise saying them until they can remember them. Select a few partners to say their sentences to the group.

6. Ask children to write their own sentences on p.38 of their *Get Writing!* Book.

DAY 4	**Day 4 timetable**	a. Daily Speed Sounds Lesson	e. Proofread – Spelling
	See guidance below for activities in **bold**. See pp.178–180 for other Day 4 activities.	b. Spell Check	f. Proofread – Grammar
		c. Grammar	**g. Write About the Marabou Stork**
		d. Vocabulary	h. Handwriting

 Grammar

1. Tell (or remind) children that we use some words to link together two parts (clauses) in a sentence. We call these words **conjunctions** or 'linking words'. On the board write the incomplete sentence: *Andean condors were almost extinct _____ too many had been hunted and killed.* **TTYP:** What 'linking word' is missing from this sentence? If necessary, give children the choice between *because, if, that*. (The most appropriate word is *because*.) Other example sentences are:

   – *The egg will break [if/when] it falls to the ground.*

   – *This is the bird [that] I told you about.*

   – *Turn left [when] you get to the tree.*

2. Ask children to turn to the Grammar activity on p.39 of their *Get Writing!* Book. Talk through the activity to check children understand it, before they start to complete it on their own.

3. Tell children to **TTYP** to check if they have written the same words and if not, to discuss which answers are correct and why.

4. Tell children the correct responses and explain any difficult points. (Children should have written: *when, because, that*. Note that one variation is possible, but these are the 'best fit' responses.)

 Vocabulary

1. Remind children that when they are reading, they may come across words or phrases that they don't understand. They can often work out a word's meaning from the sentence it is in.

2. On the board write *From wingtip to wingtip, the condor measures more than 3 metres.* Use **MTYT** to say the sentence. Underline the word *wingtip* and ask children to **TTYP** and say what it means. Draw out that it means the end of the wing that is the furthest from the bird's body when a wing is outstretched. Emphasise that even if they had not heard the word before, they could try to work it out from the context of the sentence.

3. Ask children to turn to the Vocabulary activity on p.39 of their *Get Writing!* Book. Talk through the activity, then ask children to complete the activity independently.

4. Ask children to **TTYP** to check they have circled the same words and if not, to discuss which answers are correct and why.

5. Tell children the correct responses and explain any difficult points. (They should have circled: *fly, shelf, meat, heat*.)

 Write About the Marabou Stork

Note that this activity should be started on Day 4 and completed on Day 5.

1. **TOL** about how fascinating it is finding out about different animals – how as a child, you loved visiting zoos and wildlife centres to find out more.

2. Use online file 7.10 (tab g onwards) for this activity. Explain to children that they are going to write a fact file (factual notes) about another big scavenging bird – the Marabou stork. Ask children to turn to p.41 in their *Get Writing!* Book.

3. Display the image of the Marabou stork and the accompanying information text (tab g and see the printable file in tab a). Read the text aloud. Explain that in order to write notes you need to look for key information in the text. Start reading the text and highlight the first fact about the Marabou stork: *from Africa*. Ask children what information they can find next, e.g. *the name 'undertaker bird'* and *huge, black, cloak-like wings.*

4. Draw attention to the stork fact file template (tab h onwards). **TOL** as you model writing notes under the first heading. Keep re-reading to make sure they make sense.

5. Return to tab g to display the information text. Using the questions in the *Get Writing!* Book, children should start to write their fact file in their exercise book under the heading about what the Marabou stork looks like. They can use the Useful words on p.40 of the *Get Writing!* Book to help them, and jot down ideas on p.41.

6. Repeat Steps 4 and 5 (demonstrate how you write, then ask children to write) for what the Marabou stork eats and where it lives and nests. Then draw children's attention to the last two points about the similarities and differences between the Andean condor and the Marabou stork. Ask them to use their notes and the book *Vulture Culture* to answer these questions. After discussing answers with a partner, they should complete their fact file. Some possible responses might be:

   – Similarities – similar wingspans; both have bald heads; both scavengers; both lay eggs on cliffs.

   – Differences – live in different places; lay different number of eggs; have different coloured heads.

Day 5 timetable	a. Daily Speed Sounds Lesson	d. Partner Proofread
See Day 4 for guidance on the activity in **bold**. See p.180 for other Day 5 activities.	b. Spell Test	e. Words to Keep
	c. Write About the Marabou Stork (continued)	f. Linked Text

G W **Write About the Marabou Stork (continued)**

On Day 5, children continue the writing activity that they began on Day 4.

221

A celebration on planet Zox

Teacher's Preparation

Prepare as for p.172. Print out and display the Story Green Words (see online file '7.11 A celebration on planet Zox', starting with tab a): *section, exhaustion, completion, exploration, presentation, preparation, decoration, arrive, conversation, tradition, ambition, underneath, indigestion, portion, cyber, condition, injection, mention, attention, solution, honour*, relations.* Note that Challenge Words are marked with an asterisk.

Display the Red Word cards: *caught, worse, come, call, was, said, their, great, everyone, should, who, here, watch, all, they, of, you, were, there, another.*

DAY 1			
Day 1 timetable	a. Daily Speed Sounds Lesson	g. **Story Introduction**	
See guidance below for activities in **bold**. See pp.172–175 for other Day 1 activities.	b. Speed Sounds from the Storybook	h. First Read – Children	
	c. Story Green Words	i. Read Aloud – Teacher	
	d. Speedy Green Words (online file 7.11b)	j. **Red Rhythms – Spelling Red Words**	
	e. Red Word Cards	k. Handwriting	
	f. Partner Practice		

Story Introduction

Do you remember Cosmic Clare and Radar Rob, who were playing dare games on planet Zox? Well, in this story, Clare's dad, Cosmic Clive, has just come back from a long space trip. He has been exploring Planet Pixel. Everyone is thrilled to see him!

On the day of his return, Clare went with her relations to greet him at the space station. As Clive stepped off the spacecraft, no one noticed that his face was pale green with exhaustion. The King of Zox gave Clive a bunch of green carnations and a glistening golden space watch. "I name you Zoxonaut of the Year!" he announced.

Clare's mum, Cosmic Cath, cheered, "This calls for a celebration!" She rushed home to start the preparations.

There was a lot to do. Clare helped Cath to hang the decorations and together they made a big banner, which read: "Congratulations to Cosmic Clive – Zoxonaut of the Year!" Clare planned some games, and Clive stayed up all night writing his speech.

The day of the party arrived and everyone was having a great time. But when Clive stood up to make his big speech, something awful happened...

TTYP: What do you think happened?

Red Rhythms – Spelling Red Words See *Get Writing! Grey*, p.43.

DAY 2			
Day 2 timetable	a. Daily Speed Sounds Lesson	f. Second Read – Children	
See guidance below for activities in **bold**. See pp.175–176 for other Day 2 activities.	b. Speedy Green Words (online file 7.11b)	g. **Fred Fingers – Spelling Green Words**	
	c. Red Word Cards	h. Red Rhythms	
	d. Partner Practice	i. **Hold a Sentence – 1 and 2**	
	e. Jump-in	j. Handwriting	

Fred Fingers – Spelling Green Words See *Get Writing! Book*, p.43.

Hold a Sentence – 1 and 2

1. "Can we have a celebration?" asked Cosmic Cath.

2. "Get him to the hospital for an operation!" cried Meteor Meg.

See *Get Writing!* Book, p.42.

 DAY 3

Day 3 timetable	a. Daily Speed Sounds Lesson	e. Questions to Talk About
See guidance below for activities in **bold**. See pp.177–178 for other Day 3 activities.	b. Partner Practice	f. Questions to Read and Answer
	c. Think About the Story	**g. Build a Sentence**
	d. Third Read – Children	h. Handwriting

 Think About the Story

p.9 **TOL** about how we know that Cosmic Clive was away for a long time. *He was visiting Planet Pixel and all his relations went to greet him.*

pp.10–11 **TOL** about why they were celebrating. **TOL** about how they prepared for the celebration.

p.12 **TOL** about how everyone had a good time at the party.

p.13 **TOL** about what happened to Cosmic Clive. Freeze Frame everyone's expression. **TTYP:** How were they feeling, and why? *Shocked/Worried because Clive looked so ill.*

p.14 **MTYT** (with feeling): *"His condition's getting **worse**!" cried Meteor Meg (who used to be a nurse). "We **must** get him into astrohospital!"* **TOL** about what the doctor said was wrong with Cosmic Clive.

p.15 **TOL** about what Cosmic Clive did while he was in hospital. Freeze Frame Clive's expression. **TTYP:** How was he feeling? *Pleased that he was feeling better/Loved everyone being with him.*

 Build a Sentence

Tell children that tomorrow they will start writing a story about when they went on a school trip, but felt unwell, so they had to go home early. Explain that today you are going to help them build some sentences about feeling unwell on the bus.

1. Use **MTYT** to say the sentence starter: *Sitting on the bus, I suddenly felt unwell.*

2. **TTYP:** How did you feel unwell? *Dizzy/Sick/Hot/Headachy.* Show how to incorporate some of the children's ideas into the sentence, e.g. *Sitting on the bus, I suddenly felt dizzy and hot.*

3. **TTYP:** What did you think? *Oh no!/I can't be sick now/I'll sit still and hope I feel better soon/I've eaten too many sweets.* Model how to expand the sentence, e.g. *Sitting on the bus, I suddenly felt dizzy and hot. 'Oh no, I can't be sick now,' I thought.*

4. **TTYP:** What did your friend say? *What's wrong?/You look awful/I'll get the teacher/Please don't be sick on me!* Demonstrate how to expand the sentence further, e.g. *Sitting on the bus, I suddenly felt dizzy and hot. 'Oh no,' I thought. 'I can't be sick now.' My friend Alex said, "You look awful."*

5. Ask partners to decide on their own sentences and to practise saying them until they can remember them. Select a few partners to say their sentences to the group.

6. Ask children to write their own sentences on p.42 of their *Get Writing!* Book.

Day 4 timetable	a. Daily Speed Sounds Lesson	e. Proofread – Spelling
See guidance below for activities in **bold**. See pp.178–180 for other Day 4 activities.	b. Spell Check	f. Proofread – Grammar
	c. Grammar	**g. Write About Being Poorly on a School Trip**
	d. Vocabulary	h. Handwriting

DAY 4

GW Grammar

1. Tell (or remind) children that an **adjective** can tell us more about a noun. Write *the gold watch* on the board and use **MTYT** to say it. Ask children which word in this phrase is a noun *(watch)*. **TTYP:** Which word in this phrase is an adjective? *(gold)* Discuss alternative adjectives that could be used in this phrase, to describe different watches, e.g. *blue/circular/plastic/square/digital/diamond/waterproof.*

2. Ask children to complete the Grammar activity on p.43 of their *Get Writing!* Book. If necessary, remind them to look for a word that describes a noun.

3. Tell children to **TTYP** to check they have underlined the same words and if not, to discuss which answers are correct and why.

4. Tell children the correct responses and explain any difficult points. (They should have underlined: *big, green, good, great, long, huge.*)

GW Vocabulary

Remind children that there are groups of words that have the same ending.

1. On the board write -tion. Ask children how to say this ending *(shun)*.

2. **TTYP:** Can you think of a word with this ending? Remind children of the -tion words they were taught in the Speed Sounds lessons, drawing out as many examples as possible, e.g. *station, ambition, action, celebration, relation.* The words do not have to be just from the Storybook. Use **MTYT** to revise these words.

3. Ask children to turn to the Vocabulary activity on p.43 of their *Get Writing!* Book. Draw attention to the words in the box. Talk through the activity, ensuring children understand what they need to do.

4. After completion, ask children to **TTYP** to check if they have inserted the same words and if not, to discuss which answers are correct and why.

5. Tell children the correct responses and explain any difficult points. (They should have written: *indigestion, exhaustion, ambition, tradition, completion.*)

GW Write About Being Poorly on a School Trip

Note that this activity should be started on Day 4 and continued on Day 5. If necessary, allow another writing session on another day for children to complete their work.

1. **TOL** about how disappointed everyone felt when the celebration was stopped because Cosmic Clive was ill. Tell the children about a time when you were looking forward to an event and then you couldn't go because you were poorly.

2. Use online file 7.11 (tab g onwards) for this activity. Explain that children are going to write a story about looking forward to a school trip, then being ill on the journey and having to go home early. Explain that the story can be a real experience or one that they make up, or based on other people's ideas. Tell them that they need to build up a sense of excitement at the beginning of the story, so that the reader will feel disappointment when they find out the writer had to go home early.

Ask children to turn to p.45 in their *Get Writing!* Book. Draw attention to the question prompts and the sentence starters. Tell them that they can use these as a guide to writing their own story and write notes here.

3. Go through all the questions orally with children, encouraging them to create their own responses, but giving guidance or using **MTYT** to build full sentences where necessary:

   – **TTYP:** Where were you going on the school trip? *We were going to... a castle/a wildlife park/the seaside/the countryside/the theatre.*

   – **TTYP:** What did you have to take with you? *I had to pack... a lunch/a drink/some money.*

   – **TTYP:** What did you have to wear? *I had to wear... a sunhat/a hat and gloves/a warm winter coat/sandals/a long-sleeved top/a jumper/shorts/trousers/trainers/my school uniform.*

   – **TTYP:** How did you feel the night before the trip? *The night before the trip, I felt... excited/nervous/happy/wide awake/keen to go.*

Continue with the rest of the questions.

4. **TOL** about the destination of the school trip. Use the online file (tab g) to model how to write your first lines. **TOL** about your choice of words, spelling and punctuation. Keep re-reading to make sure your writing makes sense.

5. Hide your writing. Ask children to decide on their own first paragraph and practise saying it aloud with a partner until they can remember it. Select a few partners to say their sentences to the group. Then children can write their own sentences in their exercise book. Point out the Useful words on p.44 of the *Get Writing!* Book.

6. Repeat Steps 4 and 5 (demonstrate how you write, then ask children to write) for the other paragraphs. Some children may be able to complete the remaining paragraphs without teacher support.

Day 5 timetable	a. Daily Speed Sounds Lesson	d. Partner Proofread
See Day 4 for guidance on the activity in **bold**. See p.180 for other Day 5 activities.	b. Spell Test	e. Words to Keep
	c. Write About Being Poorly on a School Trip (continued)	f. Linked Text

 Write About Being Poorly on a School Trip (continued)

On Day 5, children continue the writing activity that they began on Day 4. If necessary, allow another writing session on another day for children to complete their work.

A very dangerous dinosaur

Teacher's Preparation

Prepare as for p.172. Print out and display the Story Green Words (see online file '7.12 A very dangerous dinosaur', starting with tab a): *ferocious, stalking, vicious, mountainous, suspicious, curious, furious, herbivorous, protect, precious, gorgeous, marvellous, monstrous, hideous, scrumptious, ridiculous, idea* scissors*, rumour*, thundered, lumbered, anxiously, cautiously.* Note that Challenge Words are marked with an asterisk.

Display the Red Word cards: *talk, thought, there, where, all, through, one, would, two, was, they, other.*

DAY 1

Day 1 timetable	a. Daily Speed Sounds Lesson	g. **Story Introduction**
See guidance below for activities in **bold**. See pp.172–175 for other Day 1 activities.	b. Speed Sounds from the Storybook	h. First Read – Children
	c. Story Green Words	i. Read Aloud – Teacher
	d. Speedy Green Words (online file 7.12b)	j. **Red Rhythms – Spelling Red Words**
	e. Red Word Cards	k. Handwriting
	f. Partner Practice	

Story Introduction

Did you know that there were two sorts of dinosaurs? Some only ate plants: they were called herbivorous dinosaurs. Some ate animals: they were called carnivorous dinosaurs.

This is a story about a group of herbivorous dinosaurs – Stegosaurus, Torosaurus and Brachiosaurus. They were all very worried. A new kind of dinosaur had just arrived in the forest and he liked eating dinosaur eggs! What kind of dinosaur was he?

They called him Snatchosaurus. He was the most vicious and ferocious dinosaur in the forest. The herbivorous dinosaurs held a meeting.

"What a cheek!" bellowed Brachiosaurus. "We herbivorous dinosaurs can't protect our eggs from the likes of him."

This was serious, they decided, but they didn't know what to do. Soon things started to get worse. The Snatchosaurus lay in wait by their nests. When the herbivorous dinosaurs went in search of food, the Snatchosaurus would gobble up their precious eggs!

"Don't leave the nest!" Brachiosaurus told her baby. "You must stay and look after the eggs!" But when she came back, she found Baby hiding in a cave, shaking from nose to tail. Something had to be done...

TTYP: What do you think the dinosaurs should do to protect themselves?

Red Rhythms – Spelling Red Words See *Get Writing! Grey*, p.47.

DAY 2

Day 2 timetable	a. Daily Speed Sounds Lesson	f. Second Read – Children
See guidance below for activities in **bold**. See pp.175–176 for other Day 2 activities.	b. Speedy Green Words (online file 7.12b)	g. **Fred Fingers – Spelling Green Words**
	c. Red Word Cards	h. Red Rhythms
	d. Partner Practice	i. **Hold a Sentence – 1 and 2**
	e. Jump-in	j. Handwriting

Fred Fingers – Spelling Green Words See *Get Writing!* Book, p.47.

Hold a Sentence – 1 and 2

(**1**) The dangerous dinosaur thought the precious eggs were delicious.

(**2**) "We need to find an even more dangerous dinosaur to catch him."

See *Get Writing!* Book, p.46.

Day 3 timetable	a. Daily Speed Sounds Lesson	e. Questions to Talk About
See guidance below for activities in **bold**. See pp.177–178 for other Day 3 activities.	b. Partner Practice	f. Questions to Read and Answer
	c. Think About the Story	**g. Build a Sentence**
	d. Third Read – Children	h. Handwriting

 Think About the Story

p.9 **TOL** about the new rumour going round. Freeze Frame the expression on the dinosaurs' faces.
TTYP: How were they feeling? *Worried/ Anxious/Frightened.*

p.10 **TOL** about what made Snatchosaurus so frightening. **MTYT** (with feeling and one line at a time): *"Vicious Snatchosaurus prowls through our lands, With spikes on his feet, and claws on his hands, Crashing through the treetops on mountainous legs, Making his dinner from **dinosaur eggs**!"*

p.11 **TOL** about why Brachiosaurus was worried about Snatchosaurus.
MTYT: *"We herbivorous dinosaurs can't protect our eggs from the likes of him."*

p.12 Freeze Frame Stegosaurus's expression while she was away from her precious nest.
TTYP: How was she feeling, and why? *Anxious/Worried because of the unprotected egg.*

p.13 Freeze Frame Torosaurus's expression while she was away from her two fine eggs.
TTYP: How was she feeling and why? *Excited because she was looking forward to having two tiny Torosauruses.*
Freeze Frame her expression when she returned.
TTYP: How was she feeling and why? *Horrified because Snatchosaurus was spitting out bits of shell.*

p.14 **TOL** about what happened when Brachiosaurus went into the forest.

p.15 **TOL** about how they got rid of Snatchosaurus.

[GW] **Build a Sentence**

Tell children that tomorrow they will describe some (fictional) dinosaurs which have interesting names. Explain that today you are going to help them to build up some sentences about another dinosaur – the Ferociousaurus.

1. Use **MTYT** to say: *Beware of the Ferociousaurus.*

2. **TTYP:** How does it move? *It strides/stomps/crashes/clomps/trudges/tramples.* Model how to incorporate some of the children's ideas into the sentence, e.g. *Beware of the Ferociousaurus, stomping through the forest.*

3. **TTYP:** What sound does it make? *It grunts/growls/snarls/hisses/roars.* Model how to expand the sentence further, e.g. *Beware of the Ferociousaurus, stomping and snarling through the forest.*

4. **TTYP:** What does it do? *It searches for prey/scavenges for its next meal/scares the other animals.* Expand the sentence further, e.g. *Beware of the Ferociousaurus, stomping and snarling through the forest, scavenging for its next meal.*

5. Ask partners to decide on their own sentence and to practise saying it until they can remember it. Select a few partners to say their sentences to the group.

6. Ask children to write their own sentence on p.46 of their *Get Writing!* Book.

Day 4 timetable	a. Daily Speed Sounds Lesson	e. Proofread – Spelling
See guidance below for activities in **bold**. See pp.178–180 for other Day 4 activities.	b. Spell Check	f. Proofread – Grammar
	c. Grammar	**g. Write About New Kinds of Dinosaurs**
	d. Vocabulary	h. Handwriting

GW **Grammar**

1. Remind children that we use the **past tense** of verbs to describe things that have happened earlier (in the past). Write on the board *There is a rumour in dinosaur land.* Use **MTYT** to say the sentence. Ask children to **TTYP** to identify the verb *(is)*. Emphasise that this sentence is in the present tense – it is happening now. **TTYP:** How would you change this sentence into the past tense? *(There was a rumour in dinosaur land.)*

2. Remind children that many past tense verbs end in -ed, such as *prowled, bellowed, squeaked,* but not all of them, e.g. *saw, taught, ran.*

3. Tell children to turn to the Grammar activity on p.47 of their *Get Writing!* Book. Talk through the activity, explaining any words that they are unsure of. Then ask children to complete the activity.

4. Ask children to **TTYP** to check they have written the same words and if not, to discuss which answers are correct and why.

5. Tell children the correct responses and explain any difficult points. (They should have written: *sounded, left, returned, made.*)

GW **Vocabulary**

1. Explain that we are very lucky to have so many words in the English language because it means that, as writers, we have a lot of choice. When we want to write or say something, there are usually many different ways that we can write it.

2. Write three words on the board: *cautiously, bravely, carefully.* Use **MTYT** to say all three words. Ask children to **TTYP** and say which word is the odd one out, because it means something different *(bravely).*

3. Ask children to turn to the Vocabulary activity on p.47 of their *Get Writing!* Book. Talk through the activity, explaining any words that they are unsure of. Then ask children to complete the activity.

4. Ask children to **TTYP** to check they have underlined the same words and if not, to discuss which answers are correct and why.

5. Tell children the correct responses and explain any difficult points. (They should have underlined: *delighted, flat, show, contented.*)

 GW **Write About New Kinds of Dinosaurs**

Note that this activity should be started on Day 4 and completed on Day 5.

1. **TOL** about how the word *dinosaur* comes from two words that mean 'terrible lizard'. Go through the names of the dinosaurs in the story. Explain that the last part of each name – saurus – means lizard, but the first part of each name describes something particular about that dinosaur.

228

For example, *stegosaurus* means 'covered lizard' because it is covered in bony plates along its back; *torosaurus* means 'holey lizard' because it has two big holes in the 'frill' around its neck; *brachiosaurus* means 'arm lizard' because its neck is long and thin like an arm.

2. Use online file 7.12 (tab g onwards) for this activity. Explain to children that they are going to write about some new (made up) dinosaurs. Ask children to turn to p.49 in their *Get Writing!* Book. Point out the pictures and names of the new dinosaurs.

3. Display the image of the Courageousaurus (tab g). Ask children the questions (tab h). This should prompt ideas and stimulate suitable vocabulary for their writing. If necessary, use **MTYT** to help children to form complete sentences, using their ideas.

   The questions and responses about the Courageousaurus might follow the lines below.

   TTYP: What does the dinosaur look like? *It has big eyes/large ears/a strong/determined/serious expression.*

   TTYP: How does it move? *It moves steadily/strongly/slowly.*

   TTYP: What does it sound like? *It sounds loud/confident.*

   TTYP: What does it eat? Is it herbivorous or carnivorous? *It's herbivorous and eats berries/grass/ leaves/bushes.*

   TTYP: Why does it have this name? (In what ways is it courageous?) *It always protects its family and friends/fights off enemies/tells off bullies.*

   TTYP: What do the other dinosaurs think about it? *They like it because it is friendly/brave/ sensible/caring/kind/fair.*

4. **TOL** as you use the online file (tab h) to model on the board how to write about the Courageousaurus. Draw on the children's earlier oral responses to build up your writing. Keep re-reading to make sure it makes sense.

5. Hide your writing. Ask children to decide how to describe the dinosaur and practise saying their descriptions aloud with a partner until they can remember them. Select a few partners to say their sentences to the group. Then children can write their own sentences about the Courageousaurus in their exercise book. Point out the Useful words on p.48, and space to make notes on p.49 of their *Get Writing!* Book.

6. Repeat Steps 3, 4 and 5 (ask each question, demonstrate how you write, then ask children to write) with the Furiousaurus and Silliosaurus, decreasing the amount of support you give, depending on the children's needs. Children who work quickly could also write about Gorgeousaurus and Hideousaurus, or another dinosaur of their own creation.

DAY 5	**Day 5 timetable**	a. Daily Speed Sounds Lesson	d. Partner Proofread
	See Day 4 for guidance on the activity in **bold**. See p.180 for other Day 5 activities.	b. Spell Test	e. Words to Keep
		c. Write About New Kinds of Dinosaurs (continued)	f. Linked Text

 Write About New Kinds of Dinosaurs (continued)

On Day 5, children continue the writing activity that they began on Day 4.

229

The invisible clothes

Teacher's Preparation

Prepare as for p.172. Print out and display the Story Green Words (see online file '7.13 The invisible clothes', starting with tab a): *vain, weave, thread, length, course*, suit*, Emperor, China, tailor, servants, finest, procession, incredible, remarkable, imaginable, miserably, unbelievable, unforgettable, suitable, uncontrollably, unbearable, announced, admired, whispered.*
Note that Challenge Words are marked with an asterisk.
Display the Red Word cards: *love, wear, some, could, buy, bought, thought, everyone, father, any, whole, one, you, said, was, through, there, they, were, walk.*

DAY 1

Day 1 timetable	a. Daily Speed Sounds Lesson	**g. Story Introduction**
See guidance below for activities in **bold**. See pp.172–175 for other Day 1 activities.	b. Speed Sounds from the Storybook	h. First Read – Children
	c. Story Green Words	i. Read Aloud – Teacher
	d. Speedy Green Words (online file 7.13b)	**j. Red Rhythms – Spelling Red Words**
	e. Red Word Cards	k. Handwriting
	f. Partner Practice	

Story Introduction

> The Emperor of China was a very vain man. He loved to organise grand processions where he could show off his remarkable silk suits.
>
> One day, a tailor came to see him. He offered to make him the finest suit imaginable, from a rare and wonderful new cloth he had invented. The Emperor agreed straight away and gave the tailor six bags of gold, so he could buy the most valuable silk thread he could find.
>
> "I haven't told you the best thing about this cloth," said the crafty tailor, slipping the gold into his pocket. "If a stupid person looks at it – it will seem to be invisible!"
>
> The next day, the Emperor went to see the suit. The tailor pretended to spread a length of the cloth over a chair and asked, "Isn't it incredible?"
>
> Not wanting to seem stupid, the Emperor pretended he could see the cloth and said, "It's unbelievable!" He gave the tailor six more bags of gold to buy delicate needles, suitable for such fine cloth.
>
> When the tailor announced that the suit was ready, the Emperor pretended to try it on. "Very comfortable!" He said, admiring himself in the mirror. "I will march through the city in my new suit!"
>
> **TTYP:** Do you think the Emperor will realise what's going on before it's too late?

Red Rhythms – Spelling Red Words See *Get Writing! Grey,* p.51.

DAY 2

Day 2 timetable	a. Daily Speed Sounds Lesson	f. Second Read – Children
See guidance below for activities in **bold**. See pp.175–176 for other Day 2 activities.	b. Speedy Green Words (online file 7.13b)	**g. Fred Fingers – Spelling Green Words**
	c. Red Word Cards	h. Red Rhythms
	d. Partner Practice	**i. Hold a Sentence – 1 and 2**
	e. Jump-in	j. Handwriting

Fred Fingers – Spelling Green Words See *Get Writing!* Book, p.51.

Hold a Sentence – 1 and 2

(1) Why are the clothes invisible?

(2) Why did the Emperor feel miserable?

See *Get Writing!* Book, p.50.

Day 3 timetable	a. Daily Speed Sounds Lesson	e. Questions to Talk About
See guidance below for activities in **bold**. See pp.177–178 for other Day 3 activities.	b. Partner Practice	f. Questions to Read and Answer
	c. Think About the Story	**g. Build a Sentence**
	d. Third Read – Children	h. Handwriting

 Think About the Story

p.9 TOL about how the tailor persuaded the Emperor to buy a new suit. *He appealed to his vanity, by saying it would be the 'finest suit imaginable'.*

pp.10–11 TOL about what the crafty tailor told the Emperor was special about the cloth.
MTYT (with feeling): *"I haven't told you the **best** thing about this cloth. If a stupid person looks at it – it will seem to be **invisible**!"*
TTYP: What was the crafty tailor thinking?

p.12 TOL about why the Emperor pretended he could see the cloth.
Freeze Frame the Emperor's expression when he realised that he couldn't see the cloth.

TTYP: How did he feel, and why?
TTYP: What did the crafty tailor think?

p.13 TOL about how the tailor persuaded the Emperor to give him even more money.

p.14 TOL about why the Emperor decided to march through the city.
Freeze Frame the Emperor's expression.

p.15 MTYT (with feeling): *"The Emperor isn't **wearing** any clothes!"*
TTYP: How did the Emperor feel when this was shouted out, and why?
TOL about why the small boy was brave enough to say something.
TTYP: What do you think the Emperor learnt about himself? How do you think he might change?

 Build a Sentence

Tell children that tomorrow they will role-play two different people: someone vain and silly like the Emperor, and someone kind and sensible. Explain that today you are going to help them build up some sentences that a vain, boastful child might say when showing off something new that they are wearing.

1. Use **MTYT** to say: *Look at me!*

2. **TTYP**: What is he/she wearing? For example, *trainers/T-shirt/sweatshirt/jeans.* Demonstrate how to build the children's suggestions into the sentence, e.g. *Look at me in my trainers!*

3. **TTYP**: What do the trainers look like? *They have white/silver stripes/thick laces/flashing lights/ green soles/wheels.* Build the children's responses into two or three sentences, e.g. *Look at me in my trainers. Spot the thick laces and the flashing lights. Look at the green soles and the white stripes.*

4. Ask partners to decide on their own sentences and to practise saying them until they can remember them. Select a few partners to say their sentences to the group.

5. Ask children to write their own sentences on p.50 of their *Get Writing!* Book.

DAY 4	**Day 4 timetable**	a. Daily Speed Sounds Lesson	e. Proofread – Spelling
	See guidance below for activities in **bold**. See pp.178–180 for other Day 4 activities.	b. Spell Check	f. Proofread – Grammar
		c. Grammar	**g. Write About Choosing a Mayor**
		d. Vocabulary	h. Handwriting

 Grammar

1. Remind children what a **verb** is (a word that tells us what someone or something is doing, e.g. *make, hop, pretend*). **TOL** about how verbs can appear in different forms and tenses, e.g. the verb *say* can change to *said, saying* and *says*.

2. On the board, write *The boy whispered to his father.* Use **MTYT** to say the sentence. Ask children to **TTYP** to say which word is the verb *(whispered)*. Encourage children to explain how they recognised it (e.g. because of the -ed past tense ending, or simply because it is a 'doing word').

3. Ask children to complete the Grammar activity on p.51 of their *Get Writing!* Book.

4. Ask children to **TTYP** to check they have underlined the same words and if not, to discuss which answers are correct and why.

5. Tell children the correct responses and explain any difficult points. (They should have underlined: *wore, came, gave, spread, admired, wept.*)

 Vocabulary

1. Remind children that when they are reading, they may come across words or phrases that they don't understand. They can often work out something's meaning from the sentence it is in.

2. On the board write *The tailor announced that the suit was ready.* Use **MTYT** to say the sentence. Underline the word *announced* and ask children to **TTYP** and say what they think it means (*to say out loud in front of people*). Emphasise that even if children hadn't heard the word before, they could try to work it out from the sentence.

3. Ask children to turn to the Vocabulary activity on p.51 of their *Get Writing!* Book. Talk through the activity, then ask children to complete it independently.

4. Ask children to **TTYP** to check they have circled the same words and if not, to discuss which answers are correct and why.

5. Tell children the correct responses and explain any difficult points. (They should have circled: *expensive, parade, said again, difficult.*)

Write About Choosing a Mayor

Note that this activity should be started on Day 4 and completed on Day 5.

1. **TOL** about how some children and adults are a bit like the Emperor. They believe that if they have expensive clothes and belongings, people will think that they are special. Point out that some people spend a lot of money on particular things like trainers or dresses. **TTYP:** Why do you think people do this? *To make themselves feel proud/Because they want to feel good.*

2. Use online file 7.13 (tab g onwards) for this activity. Explain to children that they are going to role-play two different people: Vain Vincent (who is vain and proud) and Normal Nancy (who is kind and sensible). These two people both want to be voted mayor of their town. Explain that Vincent and Nancy are going to be interviewed (asked questions), so that people in the town can decide who to vote for. Ask children to turn to p.53 in their *Get Writing!* Book. Point out the question prompts that will help them to write (in role) about themselves. Remind them to respond in the first person, using the word *I*.

3. Display the image of Vain Vincent (tab g). Ask children to imagine they are Vain Vincent. Tell them to think about his character and what he is like – vain, boastful, selfish, proud and probably a bit silly! Explain that you are going to ask him some questions and they should respond in role to their partner. Encourage them to be boastful and over-the-top. Use **TTYP** to draw out responses and **MTYT**, if necessary, to build full sentences from children's ideas.

   – What do you do at the weekend? *I go shopping for new clothes/stand in front of the mirror/ wear my most expensive clothes/take photos of myself looking smart.*

   – What's the most expensive thing you have bought? *The most expensive thing I've bought is designer trainers/a hundred-pound watch/a sports car/a multi-million-pound house.*

   – What will you do if you become mayor? *If I become mayor, I'll get a big gold chain to wear/ buy more robes/give lots of speeches/invite people to give me presents/have a big picture of me painted/have a statue of me made.*

   – What's the kindest thing you have ever done? *I have let people take photos of me/let people borrow my things – for a small fee/let my friend come with me to carry my bags and drive my car/let people into my house to admire it.*

   – What do you think you are good at? *I am good at telling other people what to do/explaining how great I am/spending money on fine clothes.*

   – What do other people say about you? *Other people say that I am a great person/good-looking/ They like me because I buy them expensive presents/I have good fashion sense.*

4. Read out the first question again and remind children of their answers. Use the online file (tab h) to model how to write the first sentences. **TOL** as you write. Keep re-reading to make sure it makes sense.

5. Hide your writing. Ask partners to decide on their own sentences and to practise saying them until they can remember them. Select a few partners to say their sentences to the group. Then ask children to write their own sentences into their exercise book. Refer them to the Useful words on p.52 of the *Get Writing!* Book and remind them that they can make notes on p.53.

6. Repeat Steps 3, 4 and 5 (ask each question, demonstrate how you write, then ask children to write) with children responding in role as Normal Nancy. Nancy's responses should be thoughtful and unselfish.

DAY 5	**Day 5 timetable**	a. Daily Speed Sounds Lesson	d. Partner Proofread
	See Day 4 for guidance on the activity in **bold**. See p.180 for other Day 5 activities.	b. Spell Test	e. Words to Keep
		c. Write About Choosing a Mayor (continued)	f. Linked Text

 Write About Choosing a Mayor (continued)

On Day 5, children continue the writing activity that they began on Day 4.

A job for Jordan

For ease, we have continued to refer to 'Story' Green Words in the non-fiction lessons.

Teacher's Preparation

Prepare as for p.172. Print out and display the Story Green Words (see online file 'NF7.1 A job for Jordan', starting with tab a): *Mark, Dawn, dog, pup, read, born, lead, each, lie down, worn, deal, act, team, sight, floor, speak, guide*, Jordan, Labrador, report, behave, after, harness, command, owner, traffic, until, sponsor, support, website, because*, trained, paws, lessons, bumping.*
Note that Challenge Words are marked with an asterisk.
Display the Red Word cards: *all, are, come, do, some, they, to, want, who, you.*

DAY 1

Day 1 timetable	a. Daily Speed Sounds Lesson	g. Book Introduction
See guidance below for activities in **bold**. See pp.172–175 for other Day 1 activities.	b. Speed Sounds from the Storybook	h. First Read – Children
	c. Story Green Words	i. Read Aloud – Teacher
	d. Speedy Green Words (online file NF7.1b)	**j. Red Rhythms – Spelling Red Words**
	e. Red Word Cards	k. Handwriting
	f. Partner Practice	

Book Introduction

Have you ever seen a guide dog? Guide dogs are extremely special dogs. They are very clever and are trained to help people who are blind or partially sighted. They are also trained to help people with hearing problems and other disabilities that make crossing roads and other everyday tasks difficult.

Labradors are the most popular dog breed to be used as guide dogs, but other dogs, such as German Shepherds and Golden Retrievers are often used, too.

They start training as puppies, as soon as they are six to eight weeks old. Training begins with short trips out on the lead each morning where they learn to do things on command: sit, lie down, stay and come. Eventually, they learn more complicated things, like how to wait before crossing a road, when to go left or right and how to stop their owners from bumping into things.

In the UK, there are over 4800 people who rely on guide dogs to help them through their everyday lives. In this book, we will meet Jordan, a Labrador puppy who is just about to start his guide dog training.

TTYP: How do you think a blind person might feel about their guide dog?

Red Rhythms – Spelling Red Words See *Get Writing! Grey*, p.55.

DAY 2

Day 2 timetable	a. Daily Speed Sounds Lesson	f. Second Read – Children
See guidance below for activities in **bold**. See pp.175–176 for other Day 2 activities.	b. Speedy Green Words (online file NF7.1b)	**g. Fred Fingers – Spelling Green Words**
	c. Red Word Cards	h. Red Rhythms
	d. Partner Practice	**i. Hold a Sentence – 1 and 2**
	e. Jump-in	j. Handwriting

Fred Fingers – Spelling Green Words See *Get Writing! Book*, p.55.

Hold a Sentence – 1 and 2

(**1**) It's very important for a guide dog to behave.

(**2**) The dog and its owner must act as a team.

See *Get Writing!* Book, p.54.

 DAY 3

Day 3 timetable	a. Daily Speed Sounds Lesson	e. Questions to Talk About
See guidance below for activities in **bold**. See pp.177–178 for other Day 3 activities.	b. Partner Practice	f. Questions to Read and Answer
	c. Think About the Information	**g. Build a Sentence**
	d. Third Read – Children	h. Handwriting

 Think About the Information

p.9 **TOL** about what sort of dog makes a good guide dog.

p.10 **TOL** about why a guide dog pup has to behave well.

p.11 **TOL** about what a guide dog is trained to do.

p.12 **TOL** about other skills the guide dog has to learn.

p.13 **MTYT:** *They are shown how to act as a team.*
TTYP: What does 'acting as a team' mean? *Working together.*

p.14 **TOL** about what a guide dog does when he is not needed.

p.15 **TOL** about what you should not do if you see a guide dog with its owner.
MTYT: *Let it do its job.*

 Build a Sentence

Tell children that tomorrow they will write some instructions about looking after a dog. Explain that today you are going to help them build up some sentences about what you should and should not do if you meet someone with a guide dog.

1. Display the picture of Jordan with his owner (online file NF7.1d). Use **MTYT** to say: *If you see a guide dog…*

2. **TTYP:** What should you NOT do? *Pat him/Talk to him/Play with him/Give him anything to eat.* Model how to incorporate the children's ideas into the sentence, e.g. *If you see a guide dog, do not pat him or talk to him.*

3. **TTYP:** What should you do? *Let him do his job/Give him space/Talk to the owner, not the dog.* Demonstrate how to build the ideas into a full sentence, e.g. *If you see a guide dog, do not pat him or talk to him. Give him space and let him do his job.*

4. Ask partners to decide on their own sentences and to practise saying them until they can remember them. Select a few partners to say their sentences to the group.

5. Ask children to write their own sentences on p.54 of their *Get Writing!* Book.

DAY 4	**Day 4 timetable**	a. Daily Speed Sounds Lesson	e. Proofread – Spelling
	See guidance below for activities in **bold**. See pp.178–180 for other Day 4 activities.	b. Spell Check	f. Proofread – Grammar
		c. Grammar	**g. Write About Looking After Your Dog**
		d. Vocabulary	h. Handwriting

GW Grammar

1. Remind children that there are four different types of sentence:

    – questions (which end with a question mark, e.g. *Are you ready?*)

    – exclamations (which end with an exclamation mark, e.g. *How cold you are!*)

    – statements (which tell us something and end with a full stop, e.g. *I like dogs.*)

    – commands (which tell us to do, or not do, something. They usually start with a verb that gives an order, e.g. *Put that down.*)

2. Explain to children that they are going to look at two of these sentence types: statements and commands. Ensure that they understand the difference. **TTYP** and give an example of a question, e.g. *What time is it?* **TTYP** and give an example of a statement, e.g. *It is time for lunch.*

3. Ask children to complete the Grammar activity on p.55 of their *Get Writing!* Book.

4. Tell children the correct responses and explain any difficult points. (They should have ticked: *Statement, Command, Command, Command, Statement.*)

GW Vocabulary

1. Remind children that when they are reading, they may come across words that they don't understand. They can usually work out the meaning of the word from the sentence it is in.

2. On the board write *Labradors make good guide dogs.* Use **MTYT** to say the sentence. Underline the word *Labradors* and ask children to **TTYP** and say what these are *(a breed of dog)*. Emphasise that they can work out the meaning by looking at how it works in the sentence.

3. Ask children to turn to the Vocabulary activity on p.55 of their *Get Writing!* Book. Talk through the activity, explaining any words that they are unsure of. Then ask children to complete the activity.

4. Ask children to **TTYP** to check they have circled the same words and if not, to discuss which answers are correct and why.

5. Tell children the correct responses and explain any difficult points. (They should have circled: *bad, information, set of straps, instructions.*)

GW Write About Looking After Your Dog

Note that this activity should be started on Day 4 and completed on Day 5.

1. **TOL** about how you (or a friend) had a dog when you were a child and how much time you spent looking after it. Talk about feeding it twice a day, giving it fresh water, taking it on lots of walks, grooming and cuddling it. Also mention how you helped to train it to make sure it was always under control and behaved well with people and other dogs.

2. Use online file NF7.1 (tab g onwards) for this activity. Explain to the children that they are going to write some instructions about how to look after a dog. Display the images to help prompt ideas (tab g onwards). Tell children that you are going to talk through ideas first, then you are going to show them how to write those ideas down as a set of instructions (commands). Ask children to turn to p.57 in the *Get Writing!* Book.

3. Ask children to **TTYP** to answer the questions. If necessary, use **MTYT** to model how to create full sentences with their ideas.

– **TTYP**: What should you feed a dog? *You should give a dog... food from a pet shop, rather than scraps of human food/a few dog treats.*

– **TTYP**: What does a dog drink? *A dog needs to drink fresh water every day.*

– **TTYP**: What exercise does a dog need? *You must... take it for walks/let it run off the lead/ encourage it to jump/run around and play with it/throw balls and other toys for it to fetch/let it paddle or swim if there is somewhere safe.*

– **TTYP**: How do you keep a dog healthy? *To keep a dog healthy... check its eyes and nose aren't runny/groom it/check its nails/bath it if it gets muddy or smelly/make sure it has injections against disease/take it to the vet if it's unwell.*

– **TTYP**: What should you train a dog to do? *Train your dog to... sit/lie down/not bark at other dogs or people/walk beside you/not pull on the lead/not bite/to listen to you.*

– **TTYP**: What commands should your dog be able to follow? *Your dog should follow commands such as: Come/Fetch/Wait/Drop the toy/Be quiet.* Emphasise that these are all instructions.

4. Go back to the first question and use the online file (tab i) to model how to write the first instruction, drawing on some of the children's ideas. **TOL** as you think about which verb (imperative) to use, such as *feed...* or *give...* **TOL** as you write the sentence and keep re-reading it to check it makes sense.

5. Hide your writing. Ask children to practise the first instruction they want to write by saying it aloud to their partner until they can remember it. Select a few partners to say their instructions to the group. They should write their instructions in their exercise books. Point out the question prompts (where they can also make notes) on p.57 of the *Get Writing!* Book and the Useful words on p.56.

6. Repeat Steps 4 and 5 (demonstrate how you write, then ask children to write) for the remaining instructions, giving children as much support with modelling, writing and vocabulary as they need.

Day 5 timetable	a. Daily Speed Sounds Lesson	d. Partner Proofread
See Day 4 for guidance on the activity in **bold**. See p.180 for other Day 5 activities.	b. Spell Test	e. Words to Keep
	c. Write About Looking After Your Dog (continued)	f. Linked Text

GW **Write About Looking After Your Dog (continued)**

On Day 5, children continue the writing activity that they began on Day 4.

A place in space: the Moon

Teacher's Preparation

Prepare as for p.172. Print out and display the Story Green Words (see online file 'NF7.5 A place in space: the Moon', starting with tab a): *Moon, plane, shape, dark, huge, speed, tanks, north, south, poles, brave, date, fact, Earth*, American, Armstrong, Aldrin, Apollo 11, reflected, diameter, module, December, lunar*, humans*, astronaut*, craters, objects, hitting, orbits, shines, tides, formed, landed, patches.*

Note that Challenge Words are marked with an asterisk.

Display the Red Word cards: *any, do, does, other, there, they, was, water, were, what, who, to, of, ball.*

Bring in one of your favourite information books. If possible, one from your childhood, or alternatively one that you particularly like now.

DAY 1

Day 1 timetable	a. Daily Speed Sounds Lesson	g. **Book Introduction**
See guidance below for activities in **bold**. See pp.172–175 for other Day 1 activities.	b. Speed Sounds from the Storybook	h. First Read – Children
	c. Story Green Words	i. Read Aloud – Teacher
	d. Speedy Green Words (online file NF7.5b)	j. **Red Rhythms – Spelling Red Words**
	e. Red Word Cards	k. Handwriting
	f. Partner Practice	

Book Introduction

When it's not too cloudy, and if the curtains are open, you might be able to see the Moon from your bedroom window as you're drifting off to sleep. It's a very long way from the Earth, but you can see the light shining off it at night.

Have you ever thought about what the Moon might be like? If you look at it through a telescope you'll see lots of light and dark patches. These are steep hills and deep craters caused by meteors from outer space crashing into the Moon.

Did you know that astronauts have travelled to the Moon? It is the only place in space where humans have landed. They have to carry air with them, stored in tanks on their backs, because there is no oxygen on the Moon.

No oxygen means there isn't any life on the Moon, so you would never spot a bird flying about or a squirrel nibbling some nuts! However, there is water, which has been found at the north and south poles, the coldest areas.

In this book, you will find out many more facts about the Moon.

TTYP: Would you like to go to the Moon? Why or why not?

Red Rhythms – Spelling Red Words See *Get Writing! Grey*, p.59.

DAY 2

Day 2 timetable	a. Daily Speed Sounds Lesson	f. Second Read – Children
See guidance below for activities in **bold**. See pp.175–176 for other Day 2 activities.	b. Speedy Green Words (online file NF7.5b)	g. **Fred Fingers – Spelling Green Words**
	c. Red Word Cards	h. Red Rhythms
	d. Partner Practice	i. **Hold a Sentence – 1 and 2**
	e. Jump-in	j. Handwriting

Fred Fingers – Spelling Green Words See *Get Writing! Book*, p.59.

Hold a Sentence – 1 and 2

> **1** Craters were formed by space objects hitting the Moon at high speed.

> **2** There is no air on the Moon but there is water.

See *Get Writing!* Book, p.58.

Day 3 timetable	a. Daily Speed Sounds Lesson	e. Questions to Talk About
See guidance below for activities in **bold**. See pp.177–178 for other Day 3 activities.	b. Partner Practice	f. Questions to Read and Answer
	c. Think About the Information	**g. Build a Sentence**
	d. Third Read – Children	h. Handwriting

 Think About the Information

p.9 TOL about the shape and appearance of the Moon.

pp.10–11 TOL about how the Moon moves in relation to the Earth.
TOL about how a 'fact' is information that can be proved.
MTYT: *The Moon's **diameter** is about 3475 km.*

p.12 TOL about the subheading (both on this page and other pages). Draw out that these subheadings help to group information together and help readers find answers that they are looking for.

p.13 TOL about other Moon facts, e.g. how far it is from Earth, the presence of ice.

p.14 TOL about how many times astronauts have been to the Moon.

p.15 TOL about the first men to land on the Moon.
TTYP: What is the ground like on the Moon? *Dusty/Rocky/Grey-looking.*

  Build a Sentence

Tell children that tomorrow they will start writing a fact file about the Moon. Explain that today you are going to help them build a simple sentence about the men who landed on the Moon.

1. Display the pictures of the men on the Moon (online file NF7.5d). Use **MTYT** to say: *Astronauts landed on the Moon.*

2. **TTYP:** Who were they? *Neil Armstrong and Buzz Aldrin.* Which country did they come from? *America.* Model how to build up the basic sentence with additional information, e.g. *Two American astronauts, Neil Armstrong and Buzz Aldrin, landed on the Moon.*

3. **TTYP:** When did they land? *July 1969.* Add the information to the sentence, e.g. *Two American astronauts, Neil Armstrong and Buzz Aldrin, landed on the Moon in July 1969.*

4. **TTYP:** How did they get there? *The lunar module of Apollo 11.* Add another full sentence to the original one, e.g. *Two American astronauts, Neil Armstrong and Buzz Aldrin, landed on the Moon in July 1969. They landed in the lunar module of Apollo 11.*

5. Ask children to repeat their own sentences to their partner, then write them on p.58 of their *Get Writing!* Book.

DAY 4	**Day 4 timetable**	a. Daily Speed Sounds Lesson	e. Proofread – Spelling
	See guidance below for activities in **bold**. See pp.178–180 for other Day 4 activities.	b. Spell Check	f. Proofread – Grammar
		c. Grammar	**g. Write a Fact File about the Moon**
		d. Vocabulary	h. Handwriting

GW Grammar

1. Tell (or remind) children that a **noun phrase** is a group of words that has a noun as its main word, with other words telling us more about that noun.

2. On the board write _Brave astronauts visited the Moon._ Use **MTYT** to say the sentence. Point out the underlined noun phrase. Ask children to **TTYP** to say which word is the noun _(astronauts)_. Explain that the other word, _brave_, is an adjective that tells us more about the astronauts (i.e. that they are brave people because it is a dangerous trip).

3. Ask children to complete the Grammar activity on p.59 of their _Get Writing!_ Book.

4. Ask children to **TTYP** to check they have underlined and circled the same words and if not, to discuss which answers are correct and why.

5. Tell children the correct responses and explain any difficult points. (They should have identified these noun phrases: _dark_ **patches**; _huge_ **craters**; _The first_ **humans**.) Note that determiners, such as _the_, also form part of the noun phrase.

GW Vocabulary

1. Explain that non-fiction texts often use special vocabulary (technical terms) to explain the topic.

2. On the board write the word _diameter._ **TTYP:** What does this mean? _The distance across a circle or circular shape._ **MTYT:** _The Moon's_ **diameter** _is about 3475 km._

3. Ask children to turn to the Vocabulary activity on p.59 of their _Get Writing!_ Book. Talk through the meaning of the words _craters, orbits, tides, reflected, Apollo._ (Note that _Apollo_ was the name given to a series of space missions organised by the American space agency, NASA.)

4. Ask children to complete the activity in their _Get Writing!_ Book. (They should have written: _orbits, tides, Apollo, craters, reflected._)

Write a Fact File about the Moon

Note that this activity should be started on Day 4 and completed on Day 5.

1. **TOL** about one of your favourite information books that you had at home as a child. (If possible, bring it in, or something similar.) It might be about animals, or vehicles, or great buildings. Explain why you liked it, e.g. because of all the pictures and the amazing facts that you learnt. Recall having some fact file cards which gave key information about your favourite animals/cars/buildings. (Compare with 'Top Trumps' cards if the children are familiar with them.) **TTYP:** What do you like reading about in information books or fact files?

2. Use online file NF7.5 (tab g onwards) for this activity. Explain to children that they are going to write a fact file about the Moon, using what they have learnt from the non-fiction book they've just read. Tell them that first you will talk about the information, then guide them to write it down in their own fact files. Ask children to open their _Get Writing!_ Book at p.61.

3. Remind children how the information in the book was divided into sections under different headings. **TTYP**: What headings shall we include in the fact file? Draw out ideas such as *What shape and size is the Moon? Where is the Moon? What's on the Moon? Who has been to the Moon?*

Now ask detailed questions under each heading to draw out specific facts, using the prompts provided. Ask children to **TTYP** to answer the questions. If necessary, use **MTYT** to model how to create full sentences with their ideas.

TTYP: Is the Moon a circle, sphere or crescent? *Sphere/Like a ball/Looks like a circle in the sky/ Looks like a crescent if there is a shadow over part of it.*

TTYP: What is the diameter of the Moon? *3475 km in diameter.*

Talk through the other questions and possible responses.

4. Go back to the first question and use the online file (tab g) to model how to build the children's responses into a full sentence. **TOL** as you write and keep re-reading to make sure that your writing makes sense.

5. Hide your writing. Ask children to practise their own sentences with a partner until they can remember them. Select a few partners to say their sentences to the group. Then children can write their own sentences in their exercise book. Draw their attention to the question prompts on p.61 of their *Get Writing!* Book (where they can make notes) and the Useful words on p.60.

6. Repeat Steps 4 and 5 (demonstrate how you write, then ask children to write) for the remaining sections. Encourage children to use their own ideas as they complete their fact file. Allow time to discuss what pictures or diagrams they would like to include.

Day 5 timetable	a. Daily Speed Sounds Lesson	d. Partner Proofread
See Day 4 for guidance on the activity in **bold**. See p.180 for other Day 5 activities.	b. Spell Test	e. Words to Keep
	c. Write a Fact File about the Moon (continued)	f. Linked Text

GW **Write a Fact File about the Moon (continued)**

On Day 5, children continue the writing activity that they began on Day 4.

Red Words with circled graphemes

I th(e) y(ou) y(our) s(ai)d w(a)s
(are) o(f) w(a)nt wh(a)t th(ey) t(o)
h(e)* m(e)* w(e)* sh(e)* b(e)* n(o)*
s(o)* g(o)* (o)ld* h(er)*
d(o) d(oe)s (a)ll c(a)ll t(a)ll sm(a)ll
m(a)ny (a)ny (o)ne (a)ny(o)ne s(o)me c(o)me
w(a)tch (wh)o wh(ere) th(ere) h(ere) w(ere)
br(o)ther (o)ther m(o)ther f(a)ther l(o)ve ab(o)ve
tw(o) (o)nce b(uy) w(or)se w(a)lk t(a)lk
b(ough)t c(augh)t thr(ough) th(ough)t (wh)ole w(ear)
c(oul)d w(oul)d sh(oul)d gr(ea)t s(aw)* wh(y)*
n(ow)* h(ow)* d(ow)n* ov(er)*
m(y)* b(y)* s(o)n w(a)ter s(ch)ool* b(a)ll
every(o)ne th(eir) p(eo)ple

(*= red for while)

Simple Speed Sounds Chart

Consonant sounds – stretchy

f	l	m	n	r	s	v	z	sh	th	ng nk

Consonant sounds – bouncy

b	c k	d	g	h	j	p	qu	t	w	x	y	ch

Vowel sounds – bouncy   **Vowel sounds – stretchy**

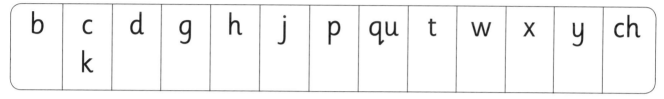

a	e	i	o	u		ay	ee	igh	ow

Vowel sounds – stretchy

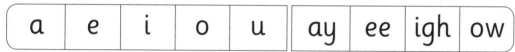

oo	oo	ar	or	air	ir	ou	oy

Complex Speed Sounds Chart

Consonant sounds

f ff ph	l ll le	m mm mb	n nn kn	r rr wr	s ss se c ce	v ve	z zz s se	sh ti ci	th	ng nk

b bb	c k ck ch	d dd	g gg	h	j g ge dge	p pp	qu	t tt	w wh	x	y	ch tch

Vowel sounds

a	e ea	i	o	u	ay $\widehat{a\text{-}e}$ ai	ee $\widehat{e\text{-}e}$ y ea e	igh $\widehat{i\text{-}e}$ ie i y	ow $\widehat{o\text{-}e}$ oa o

oo $\widehat{u\text{-}e}$ ue ew	oo	ar	or oor ore aw au	air are	ir ur er	ou ow	oy oi	ire	ear	ure